72432

SOCIALISM AND THE ETHICS OF JESUS

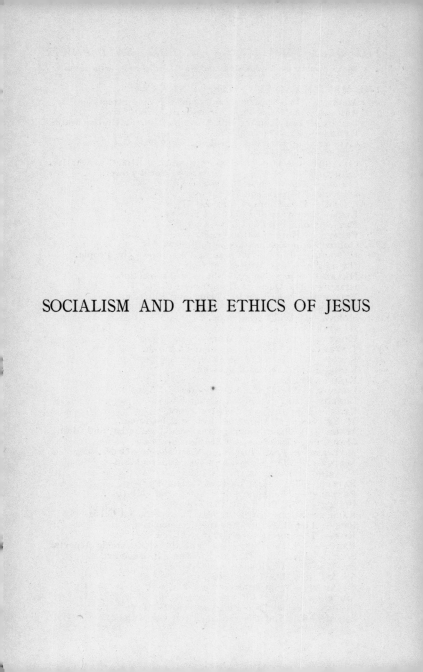

THE BEST NEW BOOKS AT THE LEAST PRICES

Each volume in the Macmillan Libraries sells for 50 cents, never more,
wherever books are sold.

THE MACMILLAN STANDARD LIBRARY

ADDAMS — The Spirit of Youth and the City Streets.
ADDAMS — A New Conscience and an Ancient Evil.
BAILEY — The Country Life Movement in the United States.
BAILEY — The Practical Garden Book.
CAMPBELL — The New Theology.
CLARK — The Care of a House.
CONYNGTON — How to Help: A Manual of Practical Charity.
COOLIDGE — The United States as a World Power.
CROLY — The Promise of American Life.
DEVINE — Misery and Its Causes.
EARLE — Home Life in Colonial Days.
ELY — Evolution of Industrial Society.
ELY — Monopolies and Trusts.
FRENCH — How to Grow Vegetables.
GOODYEAR — Renaissance and Modern Art.
HAPGOOD — Lincoln, Abraham, The Man of the People.
HAULTAIN — The Mystery of Golf.
HEARN — Japan: An Attempt at Interpretation.
HILLIS — The Quest of Happiness.
HILLQUIT — Socialism in Theory and Practice.
HODGES — Everyman's Religion.
HORNE — David Livingstone.
HUNTER — Poverty.
HUNTER — Socialists at Work.
JEFFERSON — The Building of the Church.
KING — The Ethics of Jesus.
KING — The Laws of Friendship.
KING — Rational Living.
LONDON — The War of the Classes.
LONDON — Revolution and Other Essays.
LYON — How to Keep Bees for Profit.
MCLENNAN — A Manual of Practical Farming.
MABIE — William Shakespeare: Poet, Dramatist, and Man.
MAHAFFY — Rambles and Studies in Greece.
MATHEWS — The Church and the Changing Order.
MATHEWS — The Gospel and the Modern Man.
NEARING — Wages in the United States.
PATTEN — The Social Basis of Religion.
PEABODY — The Approach to the Social Question.
PIERCE — The Tariff and the Trusts.
RAUSCHENBUSCH — Christianity and the Social Crisis.
RIIS — The Making of an American Citizen.
RIIS — Theodore Roosevelt, the Citizen.
RYAN — A Living Wage: Its Ethical and Economic Aspects.
SCOTT — Increasing Human Efficiency in Business.
ST. MAUR — A Self-supporting Home.
ST. MAUR — The Earth's Bounty.
SHERMAN — What is Shakespeare?
SIDGWICK — Home Life in Germany.
SIMONS — Social Forces in American History.
SMITH — The Spirit of the American Government.

THE BEST NEW BOOKS AT THE LEAST PRICES

SPARGO — Socialism.
TARBELL — History of Greek Art.
TRASK — In the Vanguard.
VALENTINE — How to Keep Hens for Profit.
VAN DYKE — The Gospel for a World of Sin.
VAN DYKE — The Spirit of America.
VEBLEN — The Theory of the Leisure Class.
VEDDER — Socialism and the Ethics of Jesus.
WALLING — Socialism as it Is.
WELLS — New Worlds for Old.
WEYL — The New Democracy.
WHITE — The Old Order Changeth.

THE MACMILLAN FICTION LIBRARY

ALLEN — A Kentucky Cardinal.
ALLEN — The Reign of Law.
ATHERTON — Patience Sparhawk.
CHILD — Jim Hands.
CRAWFORD — The Heart of Rome.
CRAWFORD — Fair Margaret: A Portrait.
DAVIS — A Friend of Cæsar.
DRUMMOND — The Justice of the King.
Elizabeth and Her German Garden.
GALE — Loves of Pelleas and Etarre.
HERRICK — The Common Lot.
LONDON — Adventure.
LONDON — Burning Daylight.
LOTI — Disenchanted.
LUCAS — Mr. Ingleside.
MASON — The Four Feathers.
NORRIS — Mother.
OXENHAM — The Long Road.
PRYOR — The Colonel's Story.
REMINGTON — Ermine of the Yellowstone.
ROBERTS — Kings in Exile.
ROBINS — The Convert.
ROBINS — A Dark Lantern.
SCOTT — Waverley Novels (25 vols.).
WARD — The History of David Grieve.

THE MACMILLAN JUVENILE LIBRARY

ALTSHELER — The Horsemen of the Plains.
BACON — While Caroline Was Growing.
CARROLL — Alice, and Through the Looking Glass.
DIX — A Little Captive Lad.
GREENE — Pickett's Gap.
LUCAS — Slowcoach.
MAJOR — Bears of Blue River.
MAJOR — Uncle Tom Andy Bill.
MABIE — Book of Christmas.
NESBIT — The Railway Children.
WRIGHT — Dream Fox Story Book.
WRIGHT — Aunt Jimmy's Will.

THE MACMILLAN COMPANY
NEW YORK · BOSTON · CHICAGO
SAN FRANCISCO

MACMILLAN & CO., Limited
LONDON · BOMBAY · CALCUTTA
MELBOURNE

THE MACMILLAN CO. OF CANADA, Ltd.
TORONTO

SOCIALISM

AND THE

ETHICS OF JESUS

BY

HENRY C. VEDDER

PROFESSOR OF CHURCH HISTORY IN CROZER
THEOLOGICAL SEMINARY

New York

THE MACMILLAN COMPANY

1914

Norwood Press
J. S. Cushing Co. — Berwick & Smith Co.
Norwood, Mass., U.S.A.

AH LOVE! COULD THOU AND I WITH FATE CONSPIRE
TO GRASP THIS SORRY SCHEME OF THINGS ENTIRE,
    WOULD WE NOT SHATTER IT TO BITS — AND THEN
REMOULD IT NEARER TO THE HEART'S DESIRE!

CONTENTS

CHAPTER III

LASSALLE: THE FIRST STAGE OF GERMAN SOCIALISM

The two founders — Contrasted characters — Lassalle and
Bismarck — Birth and training — Writings — The Hatzfield case — Two great careers — Lassalle's work — "The
working-men's programme" — "An open letter" — The
Frankfort speech — The working-men's union — Lassalle's
death — Character — A revolution demanded — "The iron
law of wages" — Ricardo's fallacy — An automatic regulation — The "law" only a historical generalization —
Wants essential to progress — Not an "iron" law, but
elastic — Lassalle's oratory — His programme and Louis
Blanc's — No real solution — Liebkneckt — Bebel — His
atheism — Source of error — Socialism and marriage —
Governments roused — Bismarck's repressive measures —
His socialistic legislation — Results — State Socialism in
Germany: railways — Telegraphs and telephones — Mu-

CHAPTER IV

KARL MARX AND MODERN "SCIENTIFIC" SOCIALISM

CHAPTER V

ANARCHY: THE SCHOOL OF PROUDHON AND KROPOTKIN

CHAPTER VI

SOCIALISM IN ENGLAND

CHAPTER VII

SOCIALISM IN AMERICA

CHAPTER VIII

THE IDEALS OF SOCIALISM — ARE THEY PRACTICABLE?

CHAPTER IX

THE SOCIAL TEACHINGS OF JESUS — GENERAL PRINCIPLES

Need of inductive study — True criticism and false — Need of
sympathetic study — Exegesis that misleads — Practical
ethics, not scientific — Ethics of Jesus grounded in religion
— Jesus' conception of his mission — Salvation — The

CHAPTER X

THE SOCIAL TEACHINGS OF JESUS — APPLICATIONS

Not Reformer, but Revealer — Uniqueness of method — His
social ethics fundamental — The social unit, the family —
Marriage a divine institution — Rooted in human nature
— Not a concession to weakness — Monogamy — The
union of spirit — Divorce — Wrong exegesis — What
Jesus forbade — His significant silence — Our problem —
Ethics not too severe — Persistence of his ideals — The
modern divorce problem — The false ideal of happiness —
Effect on family life — A misinterpretation — When one
must " hate " — The sanity of Jesus — Slavery — Mohammed — Drunkenness — What is moderation ? — Jesus and
wealth — Providence — " Be not anxious " — Jesus not
fanatical — His teaching interpreted by his conduct — The

CHAPTER XI

THE SOCIAL FAILURE OF THE CHURCH

CHAPTER XII

THE ATTITUDE OF CHURCHES AND MINISTERS TO SOCIAL QUESTIONS

BY WAY OF INTRODUCTION

BIBLIOGRAPHY

Some general works by socialists : —

KAUFMANN, What is Socialism? New York, 1910.

SPARGO, Socialism. New York, 1906.

KELLY, Twentieth Century Socialism. New York, 1910.

Critical but non-partisan : —

KIRKUP, History of Socialism, 4th ed. New York, 1908.

GRAHAM, Socialism New and Old, "International Scientific Series," 1891.

STODDART, The New Socialism. New York, 1910.

SKELTON, Socialism : a Critical Analysis. Boston, 1911.

Critical and hostile : —

SCHAEFFLE, The Quintessence of Socialism, "Social Science Series," 1908.

FLINT, Socialism. New York, 1895.

NOTE. — It would have been easy greatly to extend these bibliographies, but it was believed that they would be more helpful to the largest number of readers, if limited mainly to books of recent publication, easily accessible, and wholly limited to books in the English language.

BY WAY OF INTRODUCTION

I PURPOSE in the following chapters to attempt three things: first, to sketch briefly the history of socialistic principles and parties in modern times; second, to examine with sufficient thoroughness the fundamental principles of present-day Socialism; third, to inquire in what respects these principles correspond to the ethics of Jesus, and wherein the two differ. I purpose to make this investigation, not as the champion of any social theory, or the briefed defender of any social system, but in as impartial and candid a spirit as possible, as a student of history, of the Scriptures, of economics, of social institutions.

The critical examination of the principles of Socialism will come later, but at the very outset of our inquiry some definition of our subject-matter is highly desirable. There is great mental confusion concerning the nature of Socialism, and we must try to comprehend clearly just what we are to study. Socialism is first of all a philosophy, a theory by which the phenomena of society are explained. More precisely, it is the philosophy of the effective production and distribution of wealth, and the results thereby produced on all social institutions. Socialism is also a practical movement, intended to bring about the condition of things required by the philosophy. We shall be compelled to give our attention to both these phases of Socialism; for it is impossible to understand

3

either theory or movement, unless they are studied together.

Since Socialism is at bottom a philosophy, it has no programme, properly speaking. Some socialistic groups have a programme, and in the past socialists have quite generally put forward programmes which we shall subject in turn to critical examination in the course of our study. But there has been a great change within a generation: intelligent socialists no longer profess a programme. They have no faith in the possibility of establishing Socialism to-morrow or next week. It is true they have a goal: a social state in which every person shall contribute to the common good in proportion to his ability, and in return shall be guaranteed an equitable share in what is produced. But this goal socialists now expect to reach by a gradual process, not by any sudden and violent overturning of existing institutions, or even as the immediate result of legislation. It is evolution rather than revolution that is their reliance.

But the socialist holds, too, that evolution may be hastened by intelligent action. Because existing social institutions are the result of age-long process of development, of which men have been hitherto mainly unconscious, it by no means follows that man is the mere sport of economic forces and may do nothing to determine his own destiny. Neither determinism nor fatalism is a necessary part of Socialism. Man has always done something, he may henceforth do much more, to direct the line of his development and the evolution of social institutions. We may steer, and not simply drift, toward the ideal social order. Accordingly Kautsky, one of the ablest of German socialist leaders, warns laborers that they have something to do besides "sit down with open mouths and wait for the roast pigeons to fly in." Just as Burbank, by careful selection of seeds and plants, and skilful cross-breeding, is able to hasten the processes of nature and produce in a few months what ordinary evolution would require years, perhaps centuries, to bring forth, so the socialist believes that if we can gain a clear conception of the goal to be reached, and arouse in men desire to reach it, the end may be greatly hastened. Socialism is concerned to-day, therefore, not with Utopias, but with realities. It is a purposeful attempt to assist evolution, not a vain striving to shape society after an ideal pattern.

Socialism might be more scientifically named collectivism. The key to all its theories and parties is, coöperative production and equitable distribution. It is the opposite system on the one hand to individualism, and on the other to competition. It is but carrying one stage further a process of social reorganization that has been transforming the world ever since the decay of the feudal system.

We have thus seen what Socialism is; let us still further define it by seeing what Socialism is not.

Socialism is not communism, though the two are frequently confounded, even in the encyclical of Pope Leo XIII, who misstated the essential principle of Socialism by confusing it with Communism. Of what value is infallibility to a pontiff who lacks common sense, or common knowledge? It must, however, be admitted that socialists themselves are in large part responsible for this confusion of ideas. There was a time in the movement when the name "socialist" did not have its present precision of meaning, but was used to describe persons and movements that differed widely, and sometimes were in sharp conflict with each other. To distinguish their proposals from these ill-defined schemes, when Karl Marx and Frederic Engels issued their famous declaration in 1847, well named "the birth-cry of modern Socialism," they called it "The Communist Manifesto." Their ideas were quite distinct from communism, and therefore the choice of that name was most unfortunate, since it naturally tended to prolong misunderstanding and confusion.

The two systems are easily distinguishable. Communism would distribute all wealth equally; Socialism would secure to every man as nearly as possible the full product of his own labor. Communism aims at the abolition of all private property; Socialism does not object to private property, except ownership of the means of producing wealth; these, it holds, should be owned by the whole community, and not by individuals or small groups. But wealth once produced and equitably distributed, Socialism recognizes the right of each person to his own portion; he may consume it, or he may accumulate a surplus, or he may give part of it to others. Socialism offers greater personal freedom than communism, therefore, and better opportunity for the maintenance of family life. The best examples of actual communism are furnished us in some of the religious orders of the Roman Catholic Church, in which the individual does not own even the clothes that he wears, but everything belongs to the community.

Socialism is not anarchy, but its antipodes.[1] Anarchy

[1] "Socialism is not Anarchism, but order; not Communism, but justice; it does not propose to abolish competition, but to regulate it; nor to

is the extreme of individualism, the negation of all social organization. It professes as its goal that men shall live together without government and without law. There are both evolutionary and revolutionary groups of anarchists, both individualists and communists among them. They do not oppose collectivism in production, but hold that it should be voluntary, like everything else. But while anarchy would thus entirely free men from law, Socialism would greatly extend the scope of law. So much is this the characteristic of Socialism that Herbert Spencer called it "the new slavery." Anarchy is a centrifugal force, Socialism is a centripetal. Under anarchy a man might work or not, as he pleased; under Socialism every man must be an active producer, and means must be found to persuade the unwilling and coerce the lazy. No two systems could be more thoroughly unlike than Socialism and anarchy, and there is no good reason why they should be so continually confounded. The confusion is not always honest; [1] the words are promiscuously applied as epithets of opprobrium, with so

abolish property, but to consecrate it; nor to abolish the home, but to make the home possible; nor to curtail liberty, but to enlarge it." — Edmond Kelly, p. 7. "Nor to abolish religion," he might have added, "but to make it practical."

[1] The Republican platform for 1908 contained these words: "Socialism would destroy wealth; Republicanism would prevent its abuse. Socialism would give each an equal right to take; Republicanism would give to each an equal right to earn. Socialism would offer an equality of possessions which would soon leave no one anything to possess; Republicanism would give equality of opportunity which would assure to each his share of a constantly increasing sum of possessions." The object of statements so notoriously false can, of course, be nothing else than to create political prejudice and influence voters against Socialism. We have come to expect this in political platforms, but it is not seldom found in what purports to be the serious literature of the subject.

much indifference and lack of discrimination as to indicate either gross ignorance or moral obliquity in those who bandy the names about so freely.

Socialism should not be confounded, as it often is, with the private and personal vagaries of some socialists. People of widely differing opinions about art, science, philosophy, and religion have agreed in approving collectivism as the most equitable principle to govern the production and distribution of wealth. Some have been atheists, but collectivism has no necessary or inherent connection with either atheism or theism. The Erfurt Congress (1891) declared explicitly that religion is a private concern of the individual, with which Socialism as such has nothing to do. Some socialists have advocated the abolition of marriage and the family, but collectivism has no essential affinity for such a theory of social reorganization. And while some socialists would substitute the ethics of the barnyard for the ethics of Jesus, that is conspicuously not true of all socialists. Since they are disagreed on this point, yet are equally socialists, the only fair deduction is that of a recent socialistic writer, "There is no such thing as a socialistic view of marriage, any more than there is a Republican or Democratic view of marriage; or any more than there is a socialist view of vaccination, vivisection, vegetarianism, or homeopathy." [1]   Among the advocates of So-

[1] Spargo, "Socialism," p. 293. In spite of numerous disclaimers of this kind from recognized authorities, the London Municipal Society in its book called "The Case Against Socialism" makes a deliberate attempt to discredit Socialism by arguing that all socialists are violent revolutionists (in the teeth of protests by leading socialists that they neither seek nor desire revolution); and that Socialism is the necessary and determined foe of marriage and the family, as well as of all religion, espe-

cialism are many orthodox Christians, and many others who, without being orthodox, are not at all disposed to surrender marriage and the family as effete institutions.

Too many Protestants are ready to define Socialism, as the Pope has defined Modernism, as "the synthesis of all errors." This frame of mind makes the pursuit of truth impossible. No helpful discussion can be conducted, still less can any helpful investigation be pursued, in this spirit of wilful or ignorant confounding of things that differ. Let us clearly comprehend, therefore, at the very outset of this inquiry, that collectivism is essentially an economic theory, with certain limited but important social and ethical implications, but that it has no direct connection with purely religious or ethical ideas and institutions. In particular, Socialism does not imply assassination, though it is true that some impatient professors of socialist ideas have betaken themselves to the bomb and the dagger. Of course, the socialist reserves the right, common to all men and asserted by all as an inalienable privilege of mankind, in the last resort to rebel against existing government and use whatever force may be necessary to establish a new order. But the right of revolution is in no sense a doctrine peculiar to Socialism.

He who cannot or will not get the point of view that has been thus indicated, will waste his time and but add to his mental fog by further attending to the subject.

cially of Christianity. The book is manifestly published in the interest of the Tory landowners; and its bitterness and mendacity may be taken to be a good measure of the present spread of Socialism in England, and its menace against the time-dishonored rule of a class whose political and social dominance is founded on the fact that while numbering one-tenth of the people they own nine-tenths of all the land in Great Britain. The landowners are certainly badly frightened.

I

SOCIALISM IN THE TIME OF THE REFORMATION

BIBLIOGRAPHY

The literature of this subject in English is very scanty.

KAUTSKY, Communism in Central Europe in the Time of the Reformation. London, 1897.

BAX, Rise and Fall of the Anabaptists. London, 1903.

HEATH, Anabaptism. London, 1895.

I

SOCIALISM IN THE TIME OF THE REFORMATION

I

IT is during the early years of the Reformation that the first groups of socialists, in the modern sense, are found. The distinctive feature of these new groups was that they proposed what was then a novel principle to govern the ownership of property and the production of wealth. They announced as their basis of social organization what has since been named collectivism. The soil, tools, and other means for the production of wealth were to be owned by the community as a whole, not by individuals, and the product of the common industry was to be shared equally by all. As the development of these groups coincided with the Reformation, it is not surprising to find these economic and social ideas combined with religion. The men who proposed this new social order were men who desired religious liberty also, and had thrown off allegiance to the Roman Catholic Church. They had studied the Scriptures diligently, if not wisely, and they had become convinced that their proposed social order was in conformity, not only to sound economic principles and natural equity, but to the teachings of Jesus and the life of the primitive Church. We need not pause here to inquire if this conviction were well founded, since inquiry into that matter is provided for in a later chapter. It is at present im-

portant only to note that this was an honest and earnest
religious belief of these people.

These socialistic groups are generally called Anabaptists in the literature of the period, a name not at
all descriptive of them as collectivists, and often in-
accurate as a designation of their religious affiliations.
That is to say, not all those composing these socialistic
groups were Anabaptists, though probably members of
that religious party were more numerous than any others
among socialists. Nor is the inference that some have
drawn warranted, namely, that most Anabaptists of
the period were socialists. Some of the most influential
men among the Anabaptists did not sympathize with
this collectivist experiment, and gave it no support.

In the earlier stages of their movement, so far as the
Anabaptists avowed any social principles, they were
inclined rather to communism than to Socialism. They
were impelled to communism by their ideal of Christian
brotherly love, and by the example of the Church at
Jerusalem. It was supposed that this example of the
Jerusalem saints laid an obligation on all Christians to
go and do likewise — that among true Christians all
things must be held in common, to the extent at least
that every brother must use his possessions for the
advancement of the common Cause and the relief of
the more needy brother. Some went so far as to say
that the law of brotherly love forbade any Christian to
be rich. But there were many among the Anabaptists,
demonstrably some of their ablest leaders, who did not
take this view of the case. The example of a single
group of believers in the apostolic age, in a peculiar
emergency, was not believed to be sufficient to impose

a universal obligation. And so we find in most of the
Anabaptist literature now extant, either silence on this
subject or opposition to communism.[1]

What is more certainly known is, that many of the
Anabaptist groups held the doctrine of non-resistance
later advocated by the Friends. The Anabaptists were
more thoroughgoing in their logical deductions than the
Friends, however, for they held that Christ's prohibition
of violence included more than the use of force to resist
personal injury, or the collective force of war — that it
also included all civil government, which rests on force.
They differed from the interpretation of Tolstoi, in that
they conceded that "the powers that be are ordained
of God," but for the world, to be administered by the
worldly. In the kingdom of heaven, "Resist not the
evil man" is to be literally obeyed. Among the saints
there is no more place for policeman and judge than
for the soldier, because no force is to be used to
repel evil, and punishment of the evil-doer is to be
left to God. As there should be no courts, there is
no need of oaths, and so "Swear not at all" is to be
literally obeyed. Consequently, the Anabaptists consistently forbade a Christian man to be a magistrate,
or to seek protection or redress through the law; while
the Friends, less consistently, accepted the protection
of the law, even while refusing to obey it. In these
doctrines certain Anabaptists anticipated modern anarchy, rather than modern Socialism.

[1] The Schleitheim Confession is silent about community of goods, and
so are the other fragmentary statements of belief in Beck's *Geschichtsbücher*. The extant writings of Denck, Grebel, and other leaders are
equally silent, and when Hübmaier was charged with advocating community of goods, he indignantly denied the accusation.

It is also an error to look for Socialism, as some recent writers have done, in the efforts of the peasant class to better their lot, culminating in the armed insurrection of 1525, known as the Peasants' War. The Twelve Articles set forth the ideals, as well as the practical demands, of the peasants' movement, and prove beyond a doubt that it had an agrarian basis rather than a socialistic. The one article that has any apparent socialistic quality is the demand that the lords restore to the people those lands that were once common, but had been appropriated by force or fraud to private use, without color of either law or equity. These common lands were meadows for grazing cattle and woodlands, and their restoration would not have advanced a particle any scheme for socialized production. Temporary communism may be found in the peasant insurrection, as at Mühlhausen during the brief domination of Thomas Münzer, but no hint of true Socialism. The same is true of the Anabaptist attempt to set up the new kingdom of Christ at Münster — communism, extending even to community of wives, may be found there, but no Socialism.

II

The first truly socialistic groups of the sixteenth century are found in Moravia, and their history begins with the coming to Nikolsberg of one Jacob Widemann, about the year 1526. This man, popularly known as "One-eyed Jacob," is said to have been a native of Ens, in Salzburg, and he had acquired some fame as a preacher among the Anabaptists before coming to Nikolsberg. Here a large number of the sect had found refuge, owing to the fact that the lords of the region, the Counts Lichtenstein, were of a mild and tolerant disposition. They showed much favor to the Anabaptists, and at length themselves joined the sect. It is probable that the Nikolsberg Anabaptists were not homogeneous from the first, but with the coming of Widemann a party developed that held strongly to community of goods as an essential tenet of the Christian faith. Widemann became the leader of this party, and in addition taught that, as non-resistants, Christians should not pay taxes, since money thus obtained is used for the support of governments and the waging of war. Taxes therefore were "blood money," he said.

Not long after Widemann came another Anabaptist leader, named Hans Hut, a wilder fanatic than the former. He was possessed with the chiliastic notions then rife, believing himself to be a prophet and his mission to be the leading of God's people in the immediate and violent establishing of the kingdom. The time was at hand when it would be the duty of all good Christians to take up the sword and smite the ungodly hip and thigh. Even in the nineteenth century, and in the midst of an intelligent community, with schools, academies, and colleges, with a free press and a free pulpit, chiliastic ideas at one time spread like wildfire and swept even educated men off their feet; we need not be surprised, then, that they found ready acceptance among an ignorant people in the sixteenth century. Hut and Widemann, notwithstanding some contradiction in their teachings, seem to have joined forces, and their followers became a serious menace to peace and good order in Nikolsberg. So much was this the case, that Hut was arrested and imprisoned for a time in the castle of Count Lichtenstein, from which he made his escape and was no more heard of in Moravia.

c

With the departure of Hut, Widemann returned to his more moderate advocacy of communism and non-resistance. For a time the greatest preacher of the Ana-baptist movement, Balthazar Hübmaier, together with the more sober of the sect, made a successful opposition, and the cause was on the wane when the Austrian gov-ernment caused the arrest of Hübmaier and soon after put him to death; after which there was no able leader left to oppose the radicals. Widemann and his party now waxed in numbers and influence, and finally became so obnoxious that Count Lichtenstein required them either to cease their disturbance or leave his domains. Having heard of a possible refuge elsewhere, they chose the latter alternative and emigrated northward to the vicinity of Austerlitz. The territorial lords here, the brothers von Kaunitz, welcomed them with a great show of favor, even sending wagons to assist in the transportation of their goods. Sites for houses were assigned them, materials were advanced for building, and they were permitted to order their life as they pleased.

The principles avowed by the party hitherto seem purely communistic, but the new community was estab-lished on a socialistic basis. The chief occupations were at first agricultural, and the soil was the prime source of wealth. But some of the members had come from the towns and had learned trades; they were set at their various handicrafts. Others were taught, and soon flourishing industries were built up. Those bred to farming cultivated the fields, and there were no more productive farms in the country than these speedily became. Horses and cattle were bred, and the stock

quickly gained a high repute for extra quality, and brought
the highest market prices. Labor was scarce in that
region, and the lords of the soil were glad to employ any
who could be spared for the purpose. The better trained
and more intelligent of the community were in demand
as managers of farms, mills, vineyards, stables. The
wares turned out were sent to the fairs and markets, and
of certain handicrafts almost a monopoly was gained.
Their tailors, smiths, and weavers were of the best. The
knives, scythes, shoes, stockings, handkerchiefs, and other
wares produced sold promptly, for the goods were honest
and the prices fair.

The Austerlitz community thus became prosperous,
and might have grown rich, but for its internal dissensions. These were partly incidental to the form of organization, and partly the result of religious bigotry. The
community formed a common "household," occupying
a common building, to the number of several hundred
souls. A general superintendent, or "householder," pre-
sided. He was chosen by general suffrage, but his authority was almost despotic and was often despotically
used. The householder was also their chief pastor or
bishop, but besides him there were several other "ministers of the word," or preachers. Others, called "ministers of necessities," or deacons, assisted the householder
in the practical work of administration. Nobody might
preach in the community, or even give private religious
instruction, until he had been formally called to this
office by the congregation. This rule was enforced against
all, no matter how famous as preachers they might have
been elsewhere. Discipline was maintained, not by ordinary expulsion from the community, but by excom-

munication — which made of the excommunicated a
heathen, to whom not even a cup of cold water might
be given by a member of the community, without his
incurring the same penalty.   Obey or starve, was the
stern edict of the society.

Under such severe and minute superintendence as
this system made possible, we need not be surprised
that the labor of all was well directed.   Each lived
for all and all for each.   The community idea
was carried into nearly every detail of living: the
household had a common kitchen, a common school-
house, a common nursery, a common sick-room, and
of course a common dining room.   But each family
had its own apartments, and the family was nominally
not divided.   Clothing, strictly personal articles, and the
furnishings of apartments were private property;   all
else was common.   Of course, the community undertook to regulate the marriages of its members, and
seeking a partner outside was punished with immediate
exclusion.

We need not be at all surprised to discover that this
rigid rule was provocative of much murmuring and dissatisfaction, with occasional open rebellion.   William
Reublin, one of the best of the Swiss Anabaptist preachers,
the man who had taught and baptized Hübmaier, found
his way to the Austerlitz society, where he was received
as a member, but forbidden to exercise his gifts until
called to the work, and Widemann's influence was sufficient to prevent him from being called.   In spite of
this prohibition, during an absence of Widemann he
presumed to hold private meetings for the study of the
Bible, to the great edification of some of the members,

and for this offence was excluded from membership.[1]
He in vain sought forgiveness and restoration, and was
on the point of starvation, when some of the members
refused to submit longer to the will of the majority and
gave him succor.

For this contumacy they, too, were excommunicated,
but this made still further trouble in the community, and
more than one hundred members resolved to stand by
Reublin. Separating from the Austerlitz brethren, they
made their way to Auspitz, nearly midway between
Austerlitz and Nikolsberg, where a convent rented them
some land and a new community was set up. These two
communities rapidly increased in number, by the coming
to Moravia of refugees from all quarters, and especially
from the Tyrol, where a bitter persecution was now raging. By 1536 there are said to have been no fewer than
eighty-six such communities in Moravia, most of them
numbering several hundred persons each, and one boast-
ing a membership of two thousand.

We have not sufficient details concerning the inner life
of most of these Anabaptist societies to decide whether
the difficulties experienced at Austerlitz and Auspitz
were common to all. These difficulties, as we have seen,
grew in large part out of the form of organization and

[1] Letter to Pilgram Marbeck, in Cornelius, *Geschichte des Münster-
ischen Aufruhrs*, Leipzig, 1855, 1860, II: 253. Reublin charges the leaders with managing the property of the community dishonestly and fraud-
ulently. They permitted the rich to have their own little houses, so that
Franz and his wife led a life like the nobles. At meals the ordinary
brethren had been content with peas and cabbages, but the leaders and
their wives had meat, fish, fowls, and wine. "Many of their wives,"
says Reublin, "I have never seen at the common table." While some
might be in want of shoes and shirts, the leaders must have coats, good
breeches, and furs in abundance. The letter is dated January 26, 1531.

the opportunities for despotic action afforded to an ambitious and self-willed leader. The spirit of the community itself was intolerant. "There was as much liberty of conscience among them as among the Papists," said Sebastian Franck, a contemporary and not unsympathetic observer. "He who will not say them yea in all things, for him hath God stopped the ears, and be he not willing to turn back they cast him out." Truly, there has seldom or never, in the history of Christianity, been so much truculent bitterness, so many hard-hearted cruelties exhibited, as were shown here in the name of brotherly love. We are not now concerned, however, with the sinfulness of such conduct, but with its effect on the community life. That it was divisive and disintegrating, and could be only such, does not need argument.

Other difficulties developed, growing out of the community life. Not a few parents strenuously objected to the community method of bringing up their children; the Scriptures, as they pointedly and pertinently said, exhort parents to "bring up their children in the nurture and admonition of the Lord," and nowhere lay that duty on others than the parents. Not only the Scriptures, but parental love, proved to be totally inconsistent with the system. Moreover, the young maidens of the community strongly objected to being assigned husbands without their consent. Widemann threatened to give the brethren "heathen wives" if the sisters continued obstinate, by which he probably meant no worse than wives from outside the community; but his intemperate language on the subject caused great scandal, and in spite of his authority the maidens remained obdurate.

It became evident in no long time that Jacob Widemann possessed the qualities of an agitator rather than
those of an organizer.   As a ruler, desire far outran performance with him.   A man better fitted for holding together and directing the communities must be found or
they would surely fall apart.   Such a man was found in
Jacob Huter, a native of the Tyrol, who had learned the
hatter's trade in Prag and practised it in various cities,
and had also become an ardent and successful Anabaptist preacher in his native valleys from about 1529.   Here
he built up a large number of Anabaptist congregations,
many of which sought refuge in Moravia after the Austrian government began a severe persecution in all its
domains, that proved especially hot in the Tyrol.   The
mediation of Huter was sought in some of these troubles
at Austerlitz, and he improved the occasion so to extend
his influence that he finally acquired the direction of
affairs, not only at Austerlitz, but at Auspitz; and in the
other communities afterward established his voice was
potent though not always controlling.   To his power of
organization much of the subsequent prosperity of these
societies was due.   At one time, their internal dissensions had so weakened the Auspitz community that they
were unable to pay their rent and were in danger of being
dispossessed; Huter brought financial aid from the Tyro-
lese Anabaptists and assisted the community in regulating their affairs.

III

It is not certain that all the Anabaptist groups in
Moravia were organized on the strict socialistic basis of
those at Austerlitz and Auspitz, but it is probable that

most of them were.   We do not hear of dissensions in the
others, whence it is fair to conclude that they were less
troubled in this way.   In general, the chronicles preserved
by these people, and the references to them in Moravian
literature of the period, warrant the conclusion that, as a
whole, they enjoyed a notable degree of economic prosperity, so long as they were not interfered with from without.   Local jealousy finally combined with religious intolerance to secure the suppression of these Moravian
communities.   We first hear of the former from a chronicle of the Brethren in 1600: "During this year a great
outcry from our adversaries has gone abroad in Moravia,
that the fraternity increases beyond measure in that
country, and by their trade do no small damage to the
commercial interests of the towns and boroughs.   For
this reason the reigning princes have resolved to forbid
us to erect new households, and yet they permit the
territorial lords to make use of the Brothers as workmen." [1]

Even before this, in the year 1567, Maximilian proposed to expel the Anabaptists from Moravia, with the
following result, according to Gindeley : —

And now a new and entirely unexpected departure from
old tradition took place on the part of the nobles.   In union
with the knights (the prelates and towns did not take part in
this petition), they begged the emperor to allow the Anabaptists to remain in their own homes.   Not because the people were still unconvicted heretics, nor because any one had
an interest in their conversion ; no, it was set on foot on far
more practical grounds, namely, that the Anabaptists were
even more profitable subjects than the Jews, and could not be

[1] Beck, *Geschichtsbücher*, p. 331.

banished without great material injuries. Catholics, Utra-quists, as well as Bohemian Brethren, bowed before the weight of their own argument. The Anabaptists were, in fact, every-where extremely industrious, thrifty, temperate, and more-over, by far the cleverest workmen in Moravia.[1]

These socialistic settlements were finally extinguished by persecution, not by any failure of their principles to work satisfactorily. Some of the communities emigrated to Russia and continued to thrive there until recent times. A branch founded in the Tyrol by Jacob Huter found a refuge in Russia in 1769, and came in a body to the United States in 1874. They have established them-selves in five communistic societies in South Dakota, where they now number nearly five hundred communi-cant members. There seems to be no reason why they should not continue to prosper indefinitely, if they can avoid religious dissensions.

Since only ten years at most of peace were given in Moravia for this experiment, much caution is necessary in any inferences that we may draw from the history of these communities. There have been instances since that day of communities that were established and flour-ished more than a decade, only to end in failure at last, and that without any external interference. Bearing this carefully in mind, what may we learn from this first experiment in Socialism, on any considerable scale, that history records?

First, it illustrates the difficulties of introducing So-cialism out-of-hand, as socialists once hoped to do. So-

[1] *Geschichte der Böhmischen Brüder*, Prag, 1857, II: 19. This testi-mony, from a historian who by no means sympathizes with the Anabap-tists, is very significant.

ciety as a whole is not yet educated up to the pitch necessary for the successful working of socialistic principles;
and not even a picked community, actuated by one of
the strongest unifying principles yet discovered — a common religious enthusiasm — is yet educated to the proper
point. The most successful communities since those of
Moravia have been communities in which religion was
the strongest bond; but not even religion has been powerful enough to restrain jealousy and strife. Brotherly
love, without the sanctions of religion, is too weak a sentiment to be seriously considered as a bond to hold men
and women long together. And if some way could be
found of introducing Socialism universally and compelling men to live under the system, would not the suffering be greater under such a system than it is now? The
study of these communities strongly urges men rather to
bear the ills they have than flee to others that they know
not of.

Indeed, so obvious has this inference become that the
Socialism of to-day fully recognizes its force. The new
man must precede the new social order; or, at any rate,
a new man must be evolved and will be evolved as fast
as the new social order, we are now assured. As the
changes occur that are to transform present society into
the socialistic order, men will become accustomed to them,
will learn to adjust themselves to them, will find their
condition constantly improving; and by the time the
evolution is complete the new man will be complete also.
Let us hope so, for if not, the new order will no sooner
be attained than it will be overthrown. The later Socialism offers to us at least a more consistent theory than
the old, in that it does not require us to believe in the

possibility of any machine-made millennium. We can afford with patience, and possibly with hopefulness, to await the evolution and see what it will bring forth.

Second, we ought to learn from this experiment that those have been too hasty who have inferred from it the economic feasibility of Socialism. It is true that if these communities were able to keep the peace within, and were allowed peace without, they always prospered. So far as food, clothing, and shelter were concerned, plenty and happiness abounded. If men had only bovine wants, and were content with a bovine life, these communities would have furnished an elysium.[1] But we must not forget that these were picked communities, containing members far above the average in moral character, and therefore capable of an abnormal economic efficiency. The proportion of those who were not able-bodied was small, and of all the difficulties they experienced, there is no mention of idleness. Everybody seems to have been both able and willing to work. Economic waste was thus reduced to the minimum, at the same time that economic efficiency was exalted to the maximum. In

[1] It is perhaps not remarkable that people who had never before known plenty should have rejoiced in the comforts of these communities. One of their number thus writes: "How we keep our table with food and drink: we have meat at supper every day, and in the mornings once twice, thrice, or four times during the week, according as the seasons serve. At the other meals we are content with vegetables. Twice every day at meals a luscious drink of wine; otherwise nothing at midday nor in the afternoon, nor in the evening; but when we go to evening prayers we receive a drink, and sometimes even have beer. With the bread, which is generally to be had in the house, we are quite content, even if we are not permitted to bake anything special during the whole year; this, however, we are permitted to do when there is any particular reason, such as for the Day of the Lord's Remembrance, or the festivals of Easter, Whitsuntide, and Christmas." — Beck, *Geschichtsbücher*, pp. 406, 407.

any organization of a socialistic nature on a large scale, including a province or a nation, or even a city, there would necessarily be a far larger proportion of the disabled, the defective, the aged, and others who could contribute little or nothing to the common wealth. It is very doubtful if a like willingness to work would be found in other communities. This Moravian experiment, in a word, does not afford a fair economic test of the theory of Socialism, for the experiment was not conducted under fairly average conditions.

Third, these communities exhibit one common defect, of a very grave nature. While they flourished, so far as to accumulate ample material possessions, there was a painful absence of the higher life. To be sure, there was religion — of a sort — narrow, intense, bigoted, and so far it was recognized that man does not live by bread alone. But aside from religion there was hardly any provision for the higher faculties. Education was provided in a common school, but what sort of education? The most elementary instruction in reading, writing, and arithmetic — enough, as we still say, to fit a man for "business," as if the chief business of a man in this world were not to live his life well, getting the most out of it for himself, that he may have the most to give to others. The need of culture, of the harmonious development of all the faculties, so as to make of a man something like what his Creator designed him to be, was not contemplated by these people.

This is due, probably, to the fact that they were so largely of the peasant and artisan class, and even their leaders were men of little education. It was different among the Swiss and German Anabaptists, where the leaders were mainly men who had studied at the best universities of the time. We cannot excuse the failure at this point of these Moravian Anabaptists on the plea of their poverty; for we remember that one of the first things that the New England Puritans did when they settled in Massachusetts was to make provision, out of their poverty, for the establishment of a college in which their youth might be trained. If the need of higher education had been felt among these people, they could have taken some step towards its supply. They were content to remain in their ignorance. Of any appreciation of literature, of art, of music, except so far as the latter might be made available in singing hymns, we find no trace among them.

Their minds were set on the lower things. The real good of life is not dependent on wealth, and therefore to get the best out of life it is not needful for a man or a community to get rich. Money will not buy a pure heart, a clear conscience, a refined nature, a trained intellect, not even a healthy body. A moderate amount of money is a great help to the acquirement and maintenance of some of these things, but that is all. Most of the things that really count, that make life worth while — religion, love of friends, art, literature, music — do not require a fortune for their possession and enjoyment. "Superfluous wealth can buy superfluities only," said Thoreau, and he proved by his life at Walden that most wealth is superfluous, and that money is not required to procure one necessary of the soul. The business of an immortal soul is with immortal values. When the absolute bodily wants have been provided, when man has food, shelter, and clothing, there is but one thing necessary to live the higher life of the spirit, and that is the desire to live it.   To one in whom the spirit is regnant, spiritual things, which most men regard as mere luxuries, are the real necessaries of life.   "The life is more than the meat," says Ruskin.   "Meat! perhaps your right to that may be pleadable; but other rights have to be pleaded first.   Claim your crumbs from the table, if you will; but claim them as children, not as dogs. Claim your right to be fed, but claim more loudly your right to be holy, perfect, and pure."

While these highest things do not cost much in money, they do cost much in leisure.   A man must have time, and a good deal of time, to loaf and invite his soul (to speak Whitmanese), if his soul is to grow.   This sort of loafing not only does not make a loafer, but a man cannot be made without it.   This is not to blaspheme the gospel of work so urgently proclaimed by Carlyle and Ruskin. Labor is something to which we ought not to submit as a curse, but to hail as a blessing.   Work is natural to man, idleness abnormal.   Labor is so physiologically necessary to health and happiness that a man who has no work must make himself some.   The "sports" of the leisure class exist in obedience to this imperious necessity.   But no man lives by labor alone; at best he may merely exist; his higher nature demands culture.   Little money will satisfy a reasonable man, but leisure he must have for his soul to enjoy its possessions and to grow heavenward.

It is the utter failure to realize these things, to make any provision for the higher life, even to recognize that there was any higher life, save in their narrow, intense, intolerant religious convictions, that these socialistic communities mutely witness. No life could be more "comfortable" than theirs, and none could be more colorless, dreary, unattractive, unendurable. The life of these Moravian socialists was thoroughly respectable and deadly dull. It was the mechanical plodding of a daily treadmill, with no touch of sentiment or beauty, with no aspiration to make to-day's accomplishment a little finer than yesterday's. Such a life raises precisely the same question as is suggested by our present civilization, Is it worth having, at the price men are called to pay for it?

It would not be fair, perhaps, to infer that all Socialism will tend in this same direction and in the end have no ideals but the sensuous. But when we find the modern Socialism mainly concerned with material things, seldom recognizing the fact that the humblest task may be shot through with the golden thread of the ideal, with small place in its programme for any but scientific and useful education, with little appreciation of culture, the best books, the best art, the best music, may not we who believe that no full and worthy life is possible without seeking after the higher things be pardoned if we look forward with some apprehension to a future in which this leaden-hued Socialism may come to prevail, as its prophets exultingly tell us it is certain to do? Is the whole world to come to the state of mind of that rich man of the third gospel, whose ground brought forth plentifully, so that he was minded to pull down his barns and build greater, and to say to his soul, "Soul, thou hast many goods laid up for many years; take thine ease, eat, drink, be merry"? If this is to be the world's ideal of felicity, then the sooner a Power outside says, "Fool, this night thy soul is required of thee," the better. If Socialism has nothing higher than this to offer, its success will be the failure of the race.

But, while it is necessary to note this defect in the Moravian communities, it would not be fair to conclude that this is characteristic of Socialism. Once more we must remind ourselves, the experiment in Moravia was too brief to offer material for definite judgment. All that we can do is, note certain defects and tendencies, as well as certain successes, guard ourselves from drawing too large inferences from our premises, and reserve judgment until we have further studied both the theories of Socialism and the workings of other socialistic experiments.

II

THE BEGINNINGS OF MODERN SOCIALISM IN FRANCE

D

BIBLIOGRAPHY

MARX, The Poverty of Philosophy.   Chicago, 1910.
JAURÈS, Studies in Socialism.   New York, 1906.
GUTHRIE, Socialism before the French Revolution.   New York,
    1907.
ELY, French and German Socialism in Modern Times.   New York,
    1886.
LAVELEYE, Socialism of To-day.   London, 1885.

II

THE BEGINNINGS OF MODERN SOCIALISM IN FRANCE

I

SOCIALISM, both as a philosophy and as a concerted movement, has its real beginning in the nineteenth century, and must be regarded as among the most remarkable developments of that age.

As a philosophy, Socialism proposes an interpretation of history that is worthy of a preliminary examination. A great evolution has been in progress for ages, of which Socialism is held to be the necessary outcome.[1] The essential feature of this long-continued movement is a reaction against the theory of imperialism, or centralized authority, embodied in the Roman Empire and continued in the Roman Church. In its successive stages this reaction has received various names: the struggle for liberty of thought was called the Renaissance; the contest for religious freedom was known as the Reformation;

---

[1] It is somewhat difficult for us to receive this interpretation of history, because the social order to which we have been accustomed from childhood seems to us a very stable thing, and we can hardly believe in the possibility of radical changes in it. But this apparent stability of society proves, on even a slight investigation, to be as deceptive as the apparent stability of the earth — it is hard to convince a child or a savage that the earth turns completely over every twenty-four hours, and is continually turning at a speed compared with which the swiftest railway train might seem to be standing still.

the attempt to win civic freedom men named the Revolution. So much as this has long been accepted as a
sound historical generalization.

But the socialist further asserts that underneath this
evolution, conditioning and controlling these outward
manifestations, was a series of economic changes in society that historians have too little recognized. When
Christianity began its career in the Roman Empire, it
found a social order based on the institution of slavery,
whose principal source of wealth was cultivation of the
soil. This society was itself an advance on the prehistoric
barbarism, in which a continual state of war prevailed.
In such wars the defeated were at first killed on the spot
by the victors, or taken prisoners only to be put to death
by cruel tortures, as with the American aborigines, or
to be eaten, as is still the custom among various African
tribes. But after a time it was discovered that the worst
use to which men could put a fellow-man was to kill
him — that it was far more profitable to spare his life
and condemn him to perpetual servitude. Greek and
Roman civilization was based on this system. At first
free labor flourished alongside of slave labor, but at length
slave labor drove out free labor and the agricultural
system of the Empire became a series of vast farms or
ranches worked by slaves. This system was falling into
decay when the irruption of the Germanic tribes precipi-
tated its downfall, and out of the ruins of slavocracy
slowly emerged another social order, feudalism.

Feudalism had the same economic basis as Roman
civilization ; the main source of wealth was still agriculture. But under feudalism arms was the only calling
of the freeborn population, and a class to cultivate the

soil was a necessity. Slavery had ceased to be profitable, and gradually became modified into serfdom. The slave's labor had been unpaid, but, on the other hand, the owner took the responsibility of the slave's maintenance. The serf was no longer a chattel, but the land was not his. He was permitted to occupy it, on condition of giving part of his labor to the feudal proprietor, and he paid the remainder of his rent in kind; that is, from the produce of the soil that he cultivated in his own time. Neither he nor his wife and children could be sold to another master without their consent, but this freedom of person was not accompanied by any great increase of comfort or privilege. It is doubtful if the serf were better lodged, better fed, or better clothed than the slave. Even his advance in personal liberty was slight, for he could not change his domicile without his lord's consent — he was *adscriptus glebæ*.

The close of the Middle Ages saw the decay of feudalism, and the rise of a new system, based on commerce. Agriculture was no longer the mainstay of European society; manufactures vied with cultivation of the soil as a source of wealth, while commerce, surpassing both, became the foundation of the new social order. We mark the growth of this new order by the upspringing of numerous crafts and guilds, by the rise of free cities that the guilds built up and sustained, and the Hansas or leagues of cities for the protection and furtherance of commerce. The first stages in the rise of modern Capitalism are found in the fortunes — great for their time — that were accumulated through this commerce. With this new commercialism came the need for facilitation of exchanges, and this produced banking, with its bills of exchange, drafts, and credits. The coining of money, almost disused under feudalism, also began anew.

The more enterprising of the serf or peasant class forsook their fields and lords, in spite of all attempts to restrain and punish them, and became artisans, tradesmen, burghers. Wealth was gradually transferred from the owners of the soil to the merchants, bankers, and craftsmen. The cities grew rich and powerful at the expense of the country, and the result was the formation of a strong middle class, which became the wealthiest and therefore the most powerful body in the state. The continued refusal to this body of political rights, the continued imposition on them of inequitable burdens by those who had been born to rank and titles, led finally to the uprising of the *bourgeoisie* or middle class, or third estate, that is known as the Revolution. The ostensible object of the Revolution was the abolition of privilege and the establishment of "liberty, fraternity, equality." But these were mere words ; the real object was the transference of political and social power from the nobility to the middle class. In this struggle the remnants of feudalism disappeared, and out of it the modern social order emerged.

II

We see, therefore, that the history of the world is the history of a struggle for wealth, power, honor — first a struggle between communities or nations or races, and then in the conquering community or nation a struggle between classes. The law of survival applies to societies as well as to individuals ; communities must be fitted to survive, class must prove superior to class, as truly as man to man. Historians have given their attention chiefly to the struggle between nations, and the wars waged between them for the control of the earth and its resources; and have too little regarded the equally un-ending social war, which, while it has been less spectacular, has had consequences much more far-reaching and important. History will for the future be less concerned with dynasties and constitutions and great battles, and investigate more carefully the economic condition and social organization of the various classes of the people. In other words, we are beginning to study the real current of the world's movements, and not the mere foam and spray.

In all these changes that we have briefly traced, we see one principle abiding: alike in the Græco-Roman civilization and in feudalism and in the triumph of the *bourgeoisie*, the individual man was always held to be the social unit. Every man fought for his own hand against the powers of nature and the encroachments of his fellows. This was modified in social life by the family, the club, and in economic activities by the guild, the firm. The principle of coöperation was beginning to develop, but it was as yet so restricted in operation that its significance was not suspected, and individual enterprise was still the general rule.

The political reaction against absolutism not only intensified this individualism, but gave for a time an exclusively political phase to the struggle to win liberty and equality. For ages the chief oppressors of men had been, or had been believed to be, their rulers; hence the attempt to rise in the scale of manhood was first of all an attack on kings and nobles, the "tyrants" and "aris-

tocrats" who had abused and abased mankind too long.
Privilege, the deadly foe of equality, was supposed to be
rooted in royalty and aristocracy — political institutions,
that must therefore be gotten rid of as a prime condition
of progress. This was true, but not the whole truth.
The long contest bred a habit of mind : a looking at all
the problems of society as questions of political organization, which would be solved by giving every man the
ballot. And thus a mischievous delusion was spread
widely : that when political oppression was destroyed,
there would be no oppression existent or possible, for
the man with the ballot could defend himself against all
oppressors.

But it was soon discovered that the new Revolution,
by breaking down the old privilege and giving every man
the ballot, had not in fact much improved the condition
of the man who must rely on daily labor for daily bread.
"Liberty, fraternity, equality," were beautiful ideals,
but they corresponded to no realities. The laborer
found that he had exchanged the feudal noble for the
capitalist, the castle for the factory. He was made
painfully aware that the old chains which bound him to
poverty and misery had been newly gilt, not broken.
What was euphoniously called "freedom" he found to
be lifelong dependence of all but a few on the will of
others, the owners of land and capital ; and to be dependent on the will of another is the essence of slavery.
Carlyle uttered a great truth when he said that the wage-
earner differs from a chattel slave in that he is bought
for a short time and the slave for a lifetime.

That he was really free, simply because he was free to
vote, the laborer soon found to be the barest and least

satisfying of delusions. What is a ballot worth to a man who has no job, and who cannot find one? What value has "freedom" for the man to whom it means only that he is free to suffer cold and hunger and live in a slum? If freedom has any real meaning, it means equality of opportunity, equality of privilege. Instead of such equality, the poor man after the glorious Revolution found himself in the same state of economic slavery as before.

Many urgently protest against that phrase "economic slavery," on the ground that a certain degree of servitude is inseparable from living in this world. Man's existence on earth will ever mean that he has the problem to solve of wresting a living from the soil. The danger of cold and hunger will ever act as a spur to exertion, and so far man is of necessity a "slave" to economic conditions. But nobody is in danger of overlooking a fact so obvious. What men see and question is the other fact, also perfectly obvious, that the man whose toil wrings wealth out of the reluctant earth is now paid least, while the largest part of what he produces by his sweat and blood goes to those who are like the lilies of the field in one respect, that they toil not, neither do they spin. The socialist admits that man must work, but from this truth he draws the corollary that all men should work. The vast majority of men now belong to the ranks of the toilers; it is better for the individual, better for society, that every capable person should produce his share, earn his own living. "If a man will not work, neither shall he eat" is good ethics. Work is a necessity, but it is not a necessity that man should be thwarted in his efforts by his fellow-man, or plundered of the fruits of his toil without redress. "All social evils and religious errors," declares Ruskin, "arise out of the pillage of the laborers by the idlers," and he does not greatly overstate the matter. According to the Declaration, man has an inalienable right to "life, liberty, and the pursuit of happiness," but life and liberty are impossible without the opportunity to labor, while the pursuit of happiness is but a mockery if a man is systematically robbed of the fruits of his labor.

The socialist finds the secret of the laborer's failure to profit by the Revolution in the impetus that great upheaval gave to individualism. Pure individualism, of course, never existed on any extended scale, or for any long time. Robinson Crusoe on his desert island might practice — and enjoy, if he could — pure individualism, but the moment his man Friday came, a society was born. Society is not a business partnership, an arbitrary invention for purposes of convenience, — the "social contract" never existed outside of the imagination of Rousseau, — but a necessity of human life. Various forms of social organization have come into being, as they were found to be efficient weapons in the struggle for existence. The biological analogy may be pushed too far in the study of society, but it is a real analogy — society is an organism, and not a mere organization.

The closest approach to individualism was when men were first emerging from barbarism, and every man made for himself whatever he required, or did without. But barter must have begun very soon after making, and with exchange of products there was an end of strict individualism. The specialization of labor into trades followed speedily, each man doing what he could do better than others, and exchanging his surplus products for the prod-

ucts of others. This state of things is found in tribes
either barbarous or semibarbarous. Commerce is merely
another trade, that of promoting exchanges. Return
even to such a state of comparative individualism as prevailed a century ago is impossible, as impossible as return to the stone age, — it is a stage of development that
has forever passed away.

To this relative individualism, as applied to the production of wealth, the Revolution gave a fresh and powerful impetus. The watchword of the industrial and
commercial world was "free competition" [1] between
individual producers. After the Revolution this became
the recognized foundation of the economic system that
prevailed throughout Europe and America, sometimes
interfered with, but even then in an almost apologetic
spirit. Among a certain school of English economists
this principle of free competition acquired almost the
sanction of a moral law, held to be as inexorable as gravitation. One may of course ignore gravitation and cast
himself down from the housetop, but broken bones will
be the penalty. So the law of supply and demand may
be obstructed, interfered with, by legislative and other
expedients, but economic penalties are invariably exacted.
Hence *laissez faire*, let things alone, became the motto
of this school; free competition under the law of supply
and demand would solve all economic problems, and it
was deemed worse than useless to seek any other solu-

---

[1] There are sharp limitations of theoretical free competition, imposed
either by natural conditions or by law. Free competition in land is made
impossible by nature — the quantity of land is limited. Free competition
in machinery is limited by legal monopolies, known as "patents." Free
competition in exchanges is deliberately destroyed by tariffs. Competition, therefore, in practice irresistibly tends to give place to monopoly.

tion. The principle was maintained with a fanatical energy of conviction that made it almost respectable. Almost, but not quite, for there were never lacking prophets, like Ruskin and Carlyle, to lift up voices in protest against this school of economics, and to proclaim its fundamental principle not only unchristian but inhuman. Though at first few would listen to such protests, an increasing number of people came to see that if the science of economics can be divorced from ethics, it should not be.

Free competition and *laissez faire* held the field a long time, however, triumphant if not undisputed; and under the sway of such ideas the capitalistic system developed rapidly. It had its beginnings, as we have seen, in the rise of commerce during the later Middle Ages, and progressed with only moderate rapidity until the nineteenth century. Then it advanced by leaps and bounds. The reason for this sudden increase was the number of inventions made late in the eighteenth century of machinery, to which steam could be applied as a motive power, among the earliest of which were the spinning-jenny and the power-loom. This combination of steam and machinery enormously increased production, through the rise of the modern factory. Hundreds of costly machines and thousands of busy laborers, assembled under one roof, have substituted socialized production for individual production.

Hitherto, hand labor had been on the whole distinctly favorable to individualism in production, and had consequently retarded the development of Capitalism. Machine labor was, on the whole, fatal to individualism in production, and made socialized production and Capitalism inevitable. Thenceforth society tended to divide

into two classes, the employers and the employed — a
distinction that had previously existed, but that now
tended to become universal and to harden gradually into
castes.   It was and still is possible, in theory, for any of
the employed class to rise and become employers; and
for any of the employer class to fall back among the employed; and the theory is justified by a certain number
of cases of both kinds.   But, taking each class as a whole,
status tends to become fixed by birth, and passage from
one class to the other becomes increasingly difficult and
infrequent.   It is likewise theoretically possible for any
male child born in the United States, if he lives, to become President; but a laborer's chance of becoming a
capitalist is nearly as remote as that of his becoming
President.

And yet men are told, with tiresome iteration, as they
have been told for generations, that any man can by
diligence and frugality rise to wealth and power.   Theoretically this is true of any given man, but it is mathe-
matically impossible for the mass.   Under present social
conditions, for one to be rich many must remain poor.
The Pennsylvania Railroad has many thousands of employees, but only one president, and the other highly
profitable posts are few.   No matter how diligent, all
of the employees cannot rise to the chief posts, until one
and one somehow make ten.   It is not the fault of the
poor that they do not rise, though some of the poor may
be at fault; it is in the nature of present conditions that
only an exceptional few can rise.   And the number of
those who can "get on" by any amount of skill and exertion relatively decreases with the increasing scale of
modern enterprise.   A generation ago, in a small business

where half a dozen clerks were employed, one of them might without much difficulty in time become a member of the firm; but put the same man now in a great department store among five thousand fellows, and what is his chance of ultimate membership in the firm? It is precisely because the present system virtually denies advancement to thrift and industry, save to a fortunate few, that its injustice is so keenly felt.

While labor was thus becoming socialized, Capitalism continued to increase along the line of individualism. Free competition was at first necessary to the development of the system, and was found to be thoroughly advantageous — up to a certain point. Only through unrestricted rivalry could some men, superior in a certain shrewdness, in power of organization, in commercial instinct, become employers of their fellows — on a small scale at first, then on a large scale — and by exploiting the labor of the less shrewd obtain the lion's share of the profits, and so build up a great industrial concern and a great fortune. This was perfectly honest, according to the prevailing ethical standards, by no means incompatible with strict integrity and even with generous philanthropy, as those words were then understood. Ethical standards are beginning to change, and men are coming to question whether this method of acquiring wealth is in accord with fundamental equity — whether the so-called "captain of industry" deserves the great share of what is produced that he has so far succeeded in annexing.

While Capitalism was thus developing, free competition in labor was essential to its interests, — that is, laborers must be permitted and encouraged to bid against each other for jobs, which would go to the lowest bidder, not the highest. But this was as much against the interest of the laborer as it was favorable to the employer. Such free competition was a very one-sided affair, for the theory that the laborer was also free, if he did not like the terms offered by one employer to seek employment elsewhere was only valid on paper, not in actual life. In the beginning of the factory system, when the amount of capital invested was small and new enterprises were easily begun on a small scale, when individual hand labor was still not impossible, though every day becoming less profitable, the employer and the employed bargained on something like equal terms. But to-day, with hand labor practically obsolete, with vast aggregations of capital invested in manufacturing plants, with men and women employed by hundreds and even by thousands in a single concern, to talk of the workman's "freedom of contract" is either silly or a deliberate attempt to deceive. The modern workman, not by statute law, but by the iron law of necessity, is as strictly bound to the factory as ever serf was to the soil. The condition of the proletarian is hardly better than serfdom in fact, whatever it may be in theory. Wage slavery is more profitable to the capitalist than chattel slavery or serfdom, but how much better it is for the worker is an unsolved question.

Absolute freedom is admittedly incompatible with life in a society, for such life of itself imposes strict obligations, from which none can free himself or be freed. But equality of opportunity to live and labor and enjoy is at least conceivable, whether realizable or not. It is promised men by the existing social order, but what is the fact? The only means of obtaining a livelihood is, for the great majority of those who toil with their hands, to obtain employment in the shop or factory, and often only a single shop is available. The employer holds in his hands, all but absolutely, the means of support — if he withholds a job, it means suffering, perhaps starvation, for the laborer. When he deals with a worker singly, he is master of the situation, and may dictate terms that the worker must accept. The worker seeking a job under such conditions bargains with his hands tied. His freedom is fairly comparable to that of the man of whom the highwayman demands, "Your money or your life!" Of course the man is perfectly free to keep his purse and lose his life. Just so free is a man out of work, with wife and children looking to him for bread, to refuse work when the owner of the shop says, "Take this wage or none!" He is free to refuse the work — and starve. If this is freedom, what would slavery be like?

It should not be forgotten, of course, that all employers have not been grasping and heartless, but it is average human nature to take advantage of the chance to make a good bargain, and to get all that may legally be had for one's money. And besides, employers who would willingly pay higher wages are often compelled to pay the lower, because otherwise they could not sell their product in competition with the less considerate employer. Only by collective dealing with the employer through their unions have workers been able to better their position and obtain something approaching justice. Otherwise there is freedom of contract only on the side of the capitalist. He controls the instruments of production, and the proletarian can find work only on the capitalist's terms. And while the proletarian must have work, the capitalist will at worst suffer financial loss if he fails to secure the labor that his business requires. Freedom of contract indeed !

Capitalism, however, found in time that free competition had its drawbacks — for the capitalist. Individualism broke down under the strain, as individualism had already broken down in the laboring class, and collectivism in capital began. Competition became so fierce that none but the strongest concerns could endure, and their profits were cut down to the vanishing point. This desperate struggle for existence among the capitalists could not go on without danger of universal bankruptcy. There was, moreover, great economic waste in competitive production, which was not appreciated in its earlier stages : duplication of plants, unnecessary investment of capital, expensive managers and salesmen. Then began a consolidation of interests, with a view to the elimination of waste, the ending of competition, and so to an increase of prices and profits — in a word, the era of the Trust.   By pursuit of this method for a generation, the production of wealth has been largely socialized, both as to labor and capital ; while the distribution of wealth remains as before.

The Trusts and great corporations have taken a long step towards collectivism ; a few hundred men now control the great mass of our industries.   Yet they insist that individualism shall continue in the distribution of wealth — there is still to be a great scramble, and every man is to get and hold what he can.   The capitalist has the same idea of free competition as before — for the laborer. He is perfectly aware that there can be no real equality of contract between men who are unequal in condition, but he insists on the maintenance of the fiction.   In order

E

to assure the continuance of unequal conditions, he is always importing fresh stocks of laborers from Europe — in defiance or evasion of the statute that forbids importation of foreign laborers under contract — lest the competition should not be "free" enough; and he contends strenuously for the "open shop" so that no union may deprive the laborer of his freedom of contract, while at the same time he demands that a high tariff shall prevent any competition with his products. He indignantly asserts that it is an outrage for the law to interfere with his business, by shortening the hours of labor for women, by preventing the employment of small children in his factories, by requiring better sanitation of workshops, and the like. All that he asks — he is a reasonable man — is to be let alone, and left to manage his own business in his own way. The capitalist has developed the same views as the anarchist — extremes meet.

III

Capitalism thus developed in the nineteenth century as the natural mode of trade — a necessary organization of the machinery of commerce that must be developed if the world was to progress. Being a necessary stage in the evolution of society, it is to be looked on as a good, not an evil. Capitalism is still a necessity and probably always will be a necessity. But, as John Stuart Mill remarked, "Capital is necessary to production, but not the capitalist." The community really creates capital, not the individual; should not capital belong to the community, then?

Socialism is nothing else than the affirmative answer to this question. It recognizes the evils inherent in the present social system, and desires to modify the system so as to retain all that is good and avoid the evil — to better social conditions in general, but in particular the lot of the workingman.   The man not born to affluence in the modern world is no longer a slave, as in the Roman world, nor a serf as in the feudal world; he is a hireling. There remains for him a further step toward emancipation, by becoming a free producer and having for himself the whole product of his toil.   At present a laboring man's family consumes but one-tenth of what he is capable of producing when regularly employed.   Socialism proposes to insure him the regular employment and permit him and his to consume ten-tenths of what he produces.

But it is not only the emancipation of the laborer that Socialism professes to seek.   There is no real liberty now anywhere, except for the comparatively small leisure class who are able to live an idle life at the expense of the world's workers.   The laborer is not free by reason of his poverty; he must work or starve.   The capitalist is not free by reason of his wealth; he must work or see his fortune disintegrate.   Socialism was proposed in the first instance, and is still urged, as the system that will set both classes free — not absolutely, for absolute freedom is not good for man, is therefore not to be desired for any, but free in the sense that moderate labor would secure to all men means enough and leisure enough to live a full, rich, worthy life.

It is not surprising, perhaps, that the first important growth of socialistic theory and of social experiment should have occurred in France.   This was the country where the Revolution began, the country in which the

greatest results were expected to follow that immense
social and political upheaval. It was believed at first
that not merely liberty but equality had been secured.
Now began that great development of modern industrialism in which France was second only to England.
The emancipated third estate seized its opportunity,
engaged in manufactures and trade, and rapidly became
wealthy. A new privilege grew up in place of the feudal
privilege that had been destroyed, the privilege of wealth
instead of the privilege of birth. The man whose sole
capital was his hands found himself at an increasing dis-
advantage, as compared with the many who possessed
capital in money or plant or goods. This fourth estate
of laborers found itself not advanced a pace in the direction of real equality by the Revolution. In the economic
contest, it was every day becoming more hopelessly the
"under dog." In this bitter disappointment we find
the roots of French Socialism.

Saint-Simon (1760–1825), a man of noble birth, who,
like Lafayette, had taken an honorable part in our American war of Revolution, abandoned a military career and
devoted himself to studies that had for their declared
object "the perfection of civilization." He took no
prominent part in the French Revolution, probably because of his noble ancestry, and he was even imprisoned
for a time on account of the suspicion then resting on all
persons of noble birth. After the Revolution he acquired
a small fortune by speculation in land, and at the age of
forty-three entered on his real career as a writer and
social reformer. His small property was soon exhausted
in his experiments, and during his later years he lived in
poverty and want, but without any relaxation of his

efforts for the betterment of humanity. His fortitude and devotion to a cause that had become sacred to him were deserving of wider recognition and higher reward.

Saint-Simon began to propound his views in 1817, in a series of books and pamphlets. He won comparatively few disciples, but he made contributions of great and permanent value to the literature of Socialism and to its philosophy. There had been communistic writers and communists in France before him, but he developed the first scheme of pure Socialism. In doing this, he opposed revolution as merely destructive, whereas he thought construction to be the thing required. He urged Louis XVIII to begin the new order, since the interests of royalty are at bottom with the "industrials," or the world's producers, and opposed to the interests of the idle class, or "do-nothings." This will, as well as anything, illustrate the impracticable ideas of the man.

The ideal of Saint-Simon seems to have been an industrial state, directed by scientific research and competent leadership. Society would be organized on a semimilitary principle, with gradations of rank and authority, a social hierarchy, depending on efficiency and worth. For he and his followers recognized the fact that there is an actual inequality in men, of which any social order must take account. It was a fundamental principle in his scheme that the products of labor should be distributed equitably among the producers; but that would not be to distribute them equally, since then the intelligent, the energetic, and the skilful would receive no more than the stupid, the slow, the lazy.

How the leaders should be selected to direct production and see that the product was equitably distributed was never clearly pointed out by him, yet this is evidently the crucial test of his system. If selected by suffrage, what guarantee is there that the best qualified would be chosen, rather than the most popular? And if the best qualified are not chosen, the system must break down. On the other hand, if the leaders are to be appointed for their fitness, where is the power of appointment to be lodged?

Here is a difficulty that we shall frequently meet in our study: the rock upon which thus far all coöperative enterprises in production have split, is equality. Socialism is, in theory at least, the sublimation of democracy. But men are not equal in ability and capacity, and differentiation of function is necessary to the practical success of any industrial enterprise. This involves the subordination of some to others. Absolute democracy is impossible in industrialism, unless the work is to be divided up among little groups, which is both costly and inefficient. Efficient business must be organized on the hierarchical principle, not the democratic. Here Socialism must either surrender something of its boasted democratic equality or meet an *impasse*.

As a preliminary to the establishment of the system, Saint-Simon demanded the destruction of the remains of privilege, and especially of inheritance, by the operation of which not only wealth but misery becomes hereditary. Hitherto man has been exploited by his fellow-man; the remedy is for associated man to exploit the earth. Hence land, capital, and the instruments of labor should become common property, wealth should be produced by the common labors of all, and should be so divided that the portion of each should correspond to his capacity and so equitably reward his labors. Women should be included in this scheme of emancipation and be made the equals of men in every respect. Saint-Simon did not, however, like some of his followers, favor the abolition of marriage. On the contrary, he believed that he was striving for a new sanctity of marriage, by making unnecessary the present prostitution of women under the form of legal marriage, when a woman sells herself for a home, for wealth, or for social position. He would have marriage become the voluntary union of two completely equal persons, who, because of their equality, would seek each other for no reason but mutual love; and their equality of function should be as fully recognized after marriage as before. Some of his followers advocated "free love"; that is, unions that should endure only so long as mutual desire for union endured; when that desire should cease, the parties would separate without any formality of divorce.

Saint-Simon did not fully work out his principle of collectivism, which does not seem to be incompatible with private property, provided there was competent industrial direction. Many of the details of his system he left in a vague and inchoate state. He is to be looked upon as the man who first began to break a road through an unknown tract of wilderness. Some of his ideas have become permanent in the social movement and literature: the dignity and sacredness of labor, the reverence due to woman, the duty of universal peace. The contention of his followers that the armies of Europe should be employed on works of public utility, instead of the destruction of both property and life, is but a modern echo of the Hebrew prophet who foretold a day when —

> Nations shall beat their swords into plowshares,
> And their spears into pruning-hooks;
> Nation shall not lift up sword against nation,
> Neither shall they learn war any more.

So far from declaring himself hostile to Christianity, Saint-Simon called his system the New Christianity. The new social order would derive all its morality immediately from the principle of primitive Christianity: men ought to regard each other as brothers.   In its modernized form this will read, "Religion must aid society in its chief purpose, which is the most rapid development in the lot of the poor."   The social question thus becomes the essence of religion.   It is a noble conception, that will make the name of Saint-Simon immortal.   His last words were, "The future is ours."

IV

Contemporary with Saint-Simon, but unknown to him, was another remarkable French socialist.   Saint-Simon was an aristocrat by birth, tracing his lineage back to Charlemagne; Charles Fourier (1772–1837) was a man of the people. Saint-Simon advocated governmental leadership and authority; Fourier urged individual initiative.   One made the State the social unit; the other would find the social unit in local groups.   One sought progress along the line of development in the past, and so was more in accord with the modern evolutionary philosophy; the other could see in the past nothing but a series of costly blunders, and would break with it altogether and begin anew.   The motive power in Saint-Simon was a warm heart, in Fourier a clear brain.   This does not imply that Fourier was more practical in his thinking, only that he was more logical and consistent.

Fourier began to write earlier than Saint-Simon (1808), but was later in getting a hearing, nor did he ever have a large following. He did not so much wish to gather disciples or form a party, as to convince a few men of property, who would be ready to put his theories into operation. Once they were tried, he firmly believed that their success would lead to general imitation; and so the new order would be naturally brought about. For the last ten years of his life he is said to have waited in his house every day, at noon, for the coming of the wealthy capitalist who should thus become the benefactor of his race. Such faith is pathetic, even though it stamps the man as an impractical dreamer. It enables us to comprehend the inherent weakness of his socialistic speculations — his too sanguine confidence in progress, his continual and fatal underestimate of the unregenerate residuum in human nature.

Harmony is the law of the universe, said Fourier, the law of life. The present social organization, which we call civilization, is a system of oppression and repression, which necessarily produces horrible discord. To restore Harmony, new social arrangements are necessary that will give free play to all of man's propensities. This can be done only by combinations of suitable numbers in communities, which he called phalanxes, housed in suitable buildings or phalansteries. Each phalange should consist of not less than four hundred families, or eighteen hundred persons; a larger number would produce discord, a smaller number would not allow sufficient combinations. It would be a waste of time to consider the elaborate mathematical computations and philosophical speculations by which these particular numbers were justified; they are of interest only as throwing light on the operations of Fourier's mind.

Assuming his "proofs," let us go on to the further elaboration of his scheme. Each phalange would occupy a square league of land, and be not only self-supporting, but self-sufficient. It would have its own farms, its own factories, its own stores. The phalanstery, or common dwelling, would have every convenience and beauty — it would cost no more to build a palace for these four hundred families than to build four hundred small and uncomfortable houses. The utmost freedom of life would prevail, and restraint would be reduced to a minimum. The relation of the sexes would be settled in accordance with these general principles, and would be free unions founded on "elective affinity."

Some internal arrangement of the phalange would, of course, be necessary to ensure Harmony. Those having similar tastes would naturally form a "series," of seven to nine members, and several series of related tastes would unite to form a "group." Each group would undertake some one kind of labor. All labor, Fourier declared, is pleasant, provided a man is not compelled to do work that he does not like, but is permitted to choose his occupation: —

The labor we delight in physics pain.

He would have agreed heartily with the English socialist, William Morris: "It is right and necessary that all men should have work to do which shall be worth doing, and be of itself pleasant to do; and which should be done under such conditions as would make it neither over-wearisome nor over-anxious." In the phalanxes, there-fore, every person would be free to join which group he pleased, or to change from group to group. A generous rivalry between groups would induce efficiency and stimulate production. In order to secure proper dis-tribution of labor, so that too many persons would not choose a single occupation, Fourier would divide labor into three classes: necessary, useful, and agreeable. The highest reward should be paid to those who do the neces-sary work, and the lowest for the agreeable; this would accord with equity, since the necessary tasks are more or less disagreeable, while the agreeable labor is in large part its own reward.

It was the opinion of Fourier and his disciples that there would be a great increase, not only of happiness, but of culture and the refinements of living, as a conse-quence of the phalanstery. And why should not this be one of the aims of Socialism? If refinement is a good thing in a countess, why not in her cook? If good man-ners are desirable in a millionnaire, why not in the mason who builds his house? But how, in the present social conditions, are cook and mason to acquire the refinements of thought and manner that are possible to the possessors of titles and millions? In a socialized State the gap between the extremes of society will be closed up; there will be leisure and culture for all who care to avail them-selves of opportunities of self-improvement. No so-cialist advocates the reign of the physical and intellec-tual superman at the cost of the worker. To be sure, differences will remain: a lapidary can polish a diamond, but not a lump of putty. Socialism cannot change natures, perhaps, but it can offer opportunities. The higher life will be opened to all, and lived by all who are capable of it, and the number of such is greater than many suspect.

Besides increasing production, the phalange was expected to avoid the waste caused by industrial and commercial competition. Fourier dwelt less on this advantage than the case warranted, for it is one of the strongest economic arguments in favor of Socialism. The present waste in competitive production is great, and recognition of that fact has stimulated the formation of the great corporations and trusts. The elimination of small concerns and the concentration of industries into a few powerful corporations, or sometimes into a single one, has been accompanied by a vast amount of lawlessness, injustice, and suffering, but its economic results have been wholly good. Yet far greater than the waste of production is the waste of distribution, as becomes evident when one considers the enormous loss implied by the vast number of retail shops. Each proprietor of such a shop must at least get a living out of his business, and the cost of supporting his family is saddled on the consumer. It is the economy of having a hundred separate shops under a single roof, each doing a separate business but all doing business in harmony, because under the direction of one mind, that makes the department store so great a success as a distributing agency, and secures not only a large aggregate profit to the proprietor, but better wages and shorter hours to the employed, and lower prices and better goods to the consumer, than a multitude of small shops scattered about a city.

The department store is thus a great object-lesson of the advantages of socialized distribution, the full value of which does not yet accrue to society, because the proprietor now takes in the form of profit an undue share of the economies effected. Add to the economic gain of such business methods the productiveness of those now uselessly employed in purely competitive effort, and it becomes evident that the wealth of society might be indefinitely increased by a complete socialization of distribution. This conclusion is strengthened when we consider another large item of expense in the present system of distribution: the cost of finding a market. This is now done by employing skilled salesmen, or by equally skilled advertising, or by a combination of both methods. These methods are very expensive, but absolutely necessary as business is now conducted. It is a maxim in business that "any fool can make goods, but it takes a smart man to sell them." A high quality of brains and training are required to find a market, and brains come higher than goods in the world's mart. This large item of expense, now paid by the consumer in the ultimate price of whatever he buys, would be practically eliminated by socialized distribution, and the great army of bright men and women now engaged in marketing products would be added to the ranks of productive laborers, to the vast gain of the world in wealth. With all his philosophizing, Fourier failed to give adequate weight to these things.

Probably with the hope of attracting his capitalist to advance means for a practical test of his scheme, Fourier made a distinct place in his theory for private property. His plan for the distribution of profits was rather complex. A minimum should be set aside for every member of the phalange, sufficient for the comfortable support of all.   The surplus, which he believed would be enormous, should be divided in the proportion of five-twelfths to labor, four-twelfths to capital, and three-fifths to talent. Saint-Simon's maxim was: labor according to capacity, reward according to service; Fourier's was: labor according to capacity, reward according to services, capital, and talent.   In the practical working of a socialistic system, we might reasonably expect these distinctions to disappear; payment according to services might endure, but special favors to capital and talent would almost certainly be refused after a time.   Saint-Simon's formula promises better as a working principle than Fourier's.

Though the expected capitalist did not come forward during Fourier's lifetime, it is a pleasure to record that after his death his faith had in part its reward.   A rich manufacturer [1] named Godin established a community at Guise for his work-people on essentially Fourier's principles, though with some modifications of detail.   The workers are housed in one huge building, with many of the comforts and elegancies that Fourier prophesied, and many of the predicted benefits of such association have been realized.   The essential condition of success in the experiment was, however, that M. Godin should reserve to himself a large part of the power of direction; and, like the prudent business man that he was, he did this.   He thus solved the crucial problem of a socialistic experiment, the securing of competent oversight.   Qualified directors

[1] The Guise community can hardly be reckoned an instance of the success of pure Fourierism, for it was one of his pet theories that agriculture is the normal and chief occupation of a regenerated society, in which manufactures would be reduced to a minimum.   The Guise community is devoted exclusively to manufactures.

of business rise to the top under the present system of competition by a natural process of eliminating the failures — the weak men go to the wall, the strong men succeed. It seems a cruel process, but it is at least effective. If the world is to go on, somehow the strong men must control affairs, either as now by a stern fight in which they conquer their rivals, or by some process of testing and promotion that will ensure the same result. M. Godin was in this case the strong man who got to the front and stayed there, and his experiment was reasonably successful. Socialistic communities that have fallen into the hands of weak conductors, or have had no conductor, have uniformly failed.

On the whole, Fourier's contribution to the cause of Socialism was mainly through the indirect influence of certain of his teachings. His ingenious and elaborate Utopia was not convincing in its totality; it too utterly disregarded the patent facts of human nature as at present constituted,[1] and it was on these reefs that most of the actual experiments in Fourierism came to grief, — egotism, selfishness, laziness. His critique of existing institutions was often acute, and he pointed out effectively the economic benefits of socialized production and distribution. Subsequent experience, as far as it has gone, has made good all his contentions under these heads.

[1] It takes a soul
To move a body : it takes a high-souled man
To move the masses, even to a cleaner stye :
It takes the ideal, to blow a hair's breadth off
The dust of the actual.   Ah, your Fouriers failed,
Because not poets enough to understand
That life develops from within.
          — Mrs. Browning, " Aurora Leigh," Book II.

He was also the first to describe with literary effectiveness the unnecessary hardships of labor and the evil consequences of unnecessary toil. This part of his teachings has had a distinctly traceable influence on the modern factory laws for the protection of the laborer, even against himself, and the shortening of the hours of work. Sanitary reforms in factories, including the prohibition of child labor and the restrictions thrown about the employment of women, had their beginning in the same source.

It would be unfair to credit Fourier with the whole inspiration of legislation of this character. Much is due to the advance in medical science, and to the quickening of the public conscience as popular knowledge has increased, on the one hand of the existing evils, and on the other of the possibility of remedying them. Enlightened self-interest has also played its part here; the well-to-do have come to realize that if factories are permitted to be breeding-places of disease, they will themselves have to pay no small part of the ultimate penalty. And above all, we must take into account the effect of those Christian ethics that Fourier so contemptuously rejected.

V

Both the men whom we have thus far studied believed that Socialism was to come by way of evolution. Louis Blanc (1811–1882) was the first to advocate revolutionary Socialism, though it was revolution without violence. Saint-Simon divorced economics from politics, and Fourier followed his example; they appealed to ideas, not to political parties. Blanc saw that if Saint-Simon's notion of governmental direction of production was ever to be realized, there must first of all be a change of political institutions. It was plain to him, as it had not been to his predecessor, that neither Louis XVIII nor any other French monarch could be rationally expected to lead, or even to countenance, such an experiment. A government representative of the people, and so in harmony with the people, must be secured first of all.

In his "Organization of Labor" (1840) Blanc effectively criticised the evils of competition. Soul and body, he said, must be developed together; moral and material progress are mutually interdependent. Man cannot live by bread alone, but he must have bread to live. The measure of man's needs is, those means that are required for his complete development, mental, moral, physical. A society that does not guarantee to every member of it his needs is a failure. The present individualism, "taking every man outside of society, renders him the sole and exclusive judge of that which surrounds him, gives him an exalted sentiment of his own rights without indicating to him his duties, abandons him to his own powers and proclaims *laissez faire* as the only rule of government." The result is want and misery, which make symmetrical development impossible. This necessitates a new organization of society. But social reform is impossible without political; successful Socialism must be State Socialism. Therefore the State must be reorganized on a truly democratic basis as a first step.

As the poor cannot combine to produce for themselves, the State must be the banker of the poor, furnish the instruments of production, and emancipate the proletariat. This it can do by establishing social workshops (*atliers sociaux*), for the first year assigning each laborer to his place, according to his ability. During this year

F

the workers will become acquainted with each other, and thereafter will be able to elect their own chiefs. The State will grant its credit to these workshops, without interest. The loans will be repaid from railways, mines, and other public enterprises. Gradually private industrial concerns will be absorbed, but none are to be forced to join the movement. The social workshop, having capital supplied *gratis*, attracting the best workmen, possessing the advantages of a vast organization, would soon make competition by private capital impossible. Thus the socialistic State will be formed, and the best interests of all the people, rich as well as poor, will be conserved.[1]

But how is the product of socialized labor to be distributed? Men differ in powers and abilities, as Blanc was quick to recognize, at the same time contending that this difference is the measure of their obligation to society. "The more a man *can*, the more he *ought;* and this is the meaning of those beautiful words of the gospel: 'Whosoever will be chief among you, let him be your servant.' Whence the axiom, From every man according to his faculties; that is our duty." At first Blanc was inclined to admit Saint-Simon's principle of pay graduated according to services; later he maintained that exceptional ability must find its reward in exceptional service. Not what one gives to society, but what one needs, is the true principle to govern distribution. Every man truly needs

[1] Yet the system Blanc had in mind seems to be distinct from what has since been called State Socialism — it might rather be called Group Socialism, the common ownership of the means of production, not by society as a whole, but by associations of workers in each trade. Its affinities are greater with the methods now advocated by Kropotkin than with the theories of Marx.

what will enable him to derive the greatest possible advantage from his faculties, so far as this will not injure others. The formula of perfect justice therefore is, that every one "produces according to his faculties, and consumes according to his wants."

But who should decide what are the wants of each individual, and therefore settle the amount of his compensation? This problem Blanc did not attempt to solve — perhaps he felt that it would find its own solution in the different wants of the workers, each gravitating to his own place and his own kind of enjoyment. Some of his followers held that the material needs of all men are the same under normal conditions. Abnormal conditions, even in the present order, are recognized as requiring abnormal methods, which now take the form of "charity," but should rather be a form of justice. Blanc himself believed that the ideas and characters of men would be greatly changed by new social conditions and new education, which is unquestionably true, but it remains a serious problem whether his system would be workable without a greater change in ideas and character than can reasonably be expected to occur in a generation or two through mere betterment of social conditions.

For it is the experience of mankind thus far that increase of material well-being does not of itself produce any marked moral advance. The morality of the well-to-do class may perhaps be conceded to be somewhat better than that of the proletariat, but the contrast cannot be called a glaring one; while the morality of the new rich in America is notoriously bad, and that of the hereditary rich in Europe is even worse. The student of mankind finds little support, either in history or in observation, for the theory that men are likely to be made better by giving them all that they desire. That is a sure way to spoil a child; can it be a good way to make a man? Wealth has made many a man worse, and few men better. Prosperity is a severer test of character than adversity.

The teachings of Blanc had much to do with the producing of the revolution of 1848, which swept away French monarchy and undid the mischief of the reaction that had followed Waterloo. Blanc played a part in the revolution sufficiently important to secure him a place in the new government, but he was not a leading spirit. His colleagues felt compelled to begin some half-hearted experiments in the direction of establishing social workshops under State patronage. The capital advanced for the purpose was insufficient, the direction was incapable, and the experiments failed. One can hardly resist the conclusion, from all the evidence, that they were not intended to succeed.

All measures of socialistic reform meet with a common reception. First they are ridiculed and criticised, declared to be spoliative, vicious, criminal, and their authors are overwhelmed with vituperation and opprobrium. As they gain a hearing in spite of these tactics, the measures are next pronounced well-intentioned but impracticable, and their authors are described as dreamers and harmless lunatics. Still they gain adherents, until the conviction forces itself on those in power that something must really be done; whereupon the wily politician professes himself to be converted to reform, takes the measures in hand, and does his best to emasculate them and make them worthless. If, in spite of him, they succeed, he claims all the credit for proposing and enacting them into law; while if they fail, as is more likely, he casts all the blame on the original authors.

VI

Socialism has not made the progress in France that was anticipated by these forerunners, yet it is to-day a formidable movement. Its slow growth for two generations was due to its prevailing Utopian character. French socialists demanded that an artificial society should be created by a ruling class that did not desire it, for the benefit of a lower class then incapable of doing anything effective for themselves. The earlier theories were weak on the constructive side; to shatter and remould society was the ideal of Saint-Simon and Fourier, but they were capable only of shattering.

The common weakness of the systems that we have examined was that they were based on abstract truths. In the estimation of men like Fourier, it was only necessary to take a principle, assumed or believed to be an "eternal truth," and from this to derive, by logical deduction, an entire system. So the details could be demonstrated like a proposition of Euclid, it was held that men must accept them. That such a system could fail at any point in practical trial was to them unthinkable. In short, in its beginnings, modern Socialism harked back to medieval scholasticism and its deductive method, and was therefore in sharp contrast, even in active conflict, with the principle of induction, on which modern thought is builded. The method was antiquated, the conclusions worthless.

It is probable that the general hostility of the French socialists to religion and marriage retarded the accep-

tance of their theories.   There was a healthy conviction
among Frenchmen that "free love," ostensibly proposed
for the freedom and elevation of woman, really meant her
degradation and enslavement.   The probable attitude of
man toward woman in the ideal social order pictured by
Fourier has been adequately described by Tennyson : —

> He will hold thee, when his passion shall have spent its
>   novel force,
> Something better than his dog, a little dearer than his horse.

Marriage dissoluble at will could hardly fail to reduce
woman once more to her Oriental position, the slave
of man's passions.   It would give her freedom — yes,
the freedom of the harlot, without the harlot's hire !
That freedom is hers now, whenever she is ready to sacrifice for it all decency and all virtue.   The only defence
of woman's purity, the only protection of her weakness,
the only guarantee of her honor and dignity, is indis-
soluble marriage.   She will be the chief sufferer, if the
specious but deceptive proffer of a larger liberty persuades
her to abandon this citadel of safety.   All her interests
demand that the bond of matrimony should be made
more strict, rather than loosened.[1]

The last two decades have witnessed a marked progress
of socialists as a power to be reckoned with in French
politics.   In the present chamber of Deputies (1910) they

---

[1] It is but fair to point out that French Socialism has in practice been
better than its theories.   When the socialists obtained control of the
municipality of Lille, some years ago, they established a free marriage
service, the municipality paying all fees.   Thousands of marriages followed with the accompanying legitimation of children — a clear proof
of the truth of assertions often made before the experiment, that the
prevalence of illicit unions had been due to poverty rather than to
immorality.

have 76 votes, of which 53 are in the United Socialist party. Besides these, many of the Radicals (246) are socialists in all but name, and may usually be relied on to vote with the socialists on all practical measures. The foremost of their leaders, Jules Guesde, has risen from the ranks of the workingmen. Since founding *L'Égalité* in 1877, he has been a great force among his class and in public affairs. He rejects the older gospel of barricades and bullets, and advocates organized industrial and political action as the means of progress. "The Social Labor Congress," which first met at Marseilles in 1879, was largely his creation, and has been a chief agency of socialistic advance.

Jean Leon Jaurès, who divides with Guesde the leadership of the socialists, is an "intellectual," not a workingman. He was graduated at the head of his class in the École Normale Supérieure, and has twice been professor of philosophy at Toulouse. He began his public career as a moderate Republican, but was elected to the Chamber of Deputies in 1893 as an avowed socialist. Acknowledged to be one of the chief orators of the Chamber, and a writer of equal eminence, he is a man of mark among the ablest in France. For some time the socialists were divided into several factions, and there was even a serious difference between Guesde and Jaurès, but there is now practical union, and at times their party has had the controlling voice in the conduct of the State. If they continue to maintain their hold on the electorate, the socialist Deputies will be able in the near future to obtain many substantial measures of social reform.

III

LASSALLE: THE FIRST STAGE OF GERMAN SOCIALISM

BIBLIOGRAPHY

Sources: —

LASSALLE, Open Letter to the National Labor Association of Germany, "International Library." New York, 1889.
——, The Working-man's Programme, *ib*.
——, Science and the Working-man, *ib*.

Biographical and expository: —

DAWSON, Lassalle and German Socialism, "Social Science Series." 1902.
——, Bismarck and State Socialism, *ib*.
BRANDES, Ferdinand Lassalle. New York, 1911.
BERNSTEIN, Lassalle as a Social Reformer. New York, 1902.

III

Two men have almost equal claims to be considered the founders of German Socialism: Karl Marx and Ferdinand Lassalle. There were some striking parallels in their lives. Both were of Hebrew descent; both were educated at German universities and looked forward to the usual career of student and scholar in their native land, with a professorship and the esteem of the learned as its reward. Both became interested in the welfare of the working-class, though their birth and interests attached them rather to the upper classes; and both sacrificed their career and prospects for what they deemed a sacred cause.

Yet, in spite of these parallels, the two men were quite different in character. Marx was by nature a scholar, philosopher, thinker, only by chance a man of action, and never quite at home in practical affairs; while Lassalle, though not without capacity for abstract thought, was by nature an orator, agitator, organizer, politician. Lassalle was intensely German, Marx was cosmopolitan. Marx was the elder of the two by nearly two decades, and had made public some of his chief ideas, though not in their fully elaborated form, before Lassalle began to write. Yet Lassalle was the first to organize a party. His Universal German Laborers' Union, out of which grew the Social Democracy of Germany, was founded

in Leipzig in 1863; while the International Working-
man's Association, which was the child of Marx's brain,
had its first meeting in London in 1864.

I

Of the two men, Lassalle is without doubt the more
striking personage. Of his personal charm and intellectual gifts, Bismarck bore testimony in a speech delivered
in the Reichstag, in 1878, which made a great sensation
in Germany at the time : —

I met Lassalle three or four times. Our relations were not
of a political nature — politically he had nothing that he
could offer me. He attracted me extraordinarily as a private
man. Lassalle was one of thè most gifted and amiable men
with whom I have ever associated — a man who was ambitious on a large scale, but not the least of a republican. He
had a very marked inclination towards a national monarchy;
the idea towards the attainment of which his efforts were
directed was the German Empire, and in this we found a point
of contact. Lassalle was ambitious on a large scale, and
whether the German Empire should close with the house of
Hohenzollern or the house of Lassalle, that was perhaps doubtful; but his sympathies were through and through monarch-
ical. . . . Lassalle was an energetic and exceedingly clever
man, and it was always instructive to talk with him. Our
conversations have lasted for hours, and I have always re-
gretted their close. . . . It would have given me great
pleasure to have a similarly gifted man for a neighbor in my
country home.

With grim humor Bismarck hinted at Lassalle's be-
setting weakness, his colossal vanity, which led him to
believe that it was really possible for a social revolution
to displace the ruling house of Germany and place him

on the throne. And yet, with characteristic inconsistency, he declared, "I have been a republican from childhood." Many believed these frequent contradictions in his teachings and actions to have a deeper cause than intellectual waywardness — that they were indicative of a deep-seated moral insincerity. In any event, we need not fear to waste our time in studying the career of one who made so profound an impression upon the most remarkable man that Germany produced in the nineteenth century.

Lassalle was born in Breslau, in 1825, the son of a wealthy Jewish merchant. He was not proud of his extraction, but with his cynical wit once said, "There are two classes of men especially that I cannot tolerate, literary men and Jews — and unfortunately I belong to both." The father wished his son trained to succeed him in his large wholesale business, and sent the lad to a commercial school. Young Lassalle showed no liking or aptitude for business, but a great fondness for study, and the father at length abandoned his plan and Lassalle was allowed to enter the University of Breslau, whence he afterwards went to Berlin. He devoted himself especially to philology and philosophy, becoming a pronounced Hegelian. His career as a student is conceded to have been exceptionally brilliant, and he was early admitted to the friendship and esteem of the most celebrated men of letters and science. Heine [1] was his friend, and Wilhelm von Humboldt called him *Das Wunderkind*. The boastful words that he once wrote were in great meas-

---

[1] Heine writes to Lassalle in 1846: "I have found in no one so much passion and clearness of intellect united in action. You had good right to be audacious — we others only usurp this divine right, this heavenly privilege."

ure justified: "Ask friends and foes alike about me, and
if they are men who have themselves learned something,
both will agree unanimously that I write every line armed
with the entire culture of my century."

After taking his doctorate, Lassalle began with the
promise of remarkable literary and professional achievement. His first book, on the "Philosophy of Heraclitus
the Obscure," was not printed until 1858, but before publication was read by many in manuscript and received
the warmest commendations. A second work, on "The
System of Acquired Rights" (1861), was pronounced by
Savigny, the great jurist, the ablest legal book that had
been written since the sixteenth century.

This latter book was the product of the first episode
that interfered with Lassalle's promising development.
The Countess von Hatzfield had the misfortune to be
married to a wealthy and brutal German nobleman,
whose conduct at length forced her to leave him. In
1846 Lassalle took up her case, studied and mastered the
German law for the purpose, conducted her cause through
thirty-six courts, and, after a contest of eight years, won
a complete triumph. At the beginning, Lassalle seems
to have acted in the spirit of a knight-errant, anxious only
to redress the wrongs of a much injured woman; but
the countess was beautiful and accomplished, and the
tongue of scandal did not fail to wag freely concerning
this intimacy. Perhaps towards the end it was less innocent than at the beginning, but there was an uncalculating
chivalry in the course of Lassalle that moves one's admiration.

Nor was this Lassalle's only trouble during this period.
He took part, as many German students did, in the Revo-

lution of 1848, and was in consequence condemned to six months' imprisonment. After 1859 he was enabled, by the intercession of Humboldt, to reside in Berlin, where he produced his "System of Acquired Rights." This learned work was an application of the historical method to legal ideas and institutions; and it may perhaps be regarded as the first step in that intellectual development which led Lassalle into Socialism, since the net result of his studies was the discrediting of the chief existing social institutions.

The year 1862 marks the beginning of the two most remarkable careers in the history of modern Germany. In that year Bismarck became chief minister of Prussia, and entered on that line of policy which issued in the re-formation of the German Empire; and in the same year Lassalle began his leadership of the German proletariat and the organization of the Social Democracy. The future may yet reverse the estimate now entertained of these two men, and the significance of their lives and achievements, and put Lassalle on the pedestal that Bismarck has now occupied for a generation.

There had never ceased to be social discontent in Germany; as the peasantry developed into the proletariat, this discontent did not lessen; but the people had become hopeless. Reformations and revolutions had passed over Germany times without number, and still the lot of the poor seemed little improved, if any — at any rate, the progress in their comfort and uplift had no just proportion to the general progress of Germany in wealth and intelligence. It was Lassalle's work to arouse these sluggish masses, to put new hope into their hearts, and to organize them for action. He did not begin with a

deeply reasoned philosophy of social life, or with any
thorough knowledge of economic conditions and economic
laws, still less with a well-considered practical programme.
He began with a heart much moved by the sufferings of
the poor, with a conviction that these were in large part
unnecessary and remediable; and gradually, observing
men and studying books as he went on, he worked out
his ideas in a series of speeches and pamphlets, arriving
at the last at a tolerably consistent philosophy and a
thoroughly practical political programme.

A lecture that he delivered in 1862 on "The Working-
man's Programme" was epoch-making — lucid in style,
scientific in treatment. He declared that men were en-
tering on a new era of history, of which the working-
classes will be the makers and representatives. He
showed most strikingly the injustice and selfishness of
present social institutions. The workers had no right to
be contented with their lot; their too easy acquiescence
was their ruin. The daring orator was prosecuted for
this offence, but was fortunate enough to get off with
a light fine. He was not lacking in audacity when he
appeared in his own behalf before his judges. "You do
not believe in revolution," he said, "but my studies have
taught me to believe in revolution. It will either come
in complete legality and with all the blessings of peace —
if people are only wise enough to resolve that it shall be
introduced in time and from above — or it will one day
break in amid the convulsions of violence, with wild,
flowing hair, and iron sandals upon its feet. In one way
or the other it will come, and when, shutting myself from
the noise of the day, I lose myself in history — then I
hear its tread."

In the following year, in "An Open Letter," Lassalle outlined a political and social-economic programme that was clear and practical. He advocated a separate political party of workingmen to secure State coöperative production as the only hope of betterment. The government should be asked, as a first measure, to pledge its credit to the working-classes to the amount of 100,000,000 thalers, to establish coöperative associations for production. To this extent Lassalle was a follower of Louis Blanc, as to practical methods. Nobody is entitled to say that the method would not succeed, until it has been fairly tried and its futility demonstrated. On the other hand, nobody is entitled to assert that the plan would succeed, because that is just what nobody knows. It is certainly worth trying, on a sufficiently extended scale to insure a fair experiment; and Germany, with her system of strongly centralized government, offers a peculiarly inviting field for the trial. Its failure would go far to prove Socialism to be economically impossible; its success would remove many of the most serious objections hitherto urged against Socialism. Is it because governments are afraid that the experiment might succeed that none of them have had the courage to try?

The idea of organizing the German workmen, and even of forming them into a separate political party, was by no means original with Lassalle. Others had preceded him in this line, and with several leaders who had the advantage of priority and a recognized position he and his projects came into violent collision. The result was for some time in doubt, and the final battle was fought at Frankfort-on-Main, May 17, 1863. Lassalle ad-

G

dressed the thirteen hundred delegates present with great
confidence and vehemence : —

If you vote against me, if the great majority of the working-class vote against me, then I shall say to Herr Schulze
[his chief opponent] : " You are right — these people are not
yet educated enough to be helped." If I thought only of myself and my natural egoism, I should be compelled to desire
ardently that you would decide against me; for if you, and
not only you, but the great majority of the working-class were
to do that, I should — justified in the eyes of science and certain of being justified by history — withdraw quietly to science; I should, with a sad smile at your unreadiness, stretch
myself out perhaps in the Gulf of Naples, and let the soft
breezes of the South blow over me; I should spare myself a
life full of torment, vexation and worry. Thus your decision would be exceedingly easy to bear. But you would lose
one of the best friends of your class, and you would not only
lose me, but perhaps for decades every one wishful to help you
would be frightened. He would say to himself, " This class
is not ready; let me be warned by the example of Lassalle."
Therefore I tell you, by all the love for the cause of the working-class which I bear in me, my whole soul hangs on your
decision.

Won by this persuasive version of "Codlin's your
friend, not Short," the delegates voted almost unanimously in Lassalle's favor, and on May 23 following the
"Universal German Working-men's Union Association"
was formed, avowing as its fundamental principle, "the
conviction that the adequate representation of the social
interests of the German working-classes and the real removal of class antagonism in society can be secured only
by universal, equal, and direct suffrage"; and as its purpose "the acquisition of such suffrage by peaceable and

legal means, and particularly by gaining over public opinion."

Universal suffrage was won in Germany in 1867,[1] three years after Lassalle's death, but though the gaining of the ballot has doubtless promoted the recent growth of Social Democracy, the first streaks of the millennial dawn are not yet visible on the horizon, even to the most hopeful eyes. The agitation thus begun went on with varying success, but the leader became despondent towards the last over the slow rate of progress. There seemed indeed some prospect that the movement might collapse, when Lassalle became involved in an unfortunate love affair, which led to a duel in which he was mortally wounded, and expired August 31, 1864. "I shall not live to be forty years old," he had prophesied. Even if the bullet of his adversary had not slain him, disease would have claimed him in a few months more. His death caused consternation and even a temporary paralysis in the party he had formed, but after a time it rallied and pursued its course.

II

Before following its later history, let us pause to consider more carefully the contribution that Lassalle made to the movement. That contribution was so overrated at the time that there has since been some danger of underrating it. Lassalle was unquestionably a man of rare abilities and force. He had tremendous energy, uncom-

[1] This is true only as to elections for the Reischstag, for which all males of twenty-five years and over may vote. Equal suffrage, that is, suffrage for women, has not been granted even in imperial affairs. In the various States of the German Empire, suffrage is limited, even for males.

mon versatility, considerable magnetism, and unbounded ambition. He lacked sobermindedness, unselfishness, sincerity, and was also greatly deficient in self-control and common sense. He was histrionic, vain, egotistic, visionary. Worst of all, his heart was not really in the cause that he had espoused; his intellect alone was interested in the cause of the working-classes, and in leadership of them he saw the best opportunity then open to him of distinction — yet at heart he was an aristocrat, without the excuse of being an aristocrat by birth. Notwithstanding this queer mixture of qualities and motives, perhaps in part by reason of such mixture, he accomplished great things, and might have done still greater had his heart gone with his head, had he joined more seriousness and sincerity to his brilliant mind and restless energy. Something of Bismarck's practical sense and steadiness of purpose would have made him the great man that he lacked little of becoming.

Lassalle's writings were mainly polemic, and so far ephemeral. He never had the time and patience to work out a full socialistic scheme, and perhaps it is quite as well so, for the defect of Socialism has always been too much "system" — an excess of philosophic abstraction, and too little contact with fact. Socialism must strive more for reality and less for theory, if it is ever to get anywhere. Briefly, as we gather them from his pamphlets and speeches, his most important ideas were these:—

The direct ownership of man (slavery, serfdom) has ceased, but there remains in society indirect ownership, in that some men have through their possession of capital or accumulated property the power of exploiting others. The present social system raises this ethical question:

Has the employer, as such, the moral right to appropriate the result of other men's labors? If he has not, as Lassalle maintained, then the present social system is fundamentally bad and demands a fundamental alteration. The Revolution overthrew feudalism, in the name of humanity and freedom, but only established on its ruins Capitalism, a new species of despotism. A new Revolution is demanded to complete the emancipation of the laborer. The proletariat is still a subject class, and has benefited little or nothing by the Revolution. Wealth, not noble birth, is now the basis of right and privilege.

This is because the laborer is held down by "the iron law of wages." As this "law" is Lassalle's principal contribution to the philosophy of Socialism, it deserves careful examination. When closely scrutinized it appears to be little else than a development or more extensive application of a principle first stated by the English economist Ricardo: "The natural price of labor, therefore, depends on the price of food, necessaries, and conveniences required for the support of the laborer and his family. With a rise in the price of food and necessaries, the natural price of labor will rise; with the fall in their price, the natural price of labor will fall." [1]

The *proton pseudos*, the radical fallacy, in Lassalle's doctrine is this notion that there is a "natural" or "intrinsic" value or price of anything in the world. "Value" and "price" are not absolute but relative things, and are in a constant state of flux. Ricardo has merely said in a pretentious way, what if put simply would not be a profound economic truth, but a bald truism: the laborer must live, and he cannot live long unless he is paid

[1] "Principles of Political Economy and Taxation," Chap. V, § 35.

a wage that will keep himself and family in the necessaries of life.   But this does not fix a "natural" price of
labor; it merely fixes a limit below which the price of
labor cannot fall without extinguishment of the laborer.
The principle has no other application than this.   Labor-
power is a commodity, and its price at any moment is
fixed by the relation of supply and demand.   Wages
depend on how many men are competing for the same
job, and what is the lowest price any of them is willing
to take, and there is no other law of wages than just this.
If the men considerably outnumber the jobs, their competition forces wages down; if the jobs outnumber the
men, wages rise.   Of course, wages cannot fall — save
in limited cases and for a limited time — below an amount
that will keep the laborer and his family, not merely
alive, but in a state of industrial efficiency.   So much
both experience and logic approve about a law of wages.

Without detecting its hidden fallacy, Lassalle adopted
Ricardo's principle as his own, and applied it with vigor
to the condition of the German laboring classes.   The
average wage, he said, is found to be the amount necessary to secure the laborer's subsistence and the propagation of his class.   Wages cannot go much above or much
below this amount.   Supply and demand limit their
rise; life and death limit their fall.   Thus there is an
automatic regulation of wages, and the efforts of the
laboring class to better their condition by uniting to
obtain higher wages and shorter hours are foredoomed
to failure — they are fighting against a law as certain
and as pitiless as gravitation.   An increasing production
of wealth brings no benefit to the workingman, except
as the general standard of living slowly rises and so necessitates an equally gradual increase of wages.

This asserted "law" is open to many objections, any one of which is fatal to its validity. In the first place, granting its truth, it might still be objected that this is a historical law, a generalized experience of what has hitherto been, not a principle founded in the nature of social facts. If valid at all, it is valid only as to past conditions, without being necessarily applicable to the future. Education and organization among working-men are limiting, and will still more limit, the power of Capitalism, and are capable of effecting considerable modifications of the interaction of supply and demand.

In the second place, the "law" is not even valid as a historical generalization. The lot of the working-man has very greatly improved since the Revolution, to go no farther back. The average wage-earner to-day has in his house comforts and luxuries that princes and nobles did not enjoy a century ago. The trouble with the wage-earner, as with nearly all other persons in modern society, is that his scale of wants has increased much faster than his possessions. This is not to his discredit, but quite the reverse. If men did not desire more than they possess, one of the strongest motives to exertion and hence to human progress would be lacking. The negro in Central Africa, where the banana grows wild, and the woods are full of game, and clothing and shelter are superfluous luxuries, has no motive for exertion; and accordingly civilization has made no progress there in four thousand years. Lassalle once put this, as he put most things, in a very effective fashion : —

You German working-men are curious people. French and English working-men have to be shown how their miserable condition may be improved; but you have first to be shown that you are in a miserable condition. So long as you have a piece of bad sausage and a glass of beer, you do not observe that you want anything. That is a result of your accursed absence of needs. What, you will say, is this, then, not a virtue? Yes, in the eyes of the Christian preacher of morality, it is certainly a virtue. Absence of needs is the virtue of the Indian pillar-saint and of the Christian monk, but in the eyes of the student of history and the political economist, it is not. Ask all political economists what is the greatest misfortune for a nation? The absence of wants. For these are the spurs of its development and of civilization. The Neapolitan lazzaroni are so far behind in civilization, because they stretch themselves out contentedly and warm themselves in the sun when they have secured a handful of maccaroni. Why is the Russian Cossack so backward in civilization? Because he eats tallow candles and is happy when he can fuddle himself on bad liquor. To have as many needs as possible, but to satisfy them in a respectable way, that is the virtue of the present, of the economic age! And so long as you do not understand that truth, I shall preach in vain.

But this gap between desire and possession, while it is a sharp spur to exertion, breeds much discontent and social turmoil.

Third, the "law," so far as it is a law, is far from being "iron," but, on the contrary, should be called the caout-chouc law. Nothing can well be more elastic than what we are pleased to call the "necessaries" of life. It is commonplace, but true, that the luxuries of one genera-tion become the necessaries of the next. Bath-rooms, hot and cold water on every floor, hot-air furnaces or steam-heating apparatus, gas, electric lights, electric bells, telephones, — some of these luxuries, most of them in fact, are demanded now in cottages or flats for work-ing-men in all our cities; they are now "necessaries," and yet fifty years ago only the very rich could have any of them, and the richest could not have some, for they were then unknown. There is equal elasticity in the opposite direction: an Italian or Hungarian immigrant can and does live on what a native American would scorn as fit only for his pigs, while a Chinaman can and does thrive on a wage that even the Italian or Hunga-rian would think was equivalent to starvation. Just what sum is necessary to enable the working-man to live and bring up children to a laboring age? It has never yet been determined, and until it has been determined, it is ridiculous to speak of the "iron" law of wages.

None of these objections were perceived by Lassalle, and he rung the changes on his "iron law" with great effectiveness, in numerous speeches and pamphlets. He had the art of so putting things as to impress the imagina-tion, and rouse the latent sense of wrong in the hearts of German laborers. He could translate abstract ideas into concrete fact in most effective fashion, and that his translation was not always accurate by no means lessened its effectiveness. In a speech at Frankfort he said: —

What is the consequence of that law, which, as I have proved to you, is accepted by all political economists? What is the consequence of the same? I ask. You believe, perhaps, laborers and fellow-citizens, that you are human beings — that you are men. Speaking from the standpoint of political economy, you make a terrible mistake. Speaking from the standpoint of political economy, you are nothing but a com-modity, a high price for which increases your numbers, just the same as a high price for stockings increases the number of stockings, if there are not enough of them; and you are swept away, your number is diminished by smaller wages — by what Malthus calls the preventive and positive checks to population; your number is diminished, just as if you were vermin against which society wages war.

He went on to show that the average of life among the laboring classes is much less than the average life of the rich, because the latter are better housed, clothed, and fed. The working-man is unable to buy sufficient food, nourishing food, for himself and family, and this means starvation.

There are, gentlemen, two ways of dying of starvation. It indeed happens seldom that a man falls down dead in a moment from hunger; but when a man is subjected to a greater expenditure of power than he is able to replace, on account of poor food or a miserable mode of life — when he gives out more physical energy than he takes in — then, I say, he dies of slow starvation.

It was no wonder that oratory like this produced a great effect among the German working-men, and that the new organization was much feared by the government. Nevertheless, the agitation was comparatively a failure; but few of the class to be benefited actually became members of the Association; and Lassalle, cha-grined and despairing, is thought to have welcomed death as an alternative preferable to the open acknowl-edgment of failure. His practical programme was es-sentially that of Louis Blanc, to abolish the distinction between capitalist and laborer by making all men both laborers and capitalists. Productive association with State capital was the magic wand by which he proposed to effect this transformation. He advocated this idea with all the powers of persuasive oratory. He scouted the theory of the State that would limit its function to protection of life and property, — this he called the "night-watchman" theory. He held, on the contrary, that the State is an "institution in which the whole virtue of humanity should be realized." The end of the State is the education and development of the race, enabling each man to reach a height of culture, power, and freedom which would be unattainable through individual struggle. This is, at all events, a nobler conception than the Manchester theory of the State, with its doctrine of *laissez faire*, which is polite French for the ruder "devil take the hindmost" of the vernacular — though both mean the same thing, since both imply a brutal, cutthroat competition and the survival of the fittest, *i.e.* the strongest.

Even had he been able to persuade the government to make trial of his scheme, — and he seems to have labored earnestly to persuade Bismarck to commit Prussia to an experiment, — it would not have proved a solution of the social problem; it could have been nothing better than a soothing plaster on the great running sore of society. A real solution could be hoped for, if at all, only in a universal collectivism, not a few sporadic experiments at coöperative production. Lassalle accomplished nothing but the better organization of German working-men and the making of a political issue out of the abstract question of Socialism. But that was an accomplishment which has seemed of greater significance with every decade that has elapsed since his death.

III

For some years Lassalle's organization maintained a precarious existence, and then was absorbed by the Social Democratic Working-men's Party, formed in 1869 at Eisenach. The leading spirits in this party were Wilhelm Liebknecht and Ferdinand August Bebel.

Liebknecht was born in 1826, and descended from a family that for several generations had been in the civil service. He early decided that such a career was unworthy of a freeman and was therefore not for him. After graduation from the gymnasium he studied at the universities of Giessen, Marburg, and Berlin. A rebel against social institutions by nature, he made himself even less reconcilable with existing things by refusing all *Brodstudien*, and studying only what pleased his whimsical tastes. He took part in the Revolution of 1848, and in consequence spent thirteen years in exile, first in Switzerland, and later in London. Permitted to return by a general amnesty on the accession of William IV as king of Prussia, he threw himself into the cause of the Social Democracy.

Personally upright and honorable in his relations with individuals, as a leader of his party Liebknecht was utterly without moral scruple. During his later years he served in the Reischstag, but more effectively as editor of the socialist newspaper, *Vorwärts*. He also contributed several books of value to the literature of the movement, and continued in active service until his death in 1890. He had none of the personal charm of Lassalle, and there was an element of malevolence and savage temper in his writings that limited their effectiveness for making converts to Socialism, though they did much to embitter class feeling in Germany, and to widen the chasm between the working-classes and those who still possessed the greater share of wealth and political power.

Herr Bebel, born at Cologne, in 1840, was a man of altogether different type, the first of the leaders of the German working-men to come from their own ranks. He set up as a master-turner in Leipzig, in 1864, and gradually built up a large and successful business, in which several hundred men are employed. Here was a socialist, protesting against the exploitation of the laboring man, himself become an exploiter! His enemies and political opponents have not been slow to seize upon this inconsistency and make the most of it. The inconsistency is more apparent than real, however. All intelligent socialists now admit that the individual is powerless to alter the system in which we all find ourselves, neither responsible for the existing order nor able separately to do anything effectual to modify it. All that any one of us can do is, strive to rouse the people to make a united effort for the betterment of society; and in the meantime one must live his own life as he best can under existing conditions, doing as little harm and as much good as he may to his fellows.

In 1872 Bebel was found guilty of the double charges of treason and *lèse majesté*, and imprisoned for two years and nine months — too brief a time for one really guilty of treason, and too long for the mere offence of political agitation, which was his real crime. This persecution made him a martyr in the eyes of German working-men, and he has been their political idol ever since. He has held a seat continuously in the Reichstag, and has developed considerable power as an orator, while by a certain rugged sincerity he has gradually gained the confidence of all classes, and is given a respectful hearing whenever he speaks, such as is commanded by hardly any other member, even government officials. He has developed equal effectiveness as a writer, and several books attest his industry, as well as set forth his idea of socialistic doctrine and policy.

Some of Bebel's views are worth noting here, because they differ from those of many other socialists. In defining the objects of Social Democracy he says: "We aim in the domain of politics at Republicanism; in the domain of economics at Socialism; and in the domain of what is to-day called religion, at Atheism." [1] In this he is practically at one with the greatest of modern socialists, Karl Marx, but there is a decided difference between them in temper. Marx was tolerant of the beliefs of others; Bebel is intolerant. Marx for himself rejected Christianity; Bebel is bitterly hostile to it. Of course, this attitude on the part of the leader has had a marked effect on German socialists, and as a class they are more openly antichristian than the socialists of any other country. There can be little doubt that, could Bebel and his like have their will, Social Democracy in the hour of its triumph would prohibit the profession of any form of religion. This denial of religious liberty is in glaring opposition to what is always declared to be the fundamental principle of Socialism: to gain for every man the largest possible liberty, a much larger liberty than any man now enjoys. Bebel has also proclaimed an equally thorough hostility to marriage as a legalized institution: —

[1] Speech in the Reichstag, March 31, 1881.

The *bourgeois* marriage is a consequence of *bourgeois* property. Marriage, standing as it does in the most intimate connection to property and the right of inheritance, demands " legitimate " children as heirs. It is entered into for the purpose of obtaining them, and the pressure exercised by society has enabled the ruling classes to enforce it in the case of those who have nothing to bequeath. But as in the new community there will be nothing to bequeath . . . compulsory marriage becomes unnecessary from this standpoint as well as from all others.

Marriage, as at present understood, is an arrangement most closely associated with the existing social status, and stands or falls with it.[1]

Bebel has committed the common error of generalizing too freely from the social conditions with which he happens to have most personal experience. Even so, his theory is derived from the sentiments of royal and noble families, rather than from the *bourgeoisie*. With those who have titles and great estates to transmit, the birth of a legal heir is possibly the chief end in marriage — if personal happiness in the marriage relation is also obtained, so much the better; if not, it is commonly sought outside the bond of matrimony. But among the *bourgeoisie* in the larger number of cases, personal gratification in some form is the end sought; marriages not contracted on account of love have as their chief motive financial or social gain. Not the interests of property, therefore, but personal happiness, is the social foundation of marriage. But in the order contemplated by Socialism, business gain will be eliminated as a motive, as will many of the present social motives, and personal

---

[1] " Woman, her Past, Present, and Future," pp. 231, 232.

happiness will tend to become the sole motive of marriage. Then, as now, the birth of children will be regarded as the normal result, rather than the chief end, of marriage.

The opinions of Bebel regarding marriage are not peculiar to him, but it is equally the fact that many socialists do not share them. Opposition to marriage in European countries is in large part the outgrowth of social conditions that are general there. Marriages are usually arranged by parents for their children, on a cold-blooded business basis. If mutual affection follows unions thus made, well and good; in many cases mutual affection does result; but if not, breach of the seventh commandment is regarded as venial, provided it does not become publicly known. We can understand and even sympathize with the growth of a sentiment against marriages of that sort, and the resulting social ethics; but we can also see little likelihood of such a sentiment becoming strong among the socialists of America, where very few marriages are contracted for any other reason than mutual affection — or what the parties mistake for mutual affection when they pronounce their marriage vows.

IV

For several years the German States looked with much indifference on the growth of the Social Democracy, seeing in it no serious menace either to government or society. But after the establishment of the new German Empire, in 1870, the socialists increased rapidly, until in 1877 they polled nearly a half million votes and elected twelve representatives in the Reichstag. This aroused the apprehensions of Bismarck and the Emperor, and already there had been serious consideration of a policy of legal repression, when two attempts on the Emperor's life in 1878 brought the matter to an immediate decision. The Antisocialist law then passed by the Reichstag made all social-democratic organizations illegal, as well as any others intended to subvert the existing society. The police were given large powers to dissolve any societies that even, in their judgment, displayed threatening tendencies. Appeal was allowed to the courts against the prohibitions of the police, but the courts were expected to give the police the benefit of every doubt. The right of assembly was also greatly restricted. The police might dissolve any meetings in which social-democratic tendencies appeared, and no meeting could be held without permission of the police. Public processions and festivities were to be regarded as meetings. All social-democratic publications were interdicted, prohibited works were to be confiscated, and apparatus used for printing them might be seized. Any person who became or remained a member of a prohibited association was made liable to a fine of 500 marks, or three months' imprisonment. Officers of societies and speakers at public meetings might be imprisoned from one to twelve months. The circulation of a prohibited publication entailed a fine not exceeding 1000 marks, or imprisonment up to six months. Exceptional powers were conferred on the police in cases of necessity, known as a stage of minor siege, laying additional restrictions on the right of assembly, forbidding all unlicensed circulation of publications and prohibiting the carrying of weapons without special permission.

These restrictive measures, obviously formed upon

H

the methods of the mediæval Inquisition in dealing with heresy, proved so utterly ineffective for the suppression of Socialism that in 1893 the total vote of the Social Democrats had risen to 1,876,738, and their representation in the Reichstag to fifty-four. In the meantime, Bismarck had undertaken to "dish" the socialists by adopting as government measures certain features of their programme. In 1883 an Act providing for insurance against sickness was passed, which included all wage-earners in its scope. A fund was created by weekly contributions, of which at first the workman paid three-fourths and the employer one-fourth. Later the proportion was changed to two-thirds and one-third, while the State added a subvention. In 1884 an accident insurance law followed, which laid on employers the total burden of providing for injured workmen. In 1889 old age insurance was provided by law, making provision for every workman on the completion of his seventieth year. The burden of providing this fund is laid equally on workmen and their employers.

There has hardly been time to test these schemes fully, and different views regarding them are found in the ranks of German socialists, as well as outside. On the whole, it seems clear that they have done much to relieve misery among the working-class, and make their poverty more endurable; but they have proved to be mere palliatives and have therefore disappointed those who expected them to make a real contribution towards the solution of the social problem. At the same time, the principle of the laws is a distinct recognition of State Socialism, and a step in that direction of no little importance. These Bismarck laws of Germany have been duplicated in nearly every country of Europe, so that working-men no longer have to face injury without compensation or an old age of either starvation or pauperism.

Germany has taken other long strides in the direction of State Socialism. Forestry has been under State control for generations, and even on private land a man may not cut his timber save under certain regulations and restrictions as to age of trees, quantity, and immediate reforestation. Canals and canalized rivers are under State control. The acquisition of railways by the State has been vigorously pushed since the Franco-Prussian War, until now not more than one-tenth of the total mileage is in private hands, and these are mostly unimportant side-lines. And in no country in the world is the train service more prompt and convenient, nowhere is the comfort and safety of the passenger more carefully looked after, nowhere are baggage and freight handled more expeditiously and safely. Passenger rates for first and second class are about the same as in America for equal accommodations, and a third class is provided, with plainer cars, at considerably lower rates than any American railway offers, save in the "immigrant" trains, which Germans would think fit only for cattle.

The post has long been a government enterprise, as with us, but the cheap rates for carrying parcels by post make express companies a superfluity; and the telegraph and telephone lines have been made an adjunct of the post, so that in a single building one may send his message by which of the three routes he may please. Telegraph rates are considerably lower than with us. The State mans these services, in large part, with veterans from the army and navy, which partly accounts for the precision of the service and the mingled air of courtesy and authority that the American traveller observes in German officials. It is impossible to travel in Germany and not become favorably disposed toward the idea of governmental ownership and operation of railways, telegraphs, and telephones, and the merging of the express service with the post. Such a change would seem to us quite a step in the direction of State Socialism, yet Germany has taken it, and real Socialism seems as far off as ever.

Moreover, German municipalities have made far greater progress towards collectivism than American. We are familiar with municipal control of the water supply, but the German towns add to their common enterprises gas and electric lighting and street railways. These latter are uniformly electric, except in a few cases where steepness of hills makes cable roads a necessity; and the cars are far more beautiful and well-appointed than is usual in the Eastern cities of the United States — about on a par with those in our more progressive Western towns : Minneapolis, Denver, Seattle. Besides such enterprises as these, most municipalities perform other functions even more socialistic in principle ; for example, they provide pawnbrokerage at cost for the poor, so that small loans can be obtained at need without recourse to money sharks. Municipal savings-banks are also common, where the smaller savings are received and the maximum of interest is offered at the minimum of risk.

And perhaps the most striking fact about this socializing of enterprises is that it has not been done by socialists. Their numerical strength would result in their capture of most of the municipal governments, but the law expressly provides that not more than one-third of a municipal council shall be socialists. In spite of this restriction, however, the great preponderance of the Social Democrats in most of the towns gives them a moral influence far beyond their votes in the council, and policies favored by them always have a good prospect of adoption. Many towns are destroying the slums by buying up the land and erecting on it model houses, which, while rented at a low rate, return a good interest on the investment. Others lease the land thus acquired, under severe restrictions as to the character of the houses and their rents. The city of Ulm, for example, is said to have acquired and now to control 80 per cent of the land within its limits.

The Social Democracy is not merely a few officers and a mob, — as a political party exists among us, — but a definite organization, with a constitution, with a roll of members who pay regular dues, with schools and periodicals. It has branches wherever there are working-men, and they elect delegates to the annual Congress, which is the governing body. The enrolled membership is considerably over half a million, and at the last election the party polled 3,250,000 votes. When the American reader considers that this is more by some thousands than the votes cast for both Lincoln and Douglas in 1860, he can better measure the strength of this party to-day in Germany. If there were a fair system of distribution of seats in the Reichstag, the party would have 115 members instead of 43.[1] The present electoral divisions were

[1] The by-elections have been almost uniformly favorable to the socialists since the return of the last Reichstag. In 1909 they won twenty-five seats in the Saxon diet, against one in 1907, and in the Baden diet they gained eight seats.

fixed in 1871, when 397 deputies were returned for a population of 39,000,000. Though the present population is 60,000,000, the number of deputies and the methods of election are unchanged. This large increase of population has been in the cities, the country population having decreased; and it is precisely in the cities where the socialists are strongest, while the country districts are favorable to their opponents. It therefore comes about that the Conservative party, though it polls only 1,000,000 votes, has 59 deputies. Similar conditions prevail in nearly every European country; the propertied class always has some advantage, either in the suffrage itself or in the distribution of seats. It may easily be supposed that this sort of unfairness does not make the socialists any more content with the present order.

The socialistic propaganda is varied and formidable. There are 65 daily papers in Germany devoted to their interests, and 12 periodicals. Their leading daily, *Vorwärts*, has a circulation of 120,000, and their comic weekly, *Der Wahre Jacob*, claims 230,000 copies. A school for the training of workers has about thirty students in regular attendance, and twenty-eight organizing secretaries are at work in the field. The reliance of the party is on education and persuasion, not on violent revolution; and they seldom indulge in spectacular demonstrations, believing that more is to be gained by parliamentary methods.

It is often urged as an objection to Socialism that socialists are not agreed among themselves. Was there ever a party that was agreed? Among all considerable bodies of men that act together, there can always be distinguished a right and left wing, radicals and conservatives, and usually a centre or moderate group. The laws of human nature cannot be altered by Socialism, and the inherent temperamental differences of men will always cause such divisions. We need not be surprised, therefore, that a group generally known as "Revisionists" has risen among the German Social Democracy, and now composes about one-third of its strength. It leader, Dr. Edouard Bernstein (b. 1850), is the editor of *Vorwärts*. He maintains that the economics and programme of Marx, which have become socialistic orthodoxy, require revision all along the line. Marx believed in an immediate revolution, which is now seen to have been an error, and the working-men are not content to see their victory postponed to a paulo-post-future, — they not unnaturally desire immediate results. The Revisionists say, "Support us, and you can obtain your social reforms by instalments." The orthodox Marxians, thus far the majority of the party, say, "Support us, and instead of a small slice off the loaf now and then, you will get the whole loaf at once." But when?

It is a well-known fact that since the Franco-Prussian War Germany has rapidly forged ahead as a manufacturing nation, and now disputes with Great Britain the commercial supremacy of Europe. Socialism cannot, of course, be credited with this advance, but a remarkable development of State Socialism has gone hand in hand with the most striking industrial progress ever witnessed in modern Europe. For this increase of manufactures is mainly due, not to any superior natural advantages of Germany, but to a systematic attempt to apply to industrialism that advance in scientific knowledge in which Germany has led the world. Continuous aid has been given by the government to investigations in applied science, and systematic encouragement and direction have been given by the State to all promising forms of new industrial enterprise. The result is that no other country has paralleled Germany's increase of exports, and every country in the world is feeling the effect of her competition.

This great industrial development has been accompanied with a concentration of wealth in the hands of a few, much as in the United States, but not in so extensive a growth of the Trust. Instead of that form of consolidation of capital, industry is rather "syndicated" in Germany. These industrial syndicates receive orders and allot them to the establishment in which they can be most economically filled. By this method of eliminating competition and securing the cheapest production possible, although raw materials cost more in Germany than in England (this is especially true of iron, most of which must be imported), and labor costs quite as much, Germany is able to rival England in the markets of the world and often to undersell the latter. The German capitalists, who did not fail to lament that they were about to be ruined by Bismarck's social schemes, have nevertheless greatly prospered under them; while the wage-earners have gained a larger share of the benefits of this industrial progress than their brothers in America.

There is an object-lesson here for American workers. They have insisted on the policy of "keeping out of politics," and have had for their only reward thus far that other parties have exploited them and contemptuously refused to do anything of value for them. The working-men deserve the contempt with which politicians

secretly, and sometimes openly, treat them. That is to
say, the man who has a ballot in his hands and is not intelligent enough to use it for his own protection, does not
deserve any political consideration and will certainly
receive none. Until the American working-man learns
from the example of his brothers abroad that he has been
quite in the wrong in this matter, that he will never get
anything of value for himself until he goes into politics
and uses his ballot to advance his interests, and not to
advance the interests of capitalists, he will make little
or no progress.

The American working-man enjoys one enormous advantage over his brother in Europe : political democracy
has been achieved here ; he may cast his ballot freely, and
it will usually be honestly counted. He has only to decide what he wishes and it is his ; he has it in his power at
any time to overturn completely existing laws and constitutions, or to modify them according to his will. His
social grievances will exist only so long as he himself does
not know what he wants. But in every European country — even France, nominally democratic, is hardly an
exception — the attainment of political democracy is yet
far off, and the working-man is compelled to struggle first
of all for that which the American already possesses, the
power to change the laws. And yet, in spite of that, it
seems not impossible that the social grievances of the
foreign working-men will be redressed first ; for they are
alive to their situation, and are intelligently taking the
right course to secure redress of grievances, while the
American worker remains blind and inactive.

IV

KARL MARX AND MODERN "SCIENTIFIC" SOCIALISM

BIBLIOGRAPHY

Sources: —

MARX AND ENGELS, The Communist Manifesto. Chicago, 1909.
MARX, Capital, 3 vols. Chicago, 1909.
——, A Contribution to the Critique of Political Economy. Chicago, 1911.
ENGELS, Socialism, Utopian and Scientific. Chicago, 1900.

Socialistic expositions: —

SPARGO, Karl Marx and his Life and Work. New York, 1910.
KAUTSKY, The Social Revolution. Chicago, 1902.
——, The Road to Power. Chicago, 1901.
LORIA, The Economic Foundations of Society. Chicago, 1899.

Critical, but judicial: —

BERNSTEIN, Evolutionary Socialism: a Criticism and an Affirmation, "Socialist Library." New York, 1909.
MENGER, The Right to the Whole Produce of Labor. New York, 1899.
SOMBART, Socialism and the Social Movement in the Nineteenth Century. New York, 1898.
SCHAEFFLE, The Impossibility of Social Democracy, "Social Science Series," 1892.
SHAW, Municipal Government in Continental Europe. New York, 1895. (An impartial scientific study of a related subject.)

IV

KARL MARX AND MODERN "SCIENTIFIC" SOCIALISM

I

KARL MARX, who is commonly regarded as the founder of modern "scientific" Socialism, is at any rate its chief prophet and spokesman. Few men of the nineteenth century had so wide an influence, for good or evil; few have been so often quoted and so loyally followed by multitudes of disciples, all admiring, if not always comprehending. And in his case there were no adventitious aids to influence. His hold on his followers was not gained by gifts of eloquence, such as made leaders of Kossuth and O'Connell; nor by skill in the leadership of men, such as made Parnell at one time the uncrowned king of Ireland. In Marx's case we behold the triumph of sheer intellect, inspired by genuine greatness of soul. Whatever his economic errors, he sincerely believed that his teachings were the truth; and to the working out of his ideas and the inculcation of them among the laboring classes, he freely gave his life. In what was to him a sacred cause, he endured much poverty and suffering, thereby again justifying the daring words of Heine: "Wherever a great soul gives utterance to its thoughts, there also is Golgotha."

Marx was born in Trèves, in 1818. His family held a good social position. His father, born a Jew, was an official in the civil service, and had embraced Christianity, possibly to advance his career, but certainly of his own accord.   Young Marx was educated for the bar at the universities of Bonn and Berlin, at the time of Hegel's ascendency, and became greatly absorbed in the study of philosophy, so that he abandoned the study of law and began to fit himself for a university chair.   Soon after taking his degree he was drawn into journalism, possibly at first as a means of support, and almost inevitably into politics.   As editor of the *Rheinische Zeitung*, he criticised the government with intolerable boldness, with the result that in 1843 the paper was suppressed.

Believing that France would afford him a better field for the propagation of his liberal opinions, and also offer special advantages for the study of political and social questions, Marx went to Paris.   Here he formed a close intimacy with another German, hardly less noteworthy than himself, with whom his future was to be closely united, Frederic Engels.   Banished from France by Guizot, then prime minister, because of his persistent criticism of the government of Prussia, Marx went to Brussels.   Here there was a decided advance in his opinions towards radicalism, and he avowed himself a communist — by which, however, he meant what is now called a socialist.   Together with Engels he issued "The Communistic Manifesto" of 1847, which concluded with the words often since quoted in socialistic literature : "The proletarians have nothing to lose but their chains; they have the world to gain.   Proletarians of all lands, unite."

Marx then returned to Germany and founded a new journal, the life of which was extinguished by the Revolution of 1848, and its editor was banished.   He soon after took up his abode in London, where he lived until his death in 1883.   In 1869 he was joined by his friend Engels, before which time they had together founded the International Working-men's Association (1864).   Marx drafted the constitution, and the founding of the International must be regarded as his chief contribution to the organized Socialism of his generation.   Considered as a practical movement, the International was a magnificent failure.   It did little more than provoke the exaggerated fears of half the governments of Europe.   Six conventions were held before the Paris Commune (1871), which was in no official way connected with the International, but was generally believed to be a legitimate development of its principles.   In these later years Marx lost his hold on the organization and came to regard it as a Frankenstein monster, of which he was somewhat fearful. He did not himself favor or expect a violent revolution for the establishment of the social State, but believed that the new order was rapidly coming by the way of peaceful evolution.   Engels survived his friend till 1895, becoming his biographer and editor.

II

The most important contribution of Marx to Socialism was not in the field of organization and propagandism, for which he had little fitness, but in the field of literature. In 1859 he published his "Contributions to the Criticism of Political Economy," which was important not so much for his discussion of purely economic theories, as for the working out of a new interpretation of history in terms of economics.   His theory has become generally known, especially in socialistic literature, by the unfortunate title of "the materialistic interpretation of history." It is, in brief, this : The basic problem of man, in all ages, has been the problem of subsistence, how to get a living out of the earth. This primal necessity has conditioned and directed all social development. The conditions of physical life, the relations of production to consumption, are the prime factors in human progress. The transformations of society, the growth of institutions, are all traceable to economic conditions ; and all history is, at bottom, the story of an unending struggle between nations and classes for the control of the means of subsistence. We have already considered this theory, and some of its applications, and need only add that since first propounded by Marx it has had an increasing influence on all study of history.

Marx was an industrious writer, but we need not concern ourselves with the mass of his work ; for easily his most important book was his treatise on Capital.[1] Indeed, it is the greatest book, in more than one sense, that the socialistic movement has yet produced. So wide has been its vogue that it has often been called the Bible of Socialism, and it perhaps justifies the title, in that it is more revered than read. Few socialists possess a copy of this costly three-volume work, and still fewer are personally familiar with its contents. It would not be surprising to discover, in truth, that "Capital" has been, and still is, read more extensively outside the

[1] The first part of "Capital" appeared in 1867, and a second edition was published by the author in 1873. The second part was edited by Frederic Engels and issued in 1885, two years after the author's death, while the third and most valuable part was delayed until 1894.

ranks of avowed socialists than inside. But that is by
no means to deny the extent of its influence among socialists themselves. The teachings of Marx have been popu-
larized and scattered abroad, through speeches, tracts,
and other means, until not only socialists themselves, but
many others, have become familiar with his chief ideas,
even when they do not clearly know whence the doctrines came.

One who studies "Capital" carefully — and he must
study it, to get anything from it — will be likely to come
to the conclusion that the author owes no small part of
his fame for originality to his invention of a new ter-
minology for old economic ideas. The rest of his great
repute as a socialistic economist is mainly due to his
ability to say a small thing in a very large way. It is
truly marvellous how Marx can take an economic truism,
wrap it up in cumbrous jargon, half philosophic, half
scientific, add a show of elaborate mathematical demonstration that $2 + 2$ really does equal 4, and present his
conclusion in the guise of a profound truth, a contribution to human thought of the greatest possible value. It
is time that somebody punctured this swollen German
windbag and reduced it to its natural proportions. The
involved style of the book makes it very difficult reading,
even in the English translation, but there is generally
light enough to make the darkness visible, and by hard
struggling one may usually come at the meaning — when
there is any.

III

The foundation of Marx's system, as of all systems of
economics before him, is a series of definitions, from
which everything is deduced. These must be scrutinized,

I

therefore, with the greatest care. In the opening sentence of his book he defines wealth as "an immense accumulation of commodities," and a commodity is defined as an object that satisfies a human want. That definition of wealth was once valid, perhaps, but no longer applies to social conditions. Hoarded supplies of surplus products now constitute a small part of wealth. The wealth of a Rockefeller or a Carnegie is not measured chiefly by the quantity of oil or steel or other commodities that they own, but by what we call "securities," certificates of stock, bonds, mortgages, etc. These securities are titles to the possession, on an enormous scale, not of an immense accumulation of commodities, but of the means of producing commodities; and the social significance of such possession is that it enables men of wealth to command the labor or services of other men.[1] Nine-tenths of mankind, in other words, live by the sufferance and at the will of the other tenth, who possess practically all the means of living. The entire significance of Socialism is that it challenges this state of things and asks, On what ethical theory can such monstrous inequality of lot among men be justified?

Of greater importance than his theory of wealth is Marx's theory of value. He finds that there are three kinds of value: use-value, exchange-value, and surplus-value. As this theory is the corner-stone of his system, we must examine it with exceptional care.

[1] This had been pointed out by Ruskin, as early as 1862, in "Unto This Last," Essay II, "On the Veins of Wealth." It used to be the fashion to ridicule Ruskin as an economist, but of late he has been coming to his own. He was among the first to insist that economic facts and forces have a social significance, and must be subjected to ethical standards.

The use-value of a commodity is what other economists call utility, its capacity to satisfy a human want of some sort. Exchange-value, on the contrary, appears at first sight to be something quite apart from commodities, viz. a proportion in which values of one sort are exchanged for values of another sort. Since this proportion is constantly changing, it seems to be accidental and purely relative. But a closer analysis shows that when we say one commodity is equal in value to another commodity, this equation is possible only by the existence of something common to both as a term of measurement. Each of the two members of the equation must be reducible to this common element before equality can be affirmed between them. In general, therefore, exchange-values must be capable of expression in terms of something common to all, of which they represent a greater or less quantity. This common element in all commodities, by which they may be measured, must be labor; since all are products of labor that is the one invariable element that enters into all, and by which they may be measured and compared. Two sentences sum up this theory of value: "A use-value or useful article, therefore, has value only because human labor in the abstract has been embodied or materialized in it."[1] "That which determines the magnitude of value or exchange-value of any article is the amount of labor socially necessary for its production."[2]

1. This theory of value contains a self-contradiction. Marx begins by saying that the utility of a commodity constitutes its use-value — that is, the capacity of the

[1] "Capital," p. 5.
[2] *Ibid.* p. 6.

thing to satisfy a human want. Later he says that use-value exists only because human labor has been embodied in the commodity. Both cannot be true. As a matter of induction from experience, the first statement stands as true : the use-value of any commodity is its capacity to satisfy a human want, quite irrespective of the labor embodied in it. For example, a man opening an oyster finds a fine pearl — that has frequently happened. Another man spends days in hard work, digging a well, but fails to find water — many a farmer has had that experience. The first man has expended no labor, but he has something that satisfies a human want and so is very valuable. The second man has expended great labor, but that empty hole in the ground satisfies no human want, and is utterly without value. An American disciple of Marx virtually surrenders the whole contention that labor is the source of value, when he says : "If I make something to satisfy some want of my own, it will have no value unless it will satisfy the want of some one else also." [1] A useful article has value, not because labor has been embodied in it, but because it is useful. All the labor of mankind since the creation could not make a thing valuable if it were not useful. The backache value of an article may or may not be actual value, — it depends on whether the backache has been wisely incurred.

2. Marx's theory of value notably fails to correspond to fact when applied to land. Land should be worth, according to the theory, — which entirely ignores what nature contributes to the value of any commodity, — the amount of labor that has been expended on it; in

[1] Spargo, "Socialism," p. 240.

other words, what we call "improvements." But this
is notoriously not the fact.   Land is usually worth much
more than the improvements ; in exceptional cases it may
be worth much less.   Even the improvements themselves
are not valuable according to the labor embodied in them.
Those made by one occupier of the land may be considered
undesirable by the next occupant, in which case they will
be worthless and may even be an encumbrance.[1]   On the
other hand, it often happens that land on which the owner
expends no labor whatever continually increases in value,
simply because population increases in that locality and
so the demand for land tends steadily to surpass the
supply.[2]

The thing that makes land valuable anywhere is that
somebody wishes to occupy it.   Whether labor has or
has not been expended on it, is an irrelevant circumstance.
Witness the fact that in New England there are to-day
hundreds of abandoned farms, on which the labor of
generations has been expended — abandoned because
nobody cares to live on them, or is willing to buy them at
any price.   But besides this qualitative factor in the
value of land there is a quantitative : land is limited, and

---

[1] "Improvements" are to a certain degree, though to a less degree than
the land itself, subject to the same law of value.   Let a rich man build a
"palace" on Fifth Avenue, in New York, and an equally costly "cottage"
in a remote spot by the sea.   The house will be worth more than the
cottage at a forced sale, simply because it is desired by more people, since
it stands in the most fashionable location of the largest city in America.
The "palace" will therefore bring under the hammer something like its
cost, while the lonely "cottage" will sell for a small fraction of its cost.

[2] This increase in the value of land without the owner's labor is now
generally known as "the unearned increment," and a heavy tax is levied
on it in the famous Lloyd-George budget of 1909, as well as in some of
our American States, on the ground that society at large has a right to
take back at least a portion of a value that society at large has conferred.

so capable of being appropriated, as the other bounties of nature, the sea and the atmosphere, are not. These two factors — the strength of human desire for possession of the soil, and the limited quantity — determine the value of land, usually without any question of the labor expended on it.

3. Marx's theory contradicts universal experience regarding things produced by human labor. The value of each article, he tells us, must be scientifically determined by the amount of labor-time required for its production. In general, the greater the productiveness of labor the less labor-time is required to produce a given article, the less is the amount of labor-material in the article, and the less therefore is its value. *Per contra*, the less productive labor is, the more labor-time is required to produce a given article, and the greater is its value. We are able, therefore, to state this general formula for value : The value of a commodity varies directly as the quantity and inversely as the productiveness of the labor incorporated in it.

This is a good example of Marx's impressive quasi-mathematical "proofs" of his theories. The formula has a very convincing air and is well calculated to make the thoughtless believe that here is a law quite as true and nearly as important as gravitation, and that the name of Marx should be ranked alongside of Newton's among the great men of science. But the difference between Marx's formula and the law of gravitation is that Newton's law will bear every test, while Marx's breaks down at the first attempt to apply it. For this is what the Marxian law means, in a practical case : the more unskilful a shoemaker, the more valuable will be the shoes that he makes; if he puts twice as much labor into making a pair of shoes as his more skilful neighbor, his shoes are just twice as valuable; even though the latter makes his in half the time and makes them better, they are less valuable, because they embody less labor. A watch made by hand is more valuable than a watch made by machinery, though the latter is the better timepiece, because the former represents more labor. Or, reducing the formula to its ultimate absurdity, in a shop where men of different capacities are employed, the better the workman and the faster he turns out good product, the less he ought to be paid; while the more stupid and slow he is, the more valuable is his product!

It may be that Marx perceived the absurdities involved in his formula; at any rate he devised a modification of it that was believed to free it from undesirable inferences: value is to be measured by the average labor-time socially necessary for the production of an article. And his illustrations of his principle make it plain that he means by "average labor-time socially necessary" exactly what previous economists meant by the term "lowest cost of production." The exchange value of any article tends to be lowered by competition to somewhere near the least amount for which it can be made. This will, of course, be the general effect of competition under the law of supply and demand. But what is left of the theory that labor is the exclusive source of value?

4. The theory neglects some factors of value that must be taken into consideration. So far from labor constituting the total element of value, nature always contributes something, generally a great part, and sometimes by far

the larger part, of value. Take coal, for example; the labor of mining coal is considerable, but its fitness for fuel is wholly nature's gift, and constitutes its chief value. The same is true of the placer-mining of gold : the chief value of the gold lies in the intrinsic qualities of the metal ; comparatively little labor brings it to light and makes it available. So with manufactured articles. A pair of shoes embodies considerable labor, but the chief value of the shoes lies in the fact that nature has given qualities to the skins of animals that cannot be found in any other material; men demand shoes made of leather, and will accept no substitute. Marx's contention is contradicted by a thousand everyday facts. Labor without nature is only a beating of the air, and can never create value.

As in the case of land, so with all other commodities, one factor of value is the limitation in the quantity of a useful article, so that human desire is never fully satisfied. Nothing can be more useful to man, absolutely indispensable indeed, than air and water, but as they exist in practically unlimited quantities they have no economic value. When, in peculiar circumstances, water becomes scarce and is desired at the same time by many people, it at once becomes valuable. The man who then has control of a supply, which may not have cost him a particle of labor, — it may be a natural spring, — can sell it to men who have no water and must have some, for practically any price he chooses to demand. So when Mr. Spargo tells us that "the value of diamonds is determined by the amount of labor-expenditure necessary on the average to procure them," he contradicts every known fact about gems.[1] Much more to the point was this

[1] Spargo, "Socialism," p. 254.

dialogue in a recent daily newspaper: "Hobbs: What is the best way to find out what a diamond is worth? Dobbs: Try to sell it." Now this, which was printed merely as a jest, is sound economics. To try to sell a diamond is, in fact, the only way to determine its value. That value is not in the least dependent on the amount of labor embodied in the stone; it depends first, on the desire of men (and more especially women) to possess diamonds, which is what economists mean by their utility, and secondly, on the comparative rarity of the gem. The labor required to mine a diamond at Kimberly will mine many tons of coal at Scranton; but carbon in the form of coal is plentiful, while the crystallized carbon of the diamond is exceeding scarce — hence there is no comparison between their values.

5. The distinction that Marx attempts to establish between use-value and exchange-value does not exist, or rather it has no significance. Use-value is applied to an article useful to the producer, and not intended for another purpose, as the stone axe of a savage. Exchange-value is applied to an article that will be useful to some other than the producer and is intended for sale, as the modern steel axe. But value in either case depends on utility — in the one case to the producer, in the other to the prospective buyer. The two values are identical in nature, and the distinction is a purely verbal one, corresponding to no social realities. By such jugglings with words do the Marxians deceive themselves — and others.[1]

---

[1] Marx makes the ridiculous statement that "one use-value is just as good as another," and it is probably his failure to see the absurdity of that assumption that led him so astray in his whole theory of value. "What man is there of you, who, if his son shall ask a loaf, will give him a stone?" But why not, if one use-value is as good as another?

It becomes clear in the end that Marx has defined not what value is, but what he wishes it to be. Ruskin, with a similar purpose, offered a better definition, when he said that "Just payment of labor consists in a sum of money which would approximately obtain equivalent labor at a future time." [1] This definition would hold good if all labor were wisely directed to the production of articles fitted to satisfy human wants; but, whether from bad calculation or from unskilful effort, much labor is ill-directed and results in production of articles unfitted, or imperfectly fitted, to supply wants. Or, possibly the articles are good in themselves, but more of certain sorts have been produced than are necessary to supply the wants of men at that time. In such cases, the labor cannot be paid a sum that would procure its equivalent at another time, because it has been wasted, in whole or in part. Both Marx and Ruskin were, however, really defining as value or wages the *cost of production*. The only relation of labor to value is as a check upon wasteful production. If a man finds that it costs him more in material and labor to produce a given article than he can get for it in the open market, he ceases making that article and turns his labor into some more remunerative channel. Thus labor acts as a brake or regulator on the machinery of production, and in the long run equalizes inequalities, but it does not determine the value of any product or have any direct influence on such determination.

To go back to the beginning of Marx's theory, he was right in saying that, since we equate various articles and pronounce them identical in value, there must be some

---

[1] "Unto This Last," Essay III, *Qui judicatis terram.*

common denominator of commodities. But he was wrong in saying that this common element can be nothing else than labor — it can be something else, because it demonstrably is something else. The fact that all commodities have been produced by labor has no more social significance than the fact that they are all composed of matter. The one element of social significance common to all commodities is that all are capable, in varying degrees, of gratifying some desire of man — or, in economic phrase, they possess utility. In this variation of capacity to satisfy desire, combined with the difficulty of attainment, we have the whole explanation and the sole explanation of differences in value. A thing is worth whatever somebody else will give in exchange for it — no less, no more. In other words, value is exchangeability.

The ideas connoted by "labor" and "value" are incommensurable, and they can never be equated. "Labor" is something positive, definite, stable; "value" is relative, variable, and always varying. Labor no more produces the value of a pound of sugar than it produces its sweetness; labor can as easily produce the brilliance of the diamond as its value. No theory of value could more uniformly and more violently contradict every fact of experience, every principle that governs the ordinary transactions of business, the daily buying and selling that is so intimate a part of our lives, than does this theory of Marx that commodities derive their value from the labor required to produce them.

IV

Before we consider Marx's theory of surplus-value, it is necessary to inquire more particularly just what meaning he attaches to the term "labor." This is necessary, because it has been often charged against him that he recognizes only manual labor, and this would, of course, be a fatal defect in his "scientific" socialism. For only the simplest forms of manual labor are possible without mental effort — a fact that is universally recognized in the distinction between skilled and unskilled labor, for "skill" is something more than mere manual dexterity. The man who shovels dirt into a cart needs and uses little more mind than the horse that draws it, but the machinist at his lathe must have and use a high quality of mental power. The factory organization tends, it is true, to minimize all effort of mind, and to reduce all workers to the level of machines, but somewhere in the process of making every article mental power is urgently required.[1]

Marx seems to recognize this fact, when he says, "By labor-power or capacity for labor is to be understood the aggregate of those mental and physical capabilities existing in a human being, which he exercises whenever he produces a use-value of any description." [2]   A few pages further on he says again: "Labor is, in the first place, a process in which both man and nature participate, and in which man of his own accord starts, regulates, and controls the material reactions between himself and nature. He opposes himself to nature as one of her own

---

[1] Evolution is pushing the capitalist out of industry; many of the large concerns are managed by paid presidents and superintendents; in time all will be so managed. The capitalist more and more becomes a promoter and manipulator of securities. He has so organized industry that he is on the point of organizing himself out of it and becoming a mere owner.

[2] "Capital," p. 145.

forces, setting in motion arms and legs, head and hands, the natural forces of his body, in order to appropriate nature's productions in a form adapted to his own wants." [1]

But while he thus makes a formal recognition of mental labor, throughout his discussions Marx practically ignores it. The above extracts are his only explicit declarations on the subject, and it is doubtful if these mean anything else than the necessary mental effort that accompanies manual labor. Pure mental labor receives from him not even formal recognition. The services of superintendence, the designing of machinery and buildings, the creative activity of invention — all such mental labor is unrecognized in his whole treatise, appears to be excluded from his arguments, and would apparently find no reward in a social state organized according to his ideal. It does not seem an exaggeration, therefore, of the practical effect of his teaching to represent Marx as holding that wealth is produced by manual labor alone, and therefore of right belongs entirely to the manual worker.

Here again the system of Marx is based on theoretic deductions, rather than on an induction of facts, contradicts universal human experience, and is fundamentally defective. The chief element in the creation of value is not manual labor, but intelligence or mental labor. Labor undirected by intelligence is of little worth — that is why skilled labor is paid more than unskilled, and that is why the director of work, who performs mental labor only, is the most highly paid of all. Recent socialists, like Mr. Spargo, have been compelled to abandon Marx

[1] "Capital," pp. 156, 157.

at this point (protesting, however, that their master has been misinterpreted) and teach explicitly that labor must be held to include all productive energies, whether mental or physical.[1] They recognize the truth, which cannot be denied without disaster, that the man who designs a locomotive is a laborer equally with the men who build it; the man who organizes and directs a business is a laborer no less than the man who works at lathe or loom. They even go further and admit that this is the higher form of labor, requires the rarer gifts and training, and is the more important factor in the production of wealth. In this, the later Socialism is distinctly more scientific than that of Marx.

We are now ready to consider the theory of surplus-value (*Mehrwerth*), the capstone of Marx's "scientific" Socialism. Under the present capitalistic system, instead of individuals working separately we have men employed by a capitalist, who buys their labor-time or labor-power like any other commodity, paying for it its exchange-value or market price.[2] But labor-power differs from other commodities in creating new values in the process of being used up. The laborer is paid his wages, the price of which is fixed by the law of supply and demand at an amount that will maintain the worker and his family in a state of efficiency. But his labor produces more value than these wages represent, so that while the capitalist pays for the labor-power its exchange-value,

[1] Spargo, "Socialism," pp. 226–228.

[2] Economists generally speak of labor as a "commodity." As a matter of fact, there is no such thing as "labor" — the working-man sells to his employer his own body and soul for a given time, an inseparable part of himself. It is this vital human element that must be reckoned with, and this constitutes the difference between the different grades of "labor."

he obtains for himself its use-value. Suppose that the laborer requires for his daily support a certain quantity of goods that we may represent by A, and can produce this value in six hours. The employer has bought his entire labor-power and can require him to work six hours more, making his product for the day $A + b$. This b is surplus-value, which the capitalist acquires at the laborer's expense and appropriates to himself. This the capitalist is able to do because he possesses the means of production — tools and raw materials, which he has acquired through his money-capital. The laborer would be glad to work for himself, without dependence on the capitalist, but he has neither money to buy materials nor machinery to turn out product. He must accept the capitalist's offer of employment and wages, or starve. The capitalist finds for him the market for his commodity, labor-power, for which he pays its value in exchange, pocketing the difference.

This transaction, Marx maintains, is only a legalized form of robbery.[1] Society ought to be so organized that the whole of a man's labor, and not a part merely, should inure to his own advantage. There ought to be no capitalist employer to take from the poor man half of his earnings, without rendering to the poor man anything in return, save that which is already his own inalienable right as a man, the right to earn his living by his own labor. Therefore, the ideal at which society should aim is coöperative production, and coöperative production on a universal scale is the essence of Socialism — from which

[1] "Capital is dead labor that, vampire-like, only lives by sucking living labor, and lives the more, the more labor it sucks." — *Das Kapital*, Vol. I, Chap. X.

equitable distribution is a corollary. Capital, now in individual hands, owes its existence to society as a whole, and should rightfully belong to society as a whole. Owned in common, it would be administered for the common good. Labor would then be paid its use-value and not its exchange-value. The full product of labor would be divided among the laborers themselves, and there would be no favored class to seize the lion's share of wealth towards the production of which it had contributed nothing.

What Marx calls "surplus-value" is evidently precisely what other economists call profit. Marx has used a great number of pages to describe in wearisome detail the capitalistic method of creating and appropriating surplus-value, and the whole pretentious discourse, with its philosophical jargon and mathematical formulas, reduces itself to the simple proposition that every capitalist expects to sell his goods for more than the cost of production and so make a profit. But what sane man ever dreamed of questioning this? Why all this pother to prove that men do not engage in business for the mere benefit of their health? It would have been simpler, and honester too, to say that the laborer has a moral right to the entire product of his labor and that profit is ethically wrong.[1] Profit makes possible the exploitation of labor; Socialism proposes to abolish profit.

But here are two separate propositions, and a motion

[1] The right to the whole product of labor, first clearly asserted by Rodbertus, is individualistic anarchism, not pure Socialism. It was modified in the Gotha programme (1875), into the assertion that the whole product of labor, being possible only through society, belongs to society; and its ultimate distribution is determined, not by the ethical right of the producer, but by the claims of society.

to divide the question is in order.   That the laborer has a right to the entire product of his labor is an ethical principle so evidently correct that nobody is likely to dispute it as an abstraction; but, as Captain Cuttle says, "The bearings of this observation lays in the application on it." Is all of $A + b$ the production of the laborer?   Are there not other factors contained in this product besides the labor-power of the worker?   There is, first of all, as we have had occasion to note before, the gift of nature: the raw materials, plus whatever labor has been necessary to bring them to the factory and make them available. The working-man did not acquire these; why should he be paid for them?   The "surplus-value" in a suit of clothes — *i.e.* their value over and above what has been paid for labor all the way up from the birth of the lamb to the sale of the suit — does not consist chiefly in unpaid labor.   By far the largest part of this value consists in the fact that wool is the one material that satisfies a general want of mankind — the universal conviction that "all wool" clothing is the best of all.   An analysis of the process of bringing this suit of clothes to the wearer will show that capitalist and laborer have united to exploit nature, and have shared in the result in certain agreed proportions.   The equity of the respective shares is open to question, but it cannot be maintained that all of b belongs to the laborer, for he did not produce all.

If this be admitted, and the contribution of nature be subtracted from b, there remains the further factor of the "plant."   It is absurd to say that a man who stands over a machine and feeds raw material into it should be credited with the full value of the finished product, less the raw material.   On the contrary, the machine has done

K

most of the work and therefore has contributed most of the value. Another subtraction must be made.

There remains still the factor of superintendence or direction, for which Marx appears to make no provision whatever, but which is nevertheless the vital factor in the production of value. Here is a common business phenomenon : Two factories or shops are located side by side, making the same commodities, say shoes. They pay the same wages precisely to employees. One barely keeps going; the proprietor of the other gets rich. How has the latter robbed his laborers? He has made his profit by superior intelligence, buying better or cheaper raw materials, using superior machinery, having a better manager, or marketing his product with greater skill. On the Marxian theory, neither could be more nor less a robber than the other, since both pay the same market price (exchange-value) for labor-power and both presumably have in return the same use-value. Yet the b is very different in the one case from the other, and the cause of the difference can be nothing else than mental labor in the direction of the business. The quantitative value of b depends less on the laborer than on the skill, foresight, and energy of the director. If he is lacking in these qualities, part or all of b disappears, and the result is bankruptcy.

Not only is this the most important factor in present industrial enterprises, but it will be equally important in a system of Socialism. If men are to get their full return for labor in coöperative production, there must be skilled direction, and this direction must be paid for in some way. Now the capitalist pays himself, and it is of course a fair question for inquiry whether he does not overpay himself —

whether the present system does not pay too great wages for superintendence. But that is a very different proposition from that of Marx — as much different, to put the matter in the plainest words, as the ethical margin between saying that every capitalist is a robber, and saying that the products of industry might be more equitably divided than they are at present.[1]

That the laborer should have the entire product of his labor is, as we have conceded, a proposition ethically unimpeachable, but it is valid only in abstract ethics. It is a principle that will be practically unworkable in any society. Even in the socialized State to which the followers of Marx look hopefully forward, this can never be more than an ideal. The laborer can never hope to receive the whole of b. In a socialized State there will perhaps be no taxes, but there must be an equivalent: some means by which a fixed portion of the common product shall be reserved for the common profit and the common expenses. There must be another reservation for renewal of plant and extending enterprises for the common good. Society itself will always insist, and rightly insist, on having a share of that product which only society makes it possible for the laborer to produce. That is the inevitable penalty of living in a society. Only

---

[1] Marx is fond of illustrating his propositions by mathematics, which makes appropriate a proof of the mathematical absurdity of his theory of capitalistic robbery. X has a capital of $10,000, and engages in making tinware, in which he employs ten men ten hours a day. He sells at a small advance, and at the end of a year has a profit of $500. According to Marx he has "robbed" each tinner of $50. Y has a capital of $100,000, engages in manufacturing jewellery, also employing ten men eight hours a day. He sells at a large advance, and at the end of a year has a profit of $5000. According to Marx he has "robbed" *his* ten workers of $500 each!

in a state of barbarism, or by living as a hermit, can a man have absolutely the whole product of his labor. It becomes then merely a question whether society will take from b more or less than the capitalist now gets as net profit, and how much will therefore be left for the laborer to enjoy. At present a good share of b goes to pay interest on capital and for rent, but Socialism will abolish these payments, and theoretically the laborer should get the benefit of this economy. Whether he would actually get it, nobody knows — it can be determined only by experiment.

Moreover, it is plain that the formula $A + b$ represents only the labor-cost of production, which in a socialized State would be the total cost. But even in a socialized State this cost of production would not decide the value of commodities — that would still depend on the fitness of the commodities to satisfy human wants. If production should be badly directed in a socialized State, the result might be the manufacture of articles that could not even be given away, because nobody would want them.

Under the present system the laborer is really "exploited" or "robbed" only in those cases in which the capitalist succeeds in getting an undue share for his services, or as rent or interest on capital. Many manufacturing concerns, in these days when merciless competition still widely prevails, are run on a very small margin of profit, and sometimes for periods of months at an actual loss. The vast majority of corporations pay small dividends or none. Great fortunes have, as a rule, been made by some other means than direct exploitation of the working-man — means that much more closely resemble highway robbery and swindling. It is this general experience of vanishing profits that has encouraged the rapid growth of the Trust in the last few decades, if it has not actually produced it.

There is no end to the absurdities of the Marxian system. Into many of them he was led by his undue dependence on Ricardo and Smith. Ricardo had said that profits decrease in proportion as wages increase; and Marx accepted this without question — indeed, it is the necessary foundation of his doctrine of surplus-value. But it is flatly contradicted by the economic experience of the past century. If surplus-value were the sole or chief source of capitalist profit, every rise of wages would involve loss of profit. Yet it is notorious that, during the last fifty years, wages have steadily risen in Germany, in England, and in the United States, while in spite of such rise capitalists have reaped enormous profits in all three countries.

If unpaid human labor is the sole source of capitalistic profit, why should capitalists have deluded themselves with the notion that they increase their profits by introducing more machinery and reducing the number of human laborers? They ought rather to employ twice the number of men and so double their profits! Only one who carefully shut himself away from the world of fact, and employed deduction to the exclusion of induction, could elaborate a theory so at variance with economic experience. Marx, in fact, abandoned his whole theory and made waste paper of his treatise when he wrote: "The profits of an undertaking are independent of the quantity of capital employed in it and are not in proportion to the quantity of unpaid labor," [1] — that

---

[1] *Das Kapital*, Vol. III, Chap. VII (Appendix).

is, profit is dependent on skill of management.   "Scientific" Socialism, forsooth !

V

Marx failed in his analysis of economic conditions, in part because he was at heart an agitator rather than a man of science.   He was essentially a revolutionary, full of gall and bitterness against men of wealth.   But his deepest source of failure was that he had been trained as a philosopher and not as a man of affairs, and had not the practical experience of life that is essential in an economist.   It is a venerable story — and it would be an affront to the intelligence of one's readers to repeat it — that relates how the German evolved the camel from his inner consciousness.   That is exactly the history of Marx's "scientific Socialism."   He made no inductive study of social facts.   He had no equipment of training in business, no life as a proletarian to supply, in some sort at least, the material of fact that he needed.   He employed the same old deductive methods, and first of all set himself the task of making definitions, without due study of the things to be defined.   To deduce an entire system from a few definitions was an easy task for one trained in logic.   He did it.

Even his defective definitions would not have led to results so erroneous, had not Marx fixed his eyes so exclusively on a single class of social facts, that branch of industrialism concerned chiefly with factories and machinery.   Land and the workers of the land are wholly left out of his calculations.   This is a fatal defect of his socialistic scheme, for the agrarian problem is quite as serious as the industrial, and much the older of the two.

The supply of food is the one matter that cannot be neglected in any scheme for the future of society, but it has no place in the system of Marx. The agrarian problem is also a problem of capitalism, since capitalists are rapidly acquiring possession, not only of all tools, but of the land, the ultimate source not only of food but of all other forms of wealth. By this possession of the soil, modern Capitalism is becoming rapidly transformed into a new feudalism, as much more powerful than the old as it is more wealthy.

This evil and its social results were clearly seen by Henry George, and he proposed as an adequate remedy the single tax on land, all revenues of government to be raised by progressive taxation of land values until the full rental value was reached. By thus making land valueless, save for actual occupation and use, Mr. George maintained that the State would make access to the land equally free to all, and the monopoly of productive machinery would become impossible — the man who was unable to find profitable industrial employment could always turn to the soil and make a living. This would doubtless remain true until the occupation of all soil that could be profitably worked, and then all the present difficulties would reassert themselves. The socialist is right in objecting to the single tax, that it is only a palliative, not a solution.

The system of Marx, based on the old scholastic method, is as unsubstantial as moonshine. The real basis of Socialism is not scientific, but ethical. It outrages men's sense of justice that the division of the product of labor should be so unequal as it now is. Every man with a healthy moral sense is conscious that there is something wrong in a social system that permits the iniquities to

which he cannot shut his eyes if he would, though he may
hesitate much when asked to say just where the wrong
is, and is likely to hesitate still more when asked to propose a remedy.   When Socialism appeals to that latent
feeling, its appeal is irresistible, provided it does not
violate other ethical ideas in making it.   The only effective argument for Socialism drawn from economics alone
is made by pointing out the unnecessary and gross wastefulness of the present system, especially in distribution,
and by showing how this waste could be eliminated by
the socialization of both the production and the distribution of wealth.

But while Marx's theory of value, and the deductions
from it, which occupy the whole of his first volume on
"Capital," must be pronounced thoroughly unscientific
and misleading, his analysis of capitalistic production
in the second volume is of high value.   He explains clearly
the nature of over-production, the periodicity of commercial crises and panics, and makes it plain that these
arise from a superabundance of wealth badly distributed.
He was the first economist to detect and appreciate the
drift towards socialized production; and he predicted
twenty-five years ago, with astonishing accuracy, the
line along which further development would take place.
Many things that have since occurred he clearly fore-
saw, especially the present era of the Trusts, or the consolidation of capital and the consequent socialization of
production on a large scale.   This prophetic vision constitutes the real claim of Marx to eminence in economic
science; and the justification of his predictions by the
event has given him a very high repute and imparted to
Socialism the greatest impetus it has ever received, especially in England and America.

Next to this, perhaps his service was greatest in sub-
stituting evolution for revolution as the ideal of socialists, a peaceful and irresistible development of forces and
institutions already working under our eyes, rather than
a violent overturning of existing institutions and the immediate establishment of a new social order on the ruins
of the old.   For this change in the spirit and aims of
socialists we have to thank Karl Marx more than any
of their leaders.

But he must at the same time be held responsible for
a good deal of the bitterness of class-feeling that prevails
among socialists, especially such as belong to the class
of manual laborers.   He chose deliberately to excite and
deepen this class-feeling, in order to gain followers and
promote the agitation necessary to get a hearing and insure the acceptance of socialistic principles.   He was
led to this policy by his study of history, in which he
found class-struggles to be so continuous a method of progress ; and he became convinced that future progress is
to be reached only in this way.   The cultivation of class-
consciousness, and the class-struggle of the proletariat,
seemed to him the sole path by which social advance was
to be hoped.[1]   All measures of social amelioration he

[1] In any event it may be questioned if Marx's method is a fortunate
one.   If one wished to induce a friend to taste strawberries for the first
time, one would not sprinkle quinine over them — the experience of generations is that sugar will make them much more attractive.   Which is a
parable.   Class-feeling has probably prejudiced more people against
Socialism and prevented them from giving its claims fair consideration,
than it has ever drawn to its ranks.   It is because a new group of socialistic writers and speakers have risen within the last two decades, who
appeal to reason and not to passion, to love and not to hate, that Socialism is just beginning to get a serious hearing.   For none of this can Marx
be thanked.

regarded as mere tubs to the whale — they were an evil, because they diverted attention from the true method of progress and were of the nature of a bribe. Some of his followers have pushed the doctrine of the class-struggle to such an excess that they would restrict the socialistic movement to wage-earners; but others are wise enough to see that if it is to succeed, Socialism must win also the small farmers and shopkeepers, as well as the intellectual and moral *élite*. Socialists often assert that, with the victory of their cause through class-consciousness and the class-struggle, the future will see the entire disappearance of classes. What they evidently mean is, that the proletariat will after its rise to power absorb or extinguish other classes. The "disappearance" will take place *à la* Jonah. But what guarantee would there be that classes would not speedily reappear, also *à la* Jonah?

Though Marx proved a true prophet in the matter of the Trust, he as conspicuously failed in another matter of equal importance: he agreed with the Premillenarians that the world is getting worse, and that it must continue to get worse before it can get better. In the increasing misery of the workers he saw the sure sign of impending social revolution, just as the Premillenarians see the signs of the speedy coming of the Lord in the growing wickedness of the world. Marx fared no better and no worse than others who have predicted the immediate end of the age, — all have in turn been alike discredited by the event. He believed that the lot of the wage-earner would become so rapidly worse as to compel a social change in the near future; and if he were still living, he would be a greatly disappointed man, in that the wage-earner's condition has distinctly improved and the so-

cial change has been indefinitely postponed. The new
heavens and the new earth are not yet.

VI

We need not linger long over the hotly-debated question of the originality of Marx.   There is much truth in
Lowell's lines : —

> Though old the thought and oft expressed,
> 'Tis his at last who says it best —

and who may have said it first is of little moment.
Charges of unfair borrowing of ideas have been frequent
among socialistic writers.   Marx charged that Lassalle
ploughed with his heifer ; Rodbertus, the predecessor of
both, complained freely, and at times bitterly, that the
best ideas in Marx's writings had been taken without
credit from him.   In both cases the verdict must be that
the charge was substantially true ; and in both cases it
must be added that the idea was bettered by the borrower
— just as Rodbertus himself borrowed and used more
effectively ideas of Ricardo and Mill.   The fact seems to
be just this : each economist took the work of his predecessor and carried it a step farther — Ricardo improved
on Smith, Mill on Ricardo, Rodbertus on all three, and
Marx on Rodbertus.   Some were careful to give credit
to their predecessors ; others were less scrupulous.   If
any of them need any further defence, it may best be
made in certain well-known lines of Mr. Kipling : —

> When 'Omer smote 'is bloomin' lyre
> He'd 'eard men sing by land an' sea,
> An' what 'e thought 'e might require
> 'E went an' took — the same as me.

As matter of fact, the real originator of Marx's theory of value was Adam Smith, in his "Wealth of Nations," and much good may the honor do him.   He said : "What everything really costs to the man who wants to acquire it, is the toil and trouble of acquiring it.   What everything is really worth to the man who has acquired it and who wants to dispose of it or exchange it for something else, is the toil and labor which it can save to himself, and which it can impose on other people."   The first proposition is generally true ; the second is only sometimes true, quite as often untrue, since all depends, when a man comes to dispose of that which he has acquired, how much some other man wants it.   Many things enter into the other man's desire besides the amount of labor required to produce the article.   Smith illustrated his second proposition thus: "If among a nation of hunters, for example, it usually costs twice as much labor to kill a beaver which it does to kill a deer, one beaver would naturally be worth or exchange for two deer."   On the contrary, as any hunter could have told Mr. Smith, if the deer is twice as useful for food and clothing as the beaver, it will be valued accordingly, and one deer will exchange for two or more beaver.   If, however, beaver become very scarce and men desire their fur greatly, then two deer might be given for one beaver, again irrespective of the labor involved in capturing either.   It is what the animal is worth in satisfying human wants after the hunter has killed him that determines his value, not the labor of the capture.   Anybody but an economist would have known that.[1]   Utility, not embodied labor,

[1] A recent socialist writer makes this attempt to justify the Marxian theory of value : Primitive man makes a bow that costs him a day's

determines desire; and the proportion of supply to demand determines the ratio of exchanges, the world around, and such has been the case since the earliest savages began to barter. No trade was ever made since the world began on any other principles.

VII

The Marxian system should be called, not "scientific" Socialism, but dogmatic Socialism, for it has come to have in the minds of his followers almost the force of a religious dogma, and is asserted by many of them with the full force of religious bigotry. Marx did not take himself as seriously as his followers, and with rare humor once remarked to a friend, "I am not a Marxist myself," — *Je ne suis pas Marxiste, moi.* At every point, with a single exception, as we have discovered in our examination, reason or experience or both discredit his conclusions — the tooth of time has eaten away every laurel leaf save one from the crown that his admirers placed on his brows. His interpretation of history is a system of economic determinism, Calvinism without God. His idea of the inevitableness of historical events, if it were true, would leave no place for the ethical indignation that he frequently displays over economic wrong-doing. His heart frequently got the better of his philosophy, as has been the case with many determinists. Starting his inquiries with the philosophic presuppositions of the neo-Hegelian

work, and exchanges it for as many arrows as could be made in a day. (Kaufmann, " What is Socialism ? " p. 35.) No barter was ever made on that principle; the only question ever asked in a trade is, What will you give? What will you take? That is to say, in the supposed case, how much A wants the arrows and how much B wishes the bow, will decide the terms of the exchange, not the question of labor.

school, his materialistic philosophy of wealth-production and wealth-distribution precluded him from making any but an inconsiderable contribution to the solution of the social problem.   That problem is not, as he assumes, primarily a stomach-question;   it is a mind-problem, a heart-problem.   Men are not so constituted that they will become and remain happy when they are merely fed, clothed, and warmed, which is all that Marx promises them, all that he seems to take into consideration.

V

ANARCHY: THE SCHOOL OF PROUDHON AND KROPOTKIN

BIBLIOGRAPHY

Sources: —

PROUDHON, What is Property? Boston, 1876.
BAKOUNINE, God and the State. New York, 1902.
KROPOTKIN, Memoirs of a Revolutionist. New York, 1899.
——, Fields, Factories, and Workshops. New York, 1899.
——, The Conquest of Bread. New York, 1907.
TOLSTOI, My Confession. New York, 1886.
——, What To Do. New York, 1889.

Sympathetic expositions: —

TUCKER, Instead of a Book. New York, 1902.
ELTZBACHER, Anarchism. New York, 1908.

V

ANARCHY: THE SCHOOL OF PROUDHON AND KROPOTKIN

I

A STUDY of Socialism necessarily includes some examination of Anarchy, partly because the two systems are
so frequently confounded, partly because they really have
common elements, especially in the sphere of economics.
The origin of Anarchy as a distinct system is generally
ascribed to Pierre Joseph Proudhon (1809–1865). He
was a native of Besançon, and partially completed his
education at the university of that town, but was compelled to seek means of self-support and learned the com-
positor's trade. He continued his studies, acquired a
smattering of several languages, including Hebrew, and
began to compare them with the French. In 1838 he
published an *Essai de Grammaire Generale*, for which the
Academy at Besançon rewarded him with a pension.
It was an ambitious but worthless book, because the aspiring author had no adequate knowledge of philology.
Its publication is a good illustration of the intellectual
restlessness and audacity that were Proudhon's chief
characteristics.

In 1839 Proudhon went to Paris, and in the following
year published his most famous book, "What is Property?" His answer to the query appears on the first
page of the treatise: *La Propriété, c'est le vol*, property is
theft; and the entire book is devoted to a justification

of this thesis. Among the other books of this industrious writer, which were of value in making known his
ideas, are: "System of Economic Contradictions" (1846),
"Interest and Principal" (1849), and "Justice in the
Revolution and the Church" (1858). In 1849 Proudhon
attempted to found a "Bank of the People," with the
purpose of abolishing interest, and eventually capital,
also. The project came to grief almost as speedily as his
critics predicted. Later he was imprisoned three years
for violation of the press laws in connection with a journal
that he had founded, called *The Representative of the People*. On his release he went to Belgium (1852); here he
remained until an amnesty in 1860 permitted his return
to Paris, where he lived and continued to compose books
until his death.

Proudhon set up as a teacher of economics on as slender
a capital as he had when he undertook to be a philologist.
He never worked out a complete system. Like his predecessors in France, he had a logical mind, which took
naturally to the deductive method, and all his ideas are
inferences from a few fundamental principles, ethical
rather than political or economic, in which he firmly believed. Justice, liberty, equality, were the foundations
of his reasoning regarding society. In an ideal society,
he held that there would be perfect equality of payment
for service, and this would be just, because at the same
time inequality of talent and capacity would be reduced
to an inconsiderable minimum. The latter proposition
is exceedingly dubious; it contradicts present experience
and reasonable forecast of the future. Not only are great
inequalities of talent and capacity now observed to exist,
but it is only reasonable to suppose that, with perfect

liberty and the consequent opportunity of every one to
develop himself to the utmost (which practically nobody
has now), the inequalities would become greater, not less.
It is true that liberty and equality would enable many to
rise who are now ground down and crushed by poverty,
but that is beside the point. Until some process is found
for bringing men into the world with equal mental and
physical endowments, there can be reasonably expected
no material diminution of present inequalities of talent
and capacity. Under liberty and equality we might
reasonably expect a vast increase of talent and capacity,
of all grades, and that is all.

But to Proudhon, justice, liberty, and equality seemed
to demand that all men share alike in the returns of labor.
The appropriation of an undue share by individuals, the
right of property, he compared to the right of *aubane* in
French law, — the sovereign's claim to the property of
a deceased foreigner, — a legal right founded simply on
force, not on any ethical principle. Private property
has a like power of appropriating values, in the form of
rent and interest. It reaps without labor, it consumes
without producing, it enjoys without exertion. Private
property is therefore indefensible on any ethical ground.
Property in the form of land is robbery, because God
made the earth, and his gifts are free; the common right
to the soil can no more be surrendered or taken away
than other fundamental rights, like life and liberty.
That only is one's own which he actually produces, and
the right to any portion of the soil expires the moment
one ceases to cultivate it. Thus far Socialism would
assent to the doctrine of Proudhon; it makes a clear
distinction between property in means of production,

and property in means of consumption. Private property in the former is theft; private property in the latter wrongs no one and may be permitted.

Property in the form of capital is also robbery, Proudhon argued, because it enables one who has produced nothing to consume the fruits of others' toil. It thus becomes the plundering of the weak by the strong. But would it be a remedy merely to reverse the injustice and permit the strong to be plundered by the weak? This is but to perpetuate the present slavery, the only difference being that we should have many masters instead of one. Again, the law of the manna would be the ideal law of property : every man should gather and keep what his family needed and no more; to gather more is to deny the equal rights of some other family. But how to apply this principle to the conditions of modern society is the difficulty, and at that point Proudhon offers no valuable suggestion. He merely maintains that possession is the synthesis of the contradiction : the instruments of labor are mine while I use them; a piece of land is mine while I cultivate it. An analysis of Proudhon's arguments makes it clear that what he is really opposing as unjust is, the profits of capital: rent, and interest. His ideas of economics reduce themselves to the demand for the abolition of these, nothing more.

The practical means proposed by Proudhon for realizing his ideas was the establishment of a great national bank to facilitate exchanges. This bank was to issue paper-money, or labor-checks, on all articles offered, on the basis of the labor-time expended in their production. These checks would entitle the holder to any other articles of equal value; that is, articles that required the same labor-time for production. Products were to be exchanged for products, the checks merely making exchanges easier than barter. This scheme, with its ultimate reduction of interest to zero, and the disappearance of rents and profits, he called mutualism.

There is a science of society, thought Proudhon, which we have not to invent, but to discover. He had little respect for what others had claimed to discover concerning this science. "Political economy," he said, "which is regarded by many as a philosophy of wealth, is in fact nothing but an organized practice of robbery and misery." Hence he disagreed with his predecessors, chiefly because they believed it possible to regenerate society according to some ready-made programme. This notion he called a "cursed lie." He had no Utopia, but believed in the gradual evolution of society, in accordance with its fundamental laws, into collectivism and finally into Anarchy, a social condition in which government and law would be no longer necessary. Such a social condition seemed to him a clear deduction from the idea of liberty, and he was right if liberty and individualism are identical. Anarchy is simply the logic of *laissez faire* pushed to its extreme conclusion. If the best government is that which governs least, as the Manchester school maintained, then a still better would be one that did not govern at all — no government, that is to say. And if government is simply organized injustice, all the more it should be abolished. Said Adam Smith : "Civil government, so far as it is instituted for the security of property, is in reality instituted for the defence of the rich against the poor, or of those who have some property against those who have none at all." Frank confession ! How can the poor be expected to respect such law and government? Why should not their abolition be thought most desirable? It is perhaps not wonderful that Proudhon failed to perceive one implication of this doctrine of Anarchy: it is the negation of all society; perfect liberty of the individual may be wholly desirable, but it is necessarily incompatible with any form of social order.

Proudhon's importance in the development of Socialism is that this doctrine of property suggested to Marx his notion of the nature of capital: it is acquired by robbery, by the power of exploiting the worker through appropriation of the total result of productive labor and giving the laborer only a partial equivalent, the capitalist retaining the "surplus-value" for himself. He also anticipated the doctrine regarding the ownership of land, made famous in more recent years by Henry George, though it is probable that George had never heard of Proudhon's teaching. Both agreed that the right of occupation should be substituted for ownership of land, the ownership being vested in the entire community.

One great and permanent effect seems to have followed the teachings of Proudhon, the abandonment of specific programmes, the devising of ingenious Utopias. Students of social conditions became emancipated from the enslaving notion that the millennium in five minutes is a possibility; they adopted instead the evolutionary philosophy as the basis of their thinking. Doubtless we are to ascribe this great and beneficent change chiefly to the growing prevalence of that philosophy in all forms of intellectual activity, in the latter half of the nineteenth century, but Proudhon is at least entitled to the credit of blazing out the new way.

It is also worth noting, since we shall presently see a violent contrast, that Proudhon wrote in a deeply religious spirit, if not precisely as a Christian. To his first memoir on property, he appended this prayer: "O God of liberty! God of equality! Thou God who didst place in my heart the sentiment of justice before my reason comprehended it, hear my prayer. Thou hast dictated what I have written. Thou hast formed my thought, thou hast directed my studies, thou hast separated my spirit from curiosity and my heart from attachment, in order that I should publish the truth before the master and the slave. I have spoken as thou hast given me power and talent; it remains for thee to complete my work. Thou knowest whether I have sought my interest or thy glory. O God of liberty! May my memory perish, if humanity may but be free!"

We shall do well also to note that Proudhon proposed Anarchy as a goal, not as an immediate possibility. Government of man by man, in every form, can be nothing else than oppression, he said, but man can only gradually come to that perfect society which is the union of anarchy and order. This teaching his most influential successors have repudiated, and in so doing they have gone back to the old idea of the immediate reorganization of society. Anarchists are therefore still wandering in Utopias that socialists have abandoned.

II

The first to push still further the idea of Anarchy was Michael Bakunin. He was the scion of an aristocratic family of Russia, born in 1814, and became an officer in the army. Sickened by the brutalities that he witnessed

in Poland, he resigned his commission and became a
student of philosophy in Germany, from 1841 to 1843.
He then went to Paris, the great Cave of Adullam for
revolutionists, where he became an active member of
various socialist and communist societies. Making the
acquaintance of Proudhon, he adopted the latter's
theories in part and still further developed them. The
rest of his life, after 1847, he spent in going about from
place to place, being at one time under sentence of death,
and again an exile to Siberia, whence he succeeded in
making his escape. His last days were spent in London
and Switzerland, where he died in 1876. His was a
stormy life; he aimed at great things, but accomplished
little.

Even his principal work, "God and the State," is but
a fragment. He was a bald materialist in philosophy,
hence an atheist in religion. Every form of external
authority, human or divine, provoked his unbounded
wrath, his undying opposition. Absolute liberty was
his only god, a liberty limited only by the laws of nature,
scientifically ascertained. These man cannot but obey,
for they are the laws also of his own nature. Therefore,
with knowledge of these laws, all need of political organization, administration, legislation, will at once disappear.
Of course, no privileged class should exist, — nature
decrees that men should have equal rights and opportunities. All religions are to be abolished, and science
is to be substituted for faith. Marriage will also be abolished, and absolutely free unions will take its place.

These are not mere speculations, but have become an
avowed programme. The *Alliance de la Democratie
Socialiste*, which Bakunin organized in 1869 at Geneva,

adopted as the first plank in its platform : "The Alliance declares itself atheist; it demands the abolition of all worship, the substitution of science for faith, of human justice for Divine justice; the abolition of marriage, so far as it is a political, religious, juridical, or civil institution." From this it clearly appears that liberty of conscience will not be a principle of the anarchist order; to the absolute liberty of all men which they demand, there is to be one limitation : no man shall be at liberty to have any religion. The anarchist has yet to learn that to be intolerant is to be intolerable.

In his economic ideas Bakunin agrees in the main with Marx and the "scientific" socialists, — capital is to be abolished, the community is to assume ownership of the means of production, and some form of voluntary collectivism is to be established. The details of the scheme he did not clearly work out. Anarchy bends all its energies at present to the work of destruction; the first thing is to do away with the present order; construction of another will come after that.

Some things, however, are clear. All limits of race and nationality are expected to disappear in this universal solvent of Anarchy. Patriotism is a crime, not a virtue. A universal federation of all local associations will come about naturally, and world-wide peace and order will take the place of the present international jealousies and warfare. This programme, of course, demands the merciless and complete destruction of the existing social organization, to the end that men may begin to live the life for which they were designed by nature, without government and without law. Bakunin's motto might well have been, "Whatever is, is wrong."

III

After Bakunin, the most influential anarchist leader has been Prince Peter Alexeievitch Kropotkin, born at Moscow in 1842, the descendant of an ancient Russian family that is said to have better claim to the throne of Russia than the Romanoffs. He was educated in the corps of pages at St. Petersburg, and became an officer in a regiment of Cossacks. He served for some years in Siberia, where he vainly tried to introduce reforms into the convict prisons. For scientific investigations in Manchuria he received the gold medal of the Russian Geographical Society in 1864. From childhood he had been familiar with the cruelties of private owners of the serfs, and he gradually conceived an imperishable hatred of the entire Russian social and political system. In 1874 his radical theories of social reform caused his arrest and imprisonment, but he escaped in 1876 and thenceforth became a revolutionary.

Going to Geneva, Kropotkin founded a journal called *Le Révolte*, but he was expelled from Switzerland in 1881 at the demand of Russia. He then went to England, and thence after a few years to France, where in 1883 he was arrested, tried, and condemned to five years' imprisonment for political conspiracy. He had been one of the leaders of an anarchist propaganda that resulted in an insurrection at Montceau-les-Mines, where dynamite was used for the first time as an argument in social agitation. Released in 1886, he took up his abode in London, and has contented himself since then with advocacy of anarchy through the press. To his "Memories of a Revolutionist" (1899), a portrait is prefixed which shows an elderly gentleman with a big-domed, bald head, looking out benevolently through his spectacles over a patriarchal beard — an almost ludicrous contrast to the ideal of a wild-eyed, bloody-minded anarchist that is commonly entertained.

On his trial at Lyons, Prince Kropotkin (he has renounced the title) gave a full exposition of his anarchistic views, which he has since consistently set forth with more elaboration in his books. For the ordinary reader his "Conquest of Bread" (1907) will be found quite sufficient. Like all anarchists, he demands absolute freedom, so far as law and government are concerned, with no limit on the action of man but the impossibilities of nature and the equal rights of his neighbors. Instead of legal and administrative control of men, there should be free contract, perpetually subject to revision and cancellation. Freedom and private capital are incompatible. No man has a right to appropriate anything that is the culmination of the toil of generations. "All belongs to all. All things are for all men, since all men have need of them, since all have worked in the measure of their strength to produce them, and since it is not possible to evaluate every one's part in the production of the world's wealth."

Kropotkin calls his system "anarchistic communism," and says that it is the synthesis of the two ideas pursued by humanity throughout the ages, economic and political liberty. He avows as his ideal, well-being for all — or, as he further explains, science for all, work for all, bread for all, justice for all. This, he maintains, is a possible, a realizable, ideal, and his economic justification of the theory is founded on abundant knowledge and is thoroughly convincing. He shows by elaborate calculations, founded on present production in agriculture and manufactures, how the people comprised in the city of Paris and the two adjacent departments of Seine and Seine-et-Oise, if they should declare themselves to be an anarchistic commune, could supply themselves with every comfort and luxury of life by the productive labor of all, working only five hours a day.

But a much simpler computation is sufficient to prove the economic possibility of anarchistic communism. In France to-day, as the census shows, fewer than ten persons in thirty of the population are actual producers. In England, fewer than eight in twenty-six are producers, as shown by the official census. The average day's work is probably not over ten hours in either country. It is plain, therefore, that if all the people became producers, five hours' labor a day of all would result in a vastly increased product — to take no account of what might be added by intensive culture of the soil by such an army of workers, and the improved quality of labor in factories; also leaving out of account the fact that the saving of what is now squandered every year in harmful indulgence would nearly or quite double the wealth of any nation. A single fact will show what can be accomplished by approved methods of agriculture: in ten years the agricultural products of the United States have doubled, and in 1909 their value reached $9,000,000,-000, or fully $100 each for every man, woman, and child of our population.

Kropotkin scouts the idea of attaining the goal by peaceful evolution; his hope is in a speedy revolution, with as little violence as may be, though he evidently expects not a little. He has slight hope in universal suffrage as a means by which the laborer can gain his rights, because only one voter in ten is in a position to cast a free vote. Hence, anarchists all maintain and proclaim "the sacred right of insurrection," as the last appeal of men in a state of slavery. Likewise, Kropotkin has no faith in the collectivism preached by socialists, and criticises the socialistic schemes quite as severely as he does the existing society. Nothing will free the laborer but a social system that will consist of free contracts between individuals and groups pursuing the same aim.[1] When the Revolution comes, and he thinks it is near at hand, the people are to take possession of everything, especially of food, and proceed to reorganize production on this new basis of free contract. The principle on which the common product of society ought equitably to be divided, should be that which now obtains about many things, a city water-supply, for example: no limit to an individual's consumption of what the community possesses in abundance, but an equal sharing of those commodities that are scarce or apt to run short.[2]

Political economy, as ordinarily expounded, is merely descriptive of *what is* in society, and is only a pseudo-science. For this Kropotkin would substitute a real science, which he proposes to call the Physiology of Society. Instead of beginning with a study of the production of wealth, as all economists from Adam Smith to Karl Marx have done, and coming down to its consumption, he would reverse the process. Let us first study the needs of humanity and the means of satisfying them

[1] "Conquest of Bread," p. 37.
[2] *Ibid.* p. 77.

with the least possible waste of human energy, and then make a scientific adjustment of production to the supplying of these needs.   Under the present system there is frightful waste, and men's wants are still unsatisfied. Kropotkin's method would certainly give us a new science of economics, and might give us a new social order; but that could not be Anarchy.   For no adjustment of production to needs could be made without careful calculations, and when the adjustment had been made, there must be some means of securing the proper production. That would be impossible with each man a law to himself.   Kropotkin's idea is as exactly adapted to Socialism as it is chimerical in Anarchy.

IV

Without doubt the writer who has most widely diffused ideas of Anarchy has been Count Lyof N. Tolstoi.   Born in 1828, partially educated at the University of Moscow, he entered the artillery service of the Russian army in 1851, and served in the siege of Sebastopol.   He left the army and married in 1862, devoting himself thenceforth to the management of his estates and to literature. He had already published "The Cossacks," and after his marriage he wrote "War and Peace"; by which two books, and some writings of less note, he made for himself a high place in Russian literature.   In 1875 he began the publication of perhaps his greatest work, "Anna Karenina," as a serial, and though its progress was interrupted for several months, the interest of the public showed no diminution.

It is in two books of much later date that we find the story of Tolstoi's spiritual development, "My Confession" and "My Religion" (1886), which together constitute one of the most remarkable human documents in existence. He tells us that he was christened and educated in the faith of the Orthodox Greek Church; still, when he had left the University, eighteen years old, he had discarded all belief in anything that he had been taught. "I honestly desired," he says, "to make myself a good and virtuous man; but I was young, I had passions, and I stood alone, altogether alone, in my search after virtue. Every time I tried to express the longings of my heart for a truly virtuous life, I was met with contempt and derisive laughter, but directly I gave way to the lowest of my passions, I was praised and encouraged. I found ambition, love of power, love of gain, lechery, pride, anger, vengeance, held in high esteem. I gave way to these passions, and becoming like unto my elders, I felt that the place that I filled in the world satisfied those around me. My kind-hearted aunt, a really good woman, used to say to me that there was one thing above all others that she wished for me — an intrigue with a married woman." The ethical quality of high Russian society is clearly depicted for us in that single stroke of the pen.

Instructions and examples like these bore their natural fruit: "I put men to death in war, I fought duels to slay others, I lost at cards, wasted my substance, wrung from the sweat of peasants, punished the latter cruelly, rioted with loose women, and deceived men. Lying, robbery, adultery of all kinds, drunkenness, violence and murder, all committed by me, not one crime omitted, and yet I was not the less considered by my equals a comparatively moral man. Such was my life during ten years."

During this period he began to write, partly to obtain fame and money, partly because he imagined it was his vocation to teach mankind: "I was myself considered a marvellous *littérateur* and poet, and I, therefore, very naturally adopted this theory. Meanwhile, thinker and poet though I was, I wrote and taught I knew not what. For doing this I received large sums of money. . . . Moreover, I had fame. It would seem, then, that what I taught must have been good; the faith in poetry and the development of life was a true faith, and I was one of its high priests, a post of great importance and profit." It was long before he doubted the truth of this belief, for, as he tells us again: "I was simple enough to imagine that I, the poet and thinker, was able to teach other men without myself knowing what it was that I attempted to teach."

It was not until somewhere about the year 1874 that he found a strange state of mind-torpor begin at times to grow upon him. He began to wander and was a victim of low spirits. During these periods of perplexity, which grew more and more frequent, the same questions presented themselves to him, Why? and, What after? At first these questions seemed empty and unmeaning, but no sooner had he begun to answer them than he found he was concerned with the deepest problems of life, and that he was utterly unable to find an answer. His life had come to a sudden stop. He was, indeed, able to breathe, to eat, to sleep, but there was no real life in him. The horror of great darkness had come upon him, too great to be borne, and he longed to free himself by suicide.

For a time he sought relief in study. After a long quest

he found that human learning had no answer to his questions. All science was vain. His study brought him to no conclusion, except that life is a very great evil, and annihilation is a good for which we ought to wish. Having failed to find an explanation of life in knowledge, he began to seek it by observing the life of men around him, asking himself how they lived and how they practically treated questions that brought him to despair. He found that he could learn nothing from the life of the upper classes, the rich and cultivated, with whom he had formerly associated; but when he came to study the lives and the doctrines of the common people, he became convinced that a true faith was to be found among them, which alone gave a meaning to life, and a possibility of living.

After years of scepticism, therefore, he turned once more to religion, and to the Church of his fathers. He did this in entire good faith, but in the doctrines and sacraments of the Church he found so much that outraged his reason that he obtained but partial relief. He then turned to the study of the Scriptures for himself, but he found difficulty in understanding them, and when he sought help from the writers of the Church, his difficulties were increased rather than removed. Any diligent student of theological literature will respond to this saying: "It became evident to me that if the Gospels had come down to us half burned or effaced, it would have been easier to restore the true meaning of the text than to find that meaning now, beneath the accumulations of fallacious comments which have apparently no purpose save to conceal the doctrine they are supposed to expound."

M

He at last found the key that unlocked all his mysteries in a single saying of Jesus, "Resist not evil." This he holds to be the master word of Jesus, and it made Tolstoi an anarchist. It will be seen, however, that he is an anarchist of quite different temper and spirit from Bakunin and Kropotkin, and even from Proudhon. The problem of life is to him supremely ethical, only incidentally economic; and he approaches it from the religious point of view, not the political. His method is simple: a rigid, literal interpretation of the words of Jesus. "Resist not evil" means absolute non-resistance under all circumstances, — a disciple of Christ may not use force to protect himself or his family from physical violence. Jesus says, "Judge not," and this forbids courts and judges for the punishment of criminals. No man can be a Christian and assist in the protection of person and property by governments, nor can he support governments by paying taxes.

To all objections to this interpretation Tolstoi replies by the simple assertion, "Christ must have meant what he said." Doubtless, but this does not close the question; on the contrary, it becomes the more necessary to ask, What did Christ say? Not necessarily what the words literally imply, still less what Tolstoi thinks he said. In another connection Tolstoi very truly remarks that "Resist not evil," really means, "never do anything contrary to the law of love." It is astonishing that he does not see that the law of love sometimes requires resistance to evil. And even Tolstoi does not consistently apply his theory of literal interpretation. When he comes to the injunction, "Love your enemies," he decides that "it is impossible to love your personal enemies," hence

Jesus could not have meant that. We are to understand "neighbor" as equivalent to compatriot, and "enemy" to foreigner. What Jesus says is, You must not love men of your own nation and hate all foreigners, but love all men alike, of whatever race or nation. Jesus is forbidding war, not private enmity! Thus Tolstoi does precisely what he so soundly berates the theologians for doing — he explains away the meaning of Christ's words to make them easier to obey.

But Tolstoi does not altogether overlook the economic side of the problem of life — he denies, as emphatically as Proudhon, the right of private property. "Property signifies that which has been given to me, which belongs to me exclusively; is that with which I can always do anything I like; that which no one can take away from me; that which will remain with me to the end of my life, and precisely that which I am bound to use, increase, and improve. Now there exists but one such piece of property for any man — himself." Therefore, men should labor, not to accumulate possessions, but in order to fulfil the glad law of our existence. Those who work in order to fulfil this law of toil may "rid themselves of that frightful superstition of property." But Tolstoi nowhere explains on what ground, whether of metaphysics or morals, we should refuse to call that one's own which he has gained by his own toil. "If what my hands have produced is not mine, whose is it?" the laborer may cry. "What title to it has my neighbor who has not toiled; or what title have I to the fruits of his toil?" And what is the answer?

The first principle of Christian sociology, says Tolstoi, is that money is the cause of suffering and vice among the people; and if one desires to help the poor, the first thing required of him is not to create those unfortunates whom he wishes to assist. If he would really help people, one "should not make use of money, thus presenting an inducement to extortion from the poor, by forcing them to work for him; and in order not to make use of the toil of others, he must demand as little from them as possible, and work as much as possible himself." In work Tolstoi finds the great social panacea, and the only sort of work that he seems to recognize in his later writings is manual labor. For science, art, literature, he seems to cherish only feelings of contempt; and the time spent in the writing of his novels, upon which his fame chiefly rests, he regards as wasted or worse. "Everything that we call culture — our sciences, art, and the perfection of the pleasant things of life — all these are attempts to deceive the moral requirements of man." And as far as his family would permit, Tolstoi in his later years went back to the life of a peasant — wearing the peasant's dress and working with his hands at the plough and at the cobbler's bench. The problem of life being to save the soul, a man must renounce all pleasures; he must labor, be humble, endure, and be charitable to all men. Community of property, non-resistance to evil, abstinence from all duties towards government, are the cardinal points in this theory of Anarchy. Tolstoi's literary fame and literary skill in the effective presentation of his thought have secured for him a sympathetic hearing in many quarters to which other anarchistic literature would never have been admitted. How many have believed his new gospel is another question.

V

The difficulties to be met and solved by anarchistic communism are not economic, as we have seen, but human. All attempts at revolution thus far have failed, or have at least been only partially successful, because the real problem has hitherto been misunderstood and therefore has not been attacked in the right way. The Paris Commune failed in 1871 because its members busied themselves with ideas of government, instead of proceeding at once to the industrial reorganization of society. Kropotkin believes that the people have unsuspected capabilities of organization, and could solve for themselves all the complex difficulties of a new social order. But to most persons who read this portion of his writings he will appear to be only a wild and impractical fanatic. He frankly avows himself a Utopian, and for Utopias the world at large has no longer use. The fatally weak point in his revolutionary programme is his tacit assumption that the present holders of property will sit still and permit the Revolution to despoil them, without having been first convinced that they are to be benefited by the social change, as well as the proletariat. He who believes this sets at naught all the teachings of history, and all that is known of human nature. The holders of property are in an overwhelming majority in the present social order, and until the small holders are convinced of the propriety of a change they will help the wealthy few fight for their own, if need be. The Revolution of a minority against a majority can never succeed; if it wins a temporary triumph, it will be to suffer the greater downfall. On the other hand, whenever a majority are convinced that change is expedient, the Revolution will have been virtually accomplished, and that without violence or bloodshed. The anarchist will do well, therefore, to imitate the socialist, and gain converts to his views as rapidly as he may.

Since Bakunin, one school of anarchists has pursued this policy, and they are known as philosophical anarchists. By society at large they are looked upon as a class of mild and harmless lunatics, — little children in mind, who know no better than to cry for the moon. Their theories are regarded as flatly contradicting the facts of human nature as it now exists. Their social ideal would possibly be suited to angels, but is certainly not adapted to men until the arrival of the millennium. It practically assumes, though no anarchist is absurd enough explicitly to assert, that if men were perfectly free, nobody would wrong his neighbor, nobody would commit an act of trespass or violence or passion ! Kropotkin's notion is that the working-man has something inherently noble and unselfish in his nature, that is kept down by his oppressed state, but would at once burgeon into life and fruitage if he achieved economic freedom. The employer, the capitalist, has economic freedom ; where is his noble and unselfish character ? The toiler and the employer are of the same flesh and blood — the one is just as selfish, just as greedy, just as ready to resort to violence and injustice to gain his ends, just as little likely to consider anybody but himself and his own interests, as the other — and no more so. Kropotkin has been profoundly impressed by examples of unselfish devotion shown to their fellows and their cause by some workers. But the same qualities are occasionally shown in every class, including the class of employers — *and only occasionally in any class*. It is sad, but it is true; such qualities are the exception and not the rule, in every walk of life.

Dr. Anton Menger recognizes the folly of assuming that human nature will undergo a great change for the better under Socialism or Anarchy. He assumes that human nature will remain essentially unchanged, that men will continue to be actuated by self-interest under the new order, as they have been under the old; and his speculations about the probable in a revolutionized society are based on this hypothesis, not on the assumption of a miraculously perfected humanity. This is the only rational procedure. It has sometimes happened that a group of men have found themselves relieved of all restraints of law and order — as in a mining camp, or after a mutiny at sea. The result was invariably a hell on earth. With evil passions unchained, and might making right, life became intolerable to the weak and peace-loving. There was no security for life, property, or virtue until a government was once more established, strong enough to execute justice on evil-doers and maintain order, even if it were only the supremacy of Judge Lynch. No sane man can doubt that if it were possible to establish anarchistic communism anywhere to-day, with human nature as it now is, the outcome would be some form of despotism, and that speedily. After enduring for a time the evils of a society in which the weak would be at the mercy of the strong, men would in desperation accept any authority that promised them peace and protection — and the old contest for freedom and equal rights would have to be begun over again from the beginning.

Aside from this inherent impracticability of communism is the fact that it contemplates a levelling down, rather than a levelling up, of mankind. It is like that bastard democracy, which looks at the man higher in the social scale and says defiantly, "I am as good a man as you are, any day"; while the true democracy looks at the man beneath and says, "You are, or are capable of becoming, as good a man as I am, *and here's my hand to help you rise.*" The communist, in like manner, gazes at the richer man and says, "You are my brother, therefore share your wealth with me," but never looks at the man still poorer than himself, nor thinks to say, "I am your brother, therefore share with me what I possess." Men of sense and men of heart alike have rejected communism.

VI

But there is also a party of violent anarchists, widely distributed among all the countries of Europe and transplanted to America; everywhere a source of danger, which at times becomes imminent. The most numerous group of this party is found in Russia, where it is generally known under the name of Nihilists. The name was first invented and used by the Russian novelist Turgenieff, in his "Fathers and Sons" (1861), to describe a movement for general emancipation in Russia. There had been a liberal movement, rather than a liberal party, in Russia since 1825, which became more definite in its aims from 1870 onward, largely because of the spread of the doctrines of Bakunin and Marx. This movement took its deepest hold on the young men in the universities. The publication and teaching of liberal doctrines was prohibited by the alarmed Russian government, and the policy of repression increased in energy, until in 1876 and 1877 the prisons were filled with real or suspected propagandists of political and social reform.

Such governmental tyranny led to the result that might have been anticipated, the organization of secret societies for the promotion of social revolution; and, as insurrection was an impractical remedy, in the condition of Russia, the Nihilists adopted assassination as a means of terrorizing the ruling class into acquiescence. A series of attempts on the lives of officials followed, with varying degrees of success; beginning with the shooting of General Trepoff by Vera Zasulich (January 28, 1878), and culminating in the bomb-killing of Emperor Alexander II (March 13, 1881).

The Russian government was once wittily described by Talleyrand as "an absolute despotism, mitigated by assassination," but these Nihilist killings failed to mitigate. They did not produce the expected effect. The ruling class was not terrorized, — if frightened at all, it was frightened into more extreme measures of violence and repression, instead of into yielding. Reform of any sort was further postponed, rather than hastened, by the policy adopted by the Nihilists. To quote Talleyrand again, "It was worse than a crime — it was a blunder." This is an undoubted political and social fact, that stands quite apart from the question whether the Nihilists had an abstract ethical justification for their action. It was wrong to kill the Tsar, because it was quite useless.

At the close of the Russo-Japanese War there was an astonishing social turmoil in Russia for a time, in which anything seemed possible. A dangerous mutiny in the navy, followed by a less serious outbreak in the army, was accompanied by a general strike among artisans, and threw the nation into disorder for some weeks. A repetition of the French Revolution was looked for, and by some confidently prophesied. Other countries, notably Germany, felt the influence of this Russian ferment. In a speech made at Jena, Herr Bebel said: "The struggle in Russia chills the marrow of our rulers. They have a deadly fear that the fire may cross the border. They say to themselves, 'If that is possible in Russia where there is no organization and the proletariat is comparatively small, what may happen in Germany where we have politically enlightened masses and an organized proletariat?'"

In fact, nothing did happen, even in Russia. The strength of the government was underestimated, as was the strength of Russian conservatism. The Tsar had proclaimed a sort of Constitution, the people were to have a Douma, and the storm passed. The ruling classes recovered their courage, and then their power, and the good old way of repression and imprisonments, flogging and Siberia, has been restored with greater vigor and rigor than ever. Nihilism has become quiescent for a time, but there are occasional symptoms of its revival, in the sudden and violent taking off of several peculiarly obnoxious officials.

Some Americans who have personally known many of those engaged in the Nihilist movement testify concerning them that they are men of a remarkably high type of character. Many come from the upper classes of society; nearly all are of the educated classes. They have shown themselves capable of self-sacrifice, patriotism, and devotion to their cause that have seldom been surpassed. It is difficult for Americans to judge them or their methods sympathetically and impartially, since our social and political conditions are so utterly different. Their provocations are great, their abuses cry to heaven; the character of the Russian government and laws, so unspeakable, must be taken into account. What should we do under like circumstances? We do not know, we cannot know, but we can guess.

Aside from Russia, violent anarchism is strongest at present in southern Europe, especially in Spain. Here its methods of bomb and dagger are wholly without excuse. Where a government represses freedom of speech, and punishes by foulest outrages such utterance of opinions as is tolerated in every free country, and sends to lifelong exile any who join a society of whatever sort for the promotion of social reform, violent methods may be excused if not justified. But where discussion is free, where the rights of association and public assemblage are permitted, where the ballot and representative government exist, the people have it in their power to change or overthrow existing institutions whenever they please. If institutions stand under such conditions, it is plainly because the majority will them to stand — not entirely content with them, perhaps, but not yet ready to replace them with others. In such countries violence is utterly indefensible — it can only mean the attempt of a minority to coerce the majority.

Yet there is hardly a country of Europe that has not suffered from these anarchist crimes. Unsuccessful attempts have been made on the lives of Emperor William I

of Germany (1878) and the king and queen of Spain
(1906), and four rulers have been killed : President Car-
not of France (1894), Empress Elizabeth of Austria
(1898), King Humbert of Italy (1900), and King Carlos
I of Portugal (1908). To which must be added the kill-
ing of President William McKinley in 1901. In every
one of these instances the crime was absolutely senseless
— the death of the slain ruler could by no possibility
produce a change of political policy. So far as such wanton crimes are not the result of a species of insanity, being
committed by men of weak mind, unbalanced by revolutionary teachings of anarchistic leaders — they can
subserve no purpose but a demonstration of the ability
of anarchists to kill when they choose. But nobody
doubts that. From ancient times it has been known that
any ruler could be struck down by an assassin ready to
give his own life in exchange.

There was more method in the Haymarket outrage in
Chicago (1886), by which several policeman engaged in
dispersing an anarchist gathering were killed. Public
opinion at the time demanded victims, and as the real cul-
prit could not be hanged (the man who threw the bomb
disappeared, and, though his identity became known,
was never apprehended), several persons only construc-
tively guilty and others quite innocent were convicted
and hanged, to the lasting shame of the commonwealth
of Illinois. With this exception, anarchists have engaged in no form of revolutionary violence in the United
States. There is, of course, less justification for violent
measures here, since the people have and always have had
and always may have precisely what government and
laws they desire. If our laws are unjust and our govern-

ments corrupt, as we are frequently assured is the case, and as most of us partly or wholly believe, it is because we do not care enough to have them otherwise to take a little trouble to mend them. Whenever we shall really desire a change, we shall have one speedily.

Anarchy has made little impression on the educated classes of any country but Russia, and the reason is that the theory is too exclusively negative and destructive. On the constructive side it is hopelessly visionary and impractical. Its collectivism is the only element that it has in common with Socialism, and the contact of the two systems even at that point is more apparent than real, as Prince Kropotkin makes plain. Socialism to-day does not demand, like Anarchy, the violent overthrow of existing institutions, but looks for a new and better organized society through a gradual and orderly development. While the economic basis of the two systems is not radically different, the ethical and practical aims of the two are as wide apart as the poles. Anarchy aims at a liberty as absolute and complete as is compatible with the continued existence of men in communities; Socialism aims at the fullest development of organized society, and a collectivism in the production and distribution of wealth that means less liberty of personal action in some directions than most men now possess. Anarchy is the apotheosis of individualism, the negation of organization and law; Socialism means the perfection of systematic cooperation, organization developed to its highest point of efficiency.

Anarchy has certain features that help us understand the hold it has obtained on educated and aspiring minds, combined with a certain temperamental type. A lofty altruism is at the basis of its philosophy, economics, and ethics. Whatever professes to be for the good of man, or his physical and moral uplift, is so far in harmony with all that Christians profess. The fundamental ideas of Anarchy: justice, liberty, equality, are ideals that the Christian also professes to love and to seek. Such ideas were prominent in the legislation of Moses and in the teaching of Jesus. Anarchy also builds, as on a cornerstone, on faith in the perfectibility of man. So do Christians — given time and the grace of God. The weakness of Anarchy is that it rejects both time and grace as unnecessary elements — the Revolution would instantly bring to the front and necessarily develop the best in man, while the worst, being the product of oppression, poverty, and ignorance, would at once begin to dwindle and would speedily disappear. An iridescent dream, contradicted by all human experience up to this very hour !

By its hostility to Christianity, Anarchy has rejected the only ally that promises the least encouragement to the practical working of its social theories. For, if the time ever comes when men can live here on earth in a society in which law shall be unknown and force unnecessary, it will be because the principles of Jesus Christ have become so implanted in human hearts that all men love their neighbors as themselves. Where that law prevails, it is true that no other law will be needed, and there will no longer be a social problem, because no man will look on his own things, but every man also on the things of others.

VI

SOCIALISM IN ENGLAND

BIBLIOGRAPHY

Socialistic literature: —

GODWIN, An Inquiry concerning Political Justice and its Influence on General Virtue and Happiness. London, 1793.

OWEN, A New View of Society. London, 1813.

JONES, Life, Times, and Labors of Robert Owen, "Social Science Series," 1890.

MORRIS, News from Nowhere. London, 1891.

BLATCHFORD, Merrie England. London, 1895.

——, God and My Neighbor. Chicago, 1910.

Fabian Essays. London, 1890.

Fabian Tracts, 1–136. London, 1907.

HYNDMAN, Economics of Socialism. London, 1909.

WELLS, New Worlds for Old. New York, 1908.

VILLIERS, The Socialist Movement in England. London, 1908.

Books of general information: —

BOOTH, Life and Labor in London, Part III : Religious Influences, Vols. I–VII. London, 1902.

SHAW, Municipal Government in Great Britain. New York, 1894.

Bitterly hostile: —

TOWLER, Socialism and Local Government, Handbook of the London Municipal Society. New York, 1909.

VI

SOCIALISM IN ENGLAND

ONLY within the last two decades has Socialism made any considerable progress in England. Compared with Germany, France, Italy, or even Spain, the tight little island is unfruitful soil. The British character is unfavorable to Socialism, since it is above all things devoted to the "practical," and has as little tolerance for an "ideologist" as the great Napoleon. The Englishman prides himself on being the very antipodes of a Frenchman; he does not insist on reforming an abuse because it is irrational, but because it is inconvenient. A Frenchman, on the contrary, is more annoyed by the irrationality of an abuse than by its inconvenience. Owing to this peculiar mental constitution, no people are so inaccessible to ideas as the English. They demand concrete propositions; they must be shown definite advantages to be gained; abstract principles and general truths merely irritate them.

The comprehensive revolutionary ideals of Socialism, therefore, are thus far understood only by a few of the educated middle class. Among the working-class, where Socialism might be expected to flourish, it is only just beginning to get a foothold. The British artisan is quite as conservative and insular, in his way, as the aristocracy. Talk to him of an eight-hour day, and he understands you; begin to speak of the rights of labor, and he stares at you and turns away.   Sydney Smith said that a surgical operation was necessary to get a joke into the head of a Scotchman; nothing less will suffice to get a general political or social principle into an Englishman's head. He has been slow even to give a fair hearing to the advocates of Socialism, and only the hard pounding of events has wrought in him a partial conviction.

I

The earlier English Socialism was the product of the industrial condition of the country.   England had special advantages for taking the lead in the great modern development of Capitalism.   She had control of the sea, and was able to extend and protect her commerce as no other nation could.   Her insular position was favorable to commerce, and assured her special protection in time of war; so that less of her revenues had to be expended on a standing army.   She had been ever foremost in colonization, and had markets all over the world ready to absorb her products.   She was rich in mineral wealth, and fortunate above every other nation in having coal and iron side by side, thus lessening the cost of production by economizing transportation.   She had a suitable climate, liable to the extremes of neither hot nor cold.   In short, nature and her own previous history had combined to shower upon England all possible advantages for outstripping her competitors, when the advent of machinery created a new era in the world's industrial history.

In no other country was the laboring class more stolid and stupid, less alive to its own interests, less capable of any common action to promote the common welfare. It had no voice in the government of England.   The up-

per classes had made the law, and combinations of workers were all but impossible.   Even combinations of capitalists had been illegal under the common law, a corporation being presumed to be in restraint of trade, and
so unlawful, unless it could obtain a royal charter and
so acquire a legal standing.   Public opinion at first looked
on corporations much as the Trust is regarded to-day,
when the belief widely prevails that the only good Trust
is a smashed Trust.   But the capitalists, being intelligent, set about changing both public opinion and law,
and in time succeeded.   Combinations of those having
property became possible, but combinations of those
who had no property were made still less possible.   For
the capitalists, not content with the legalizing of their
corporations, obtained the passage of the Combination
Act (1799) which made all trades-unions illegal.   Under
that oppressive statute, any persons who combined to
advance wages, or affect those who carried on manufacture or trade, in the conduct and management thereof,
might be convicted before a single justice of the peace
and imprisoned in the common jail not exceeding three
months, or be kept to hard labor in the house of correc-
tion not exceeding two months.   Surely, the tender mer-
cies of the capitalist are cruel.[1]

The better to keep the working-class quiet under such

[1] Though the Combinations of Workmen Act of 1824 repealed thirty-
four antiquated and inhuman statutes, some as early as Edward I (1304),
prescribing such penalties as imprisonment, the pillory and mutilation
for the awful crime of "conspiring" not to work but at a certain rate or
price, or to work only at certain hours, and England thus took her stand
among civilized nations, an act passed the following year declared in its
preamble that all combinations of workmen "are injurious to trade and
commerce, dangerous to the tranquillity of the country and especially
prejudicial to the interest of all who are concerned in them."

oppression, and as an anodyne for the more tender consciences among the upper classes, a system of political economy was expounded which assured the laborer that he was doing very wrong to kick against the pricks, and discouraged every attempt to alleviate his lot. Adam Smith and his successors argued that the condition of the workers was the result of the "laws" governing the production and distribution of wealth. These "laws" were asserted to be as immutable as gravitation, since they were the unvarying result of universal principles of human nature. Pupils of the greater teachers gravely expounded these "laws" to the worker, and solemnly told him that he was crying for the moon.

The two primary " laws" of this new science were: that self-interest is the sole actuating motive of all men in business transactions, and to buy in the cheapest market and sell in the dearest is, if not the whole duty of man, at least his whole aim; and second, that prices of all commodities are fixed by supply and demand, under free competition, and to interfere with free competition is dangerous — indeed, considered in its social consequences, nothing less than immoral. It was a long time before men discovered that these "laws" were the result of hasty generalization from imperfect data; that they were the laws of an imaginary world, not of this real world in which we live; that men are not moved by self-interest alone; that there never was free competition, in any society of any age; that the law of supply and demand never fully operated — in short, that the political economy of Smith and his school is nothing more than a pseudo-science, and its "laws" mostly bugaboos to frighten people in their intellectual childhood.

Among the most effective of these bugaboos was the Wages Fund; namely, the theory that there is at any given time only a certain sum existing that can be divided among the wage-earning class. This sum being fixed, the wage of each person depends on the divisor, that is, the number of laborers. It is in vain, therefore, for laborers to combine and strike for higher wages — higher wages can no more be paid than a pie can be divided into ten quarters.[1] The Wages Fund was long regarded by economists as almost on a level with the axioms of mathematics, and to question it was to cast suspicion on one's entire sanity. It was finally proved to be nothing more than a bugaboo, by the fact that, though the trades-unions were assured they could not possibly increase their wages by combinations and strikes, they did raise wages steadily by just these methods. And then the economists reluctantly gave up their Wages Fund.

While this bugaboo was still scaring nervous people, another frightful "law" was discovered, to teach the working-man to keep his place and work for his betters for whatever they chose to give him. This was the "law of population," discovered by an English clergyman named Malthus. His great discovery was that population tends to increase in a geometrical ratio, while food cannot possibly increase faster than in an arithmetical ratio. As a result, there is a constant pressure on the means of subsistence, which necessarily means distress for some. The only cure for poverty is the voluntary

[1] The suppressed premise of the Wages Fund argument was that the whole pie was actually divided — that the entire Wages Fund was paid out in wages — a thing that nobody attempted to prove, or even to state in clear terms, lest sensible people laugh at the very idea. The workers well knew that employers kept a large slice of the pie for themselves.

limiting of population, by later marriage, and cultivating a greater sense of social responsibility, which will prevent people from bringing into the world more children than they can provide for. But for the present there is no cure for poverty; it is the necessary result of reckless over-population.

Malthus was peculiarly bitter in his opposition to Socialism, and all theories of the rights of man. Man has no rights: "A man who is born into a world already possessed, if he cannot get subsistence from his parents on whom he has a just demand, and if the society do not want his labor, has no claim of right to the smallest portion of food, and, in fact, has no business to be where he is. At Nature's mighty feast there is no vacant cover for him. She tells him to be gone, and will quickly execute her own orders." [1] That is to say, he will starve, and serve him right, for being born into a world where there was no room for him.

This doctrine of Malthus is not only heartless, but irrational. Why has a child a just claim on his parents for subsistence? Because they brought him into the world; being the cause of his existence, they are bound to see that he has means to exist. But the same thing is true of society at large, not of the immediate parents only. Society was a party to their act, and cannot shirk its responsibility for the existence of the child. By encouraging men and women to marry and give life to children, society underwrites the marriage contract and assumes responsibility for children not cared for by parents. And it may well be disputed whether Malthus has cor-

---

[1] "On Population," p. 513, ed. of 1803. This heartless passage was expunged from later editions of the writings of Malthus.

rectly interpreted the voice of Nature, for he has affronted well-nigh universal instincts by the words he puts in her mouth. To the vast majority of men it rather seems that Nature says to every child born into the world: "Come to the table and take your share. It is spread for you, as much as for those who arrived before you." Not Malthus, the Christian priest, but Blatchford, the atheistic journalist, has spoken the word of truth about Nature's feast: "We say that there ought not to be any poor, and there need not be any poor, and that there would not be any poor, if our Christians were not infidels and our wealthy classes were not hogs." Bitter words, but who shall say they are not deserved?

Malthus supplemented his "law of population" with another precious "discovery," which he derived from his study of agriculture and named the "law of diminishing returns." According to this law, supplies of food can be obtained from the earth only by an increased outlay from year to year of labor and capital. The same amount of labor and capital expended year after year brings continually lessening returns. The expenditure of double the labor and capital will bring greater returns, but never double returns. Hence the increase in the production of food can never be more than an arithmetical ratio. But later economists have been compelled to recognize that this "law" is "suspended" whenever improvement in methods of culture occurs — in other words, it is no law, but only a partial induction from facts; if true at all, true only for limited times and places. It is merely a pretentious statement in "scientific" form of the fact known to everybody who has ever tilled the soil, that land tends gradually to lose its fertility, unless something is done to prevent this result. But it has also become known to cultivators that if soil is properly treated, its fertility becomes greater, instead of less.

The supposed law fails utterly to take into account the enormous rate of possible increase in the production of food by means of machinery and intensive farming. Since Malthus wrote his book, there has been such a revolution in food production as makes his prognostications of an approaching starvation of the human race as little practical as the speculations of astronomers regarding the eventual extinction of the sun. It may be that, æons hence, the sun will cease to give forth enough heat to sustain life on this planet, but such a calamity is not worth taking into account in any present computations or forecasts. That population will at some time reach the extreme limit of the capacity of the earth to produce food is arguable as an abstract proposition, but the event is too many thousands of years distant to engage the attention of any but idle people who have nothing better to occupy their minds than debating such academic questions. It is a notorious fact that wealth of all kinds, including food, has for half a century been increasing at a rate so prodigiously greater than population as to make the Malthusian theory a joke. The problem to-day, and for many a day to come, may be stated thus : not how to limit population to the means of subsistence, but how to secure a fair distribution among the population of the vast quantity of wealth produced. It was because the people of England at last got a dim inkling of the terms of this problem, and began to perceive more clearly and to feel more keenly the inequality of the present distribution, in spite of all that was preached to them in the name of political economy and in the name of Christ, that Socialism had its first beginning among them.

II

The leader in the socialistic movement was Robert Owen (1771–1858), a native of Wales, where he received the little education that he ever received in schools. The rest of his training came from life, and from books that he read in his leisure hours; and, having a mind both acute and receptive, he obtained thus a more adequate education than he could have been given at any university of his time. At nine years of age poverty compelled him to go to work. His qualities of body and mind may be inferred from the fact that, with such beginnings, he was, at the age of nineteen, the manager of a cotton mill, in which five hundred workers were employed. We are not surprised to read of him that he formed the habit of early rising, was an incessant reader as well as a diligent worker, and that his habits were faultless, — all his life he was a total abstainer from alcohol and tobacco. Such a boy was bound to rise. Even before his becoming a manager of the factory, he had borrowed a little money and established a small business of his own, in which he made a profit of £300 the first year. He thoroughly mastered the business of cotton spinning, and made his concern a model mill. As long as he remained in business, his enterprises were successful. It is important to remember that the first English socialist was not a mere man of books, an impractical dreamer of dreams, but a successful manufacturer.

These early years of Owen's experience in the cotton mill were probably the time when the laboring class of

England was at its lowest point of wretchedness. The Combination acts were in full force, and employees were completely at the mercy of the employer. The capitalist was taught by economists that labor was a commodity, like any other, and that it was his first duty to recognize and obey the great law of supply and demand. He was concerned only to get his labor at the lowest possible price and to sell his product at the highest possible price. And he was assured by the economists that to do the best for himself was in the end to do the best for others. For the welfare of his laborers he was in no way responsible. To hold that he was his brother's keeper, was to defy the sacred "laws" of political economy.

The profit of the manufacturer was enormous, incredible. Owen's biographer tells us that he was able to buy a pound of raw cotton for five shillings, and when he had made it into yarn to sell it for £9 18s. 6d. Such possible gains stimulated the greed of mill owners until their conduct passed the bounds of all belief, if the facts were not so well accredited. Employers found that child labor was most profitable of all, because it cost almost nothing. They obtained large numbers of children from the workhouses to be "apprentices." These apprentices were housed and bedded in sheds, fed upon the cheapest food and not enough of that, clothed mainly in rags, and worked in shifts night and day, so that the beds in which they slept were never cold. The sufferings of these workers were terrible, but not until disease bred under such conditions attacked the well-to-do was their attention aroused. There is no more appalling episode in the history of the English people than this condition of the factory workers a hundred years ago. Statesmen taught employers that any interference by law with such conduct of their business was curtailment of liberty; economists taught them that shortening the hours of labor necessarily meant lower wages for the workers; while their own selfishness assured them that more humane treatment of their work-people meant a lessening of their profits. What wonder the abuses continued?

Robert Owen was by nature a quiet, tolerant, patient man, the reverse in temperament of the ordinary social agitator, but he could not look on these evils and do nothing for their abatement. He set himself the life-long task of doing what he could to improve the condition of England's laboring classes. He had but to persevere as he had begun to make an immense fortune, and accomplish the ambition of most Englishmen, the "founding of a family"; that is, establishing his descendants as landowners, and possibly as nobles, thenceforth for generations to be supported in idleness and luxury by these hopeless toilers. This he could not do. On the contrary, he began to provide decent homes for the people in his mill, and to encourage them to form habits of cleanliness and thrift.

In 1800, Owen became manager of mills at New Lanark, near Glasgow, which he had persuaded some English capitalists to purchase, with a view of giving his methods a better trial. He looked upon the enterprise as a great commercial and social experiment, not a mere business, but it was necessary first of all that it should be so managed as to return a reasonable profit on the capital involved. This, from first to last, Owen succeeded in doing. He found at New Lanark a population of about two thousand, considerably below the average in moral character, as a prejudice against factory employment at that time prevailing in Scotland naturally caused the workers to be recruited from the lowest grade of the people. They were suspicious of the new manager, and slow to be convinced that he really sought their good, but in time his efforts overcame their prejudices and gained for him their devoted affection. His first task was to provide decent houses for them, and the next to establish schools in which their children might be trained. He was firmly convinced that by thus altering the conditions and surroundings of the people, teaching them cleanliness and self-respect and raising the standard of intelligence among them, a corresponding change would be effected in their character. And though all who heard of his plans regarded his scheme as visionary and impractical, he was given a free hand; and, by the testimony of all who knew the facts, he did effect a great change in the character of the people of New Lanark.

In his attempt to make his mills model concerns, Owen was forced to rebuild or rearrange them; to improve the sanitary condition of the buildings and surroundings; to secure ample light and air. No more pauper children were received; hours of labor were shortened. Finding that the local shops sold goods of poor quality, at the highest market price, the company established shops under Owen's direction, that furnished the best goods at a saving of twenty-five per cent to the workmen. But, though a good profit was returned from the business, the investors became dissatisfied at the spending of so much money in improvements, instead of distributing it as additional dividends, and twice Owen was compelled to reorganize his company and obtain the support of other capitalists. He was finally compelled to resign his position and abandon his experiment, because of the meddlesomeness of a Quaker partner in the enterprise, who was not satisfied with the quality and amount of the religious instruction given to the people.

There is no question that Owen himself was not an orthodox Christian; to-day he would probably be called a liberal Unitarian. But he did not try to propagate his views of religion among his work-people; on the contrary, he had established at New Lanark a complete system of religious liberty. Regarding persecution as a worse error than false doctrine, he held that the first duty of all men in matters of religion is a broad tolerance. It was his personal belief that men's religious ideas are the effect of the accident of birth and the resulting training — education imparts these ideas, and therefore men are not responsible for holding them. He frankly avowed to an inquirer: "I am not of your religion, nor of any religion yet taught in the world. To me they all appear united with much — yes, with very much — error." But, holding such sentiments, he yet insisted on the full right of each man to the enjoyment of the utmost liberty of conscience. And therefore he could not be persuaded to have any system of faith inculcated at New Lanark as a sort of established religion. Instead of that, he was ready to co-operate in maintaining whatever forms of worship the people themselves desired. Official investigation of the conditions there showed that he was "not known to have in any one instance endeavored to alter the religious opinions of persons in his employment; that the desires of his workmen to attend their respective places of worship are complied with and aided to the utmost extent; that

a minister has long been paid by the proprietors . . .
for performing divine service in the Gaelic tongue to the
Highland workmen; that Mr. Owen's house is a house of
daily prayer."

Owen was now fifty-seven years of age; he had gained
a modest competence, and resolved to devote himself
thenceforth to philanthropic effort. During his work at
New Lanark he had begun to write on social topics, and in
his "New Views of Society," or "Essays on the Formation of Character" (1812) and his "Book of the New
Moral World" (1826–1844), he set forth the ideas that
underlay his social experiments. It is clear that the
fundamental principle of his Socialism was a philosophic
and practical determinism. He had also been profoundly
influenced by the reading of Rousseau and other writers
of the French Deistic school, not so much by their ideas
of religion as by their theories of human nature. Environment and heredity, he believed, determine character, and of these the greatest is environment. Place men
under proper influences from infancy, so that the right
physical, moral, and social training may be given them,
and right character will result.[1] His remedy for all the
ills of society was education; but by education he meant
not merely impartation of knowledge, but the whole
process of forming character. Education in this sense he
believed to be omnipotent. His success in elevating the

[1] We might suppose that Owen had gone farther back than to Rousseau, if we had any reason to think that he was familiar with Plato. "Our
youth will dwell in a land of health, amid fair sights and sounds, and receive good in everything; and beauty, the effluence of fair works, shall
flow into the eye and ear like a health-giving breeze from a purer region,
and insensibly draw the soul from earliest years into likeness and sympathy with the beauty of reason." — "Republic," Book III.

character of the New Lanark population naturally confirmed him in these views; his theory had seemed to work well in practice.

Out of this fundamental notion grew all the practical schemes of Owen. As early as 1817, he undertook to interest the influential classes of England in making trial of his ideas, in a report submitted to the House of Commons on the Poor Law. He proposed the establishment, at State expense and under State supervision, of communities of about twelve hundred persons on from one thousand to fifteen hundred acres of land each. The people were to live in one large building, each family having private apartments, but a public kitchen, dining rooms, etc. Children were to be cared for by their parents until three years old, after that to be educated by the community in a common school. Work was to be provided for all, and all were to share equally in its fruits. Each community would be mainly agricultural, but was to own machinery and offer to its members every variety of employment, so that it would be a self-dependent unit. It is not known how far Owen had read the French socialists, but there is more than a flavor of Fourierism in this.

It seemed at first that there might be at least a chance of making an experiment along the lines thus suggested. Considerable interest was roused and fair progress was making, when rumors of Owen's lack of religious orthodoxy began to be circulated. When questioned, he frankly avowed his beliefs. Prejudice was thus excited against him, and he did not lack actual detractors among the clergy. The Bishop of Exeter went so far as to charge him with "squandering his wealth in profligacy and luxury," — a charge as absurd as it was slanderous. Those who were looking for a decent pretext to turn the cold shoulder to his enterprise, or even to offer active opposition to it, found one here; while many timid people who might have been his supporters were effectually alienated. The whole scheme proved abortive.

Owen was more successful in his attempt to secure legislation that would protect the workers against the greed of their employers. An epidemic at Manchester, in 1802, first called the attention of the English people to factory conditions, and a statute was passed regulating the conditions of employment in factories. The reforms thus made were chiefly sanitary, and the hours of work were permitted to remain at what was then customary, twelve hours a day for each worker. In 1819 a Factory Act was passed by Parliament, but it was so emasculated through the influence of the wealthy manufacturers as to give little relief. Owen had sought to make the age limit for employment in factories ten years, and the time limit ten and a half hours a day; Parliament cut the age limit to nine years, and left the day's work at twelve hours. The chief gain was that the statute applied to all factories, whereas previous laws had been of partial application. It was not until 1847 that the day's work was lowered to ten hours, and then only for women and children. In the name of "free contract," the legislators refused to limit the sacred right of men to be overworked as much as employers could compel.[1]

[1] How little is to be expected from the humanity of the capitalistic class is shown by the fact that eminent "reformers" like John Bright and Richard Cobden opposed the English statutes against child labor. It took fifty years of agitation to humanize English factories, but now they are far in advance of the United States in such particulars.

Failing to induce the English government to undertake socialistic experiments, Owen undertook them for himself. A socialistic colony, conducted on his principles, was attempted at Abram Combe, near Glasgow, but the experiment from which most was hoped was made at New Harmony, Indiana. The history of this belongs, however, to a later chapter. A bank on the principle of a universal labor exchange was another of Owen's enterprises. All of these attempts failed after a brief trial, as his critics predicted would be the case, but not for the reasons on which the predictions were based. The causes of the failure were elements that might have been and should have been excluded from the problem.

In spite of his business experience, Owen was not the man to conduct such enterprises to success. His experience had been that of a manufacturer; he knew little of trade or agriculture, less of banking and general business. He should have associated with himself one or more men of experience in those affairs of which he knew little. He was not skilled in judging men; he was too sanguine, too quixotic, too visionary. His philosophy of determinism had bred in him a faith in the essential goodness of human nature that would not permit him to see facts patent to every ordinary observer. No groups of perfectly rational and unselfish men can be created by magic out of vagrant adventurers and cranky enthusiasts, nor even out of the average stolid British worker. Every project of Owen's proved a magnet to draw to it precisely the men that would insure its failure: the over-sanguine, quick to be discouraged when their roseate fancies were not immediately realized; the odd and cranky, who will not fit into any scheme, and are everywhere a source of

o

discord; the self-willed and ambitious, who cannot be controlled and are incompetent to lead; the waifs and strays, men whose only title to success in a new venture was that they had failed in everything they had yet undertaken.

Owen's postulate that man is good by nature, and only made bad by bad surroundings; that if these were removed, man's primitive goodness will assert itself, — was not in the long run borne out by the facts. New surroundings proved in numerous cases to be nothing more than a fertile soil in which primitive badness made a flourishing growth. His other postulate, that it is only necessary to make clear to men the beauty and benefits of the socialistic order to secure its immediate adoption, also failed to justify itself in working. Like many other reformers, Owen did not take into the account that men might not care for a new order. He did not see that an existing society exists because it is still satisfactory to the class who have the power to maintain it. It is not ignorance of the good that preserves unjust institutions, so much as self-interest. The ruling class finds its profit in abuses, and reforms can be wrung from it only by force, actual or potential.

Owen also failed to see that social ideals are merely Utopian, unless they arise out of actual economic conditions and contemplate demonstrable economic possibilities — otherwise they lack reality and can never emerge from the realm of the ideal. His colonies sought industrial freedom amid competitive conditions, therefore not failure but success would have been the surprising thing. Moreover, his enterprises were attempted with inadequate capital, — or, rather, they were attempted on

a scale too large for the available capital. Coöperative
enterprises that have succeeded have begun in a small
way, proportioned to the means of their founders, and
have enlarged by degrees. That the projects of Owen
were not inherently absurd and impossible is shown by
later successes on the same principles; his experiments
were wrecked on obstacles that better directed enterprises avoided. He discovered that it is not enough to
devise social machinery; social man is needed to work it;
and social man cannot be made out of hand, — he must
be slowly developed.

Owen's significance in the history of Socialism is mainly
as a propagator of ideas. Even in this, his service was
often of doubtful value, for his frankness and benevolence
won for many of his ideas a respect that their intrinsic
quality did not deserve. On the other hand, some of his
later vagaries cast a reproach equally undeserved on his
socialistic theories. When he was past eighty he fell under
the influence of certain persons, it matters not whether
dupes or impostors, who made of him an ardent believer in
spiritualism. His lax views on marriage also did not com-
mend his Socialism to Britons of any class. It is hardly
possible to regard his career as other than a failure, in
spite of his excellent intentions, his considerable abilities,
and the correctness of some of his social theories.

III

The Reform bill of 1832 was thought by Macaulay and
the Liberal statesmen of his generation to be the proper
sequel to the Revolution of 1688; on the ground that,
while the Revolution had brought the Crown into harmony with Parliament, the bill had been necessary to

bring Parliament into harmony with the nation. But this harmony soon proved illusory. The Reform bill did away with some of the most anomalous features of the English political system. "Three niches in a stone wall" no longer sent two representatives to the House of Commons, but as a £10 qualification was still required of voters in boroughs, and for the county franchise a man must be a leaseholder or copyholder, it is obvious that only the middle class was benefited. The shopkeeper and the manufacturer had now their political rights, but the artisan and the laborer were no better off than before. What gave additional edge to their disappointment and exasperation was that the middle class had used the discontent of the working people as a means of exacting the concessions obtained, only to cease all effort as soon as their own grievance was redressed. Poor harvests and commercial depression combined to make the lot of the workers more grievous; and the operation of the new Poor Law of 1835 was deeply resented, especially in the rural districts. Instead of a cessation of the social unrest and political agitation on the passage of the Reform bill, as had been confidently predicted by its advocates, there seemed to be even greater dissatisfaction after "reform" than before, and a prospect that the agitation would be interminable.

The reign of Queen Victoria opened among such unpromising conditions, and a few weeks before her coronation a great radical meeting was held at Birmingham, at which a petition was adopted for presentation to Parliament, that afterwards became known as the Charter, while the party that advocated it were called Chartists. These demands, the people's charter of liberties, as they were then deemed, do not seem in the least radical now. Briefly summarized, the things demanded were six: (1) Universal suffrage (by which was really meant manhood suffrage); (2) equal electoral districts; (3) vote by ballot; (4) annual Parliaments; (5) no qualification for a seat in Parliament but choice by electors; (6) payment of members of Parliament. All of these were certainly fair matters of debate, reforms that might reasonably be asked and advocated by peaceful means, as is attested by the fact that all but the second and sixth of these demands have been conceded, or substantially so, and the sixth has been promised by a Liberal ministry. Yet in the thirties a storm of objection and protest and criticism was poured out on the advocates of these reforms, as if they were threatening to lay the British constitution in ruins and undermine the very foundations of society.

But if the opposition to Chartism was unreasonable, it must be confessed that its advocacy was equally without reason. More was hoped and expected from these political changes than they were in any way fitted to bestow. Now that they have been mainly granted, the condition of the poor of England is little improved, and whatever improvement there may be is certainly to be ascribed to some other source. But the most extravagant claims were put forth: "The Charter means a good home, good food, prosperity, and shorter working hours." How it could have been rationally expected to give all, or any, of these things passes comprehension. Misled by these social expectations, more than attracted by the political features of the movement, the workingmen took part almost as one man in the agitation for the proposed reforms. Immense meetings were held to advocate the Charter, at some of which a hundred thousand people are said to have been present. In 1839 the House of Commons refused even to receive a petition in favor of the Charter, and this denial of a fundamental right produced many riots in different parts of the kingdom. There was a serious prospect at one time of a general uprising of the working-class, in which event much bloodshed and suffering could not have been averted. The government acted with great firmness and energy, rather than with wisdom. The meetings of Chartists were forbidden; those held were broken up; leaders of riotous demonstrations were prosecuted, convicted, and by hundreds either imprisoned or transported. The agitation rapidly declined, leaving the working-classes greatly embittered against those who had shown that they still possessed the power of the State, and meant to use it whenever necessary to maintain their supremacy.

One of those who had a deep sympathy with the wrongs of the working-men, and wished to see them righted, was Thomas Carlyle. If his knowledge of social forces had been equal to his hatred of all injustice and oppression, he might have spoken a prophet's word to his England. The best word that he could speak was his "Past and Present," an eloquent and stimulating book in many ways, but utterly inapplicable to the social conditions, and, considered as a proposed solution of England's troubles, supremely ridiculous. For the remedy that Carlyle, in good faith, proposed for the ills under which nineteenth-century England was groaning was — a return to the England of Henry II ! He might as reasonably have proposed a return to the stone age.

Another solution offered was less irrational, but hardly more practical. It was known as Christian Socialism, and its origin is generally ascribed to Frederick Denison Maurice, though Charles Kingsley did more than any other to popularize its principles. Maurice established the *Christian Socialist* in 1848, as the organ of the movement, which, according to its founder, opposed equally "the unsocial Christians and the unchristian socialists." The Christian socialists avowed no definite social scheme, but were deeply impressed by the brutality of the doctrines taught by the English economists. Kingsley had no words adequately to express his scorn of the "narrow, conceited, hypocritical, anarchic, and atheistic scheme of the universe" that lay, as he thought, at the base of the accepted political economy of his day. "We believed," wrote Maurice afterwards, in explanation of the motives of the group, "that Christianity has the power of regenerating whatever it comes in contact with, of making that morally healthful and vigorous which apart from it must be either mischievous or inefficient. We found, from what we know of the working-men of England, that the conviction was spreading more and more widely among them, that Law and Christianity were merely the supports and agents of capital. We wished to show them both by words and deeds that Law and Christianity are the only protectors of all classes from the selfishness which is the destruction of all." [1]

Christian Socialism, therefore, as its chief advocates understood it, was the belief that the Church is intended to be an organization for the promotion of social right-

[1] "Life of Frederick Denison Maurice," 2 vols. New York, 1884, II: 92.

eousness; and that when this fact is duly recognized, the
production and distribution of wealth in Christian countries will proceed on wholly different lines from those at
present obtaining. A series of tracts was published, in
which the principles of the movement were set forth, and
a league was formed to promote coöperative societies. In
this latter direction, it does not appear that the leaders
ever succeeded in accomplishing results worth while.
As they were not men of business training, but men of
books, and did not attract to themselves as co-laborers
any notable laymen, their lack of practical success is not
wonderful and should not be charged against them.
They did the one thing for which they were fitted: a
work of education, the propagation of ideas. Their
chief desire seems to have been the socialization of industry; they do not seem to have thought necessary the
socialization of land. In short, they had learned their
Socialism, not from economists, but from Jesus. Their
text-book was not *Das Kapital*, but the New Testament.

The most effective literary expression was given to these
ideas in the writings of Charles Kingsley, especially in
"Alton Locke" (1850) and "Yeast" (1851). He advocated the duty of the Church to improve the condition
of the working-classes, as one of its chief functions; the
Church should aid the people in bettering their material
position, as well as teach them religion. That the people
were capable of elevation, which many then denied, he
strenuously maintained. "I believe," he said in his
preface to "Alton Locke," "that a man might be, as a
tailor or a costermonger, every inch of him a saint and a
scholar and a gentleman, for I have seen some such already." He scouted the postulates of political economy:

"It is my belief that not self-interest but self-sacrifice is the only law upon which human society can be grounded with any hope of prosperity or permanence." He was a strong advocate of coöperative association, and differed from those socialists who looked to the State for regeneration of the social order. Maurice thought that the State was "by nature and law conservative of individual rights and individual possessions," while the Church is communistic in principle. In the union of Church and State he therefore saw the fusion of the principles of communism and property. Kingsley had more sympathy with the political agitation then prevalent than Maurice; he was so far a Chartist that he approved all the demands of the Charter. But Kingsley was clear that legislative reform was not social reform, and that neither the hearts nor the social institutions of men are to be reconstructed by act of Parliament. If the Chartists ascribed too much importance to political reform, the Christian socialists as clearly underestimated its value. The Chartists were justified in making their appeal for manhood suffrage and the ballot, without which as its weapons democracy can make no progress save by a bloody revolution.

Both Chartism and Christian Socialism disappeared [1] for more than a generation, and for substantially the same reason in both cases: they appealed to a people unorganized, and at that time incapable of being effectively organized. But Christian Socialism, before its disappearance, accomplished one thing of no small im-

[1] An existing Christian Socialist League, composed of clergy and laymen of the Church of England, may be reckoned a belated survival of the earlier movement, though it seems to be really independent in origin. This League is distinctly a High Church affair, while the original Christian socialists were of the Broad Church Party.

portance : it destroyed in England that hostility between advanced political and social ideas and established religion, which has prevailed on the Continent between Socialism and Christianity, to the mutual injury of both. Maurice and Kingsley introduced socialistic ideas among a wide circle of Christians, both clergy and laity, who but for them would never have listened to the new theories.

IV

The Manchester school of economists concerned themselves almost wholly with the production of wealth; it seemed to them that distribution would take place, in an almost automatic manner, under the system of competition, and that the final result would be substantially just. Whatever incidental injustice might occur would be more likely to be aggravated than redressed by any governmental interference. And they were right in part. Experience showed that distribution was automatically effected — in the same way that an automatic distribution of swill is made in a hog-pen : the strongest hogs get what they want first, and the others get what may happen to be left. And that system of distribution of wealth might be satisfactory in a social order, if men were no higher in the scale of being than hogs, if they had no instincts that demand protection of the weak against the strong and equal justice for all.

But since men have such instincts, they are not satisfied with the methods of the hog-pen; they have come to see that the chief economic questions are questions of distribution — that to get wealth is less important than how to spend it. And to the solution of this problem the

Manchester school could offer nothing better than the reiteration of their great maxim, *laissez faire* — let men continue to live as if they were hogs. But men were becoming impatient of this formula; they were clearly perceiving the truth that Matthew Arnold uttered a little later: "Our inequality materializes our upper class, vulgarizes our middle class, brutalizes our lower class." They were revolted by a civilization that could show as its type and symptom a London, with its Mayfair at one end and its Whitechapel at the other.

In the sixties a voice was lifted against the hog-pen theory; a single voice, but one to which multitudes had become accustomed to listen: the voice of John Ruskin. It was not as an authority on social topics, however, that Englishmen had become wonted to listen to Ruskin; he was a writer and lecturer on art, of the first authority, but was supposed to understand little else. The time may come again when, if men continue to read Ruskin at all, they will read him chiefly as the expounder of art. But to his own generation, and to several generations following, his greatest service was and will be that of prophet and preacher. He had discovered in his study of art, that pictures and statues and music and other beautiful things, could not be understood apart from the social conditions out of which they sprang — that the production and distribution of works of art bore an intimate relation to the production and consumption of commodities in general. Not only the production, but the appreciation, of art, he discovered, is profoundly affected by social conditions. The quality of a people's life is reflected in its art; hence a noble art can proceed only from a people that are living a free, rich, and noble life.

Ruskin was thus led to study economic phenomena, the production and distribution of wealth, as social forces. He was chiefly interested in the bearing of these forces on human life and character. It was borne in upon him that the making of human souls is the most important manufacture in which a nation's energies can be engaged, and he was not greatly pleased as he contemplated the quality of souls that the England of his day was making. He hoped to rouse her to her failure and lead her to change her ways. "In some far-away and yet undreamt-of hour," he said, "I can even imagine that England may cast all thoughts of possessive wealth back to the barbaric nations among whom they first arose; and that, while the sands of the Indus and the adamant of Golconda may yet stiffen the housings of the charger, and flash from the turban of the slave, she, as a Christian mother, may at last attain to the virtue of a Heathen one and be able to lead forth her Sons, saying, 'These are My Jewels.'"

Ruskin was flouted and scorned by nearly his entire generation for maintaining that England's output of men was of greater importance than her output of iron and cotton. The four Essays that were printed in a small volume, with the title "Unto this Last," were first published in the *Cornhill Magazine*, of which Thackeray was then the editor. They provoked such a growing storm of criticism and protest that Thackeray quailed, and, though a personal friend of the author, notified Ruskin that he could print no more. If there was anything on which educated Englishmen were then agreed, it was that Ruskin knew nothing of political economy, that these writings were unworthy of his fame and unworthy of serious attention. Yet "Unto this Last" was one of the most valuable contributions ever made to the fundamental principles of economic and social science, and has done more to mould the opinions and character of readers by the thousand than any other book of its century.

The old economy of the Manchester school had taken as the foundation of its science human nature at its worst. Ruskin persisted in taking as the foundation of economics and sociology man at his best. Manchester stoutly maintained that man may always be trusted to be a selfish beast; Ruskin, denying neither the beast nor the selfishness, insisted that this is not the whole truth about man, not even the most significant truth; that man has also capacity for love and kindness and self-sacrifice is the most deeply significant fact about him. A science of economics founded wholly on man's bestial selfishness, and taking no account of his godlike qualities, ignoring his capacity to give his life for ideals of truth and goodness, is well named the "dismal science." But it ought also to be called the lying, slanderous science.

The old economy recognized consumption as the end of production. True, says Ruskin, but why stop there? Life is the end and aim of consumption. From this follows what he held to be the cardinal principle of economics: "There is no wealth but life — life, including all its powers of love, of joy, of admiration. That country is richest which nourishes the greatest number of noble and happy human beings; that man is richest, who, having perfected the functions of his own life to the utmost, has also the widest helpful influence, both personal, and by means of his possessions, over the lives of others." In other words, economics being concerned with man and his conduct must be an ethical science, and cannot be investigated as if it had to do only with the interplay of unmoral forces.

Lest men should object that his treatment of the subject was a mere prophetic rhapsody, and no guide to practical action, Ruskin was ready with a programme for the partial realization of the ideal of society that he so eloquently described. He urged four lines of social activity and reform, as a beginning: first, government training-schools, in which children should be taught the laws of health, habits of gentleness and justice, and the calling by which they were to live; secondly, state manufactories and workshops in connection with these schools, for the production of every necessary of life and the exercise of every useful art — interfering with no private enterprise, but producing good and exemplary work; thirdly, that in these industries employment should be furnished for all out of work; [1] fourthly, that for the old and destitute, comfort and home should be provided, not as a charity, but as justice. "A laborer," he said, "serves his country with his spade, just as a man in the middle ranks of life serves it with sword, pen, or lancet. If the service be less, and, therefore, the wages during health less, then the reward when health is broken may be less, but not

---

[1] To the objection always made by the "practical" man to proposals of this sort: How could the expenses of such schools and manufactories be met? Ruskin had a reply that was not only ready but conclusive: "Indirectly they would be far more than self-supporting. The economy in crime alone (quite one of the most costly articles of luxury in the modern European market) which such schools would induce, would suffice to support them ten times over. Their economy of labor would be pure gain, and that too large to be presently calculable."

less honorable; and it ought to be quite as natural and straightforward a matter for a laborer to take his pension from his parish, as for a man in higher rank to take his pension from his country."

Ruskin did not call his doctrine Socialism, nor did he call himself a socialist, nor were these terms then applied by others; but it will be seen that he anticipated many of the principles and most of the practical programme of modern Socialism. To his work as a sower of seed is to be attributed much of the harvest of Socialism in the England of a generation later.

Nor was his teaching entirely a propaganda; it bore practical fruit through the labors of a disciple, Arnold Toynbee, a graduate of Balliol College, Oxford, in 1878, and thereafter a lecturer on economics in that institution, until his untimely death in 1883. He was the inspirer in turn of a knot of young men who gathered around him, spoke on industrial questions in many of the manufacturing towns of England, and spent some of his "long" vacations among the poor of East London. After his death, Canon Barnett, rector of the parish of St. Jude's, in that part of London, suggested the establishment of a kind of "Hall," in which men might reside and do a like work for the Whitechapel poor. The result was the erection of such a building, called Toynbee Hall, in memory of the pioneer, which was opened in 1885. This was the first example of University Settlement work, which has since that time been greatly extended in England and America, and widened out into Social Settlements that have had a most beneficent effect, in spite of some shortcomings and follies.

Settlement work depends for its efficiency on the principle that education is mainly a matter of personal contact, of arousing enthusiasm and imparting ideals, not of merely conveying knowledge from mind to mind. And successful settlement work is that which has recognized that education, in this sense, is what the poor need most of all for any permanent improvement in their condition. Next to this, the value of settlement work lies in the discovery and dissemination of social facts. For the most dangerous element in social reform is sentimentalism, mere uninstructed emotionalism. One remembers the Hatter's watch, in "Alice in Wonderland." "I told you butter wouldn't suit the works," he said angrily to the March Hare. "It was the *best* butter," the March Hare meekly replied. The surprise of well-meaning people at the failure of their good intentions and best efforts at social amelioration is often equally humorous, but it is pathetic also. A little intelligence must be mingled with good intentions to make them anything else than harmful.

V

"We are all socialists now," is a remark made with increasing frequency since it was first jocularly uttered by Sir William Vernon Harcourt twenty years ago. Even when seriously spoken, the words express barely a half-truth. Many people are doubtless more hospitable than formerly to the notion of some halting steps in the direction of Socialism, but they still recoil from the thought of real Socialism. Such acceptance as socialistic ideas have to-day in England is mainly due to the rise of a new school in the eighties. The publication of *Das Kapital* produced surprisingly little effect on English thought;

its author might as well have resided in Mars as in London while writing the book. Few Englishmen read it, fewer understood it, and of these latter only here and there one was receptive.

Nevertheless, Marx did make a few ardent disciples, and in 1883 they formed the Social Democratic Federation. As one of their own votaries put it: "The socialists of the eighties came into the English world with a doctrine of coöperation and fellowship of which the nation stood in sore need, and a set of Marxian formularies which it would not have at any price." A prominent member of this group was William Morris, who had first won distinction as a poet, and later as an artist-decorator. Neither by temperament nor by education a philosopher or a politician, as a socialist he was not a doctrinaire. It became clear to him that if Socialism was to make progress in England, it must be delivered from the domination of Marx and his dogmatic trinity: the theory of value, the class war, and the catastrophic revolution. The first is unscientific, the second is immoral, and the third has been abandoned by his disciples. With some others Morris seceded from the Federation in 1885, and founded the Socialist League on broader principles. His own "News from Nowhere" was one of the most effective books ever written in advocacy of Socialism, and the *Commonweal* proved to be one of the best socialist weekly papers ever established.

Though less narrowly dogmatic than the Federation, the League is no less radical. It avows as an immediate practical programme, "stepping-stones to a happier period," the following measures: compulsory construction of laborers' dwellings, to be let at cost; free compulsory

P

education, with at least one meal a day; eight hours or less for a normal day's work; a cumulative income tax; state appropriation of railways; national banks; rapid extinction [repudiation ?] of national debt; nationalization of land.   A colleague of Morris in the League was Ernest Belfort Bax, a barrister of the Middle Temple, educated in large part in Germany, a valuable assistant in the conduct of the *Commonweal* and author of numerous books on the history and doctrines of Socialism.   Since the death of Morris he has returned to his earlier allegiance, and is now active in the Social Democratic Federation.

One of the leading spirits in the Federation from the first has been H. M. Hyndman, a graduate of Trinity College, Cambridge, and for years a brilliant journalist before avowing socialist principles.   He is probably the best-equipped writer among the English socialists, and his books are said to have made a profound and wide impression in his own country, but are little known in America.   Another influential writer is Robert Blatchford, a self-educated man, the only one among the literary group of English socialists who is truly a man of the people and has worked with his hands.   The others are what are called on the Continent "the intellectuals," and cannot know the people as one of themselves knows them.   The *Clarion*, a newspaper established by Mr. Blatchford in 1891, has been very successful and has the largest circulation and greatest influence of any socialist publication in England, by no means excepting *Justice*, the official organ of the Federation.   While men like Morris, Bax, and Hyndman were men of education and literary standing, and were read quite widely by educated Englishmen, making a considerable impression on men of wealth and social position, they did not touch the working-men. But these are the precise audience to which Blatchford addressed himself, and not in vain.

The Social Democratic Federation has remained strongly Marxian, although an admiring friend and biographer of Mr. Blatchford says that the *Clarion* man has never read *Das Kapital* and knows nothing of Marx at first hand. The Federation has also been emphatically antichristian in its spirit, and in much of its literature. Some of Blatchford's writings, and possibly some of Hyndman's also, would have exposed their author to a prosecution for blasphemy a few years ago, — in 1841 George Jacob Holyoake was convicted and imprisoned for six months for an offence much less serious.

Not only has the socialistic movement in England antagonized the middle classes by its indifference or hostility to religion, but some of its leaders have increased this odium by advocating entire freedom of divorce, and the confiscation of property without compensation. Another of their leaders, however, Mr. Bruce Glazier, in the *Labor Leader*, in answer to some of the reproaches that the movement has had to endure for these matters, which are no essential part of Socialism, has effectively retorted on the middle and ruling classes. He showed that scores of English Liberals and Tories have advocated the loosest of sex-relationships, and illustrated their theories in their lives. As to spoliation, he showed how confiscation, bribery, and corruption have built up the fortunes of half the English peerage. Even as to atheism and agnosticism he asserts, without contradiction, that for one advocate among socialists a dozen can be produced from Liberals and Tories. There has of late been a marked tendency to let this charge against English Socialism quietly lapse into oblivion. It is an ancient principle of law that one who seeks relief in a court of equity must come into court with clean hands.

What is even worse in the eyes of some Englishmen than irreligion is that members of the Federation have advocated, in their list of immediate reforms demanded, the abolition of the Monarchy. It has been urged that this is a violation of the Treason Felony Act of 1848, which makes any open speaking or writing with the object of deposing the king punishable by penal servitude. Proposing a radical change in the form of government may be a technical violation of that or some other outworn statute — though it is to be noted that deposing the king and abolition of the Monarchy are not the same thing — but no sensible government will ever elevate socialist leaders to the dignity of martyrdom by securing their conviction on such a charge. A specimen of equal political madness is the suggestion that socialists who circulate their literature in the army and navy should receive condign punishment for corrupting the services ! [1] When the ruling class of England confesses by such acts that it dare not permit Socialism to be freely discussed, its days will be numbered.

Another influential organization is the Fabian Society, formed in 1884, in order to promote the education of the people in the principles of Socialism. Its very name was a protest against the Marxian doctrine of an immediate and catastrophic revolution. The society announces as

[1] Both of these specimens of political wisdom may be found in W. Lawler Wilson's "The Menace of Socialism," New York, 1909. See especially pp. 59, 60.

its object : "the reorganization of society by the emancipation of Land and Industrial Capital from individual and class ownership for the general benefit." This should be done "without compensation, though not without such relief to expropriated individuals as may seem fit to the community." The members of the Fabian Society were mostly young men, clever, possessing considerable literary ability, and full of initiative. George Bernard Shaw, the dramatist, H. G. Wells, the ingenious spinner of more or less scientific romances, the Rev. R. J. Campbell, the famous London preacher, Mr. and Mrs. Sidney Webb, have been its most active and prominent members. A volume of "Fabian Essays" and a large number of penny tracts have done excellent service in the work of educating Englishmen in the principles of Socialism. The Society claims a membership of about a thousand, and the fact that eleven Fabians were elected to Parliament in 1908 is perhaps a good measure of the extent of their influence. These members act independently, but almost invariably vote with the Labor Party. Though sneered at by thoroughgoing Marxians as advocates of "socialism-and-water," hardly deserving the name of "comrades," the Fabians are evidently a force with which both socialists and antisocialists must reckon.

The formation of the Independent Labor Party at Bradford, in 1883, under the leadership of Keir Hardie, was the most important event in the progress of English Socialism. Working-men had discovered by a long and costly experience that they gained nothing by voting Tories out and Liberals in, or *vice versa*. Whether a man bore one party label or another, he was opposed to the interests of the working-classes, because he invariably

belonged to another class and had other interests. The
Labor Party was in no way hostile to the other organizations engaged in propagating socialistic ideas; it merely
proposed to translate some of the ideas into political
action. It was all very well to promote Socialism by
voice and pen, but why neglect its promotion by the
ballot? was its query. Mr. Blatchford and his *Clarion*
gave yeoman service from the first in the cause of the
Labor Party.

The Independent Labor Party has been vigorously
pushed by the Fabians and has shared the moderation
of that group of socialists. It has explicitly refused
to avow the Marxian dogma of the class warfare. It
cannot see the consistency of socialists declaring in one
breath for universal brotherhood and for a relentless war
of the classes. The Marxians are determined to make all
men brothers, if they must kill off half the race to do it!
The Stuttgart Congress, in August, 1907, undertook to
establish a standard of orthodoxy, and declared that only
those who avow their belief in the class struggle are entitled to bear the name Socialist. The German socialists,
who despise Christianity, are not above taking a leaf from
its history, it should seem, — already they have held
their Council of Nice and have anathematized their
Arians.

At their eighth annual conference, held at Hull, in
1908, the Labor Party adopted a resolution setting forth
their general aims and principles: "That in the opinion
of the Conference the time has arrived when the Labor
Party should have a definite object, the socialization of
the means of production, distribution, and exchange, to
be controlled by a democratic state in the interests of the

entire community; and the complete emancipation of Labor from the domination of capitalism and landlordism, with the establishment of social and economic equality between the sexes." As immediate practical measures, it demands: a maximum of forty-eight hours a week labor, with retention of all legal holidays; provision of work for all, at minimum pay of sixpence an hour, the various councils to undertake industries for the purpose; State pensions for all over fifty years of age, and adequate provisions for widows and orphans; free education, including the university for all who desire it, and free maintenance of pupils; raising the age of child labor, with the ultimate purpose of abolishing it entirely; municipalization and control of the drink traffic; municipalization of all hospitals and infirmaries; abolition of all indirect taxation and transference of public burdens to unearned incomes, with a view to their ultimate extinction; and adult suffrage.

The first general election after the organization of the Labor Party caught it unprepared; the contest came suddenly, and their organization was incomplete, their treasury empty. They made a gallant fight, but suffered a bad defeat; not a single electoral district was won, and even the one representative they had boasted, Keir Hardie, lost his seat. Chastened and instructed by this experience, the party settled down to business in dead earnest. An incessant propaganda among the working-men was maintained during the next five years. Working-men were put forward as candidates in every local election, and many of them were chosen members of local boards and borough councils. Immediate results followed in the municipalizing of many enterprises that had been conducted by private capital. Keir Hardie and John Burns continued the organization and instruction of the working-men, pressing on them as a political principle that which has long been at the basis of their trades-union bodies, "The injury of one is the concern of all." An increasing number of workers became convinced that there is no weal for any until there is weal for all.

But, as we have noted, there is little use in urging upon an Englishman an abstract idea, — he has something very like a horror of a general principle. He will not move against any social evil, however great, and particularly if it has a fine ripe flavor of antiquity, until it becomes a personal grievance. The ruling class were unwise enough just at this juncture to give the British worker a personal grievance against themselves. This was what was known as the Taff Vale decision, by which in 1901 the House of Lords decided not only that a court had a right to enjoin a union from picketing in case of a strike, but that the union could be made a party to a suit for damages; which carried with it the doctrine that the funds of every union were liable to attachment in a verdict for damages. The far-reaching effect of this decision will be better appreciated when Keir Hardie's estimate of the strength of unionism in England is scanned: the trades-unions had, when the decision was rendered, 2,500,000 members, with reserve funds amounting to £3,000,000. As a natural sequel to the decision, the Taff Vale Railway Company brought suit for damages against the Amalgamated Society of Railway Servants, and got a verdict of £28,000. The decision was seen to be a death-blow to trades-unions in England, if it stood as law. It reversed the principle hitherto accepted by English courts, that a union was a voluntary association and not a corporation, and hence could neither sue nor be sued, — the only remedy of an injured party was to sue the individuals composing the association.

The unions were now compelled to fight for their very existence, and they proceeded to fight to good purpose. In the general election of 1906, a remarkable result followed: twenty-six seats were carried by official representatives of the Labor Party, and twenty-nine others by Liberal-labor candidates, who owed their election to working-men and were pledged to support their measures in Parliament. A gasp of dismay went up from both of the old parties. The representatives of labor held the fate of ministries in their hands, and as soon as they caught their breath again both parties began to vie with each other in cultivating the good-will and securing the support of this new political power. A bill was promptly introduced by the government, providing that an action against a union, whether of workmen or masters, or against any members or officials thereof, on behalf of themselves or other members of the union, in respect of any tortious act alleged to have been committed by or in behalf of the union, shall not be entertained by any court. This Trades Disputes bill, as it was known, not only reversed the decision of the House of Lords, but gave the members of unions an immunity greater than they had ever known before. It is quite usual for the Lords to throw out any bill of a reform nature passed by the Commons, but they made haste to pass this, — there were too many Tory seats in the Commons that might be at the mercy of the working-men voters at the next election to permit any playing with them. Parliament also passed, in 1906, a Workman's Compensation Act, assuring an injured workman weekly payments not exceeding half his wages while incapacitated, and a sum equal to three years' wages to his family in case of his death.

A more recent example has been given of the willingness of the English ruling class to make quickly any reasonable concession to the growing power of the Labor Party. In what is known as the Osborne Case, the English courts decided that the trades-unions had no right to pay out of their general funds the modest salary of £200 a year to their Parliamentary representatives. The case was taken to the House of Lords, where final decision was rendered December 21, 1909 that the Trade Union Act limits the activities of such organizations to "regulating the relations between workmen and masters, or between workmen and workmen, or between masters and masters, or for imposing restrictive conditions on the conduct of trade or business. The payment of salaries to members of Parliament is *ultra vires* and void." This has made it very difficult, and threatens to make it impossible, for the Labor Party to maintain their representation in the House of Commons. Premier Asquith came to their relief in November, 1910, by announcing that if his government should be continued in power with a working majority, he would bring in a bill for the payment of members of the House, — a measure that has been refused by England's rulers to the demands of the working class for two generations. *E pur si muove*, even in England !

Much of the victory of 1906 was due to the direction of the political campaign by the Labor Representation

Committee, an organization that attempted the federation of the various bodies engaged in propagating socialistic principles. The object was not entirely successful, for the Social Labor Federation withdrew from coöperation with the others, because the latter would not explicitly declare themselves in favor of the Marxian principles and programme. The Federation has virtually proclaimed that nobody shall be recognized as an orthodox socialist, unless he will profess as his creed: "There is no God, and Karl Marx is his prophet." Socialists flout and scout the Bible as a collection of old wives' fables, but the inspiration and infallible authority, and even the inerrancy, of *Das Kapital* is an article of faith from which they will permit no dissent, on pain of excommunication. So long as they retain this fanatical and intolerant spirit, the Marxians will be a hindrance to the progress of Socialism.

VI

The English movement has avowed a practical plan of immediate legislation, upon the chief items of which all are agreed. And though this proposed legislation would involve a considerable social change, it can hardly be called revolutionary. While they differ among themselves as to the emphasis to be laid on the various items, and therefore the preferable order in which the enactment of them into law should be sought, there is substantial agreement among socialists in demanding, as rapidly as possible: the socialization of land; the nationalization of railways and expresses; the nationalization of all natural resources — mines, forests, water-power; a national banking system; the municipalizing of industries connected with the necessaries of life — water-supply, gas, bread, meat, milk, coal. All of these may be subsumed under the general principle of making public property of all monopolies. To these are added certain fiscal reforms : abolition of all indirect taxes ; a progressive income tax, a graduated inheritance tax. The objection to Socialism by its opponents that it has no practical programme is ceasing to be heard in England, — this is much too practical for the taste of the classes, but it is winning the enthusiastic support of the masses. The masses hope, and the classes fear, that, if these steps were once taken, the progress toward ultimate Socialism would become both possible and easy.

The impression made by the great political success of the working-men, and the measures proposed by them, may be gauged by the dismay that has seized the upper and middle classes and the counter measures that are proposed. In order to take the wind out of the sails of Socialism, even Tory writers now advocate a wholesale State interference with industrial affairs, the proposition of which two decades ago would have been regarded as little less than impiety. Specific recommendations of this kind have recently been made : compulsory arbitration, with voluntary conciliation councils ; encouragement of coöperation and profit-sharing ; encouragement of trade-unions, especially in a scientific scheme of pensions for the relief of old age, sickness, and unemployment ; importation of alien workers to be forbidden ; a land purchase act for small proprietors ; a house purchase act for working-men ; a thorough scheme of national sanitation ; revision of laws relating to crime and debt ; imperial colonization, to dispose of surplus population ;

fiscal reform (by which is meant a protective tariff, for the alleged benefit of working-men) ; the encouragement of intelligence by making open careers.[1]

Just what is intended by the latter proposal, or how the end sought is to be accomplished, is doubtful; but these proposals are all clearly in the direction of Socialism. No socialist can have any objections to them, viewed as steps in the right direction. But the middle class idea is evidently that the Cerberus of Socialism may be appeased by a few sops; and that, if England will give socialists, say, a quarter of what they ask, they will cease to demand the other three-quarters. The amount of political wisdom contained in such a scheme can easily be estimated by every reader, without the assistance of any further discussion of these details.

A marked advance in practical Socialism has been made within the last two decades in many municipalities and boroughs in England, by the undertaking of public enterprises for the common good that were formerly left to private initiative. Municipal and borough councils have taken possession of local tramways, or have granted franchises for limited periods and under rigid restrictions. It is claimed that as a result the English towns are far behind those of America in transit facilities, but other causes may be in great part responsible for this relative backwardness. Many cities are erecting municipal tenements, have already taken over the water and gas supply,[2]

[1] Wilson, "The Menace of Socialism," p. 416 *et seq.:* "The Alternative Policy."

[2] One of the humorous features of antisocialistic polemics is, that it is perfectly orthodox to favor municipal gas in England, but to propose municipal water is "socialistic"; while in the United States it is orthodox to favor municipal water, but distinctly "socialistic" to propose municipal

where they did not control these enterprises from the beginning; and are taking charge of the sale of milk, bread, meat, and coal. The field of public enterprise has always been larger in Great Britain than in the United States; the telegraph, like the post, is a public institution, and of late years the telephone has been added; and though Englishmen grumble at the administration, as a matter of principle, all three enterprises are as well managed and give as good service as our own post-office system, which nobody believes would be better conducted as a private enterprise. Within the past few decades, there has also been a generous provision made by municipalities for parks, playgrounds, recreation fields, museums, art galleries and libraries, on a scale never before known in England, and still paralleled in few other countries.

There is difference of opinion whether the remarkable development of coöperation in England is to be credited to Socialism or debited. The first successful attempt at coöperation was made by the Rochdale Society of Equitable Pioneers, which was begun in 1844 by twenty-eight Lancashire weavers, with a capital of $140. Its first work was to furnish provisions to the shareholders, among whom profits were to be divided in proportion to their purchases. At the end of thirteen years it had a membership of two thousand, and a capital of $75,000. The coöperative stores of the united services is a later instance of similar success on a scale even larger. It is said by statisticians that there is now a capital of $330,000,000

gas. The reason for this blowing hot and cold by opponents of Socialism is, that in England gas has from the first been generally treated as a municipal matter, while water has been furnished to cities mainly by private companies; while in America precisely the reverse is true.

invested in such enterprises, and one-sixth of the population of England shops in coöperative stores.

On the whole, it would be a moderate statement to say that the field of private enterprise is now considerably more restricted in England than in the United States, — a thing that many Americans will doubtless be surprised to learn. The socialists look with indifference, as has been intimated, on this growth of coöperation, regarding it as only another form of Capitalism, instead of seeing in it a trial of their theories on a limited scale, preparatory to trial on a universal scale. Those who engage in such experiments, say some socialists, are simply working for their own selfish profit, and the community has no more power over their industry, no more share in its prosperity, than would be the case in any other form of Capitalism. Which seems a selfish and narrow-minded, as well as short-sighted, way of regarding a very significant social experiment.

VII

SOCIALISM IN AMERICA

BIBLIOGRAPHY

Books by socialists : —

HILLQUIT, History of Socialism in the United States. New York, 1906.

HUNTER, Poverty. New York, 1907.

MYERS, History of the Great American Fortunes, 3 vols. Chicago, 1910.

Historical and expository : —

HINDS, American Communities. Chicago, 1908.

ELY, Socialism and Social Reform. 1894.

Books on the single-tax theory : —

GEORGE, Progress and Poverty. 1879.

POST, The Single Tax. New York, 1895.

Books on the Trust Problem : —

MOODY, The Truth about the Trusts. New York, 1904.

JENKS, The Trust Problem. New York, 1901.

LLOYD, Wealth against Commonwealth. New York, 1894.

GHENT, Our Benevolent Feudalism. New York, 1902.

VII

I

WHILE the development of Socialism in America has been slow, as compared with European countries, the fact is ascribable not to mental impenetrability, but to absence of motive. The abundance of unoccupied land, to be had for the asking, and the backward state of manufactures during the first half of the nineteenth century, were sufficient reasons for the failure of Socialism to make swift progress here. So long as no man need remain poor unless he chose, so long as the rapid development of our natural resources and the equally rapid expansion of our industrial undertakings opened up careers for every ambitious and alert-minded man, the pressure of the struggle for existence was not unbearable. If the poor boy of to-day might be the millionnaire of to-morrow, why discuss theories of society? But after 1870 the pressure of population on subsistence and employment began to be a severe one; immigration and the natural increase brought us face to face with social problems. Socialism had hitherto been an importation, a foreign speculation, an exotic; it now began to take root and become naturalized.

This comparatively late growth of Socialism was not for lack of socialistic literature or socialistic experiments.

227

At a comparatively early date in our history, settlements were established on a more or less complete socialistic basis.   Perhaps the earliest of these were the Moravian colonies: one in Georgia as early as 1735; another at Bethlehem, Pa., in 1741; and a third at Nazareth, in 1743.   These colonies were founded with a primarily religious object, and their community features were of secondary importance; hence they were never thoroughgoing in their socialism.   While there was community ownership of the land, and certain enterprises (like stores and bakeries) were managed by the community for the profit of all, private property and private enterprise were permitted.   In every instance, these Moravian settlements were prosperous; they accumulated wealth, maintained a high standard of comfort, established excellent schools, and vindicated the soundness of the principles on which they were founded.   The community features have been gradually abandoned, not because they were no longer profitable, but because the Moravian people could no longer resist the pressure of the surrounding communities, and have preferred to assimilate their lives to the economic and social standards of Americans in general.   The fate of these communities illustrates a serious difficulty that utopian socialists have always failed to consider: the practical impossibility of maintaining a socialistic group in the midst of a hostile society.   Sooner or later, every such group seems certain to succumb.   If all of society cannot be completely socialized, then none of it can be.

Out of the large number of groups that have been founded on a basis of religion and Socialism combined, it will be profitable to consider only a few cases.   One of the best known, the Shakers, of English origin, established themselves at Watervliet, N.Y., in 1776, whence they have scattered through nine States in fifteen societies. Fifty or sixty years ago, there was a total Shaker population of five thousand, but they have now dwindled to about a thousand. They own a hundred thousand acres, and their property is valued at several millions. But though they have thus maintained themselves for more than a century, and have been able to accumulate considerable wealth, their rapidly failing numbers admonish us that this cannot be reckoned a successful experiment in Socialism.

Several groups owed their origin to immigration from Germany. Of these the earliest, and perhaps the most important, was due to the coming to the United States, in 1804, of some six hundred Separatists from Würtemberg. They attempted to establish themselves in several fields, and finally settled at Economy, Pa., near Pittsburgh. In 1807, they became celibates, and now their steadily decreasing community is practically a capitalistic body, employing outside labor on a considerable scale, at day wages, for the benefit of the stockholders. The Socialism of these Rappists, as they are also called, has not so much failed as disappeared.

A similar colony of Germans who settled at Zoar, in 1817, did not begin as a community, but so organized themselves after two years. More than two generations of prosperity followed, and then the survivors dissolved by mutual consent, in 1898, each receiving about $1500 from the common estate.

The Amana colony, first settled near Buffalo, but afterwards removed to Iowa, where about eighteen hundred

people live in seven villages, have had a history of continuous growth and prosperity, from 1855 till the present
time. Each family has a separate house, but a common
dining-hall is maintained in each village. Marriage is
not forbidden, but seems to be discouraged among them;
as it is permitted to no man until he has reached the age
of twenty-four, and then only by vote of the elders; and
wedding ceremonies are said to be as lugubrious as a
funeral. The means of producing wealth are owned in
common; the labors of the community are directed by
the elders; and each member is given a certain credit at
the community store, where he gets what he pleases and
has it charged to his account. Many of the features of
Bellamy's "Looking Backward" are found realized in
the Amana community, which, on the whole, is probably
the most completely socialistic and the most economically
successful of all American experiments of this kind.

The most notorious of the religious-socialistic groups,
the Oneida Community, was founded in 1848 by John
Humphrey Noyes, and is the one experiment of this kind
that was conducted by people of native stock.   It has
had a remarkable record of harmony, only one member
having been expelled during its history, and has been
prosperous beyond the average. It was dissolved as a
religious community in 1880, at which time it had property valued at a million dollars, and was reorganized as
a corporation, the "Oneida Community, Limited." The
Community long ago gained a high reputation for the
quality of its manufactures, which it still retains.

Nearly all of the other religious communities, as well
as those that have been mentioned, were economically
successful. Many of them endured for half a century

or longer; several amassed much wealth. But it was true of all, as well as of the Moravians, that the religious motive predominated, and the social experiment stood in the second place. It was also true that the membership of all was carefully winnowed, so that these communities were composed of homogeneous material, industrious and frugal people, well fitted to make their way in the world as individuals before they became parts of communities. The religious bond promoted harmony; the character of the people insured success in the industrial part of the venture. And in the end, nearly all such communities that have survived have ceased to emphasize the community feature, and have become, either avowedly or in fact, mere corporations, of which the members are stockholders.

II

Contemporary with some of the later religious communities were numerous experiments due to the doctrines of Fourier. Several of these experiments were more immediately inspired by Robert Owen, who thought to find in a new world a better opportunity for the development of his ideas than was offered by any old-world society. In 1825 he came to the United States, and found at Harmony, Ind., a favorable field for his venture. The Rappists then had there a tract of thirty thousand acres, of which they had brought three thousand under cultivation, besides laying out a village. This property, on which the most difficult work had already been done, Owen acquired for $150,000. William Maclure of Philadelphia, a man of considerable culture, wealth, and ability, was his associate, and the aid of a number of men eminent in science and education was enlisted. No community began with more favorable conditions, and Owen had the liveliest expectations of a grand success, that should impress the world with the advantages of Socialism. With his usual expansiveness, he invited "the industrious and well-disposed of all nations" to find a home here and share in the coming prosperity of New Harmony.

Some of the industrious and well-disposed came, but mostly the lazy and the ill-disposed accepted the invitation, a motley and heterogeneous crowd of incongruous natures and irreconcilable aims. No pains were taken to select from applicants who offered themselves such as gave some token of fitness for taking part in such an experiment. The community so constituted was foredoomed to failure. It lasted little more than two years, and during that time had more revolutions than a South American republic, — seven "constitutions" having been tried and found wanting, an average of little more than three months for each. Twice Owen himself was "dictator," by the vote of the community, but even he could not bring order out of this chaos. The colony broke up as a community; most of its members went away, and those who remained in possession of the land relapsed into the ordinary life of the ordinary American village. A half dozen other communities, more or less of the Owen type, had a similar history.

Of all the earlier American trials of Socialism, the most famous was that of Brook Farm, in West Roxbury, Mass. This prominence was due to the personnel of the colony; nearly every man or woman connected with it was then or afterwards distinguished. The head and leading spirit was George Ripley, in after years the literary editor of the *New York Tribune*, and even then a well-known man of letters. Among the most prominent members were Nathaniel Hawthorne, Margaret Fuller, George William Curtis, Charles A. Dana, and Theodore S. Dwight. The colony had besides, as sympathetic friends and occasional visitors, a large number of the most eminent Americans of the time : the two Channings, Ralph Waldo Emerson, Horace Greeley. Hawthorne has left on record his impressions in his "Blithedale Romance," and other members of the colony have in more sober prose given us their reminiscences. All this has combined to make Brook Farm eclipse every other community experiment.

Yet of all, none achieved a more dismal failure than this. It was made up of most accomplished and amiable persons, of the least possible practical experience, none of them accustomed to earning his own living before coming to the farm, and all quite ignorant of agriculture, which was practically the only occupation offered. There was abundance of food for the mind and very little for the body at Brook Farm, no end of culture and social enjoyment, but little practical prosperity. After 1844, this became the centre of the Fourier propaganda in America ; the principal magazine was edited and published there. Money was obtained for the building of a large Phalanstery, but as this was nearing completion it was destroyed by fire (1846). The Fourier movement was already on the wane, and this misfortune was a death-blow to Brook Farm. It proved impossible to obtain money for rebuilding ; in a few months the colony broke up, and the property was sold.

Though much the most famous, this was far from the only, experiment along Fourierist lines. The diligence of investigators has recovered data of forty-one phalanxes, mostly established between 1841 and 1853, all of which were failures. The average duration of such experiments was little more than two years. They did not approach the religious communities in economic success: few of them had even moderate prosperity; most of them experienced hard labor and dire poverty. The common experience of all these attempts proved to a demonstration that the immediate establishment of Socialism, with the average human material, in the absence of religion or some other strong bond, is hopeless. The only hope of successful Socialism is in a gradual evolution.

III

The beginning of real American Socialism was contemporary with the later British; that is to say, it cannot be placed farther back than the eighties. Any socialists before that time were immigrants, mostly German, who had brought their theories along with their other scanty baggage, and were rather laughed at than taken seriously. But in the eighties Socialism began to get a hearing and to win adherents among native-born Americans. The causes of this development are not far to seek, but so many people have never comprehended them, and so many more yet refuse to consider them, that it is worth our while to give some time and space to their consideration.

The theory of American law, statute and constitutional, is that all men are free and equal. The equality predicated is, of course, understood to be, not actual equality, but equality of rights and social opportunities. Our entire system of civil and criminal jurisprudence is based on this assumption. American Socialism has grown out of the observed and experienced variance between this theory of the law and the facts; and is nothing else than an attempt to make the facts correspond to the theory. The principles of the Declaration are the principles of every socialist — what he wishes is, to give them practical effect.

The American laborer finds that he occupies two positions in the world of fact, one of which is quite irreconcilable with the theory of the law. As a citizen and voter he is free, the equal of any. He may cast his vote without hinderance, and if he is fortunate he may get it counted; he may aspire to any office, and may sometimes be elected. But as a member of the industrial community he occupies a dependent position that is incompatible with freedom —a new form of the ancient slavery, in fact. Here, too, the law makes all men equal, but Capitalism nullifies the law and makes men unequal. We may paraphrase Lincoln's words, and say that society cannot endure permanently in a state half slave, half free. Either freedom or slavery will in the end prevail. But at present this half-and-half state is the real fact, contradicting the theory of the law. Just as under the feudal system the lords held all the land, and the common people lived on it by their sufferance and on their terms, so under the capitalistic system the common people (some of them) are benevolently permitted to work (some of the time) by those who hold all the means of production. This state of things has come about, as the socialist economists maintain, because an orderly and regular development has in large measure effected the socialization of labor in producing wealth, while the private ownership of capital and the system of exchange have retained the distribution of wealth mainly in the hands of individuals.

That this wide gap between theory and fact really exists will hardly be denied. But there are obviously two ways of dealing with the problems that such a contradiction suggests. One has already been mentioned, the way of the socialist : to make an honest effort to close the gap, so that theory and fact shall correspond. The other method is, to bend all energies toward keeping things as they are, to shut one's eyes to all social inequalities and social iniquities, to denounce all who propose change as mischievous fanatics and enemies of the social order — in short, to "stand pat." The late E. L. Godkin was a type of this large and influential class of Americans. In the columns of the *New York Evening Post*, and in his published Essays, he poured out a flood of ridicule and denunciation on all who demand any serious modification of existing social institutions. "I know of no more mischievous person," said he, " than the man who, in free America, seeks to spread among them [the workers] the idea that they are wronged and kept down by somebody ; that somebody is to blame because they are not better lodged, better housed, better educated, and have not easier access to balls, concerts, or dinner parties."

But there is a more mischievous person, and that is the man of education, who should be a man of light and leading, but who spends one-half his talent and energy in telling the workers that they have no right to aspire to the pursuit of happiness, that it is their duty to accept their hard

lot without murmuring or questioning; and the other
half in administering sedatives to the consciences of the
well-to-do, so that they shall rest content with what they
have and make no effort to better conditions. Such a
man, and not the man with the bomb, is the really dangerous revolutionary. For we learn from history — well,
what *do* we learn from history? Hegel says, "We learn
from history that no one learns anything from history"
— we ought, then, to learn from history that this is the
precise way to provoke bloody and destructive revolutions.

Some maintain that history never repeats itself, but
it certainly offers some striking parallels; and if we may
reason from analogy, suggested by former revolutionary
episodes, we shall conclude that if the capitalist class of
to-day recognize the inevitable change coming, and yield
in time with just and reasonable concessions, the reconstruction of society will be accomplished by the machinery
of existing laws and government. If, on the contrary,
the policy of "stand pat" and resistance be maintained,
if wealth be used to corrupt legislatures and courts and
officials in the vain hope of resisting an irresistible tide
of social feeling, the result will be a violent explosion like
the French Revolution, involving loss of life and confiscation of property. England has avoided effusion of
blood and spoliation of one class by another, by a slow
yielding on the part of her ruling class at every crisis when
longer struggle would have meant a violent revolution.
The French nobility had no such political wisdom, and
the penalty for their obstinate resistance to the very last
was that they lost their property and their lives when the
inevitable reconstruction came. Will our ruling class

imitate the English nobility or the French? On the answer to that question hangs the peaceful character of the change impending, but that the change will come we may hold for certain.

What makes for a peaceful change is the absence of any deep class hatred. The average American may envy a millionnaire, but he does not hate him — "there but for the grace of God, go I," he says to himself. But it is a sinister fact that something very like hatred is growing in American society towards the brutality of wealth that revels in luxury and makes ostentatious display of its wicked waste while the poor starve. For they who look on at this display, as vulgar as it is wicked, know well that in order that these may enjoy what they did not produce, it was necessary for other men to produce what they are not permitted to enjoy. Yet this flaunting of wealth in the faces of the poor is not likely to result in violent revolution and spoliation, because of the political power of the poor man when he becomes intelligent enough to realize and use it. A party of socialists, let us say, strong enough numerically and otherwise to overthrow existing institutions by violence, will probably be strong enough to obtain their ends without violence. The moment a revolution becomes possible here, it has become unnecessary.[1] Bullets and bombs are for those, and for those only, who have not ballots.

Not only in a less inclination to violent measures, but

[1] A story told of two prominent advocates of Socialism indicates that they are not all of one mind regarding the future. They were guests of a certain club, and were requested to sign their names in the visitors' book with a sentiment. The first did so as follows: "Yours for the Revolution, Jack London." The other wrote under this, "There ain't going to be no revolution, H. G. Wells."

in many other particulars, American socialists differ from
those who, in Germany and France, in Italy and Spain,
and even in Great Britain, bear the same name and in
general maintain similar principles.   There has developed here a distinct type of what may be called with propriety, American Socialism.   The political and social
atmosphere is different here, and above all the religious,
and this accounts for the observed divergence of type.
The American socialist is much less grudgeful against all
existing institutions than his European prototype.   The
absence of any State Church, the prevalence of complete
religious liberty, make him far less hostile to religion than
is the case in Europe, where State Churches, both Protestant and Catholic, are regarded as chief bulwarks of
social evils.   It is true that many socialists in America
believe that organized Christianity here is the ally of
Capitalism, and therefore the foe of social progress, and
this feeling is something to be reckoned with.   This matter will be discussed more fully in a later chapter, and here
it is sufficient to remark that this feeling, though undoubtedly existent, lacks the rancor of European Socialism
towards all forms of religion, and there is no assertion of
crass atheism as part of a programme.   Since in America the marriage of convenience, though not unknown,
is not the rule, since parental coercion is so rare that we
may almost say it is non-existent, there is all the freedom
of union that even Socialism contemplates; and in many
States there is nearly as much freedom of divorce as any
socialists have demanded; therefore, the socialistic opposition to legal marriage is much less insistent in America than in Europe.   Moreover, though American socialists in the main avow themselves followers of Marx, they

have much modified his theories of labor and value.
They recognize distinctly the high value of mental labor,
the importance of direction in all industrial undertakings, and maintain that means must be found to promote
and reward this kind of labor in the new social order.

"All men are born free and equal," as the Declaration
holds, only in the sense that all are born equally men.
Because of this common manhood, each person who comes
into the world has an equal right with all others to the
life of a man, and to all that constitutes such a life.   The
"equality" contemplated by the socialist is equality of
obligation to one's fellows, to be a producer of wealth
according to ability; and society is under a correlate
obligation to guarantee to every human being who fulfils
his duty such a share of the common wealth as shall make
possible to him a life worthy of his manhood.   There
surely cannot be a nobler ideal of human existence, so
far as its material conditions are concerned, than this.
Contrast it with these facts from the census of 1900:
nine-tenths of one per cent of the population of the
United States owned 70.5 per cent of the wealth; 29
per cent owned 25.3 per cent of the wealth; while 70.1
per cent owned 4.2 per cent of the wealth.[1]   It would
be possible to furnish pages of such figures as these, as an

[1] These facts may be approximately indicated to the eye by a
diagram: —

Population		Wealth	
▬ 0.9		70.5	▬▬▬▬▬▬▬▬▬▬▬
▬▬▬▬▬ 29.0		25.3	▬▬▬▬
▬▬▬▬▬▬▬▬▬▬▬ 70.1		4.2	▬

explanation of the growth of Socialism in America, but to little purpose, for it is not enough for this or for any other worthy object merely to accumulate facts about society. Something is needed beyond an industrious observer, more even than an accurate observer. Not sight alone, but insight, must be our equipment for this study, if our results are to have any value. We shall find the spirit that moves society by a study of statistics and an analysis of social facts on the day after we discover faith, hope, and charity by the scalpel in the dissecting room.

American Socialism differs from European in that it has completely thrown off the notion that it is possible to reach the social millennium at one jump. It recognizes the folly of social Utopias, and maintains firmly that the hope of establishing a just social order lies in an evolution. It believes that there are signs all around us of a tendency in the direction of socializing industry, that may be hastened by effort and legislation, but that no sudden change to a new order is either possible or desirable. It recognizes frankly the difficulties in the way, and that time and gradual change are necessary to surmount them. It does not discourage present attempts to mitigate social suffering, provided these are recognized as palliatives, not as cures. Kind and considerate treatment of employees by employers will do much for the relief of misery, and is therefore worthy of encouragement, but it is absurd to expect from such means the removal of evils that are inherent in the capitalistic system.

Some socialists are far from cordial in their comments on the tendency among American millionnaires to devote a portion of their wealth to humanitarian enterprises —

R

hospitals, universities, libraries — and indignantly assert
that what they ask is not the doling out as "charity"
of some small part of unjustly gained wealth, but that the
power of one man to exploit another, being the tap-root
of social evils, must be abolished, and then there will be
no ill-gotten wealth and no need of charity.   This attitude cannot, however, be said to be characteristic of
American Socialism as a whole.   Rather there is a tendency to the calmer and more equitable view, that the
rich as well as the poor among us are the victims of the
social system, and powerless by themselves to cure its
evils.   The single employer can do as little as the single
employee to better the social order.   If he spends more
money on sanitation, if he employs fewer child workers,
if he pays higher than the market rate of wages, his cutthroat competitor will undersell him, and eventual bankruptcy will be the reward of his humane attempts.

But the employer can afford to support every law for
the betterment of the conditions of labor, because the law
will impose equal obligation on all his competitors.
This makes inexcusable the combination of capitalists
to resist, first the enactment, and then the enforcement
of labor-reform laws.   They have not even greed as an
excuse; it is pure inhumanity that actuates them, when
it is not blind conservatism.   But even when capitalists
favor labor legislation, the principle is still valid that, as
society as a whole has made existing institutions, society
as a whole must unmake them and remake them; and
in the meantime individuals are responsible only for making existing conditions as workable, as little oppressive,
as may be.   There is, in this view of the case, a large
field for private action looking toward the amelioration

of social conditions, while we all await, and hasten if we can, the evolution that is to result in permanent and complete betterment.

It is because of this faith in an evolution of the new social order out of existing elements, that the attitude of socialists toward the Trusts differs so widely from the attitude of the average American. Unless he is personally interested in some Trust, or is in friendly relations to some one who is personally interested, the man in the street is opposed to all Trusts. He favors every legislative measure that will limit their powers and dissolve their combinations of capital. He scorns the distinction sometimes made between the good Trusts and the bad — he believes them all bad, all formed to limit production, eliminate competition and impose higher prices on the consumer, and all, therefore, more or less setting at defiance the principles of the common law and innumerable statutes, that every combination in restraint of trade is illegal. His favorite political leader is one who has a reputation as a "Trust-buster." This same average American still believes that it is possible to pass some law, and to get some court to enforce it, by which the Trusts shall be dissolved, and the old era of competition be restored.

The socialist, on the other hand, sees in this development of the Trust an inevitable stage in the evolution of industrial society, and does not believe that any such forward step can ever be retraced. He can cite some impressive facts in support of his view. The oldest of the Trusts, the Standard Oil, was formed some thirty years ago, and ever since then the American people have been trying to secure its dissolution, yet it has grown larger and more powerful every year. More than twenty years ago, as organized in the States of Ohio and New York, it was declared illegal and commanded by the courts to dissolve. It obeyed, and immediately perfected another and more efficient organization under the laws of New Jersey. In May, 1911, it was again pronounced illegal and commanded to dissolve, by the decision of the Supreme Court of the United States. But months before it was announced that, if such a decision should be rendered, the stock of the fifty or more sub-companies will be distributed *pro rata* among the shareholders of the New Jersey concern. Ownership of the sub-companies will be as consolidated as ever, and competition will not be promoted in the least.

It is not likely that any legal ingenuity can contrive an Antitrust law that other legal ingenuity cannot evade. The Sherman law is a "rainbow-chaser," to borrow a picturesque phrase from current politics. We are not likely to go back to an era of competition, but are in all likelihood going forward to still greater consolidation. The trend of economic development is unmistakable, the advantages of consolidation are incontestable, and the force of the movement is irresistible. No law or combination of laws can do more, probably, than disturb conditions and delay progress. The breaking down of the high tariff wall might lead to the dissolution of certain Trusts, by bringing in foreign competition, but even this is doubtful; for, in the case of such alteration of the tariff, the next step would be international consolidation of industries, which is already in sight for some and, in any case, not far off for all.

Socialists recognize this inevitable trend of industrial

development, and see in it the first step to complete socialization of industry. They expect, and even hope, that the development will go on; that it will with every successive year become plainer to the people that no step backward is possible; that the Trusts cannot be legislated out of existence, but must continue to become more numerous and more powerful, until practically all branches of industry are "trustified." This is even now accompanied with inconvenience and suffering. The cost of living is soaring aloft at a rate that makes it increasingly difficult for the poor to command even the necessaries of life, to say nothing of luxuries. Capital is becoming consolidated until the most careless observer must feel alarmed at the power thus lodged in a few hands, irresponsible and unchecked in the use of this tremendous weapon for good or evil. Venice, with its oligarchy of nobles, its Council of Ten, stands as an example of the worst kind of despotism under the forms of republican government known in history. We, too, are a republic, but to-day ten men can sit around a table in New York and dictate the business policy of the nation; they can precipitate or stop a panic; they wield a power greater than that of the government of the United States, and are responsible to none but themselves, save for that indefinable yet real check on all power that we name public opinion. They can do all this, they have done and are doing all this, because of the wealth they control, — three-fourths of the entire wealth of our country. The life and fortune of half the voters of the United States are at this moment at the mercy of these ten men.

How long, asks the socialist, will the liberty-loving people of America endure this state of things, when they

once comprehend it ?   Will they not insist on taking into
their own hands this power, power that belongs to them,
since they and not these ten men have created this
wealth ?   Will they not insist that these great industries,
already so largely socialized, shall be completely socialized ?
Will they not see that it is better for the nation at large,
that the people themselves should assume the ownership
and management of industries, than to permit them to
remain in private hands ;   that industrial enterprises
should be conducted for the good of all, and not for the
profit of a few ?   And above all, will not the people see
clearly before long that, unless this is done, it will be
absurd to talk longer about "free America" — that continued freedom, in any real sense, is impossible under
such a system ?

We must in fairness consider the general denial of the
Trusts, that the rise in prices and the increased cost of
living is due to their agency.   The combination of pack-
ers popularly known as the Meat Trust, for example,
would persuade us that the high prices of meats should
be ascribed to anything and everything else than to them
— to the increased production of gold,[1] or to a decrease
in production, or to an increase of consumers, or to the
exactions of middlemen and retailers.   It is possible,
probable even, that most of these reasons for an advance
in prices have a foundation of fact; but from this
concession must be excepted the supposed decrease in
production, if figures collected by the Department of

---

[1] There can be little doubt that this is an important factor in the rise
of prices.   In 1909 the production of gold amounted to $450,000,000,
which was four times the annual average from 1860 to 1890.   This enormous production of gold has made a "back number" of the silver question, which so recently as 1896 was convulsing the nation.

Agriculture are to be trusted. The increase in cattle, other than milch cows, during the decade from 1900 to 1910, was more than 76 per cent, while the population could not have increased more than 10 per cent. During the same period, swine increased 40 per cent. On the other hand, the increase in cattle and hogs actually slaughtered was about 20 per cent during the same period. Evidence of deliberate manipulation to control the market could hardly be plainer than is afforded by these official figures. The American people are not fools: they know that no Trust or combination was ever formed for any other purpose than the prevention of competition and the increase of prices.

It is inconceivable that Americans will be long content to live under this new despotism, even though it is administered, to quote the now famous words of President Baer, of the Reading Railway, by "the Christian men to whom God, in his infinite wisdom, has given the control of the property interests of the country." If these be Christian men, the people are saying, then bring on your heathen! The truth is, that men of the Baer type have got God and the devil hopelessly mixed in their thinking. The divine right of kings, after desperate and prolonged struggles that wrecked many a throne, has passed into oblivion; the divine right of Capital, though still believed by some and advocated by not a few, is doomed to the same fate.

IV

But is Socialism all in the air? some will ask. Is there nothing more definite than vague hopes and aspirations, or empty academic discussions? What do American socialists propose to do — sit still and wait for the millennium to come? Some have even suspected that socialists are opposed to practical reforms, lest these should have a tendency to lessen the existing discontent; in other words, their policy is to refuse the half loaf, lest its acceptance cost the remainder. This, if it were true of any considerable number of socialists, would be a shortsighted policy; for there is a motive to progress at least as strong as dissatisfaction, and that is, satisfaction. Discontent might conceivably be greatly lessened by legislation; but might not a people, like an individual, be so well pleased by one step in advance, as to insist on taking a second, and a third, and so on indefinitely? Throwing a bone to a dog may not satisfy his appetite, but only give him a desire for more; and those who think of reforms as merely a means of occupying the attention of a dangerous populace, and would concede a few for that purpose, may discover too late for their own comfort that they have whetted, not appeased, a hunger.

The more thoughtful socialists of America respond to the challenge to propose a policy, by sketching a sufficiently definite programme of immediate reforms to be attempted. Not all of these are peculiarly socialistic; some are favored by socialists mainly because they promise to smooth the way for the advance of Socialism. But, at any rate, one who examines the list will no longer say of Socialism that it is vague and indefinite. These practical reforms may be considered under three separate heads.

One class of reforms demanded may be called political. In a genuine democracy, the laws must reflect the popu-

lar will. But our experience with representative government has proved beyond a doubt that representatives do
not represent, that the will of the people is as often
thwarted as executed in legislation. Shall not the people
themselves be permitted to decide whether an important
measure shall or shall not be law? Their right to decide
is recognized in the matter of amending the fundamental
law, the constitution; why should it not be recognized
in statute law? This is the *referendum*, or submission
to popular vote of all important statutes, or of any statute that a certain proportion of the voters by petition
demand to have submitted. Then, too, in a genuine
democracy, the people must have the power not only to
prevent the legislation to which they are opposed, but
to secure the legislation that they desire. Our so-called
representatives now defeat the popular desire by the
simple expedient of promising laws before election, and
doing nothing after election to procure their enactment.
Giving the people this power is the *initiative*, the right of
the people to say at any regular election, that a certain
statute shall be enacted by the legislature. And then
supposing the faithless representatives still fail to fulfil
their pledges, or any officer elected by the people is de-
linquent in his duty? One more weapon it is proposed
to put into the hands of the people, the *recall*,[1] so that if a
man chosen by the people to do their will turns out at any
stage of his service to be a thief or a "crook" or a traitor,
the same people who voted him into office may vote him
out again, and at once, instead of being compelled as

---

[1] The first case of the successful use of the "recall" occurred in Seattle,
Wash., where the mayor was removed in February, 1911, for incompe-
tence, abuse of the appointive power, and failure to enforce the laws.

now to wait until he has served his full term, and replace him with a man who may prove to be no better.

Some of our States have already adopted one or more of these methods, and a considerable number are pledged to give them a trial.[1]   They have not yet had a sufficient trial to determine their value in promoting a pure democracy; and from Switzerland, where they originated, comes conflicting testimony as to their efficiency.   Such political reforms are, in any case, rather the necessary preliminaries to Socialism, than Socialism itself.   Political democracy once attained, social democracy will follow as fast as the people are educated to demand it. This is the chief reason why these political reforms are made part of the socialistic programme.

A second series of reforms might be classified as fiscal. Socialists demand the abolition of all indirect taxes. Many who are not socialists admit that there are strong reasons in favor of direct taxes.   If citizens knew exactly what they were paying for the support of government, and knew when they were paying it, they would have a strong motive to enforce honesty and economy in governmental affairs.   The favorite argument for indirect taxes is, that "people do not feel them," but that is really the strongest argument against them.   A tax ought to be felt.   Indirect taxes make it easy to deceive the citizen

[1] Up to the close of 1910 the status of these reforms was as follows: Maine, Missouri, Arkansas, Oklahoma, South Dakota, Nevada, Oregon, and Montana have the initiative and referendum in their constitutions. Both reforms are pledged by both parties in Nebraska, Wisconsin, Illinois, Colorado, California, North Dakota, Kansas, Massachusetts, and are therefore virtually adopted by those States.   One party has pledged them in Idaho, Wyoming, Washington, Utah, Minnesota, Iowa, and Ohio, and in these States their fate may be said to be uncertain.

as to the cost of government, and so lessen his scrutiny of expenditures. They are the stronghold of all sorts of corruption. Moreover, being taxes on consumption, they fall most heavily on the small homes, on the people least able to bear them, and thus violate the fundamental principle of taxation, that it should be proportioned to ability to pay. No iniquity of a protective tariff is so great as this; what it may accomplish in the fostering of Trusts is a mere bagatelle by comparison with this wholesale plundering of the poor.

Socialists would collect all revenues for common expenses by three kinds of direct taxes: a poll tax, a progressive income tax, and a progressive inheritance tax. Such a fiscal policy would lay the burden of government on the people who are best able to bear it, by taxing men in proportion to their ability to pay and not in proportion to their necessity to consume. Socialists do not favor the Henry George idea of a single tax, levied on land, save as a temporary expedient. This is because, in their view, rent is one form of exploitation of the laborer that Socialism looks forward to abolishing; and so a system of taxation based on the rental value of land could only be temporary, and a mere amelioration of existing evils, not a permanent cure. Let no one who has not given much study to the question reply to these proposals that the revenue to be reasonably expected from these three sources would be inadequate; any one who has studied the matter will be in no danger of making such reply.[1]

[1] Those who are fond of mathematical computations may see the working out of a scheme for a progressive inheritance tax, and a demonstration of its extreme fruitfulness of revenue, as well as its inevitable effect on social inequalities, in Newton Mann's "Import and Outlook of Socialism," p. 130 *et seq.*

There is no question as to the effectiveness of the taxes, or as to their incidence. It has not escaped the notice of any reader, probably, that the rich and well-to-do object strenuously to an income tax, which shows precisely where *that* shoe would pinch. The same people object to the progressive inheritance tax that it is confiscation.

The socialist would greatly diminish the necessity of taxes by the immediate abolition of all standing armies and navies. These armaments, he believes, have grown out of the capitalistic system, which inevitably leads to clashes between nations. With the coming of Socialism and the disappearance of private capital, the motive for wars will disappear, and the need of armaments with it. It may be said in passing that this contention of socialists as to the capitalistic origin of all wars is not wholly convincing as a historical generalization, and this defect throws some doubt on the prophecy that wars will disappear with private capital. Why do savage tribes fight?

The third class of reforms urged by socialists are economic, and all have to do with some method of immediately improving the conditions of industrial and social life. The moral necessity of such reforms, as well as the economic, must be admitted. There is much force in the contention of socialist writers that for the average man at least, experience shows it is not enough for him to have the will to be good — he must have a fair opportunity also. And while it would doubtless not be true to say of the average man that at present he has no opportunity to be good, it is well within the facts to say that he has far less than he should have, far less than he needs.

This is not to assent to the argument of Bax, the English socialist, in his "Ethics of Socialism," that men can cultivate the highest ideals only when their bodies are comfortable; that is, well fed, well clothed, and well housed. Virtue, he urges, cannot be expected in those who are struggling for existence. To which the reply is, that all depends on who is struggling. The whole history of asceticism, in all ages and religions, teaches that the highest ideals of conduct and character may be successfully cultivated, independent of bodily comfort.[1] Not merely in Christianity, but in many religions, it has been repeatedly demonstrated that the higher life is compatible with an endurance of hunger, cold, and squalor, compared to which the poverty of a New York or London slum is luxury. Nay, millions of men believe to-day, mistakenly though firmly, that this is the only way by which the highest spiritual life may be attained. It is not because the working-classes feel the pinch of want that they are not more spiritual. There is no man to-day that labors with his hands, who is so poorly clothed and fed as were Bernard of Clairvaux and Francis of Assisi.

But let us ask what are the actual betterments proposed for the working-man, and return later to the spiritual question. A series of measures comprised under the general head of factory reform are proposed for immediate enactment: such as shorter hours of work wherever possible; more effective restriction of child labor; better protection of women laborers, especially prohibition of excessively long hours; better lighting, ventilation, and sanitation of factories and workshops. The better hous-

[1] It is only fair to Bax to add that he attempts to break the force of this testimony of asceticism, but without avail — it is fatal to his theory.

ing of laborers is another measure of reform demanded. Surely all these are sufficiently definite and practical, and without exception, they appeal to the general sense of justice of the people at large.   Here is a field in which Socialism and Christian philanthropy may find common ground of activity, without first settling or even trying to settle the philosophy of the social system.   It is well to note again, however, that the socialist looks on these measures as merely palliative, not as constituting substantial relief of the grievance of the working-classes.

It is also worth noting that some of these things have already been attempted, and even partially achieved, in certain States of the Union, not as a step towards Socialism, but as things just and wise in themselves.   Laws against child labor have been enacted in many States, and are vigorously pressed in the South at the present time. Oregon has passed a statute forbidding the employment of women more than ten hours a day, and the Supreme Court of the United States has sustained it as constitutional.   A similar statute has been passed in Illinois, but the Circuit Court of Cook County granted an injunction against its enforcement.   The Illinois Manufacturers Association is aiding the efforts of individual employers to nullify the law, on the ground that the sacred individual right to freedom of contract is infringed by it.   England and some of the continental States of Europe are far in advance of the United States in protecting women from overwork, and so protecting the public health.[1]

[1] Not long ago ex-President Theodore Roosevelt committed himself to this public statement: "In legislation and in our use of safety devices for the protection of workmen, we are far behind European peoples, and in consequence, in the United States, the casualties attendant upon peaceful industries exceed those which would happen under great per-

Certain Christian moralists, like Professor Flint in his book on "Socialism," are inclined to disparage all such remedial measures, on the ground that "the great bulk of human misery is due, not to social arrangements, but to personal vices." It is the old theological notion, persisting in religious circles, that everything out of joint in the social system is to be charged up to an indefinite and all-pervasive agency known as "sin." Sin in the abstract never harms society; it is when some definite person commits a precise evil act that harm is done to himself and others. And so the socialist is prone to go to the opposite extreme, and make the social order responsible for all forms of wrong-doing, almost to the elimination of personal agency and personal responsibility. To men like Professor Flint, the Wise Man spoke the whole truth when he said that "the destruction of the poor is their poverty"; for their poverty he believed them to be responsible, and from it all might escape if they would be virtuous, industrious, and frugal. The socialist holds that poverty grips most of the poor with tentacles from which they cannot free themselves, by which they are dragged down to disease and death, and that vice is largely the desperate attempt of the victims to seek some temporary relief for their sufferings, some compensation for their misery.

Probably there will never be agreement between schools of thought so fundamentally opposed; the difference is temperamental in part, and in part is due to differences

petual war." In 1911 the Court of Appeals of New York declared unconstitutional a statute for insurance of workmen against accidents, carefully drawn by some of the best legal talent of the State, and equally desired by employers and employees, on the ground that it deprived citizens of property without due process of law.

of experience and observation.   Many who once agreed
with Dr. Flint, as they have grown older and presumably wiser, and at any rate have observed more widely
for themselves, have come more and more to doubt his
contention.   Too many thoroughly industrious, temperate, honest, thrifty people are known to us, people
who have been unable by a lifetime of effort to rise above
poverty and have at times been reduced to real distress,
to make the Flint hypothesis credible.   Such people
failed of independence merely because they lacked the
money-making shrewdness, not to say unscrupulousness,
and for no other discoverable reason.   They could not
or would not successfully exploit their fellows; and, in
society as now organized, one must exploit or be exploited.

V

American politicians and newspapers frequently exhort
the people, with an earnestness little short of pathetic,
not to abandon their democratic inheritance for the
jack-o'-lantern of Karl Marx.   This but shows how blind
our political leaders and teachers are to the actual situation, and how little they comprehend the ideals and aims
of the socialist.   Socialists, whether followers of Marx
or otherwise, do not propose to abandon democracy, but
to realize it.   We have already seen how American democratic theory is contradicted by industrial fact; we
should note that it is hardly less contradicted by political
fact, and then we shall understand the recent growth of
a socialistic party in the United States.   We have always
heard that we live in a democracy, and under a representative form of government; and this has been so re-

iterated that we no more dream of doubting it than of doubting that we live in the Western hemisphere and a temperate climate. But if we lay aside political clap-trap and look resolutely and candidly at facts, not theories, we quickly learn that we are living under the least democratic system in the civilized world, outside of Russia.

Our fathers, who made the constitutions under which we live and try to do business, were deeply suspicious of the people; and they introduced into our political system a number of ingenious checks and balances that should prevent the popular will from getting itself executed — so far as such a result was possible in a state where every free male adult was a voter. The people were not permitted to choose a President directly, but an electoral college was interposed between them and the executive office. We have overcome this barrier to the popular will by our extra-constitutional device of a nominating convention and the reduction of the electoral college to a mere register of the popular vote by states. But it is still possible, under this clumsy and antiquated system, for a President to be elected by the votes of a minority of the people. Is that representative government?

The Supreme Court of the United States — within certain limits, and those limits mainly defined by itself — is the highest power in our government: above the President, above the Congress, and, of course, above the governors and legislatures of the several States. It has the power to annul any statute, or so to "interpret" it as to give a meaning never intended by lawmakers, whether enacted by State or Federal legislative body, and

s

few years pass without the exercise of such power. In every other nation, the will of the people, expressed in statute law, is supreme; in our "democratic" country, the will of the people does not obtain if five men in Washington say Nay. And these omnipotent judges are totally irresponsible to the people, who have no voice in their selection and can do nothing to secure their removal, since the Constitution provides that, once appointed, they shall serve for life or during good behavior. In all the States, also, the people were originally not suffered to elect their judges; but against this they revolted, and most judges are now elected for limited terms, though long. Yet, in spite of this reform, the most important part of our national government, the judiciary, is an oligarchy of the most pronounced type.

The Federal Senate does not represent the people; the exact fact is, that the people are misrepresented by the Senate. This, not merely because that body has come to consist almost wholly of plutocrats and their willing tools, but from the very constitution of the Senate. How ridiculous to call a legislative house representative, even if it were democratic, to which twenty-five States, that have one-sixth of the entire population, send fifty out of ninety-two Senators! One-sixth of the people outvote the other five-sixths, inevitably, on every measure proposed in the Senate. This is an evil inseparable from our system, and incurable except by constitutional amendment, for which the requisite majority of States can probably never be secured, because these twenty-five States will never voluntarily surrender the great advantage thus given them. But the fathers made the matter still worse by denying to the people the right to elect

Senators, directing the legislatures of the several States to perform this duty. As in the case of the electoral college, the people are showing themselves resolved to take and exercise this power by another extra-constitutional device: nominating Senators in primaries and securing pledges from candidates for the legislature to vote for such nominees. In this way, several States have already established the election of Senators by popular vote, and the Senate is in fair way to become as nearly a representative body as the Constitution will permit.

It is not surprising that a body, not representative, and not democratic, should have fallen under the domination of Capitalism, and that 60 per cent of the Senate to-day is composed of millionnaires and corporation lawyers. But it is surprising that in the House of Representatives, which might easily be made both representative and democratic, virtually the same proportion of rich men and lawyers should be found. For this result the voters have nobody to blame but themselves; the remedy is in their own hands. If they like to be governed by laws enacted by such representatives, there is nothing more to be said. But why should a people let themselves be persuaded or cozened into electing representatives of this kind, and go on proudly asserting that this is a democracy? Why should they send capitalists and corporation lawyers to Washington to make their laws, and then marvel that legislation for the conservation of the people's rights and interests is so hard to procure? The real marvel should be that popular legislation is not altogether impossible.

And this is to take no account of the fact that for many years past the House of Representatives has been pre-

sided over by a speaker as autocratic as a Tsar, and quite
as powerful, though himself controlled by a capitalistic
clique, — a man to whom the President himself must
come, hat in hand and with bated breath, if he would
have any law enacted in which he happens to be especially
interested.

> Upon what meat doth this our Cæsar feed,
> That he is grown so great?

Between our fathers' uneasy suspicion of what we might
do, and what in our folly we have actually done, we, the
American people, find ourselves tied like Gulliver in
Lilliput, and as little able as he to help ourselves or punish our foes.

In no other country where the rights of the people are
recognized at all, are the rights and interests of the people less protected; in no other country is the will of the
people so nearly a negligible quantity. And Americans
are themselves at fault, because they are so unintelligent
in political affairs. They wilfully refuse to see themselves
and their political institutions as they are, but insist on
living in a political fool's paradise, blinding themselves
to the realities and encouraging themselves in compla-
cence by a parrot-repetition of venerable phrases and
theories; and each year they meekly step up to the polls
and vote to continue this order of things, which they
have the power to end any day they choose. Apparently
they will never be convinced, save by bitter experience,
of the error of their ways, and they are likely to have
plenty of experience. They are beginning to feel severely
the pinch of the purse, yet they still refuse to open their
eyes. Very well, one is inclined to say, let them feel;

it is good for their souls. By and by, when they have been squeezed hard enough, until they have been made to shed not only tears but blood, they will recognize the true source of their evils and begin in earnest to abate them.

Slowest of all to see how they have been exploited by the politician, as well as by the capitalist, have been the workmen of America. Have they no perception, have they no logic, have they no sense? Will they permit themselves forever to be treated as dumb, driven cattle by political bosses? Will they continue to believe that a high tariff is maintained for their benefit, when they know well that the interest of capitalists is to make wages as low as possible? Will they continue to believe that the interest in high wages for them, which employers manifest so touchingly just before each important election, is consistent with the constant stream of cheap labor kept pouring into this country by capitalists, mostly in direct and shameful violation of the immigration laws? One hardly knows which is the more culpable, the hypocrisy of the capitalists or the gullibility of the workmen; but the latter is beyond controversy the more surprising, and the more shameful. For "there's a reason" for the attitude of the capitalist; the conduct of the workmen is the essence of unreason.

It was a dim appreciation of some of these facts, together with the disillusionment of those who had hoped for a real betterment of the workers' condition, that led to the organization of the Working-men's Party in 1876. The following year the name was changed to the Socialist Labor Party. Before this time the political efforts of working-men in the direction of Socialism have only a historic interest, and little even of that. For twenty years the Socialist Labor Party was the dominant factor in such progress as was made, a progress much limited by the fact that the leaders of the movement, as well as most of the followers, were of foreign birth and education. The result was naturally a small party, with little influence and fewer votes. The difficulty of making an advance was soon apparent, and every method was tried of enlisting the interest of native American working-men. So little success rewarded these efforts for a time that the general propaganda was practically abandoned in favor of an attempt to win over the trades-unions. The latter, however, had been so sedulously instructed that it was their duty to "keep out of politics," that this work made exceedingly slow progress. Even now, some of the most trusted leaders of the working-men cling to this policy of aloofness from politics — men like Samuel Gompers — regardless of the teaching of experience.

Some humorist has restated an old proverb in these terms: "Experience keeps a dear school, but it delivers the goods." Not always; some people cannot be taught, even by experience. In the struggle of unionism against capitalism, unionism seems certain to be defeated as long as the struggle is economic and financial only. When labor was first organized and capital was unorganized, it steadily gained, even though it sometimes sustained notable defeat. When capital became organized, labor was able to win only in a small way and under specially favoring circumstances. Between 1881 and 1900 there were 22,793 strikes, big and little, of which 50.77 per cent were successful, while 13.04 per cent partially succeeded, and 36.19 wholly failed. These, which are official figures furnished by the Bureau of Labor, seem at first sight to be quite favorable to labor. But the successful strikes were all small affairs. The great strikes during that period, where large numbers of well-organized men were arrayed against large aggregations of capital, were disastrous failures. The strike on the Gould system of railways, in 1885, failed. The great strike of telegraphers against the Western Union, in 1883, failed. The steel workers' strike at Homestead, in 1892, failed. The switchmen's strike at Buffalo, in August of the same year, failed. The carworkers' strike at Pullman, in 1884, failed. The great coal strike, of 1902, was saved from failure only by the interposition of President Roosevelt. There was one success in the great strikes during all this time, that on the Great Northern Railroad, in 1884.

The reason for this failure of working-men is that they were, in all these cases, accepting the present industrial order and fighting Capitalism on its own ground, but with greatly inferior weapons. Working-men are surprised and enraged whenever they are defeated in a great strike; what should surprise them is that they ever win. They are joining in the selfish scramble of the competitive system, with the odds greatly against them. They pit themselves at the swill-tub against hogs who have all the advantage of long possession, of being strong and well-fed, and of knowing all the tricks of the game, while they are weak, hungry, ignorant, and on the outside. The unions have been meeting competition with competition, monopoly with monopoly, tyranny with the boycott. It is war to the knife, and the knife up to the hilt, with *Vae victis* as the motto. The unions sometimes win a battle; they have never won a campaign.

Yet, impervious to the lessons of experience, the unions go on in the same old way, challenging capital to a conflict where capital is invincible, save through its own blunders, and refusing to fight capital where it is vulnerable, at the ballot box. In the ballot, the American working-man has a weapon that will insure him victory, whenever he has intelligence enough to use it. Capitalism is not afraid of strikes; it dreads the ballot, and does everything in its power to corrupt the suffrage and hinder the expression of the people's will. For Capitalism understands thoroughly what the working-man has never yet been able to comprehend, the power of the ballot. Capitalism asks nothing better than the continuance of the Gompers ideas and the Gompers policy. For that means, in the long run, the defeat of the working-men, who are morally certain to lose as often as they measure strength with capital in a great industrial contest.

But to return to our Social Labor Party. Its greatest and most dangerous antagonist proved to be the Revolutionary Socialist Party, founded by John Most, in 1881. This was really an anarchist organization, as its avowed principles showed, and Anarchy, though often confounded with Socialism, has little resemblance to it — is really its antipodes. The Haymarket affair in Chicago, in May, 1886, showed what Anarchy really meant and ended its open propagation for many years. Just as the Socialist Labor Party was rallying from this check, it was diverted from its proper purpose by the movement in New York City that resulted in the campaign of Henry George for mayor. Mr. George was not a socialist, except as to private property in land. He saw in the appropriation of land to private ownership the fundamental factor in social wrongs, and rent seemed to him the most serious form of the exploitation of the poor by the rich. He was blind to the at-least-equal evil of private ownership of tools and machinery, the factory system, nor did he see that interest and profit are as deadly means of exploitation as rent. But he favored socialization of land, through the confiscation of rent in the form of taxation, at the same time refusing to consider the remedy of socializing the other means of production. In other words, George advocated a strictly limited form of Socialism, while the Socialist Labor Party stood for a more thoroughgoing Socialism. George would abolish the landlords, but continue the capitalist, thus affording the exploited but a partial measure of relief.

But, since he did advocate some relief, and since his candidacy offered the working-men a good opportunity to "stand up and be counted," the Socialist Labor Party gave him a hearty support. He was defeated, possibly by the fraudulent counting of the vote, as his followers alleged, and this result gave the Socialist Labor Party a severe check. Nevertheless, they had the courage to nominate a Presidential ticket in 1892, and polled 21,512 votes, which increased in 1896 to 36,275, and in 1898 to 82,204. Several parties of socialists, under various names, have since then risen and declined, but the greatest success has been won by the Socialist Party, which came to the front in 1901, and polled 409,230 votes in 1904, and 420,793 in 1908. At recent elections immense gains have been made by socialists in the Middle West. In 1904 five socialists were elected to the Wisconsin legislature, and two in Illinois. In the spring of the same year, socialists elected nine aldermen in Milwaukee, and in 1910 they elected a mayor, who has accomplished the apparently impossible feat of enforcing the law against the saloons and other haunts of vice in that city.   Twelve other cities in 1911 elected socialist mayors.

These facts give some slight indication of what the working-men might accomplish, if they had but the practical sense to unite and vote for their own interests, instead of combining to support parties controlled by capital, as they have thus far continued to do.   When they show as much political insight, and as much class solidarity, as the English working-men are beginning to show, they will receive from politicians equal respect.   So long as the capitalists, and their political henchmen, can continue to hoodwink and deceive the American working-men, so long will working-men and their interests be treated by every politician with the contempt that they will deserve.

There are, however, other criteria by which the progress of Socialism should be judged, besides the number of votes polled by its candidates.   There are over fifty newspapers and periodicals published in the interests of Socialism, of which half are printed in foreign languages. Many of the organs of trade-unions are now giving at least a qualified approval to Socialism — teaching the principles, though holding aloof from the organization. A considerable native literature of Socialism in book form also exists, and is increasing in volume from year to year.   While the foreign-born element is still strong in the ranks, perhaps a numerical majority, the influential leaders are now of American birth — men of intelligence and broad education.   Socialism is winning every year recruits among the thoughtful and scholarly class of Americans, to whom it becomes increasingly plain that the capitalistic system is as much their enemy as it is the enemy of the manual worker. The ethical appeal of Socialism affects strongly the professional class, who do not respond readily to motives of personal or class interest. It thus far appeals least to those whom it promises most. There is no real solidarity among working-men; they are divided into a multitude of cliques, with conflicting aims; and underneath their cant of brotherhood is a bitter and selfish strife of the cliques. Only a common enemy and a common danger produces even a semblance of union among them.

Nor has Socialism thus far made any noteworthy progress among the other class that would be most affected by it, the farmers. Tillers of the soil have always been a conservative class, and they need to be convinced that the social revolution is for their benefit, and that their interests would be protected. There is little prospect of a successful revolution without their coöperation; their mere passive resistance, as Jaurès has pointed out, would be enough to defeat such a revolution. Ultimate socialization of the land is part of any socialistic programme; but it does not follow that the reorganization of the social system need begin at that point. It would not be necessary, and, as a practical measure, it would be manifestly unwise, to attempt the complete socialization of land at first; but the unearned increment should be taken for the community that has produced it, as one of the first measures of socialistic advance. Land would then have value merely for occupation and use, and this would be greatly to the advantage of the farmer class.   French and German socialists are making more effort than English or American to convince the small proprietor that the coming social revolution will do him good, not harm — that socialization of the land means the expropriation of the large proprietor, not the small.   Far from depriving the peasant proprietor or small farmer of his land, socialists propose to guarantee him its possession.   American socialists must follow in this line, for their cause is hopeless if they provoke the antagonism of the farmer.   He is not as yet antagonistic, but neither has his support been secured.

The future of Socialism in America depends, apart from irresistible forces of evolution, on an intelligent and persistent propaganda.   Socialists assure us that the interests of all the people, except about two hundred thousand proprietors and hangers-on, are bound up with the success of the revolution.   It ought, therefore, to be comparatively easy to win the vast majority of the people to a programme so obviously in their interest.   So long as only a small minority hold the ideas of Socialism, no progress can be expected save by the slow method of evolution ; a successful revolution, no matter how gradual and peaceful, must have behind it the will of the majority.   Socialism is gaining converts rapidly ; it is "in the air."   What a few thought yesterday, the world thinks to-day.   And what the world thinks to-day, is what the world will do to-morrow.

VIII

THE IDEALS OF SOCIALISM — ARE THEY PRACTICABLE?

BIBLIOGRAPHY

Sympathetic and favorable expositions: —
THOMPSON, Constructive Programme of Socialism. Milwaukee,
 1908.
MANN, Import and Outlook of Socialism. Boston, 1910.
HILLQUIT, Socialism in Theory and Practice. New York, 1909.
BELLAMY, Looking Backward. Boston, 1888.
BAX, Ethics of Socialism, "Social Science Series," 1907.
——, Religion of Socialism, ib. 1888.
BEBEL, Woman under Socialism. New York, 1910.
RUSKIN, Unto this Last.
GHENT, Mass and Class. New York, 1905.

Critical and hostile: —
WILSON, The Menace of Socialism. New York, 1909.
MALLOCK, A Critical Examination of Socialism. New York, 1907.
The Case against Socialism: a Handbook for Speakers and Can-
 didates. New York, 1909.
LE ROSSIGNOL, Orthodox Socialism: a Criticism. New York,
 1907.

Books on related topics: —
KOREN, Economic Aspects of the Liquor Problem. Boston, 1889.
HOPKINS, Wealth and Waste. New York, 1902.
WARNER, Social Welfare and the Liquor Problem. New York,
 1909.
REEVE, The Cost of Competition. New York, 1906.
GILMAN, Women and Economics. New York, 1902.

VIII

THE IDEALS OF SOCIALISM — ARE THEY PRACTICABLE?

I

SOCIAL discontent, properly understood, is a symptom of social health, an index of the progress of mankind. The man of to-day is a larger man than the man of fifty years ago; he is more intelligent, he is more aspiring; as a member of a more complex society, he has more wants and is dissatisfied with a standard of living that would have more than satisfied his grandfather. What makes his discontent acute is his perception of the fact that, under present industrial conditions, no effort of his can make possible to the average man the reasonable satisfaction of his new wants. Our newspaper humorists jest at the man who has "champagne tastes and a beer income," but the jocular phrase aptly describes the larger part of society to-day — all, in fact, but those who have the wealth to buy the "champagne."

The progress of civilization has consisted in the attainment of greater liberty, the successful effort of man to free himself from the restraints by which he finds himself surrounded — restraints of physical environment, restraints from his fellows, restraints of ignorance. He has progressed in civilization as he has conquered nature, established social order, and gained knowledge. With the conquest of nature has come leisure, order has given security, knowledge makes culture possible. Leisure, security, and culture are the ideals of civilization. But as yet these blessings are very imperfectly possessed, and very inequally distributed so far as possessed. Leisure is the possession only of the idle rich and the idle poor; security is the possession of any only in a relative degree; culture is possible only to the favored few. No liberty is worth having that does not bestow all three upon all. Socialism has as its ideal, in a word, the completion of what civilization has only well begun.

The present great obstacle to further progress, socialists find in Capitalism, and the competitive system that Capitalism implies and compels. Society has been struggling for ages towards the complete elimination of private war, of personal strife among men, and the attainment of absolute security of person from violence and property from robbery. The age-long struggle is not yet crowned with entire success, but, as compared with the state of barbarism from which mankind has risen, the end has been measurably attained; what we call law and order has taken the place of constant strife and violence and robbery. But society has permitted strife to continue between men in the realm of industry, and has even encouraged it. While personal violence was condemned from prehistoric times, and private war was allowed only during the prevalence of feudalism, and now the educated Christian conscience declares that even international war is wrong, industrial war is declared by that same conscience to be not only right but necessary, and even laudable. The majority of Christians refuse to believe that any better system is possible.

Society exists for the development of the race by

mutual aid and coöperation. Competition is therefore necessarily antisocial.[1] Society strives for the greatest good of all; competition means the greatest good of the smallest number. Competition inevitably makes for the things that disintegrate society and hinder the upward march of humanity. It is the flat denial of the Golden Rule. No Christian can defend competition without intellectual and moral *hara-kiri*. And the antichristian and antisocial character of competition is equalled only by its anti-economic character. The iniquity of Capitalism, even as described by its severest critics, is surpassed by its stupidity. For the competitive system is a system of wanton wastefulness. The only possible way by which a community can learn that it does not need more of a certain article is by producing more than it needs, and the process of learning drives employers into bankruptcy and employees into want. "Business" is nothing more than a gigantic gamble.

For this rule-of-thumb method Socialism proposes to substitute scientific methods: the definite ascertainment of the needs of the community, and the adjustment of production to need. Over-production, in any embarrassing sense, would be impossible under Socialism; because, though an exact adjustment of production to need would not be possible, any surplus of production in any single line during one year would be relatively small, and could mean only so much accumulated wealth for the whole community, and therefore so much less labor required in that line for the coming year. The waste of human energy and the cost of human agony that are inseparable

---

[1] This applies to all forms of hostile competition. Emulative competition is wholesome and ethical, and society should encourage it.

T

from the competitive system ought to be a sufficient motive to induce every man with a heart in his bosom to look favorably on any proposal for the coöperative, social production and distribution of wealth, and to inquire carefully into its merits.   Many a man excuses himself from this task on the ground that the present system, with its admitted evils, has also its good points.

For one thing, as the business man often complacently remarks, the competitive system "makes character." Yes, but what sort of character?   Can a really admirable sort of character be produced by a system that reduces the worker to an economic condition lower than prevailed in slavery?   For the slave had one great advantage over the working-man : he was never unemployed, and never lacked the necessaries of life.   The owner was compelled to feed his slaves, to clothe them, to provide them shelter, in order to secure their economic efficiency, and for the same reason he must care for them when they fell ill. The modern factory-owner is hampered by no such necessity of being humane for his own interest; when slow starvation or illness caused by insufficient clothing causes a worker to drop from the ranks, three others stand ready to take his place.   If the slave-holder failed in his obligations to his slaves, their labor became unprofitable; by neglecting his moral obligation to his employees, the modern factory-owner makes a great fortune.   In many important respects, the prevailing industrial system is less humane than a state of slavery. Only an advanced civilization, that boasts of liberty for all, is capable of condemning a willing worker to starve and shiver.   There is plenty of work to be done, but he cannot find it; there is plenty of food to be eaten, but he is denied it; the shops and warehouses are bursting with warm clothing, but he and his wife and babes can have none of it. Is it not a bitter irony to call such a state of things, which is chronic among us, a "social system"?

A rate of wages so low that it will drive men into crime and women into prostitution is declared by manufacturers and storekeepers to be absolutely necessary to the continuance of their business. If they raised wages, their competitors would underbid and undersell and eventually ruin them. They speak the truth: the continuance of "business" requires this awful sacrifice of human bodies and souls. As Charles Booth says, "Our modern system of industry will not work without some unemployed margin, some reserve of labor." Translated into plain words, that means: to keep the present system in working order, it is necessary to have in the United States about two million workers in a constant state of partial starvation, in order that they may be ready to compete with those employed and keep wages down to a standard that will be profitable to capital. The "scab" and the "open shop" are a necessity of "business." The mere statement of the thing, socialists believe, should be enough to convince any person of humane instincts that the present system is rotten and iniquitous to the very bottom, and must be reconstructed.

Thrift is no remedy for such social evils. Thrift will elevate a few individuals above the mass, but if it were generally practised it would reduce consumption and cause additional misery. We need a remedy that will produce more consumption, not less, by making it possible for more people to consume an amount equal to their reasonable wants. And, of course, we need a remedy that will stimulate production to the point of satisfying all reasonable wants. Competition is notoriously incapable of doing either; Socialism professes as its ideal the doing of both, and asserts its ability to accomplish both. Are not such claims worthy of impartial examination, rather than scornful rejection without inquiry?

We cannot hope for any essential modification of the present system through the efforts of good men. Not all capitalists are greedy and selfish; not all men engaged in competitive business are careless of every consideration save the making of the largest possible profit. Many men under the present system are actuated by lofty Christian principles, and are sincerely anxious for the welfare of their employees, and are honestly striving to do what is best for them, as well as best for themselves. But such men will necessarily be exceptions, under a system that is founded on greed and encourages every man to destroy his competitor. The heartiest of goodwill can do no more than palliate some of the worst evils of the present system. "We ought never to trust to the justice and humanity of men whose interests are furthered by injustice and cruelty. The slave-owner in America, the manufacturer in England, though they may be individually good men, will, nevertheless, as slave-owners and masters, be guilty of atrocities at which humanity shudders." These words are as true to-day as when they were spoken, in 1869, by J. A. Roebuck, the English agitator and economist.

Wealth, in the last analysis, is the power of controlling the services of others, through the possession of things that are objects of desire to others. Hence the accumulation of wealth in private hands is incompatible with equal liberty among men — it infallibly leads to the practical enslavement of the poor by the rich. The production and distribution of wealth must be controlled by society, or liberty is possible only to some, not to all. Hence the essential feature of all socialistic theories, however much they differ in details, is a system of coöperation based on the common ownership of land and capital. Private wealth is not so much prohibited as made practically impossible at the same time that the chief motives for the accumulation of private wealth are removed. This coöperative production and distribution of wealth is the economic goal of all Socialism, and the particular means of its attainment, by state action or otherwise, by quick revolution or slow evolution, are mere questions of detail not involving fundamental principle, but relating mainly to views of expediency or practicability.

Socialism is really based on two very simple principles : First, every man must work. In an ideal state of society, there can be no idle class. Every man comes into the world sentenced to hard labor for life. The noble, at one end of the social scale, and the tramp at the other, are equally parasites, consumers who do not produce, and must be eliminated. This is at once sensible and Christian. Daily bread is the product of daily labor; and only he can honestly offer the prayer, "Give us this day our daily bread," who is ready to do the work needed for its production. Paul correctly interprets this prayer when he says, "If a man will not work, neither shall he eat." Jesus is with the men who labor, not with the idlers who live on the labor of others. We need to learn that hereditary privileges that one has not earned, and that exempt him from the common lot, are not honorable but disgraceful; hereditary wealth, or wealth for which no adequate service has been rendered to society, is a badge of shame, not of honor.

The second principle is, that every man should enjoy the fruits of his labor, subject only to the superior rights of the whole community. What a man produces is justly liable to taxation for the general good, even more truly under a socialistic system than under the present, but it should not be wrested from him, as now, by those who are stronger than he. In other words, production, which is now mainly for the benefit of the landlord and capitalist, should be for the benefit of the producers, that is to say, of the entire community. Socialism involves, therefore, the abolition, not of capital, but of the capitalist. It would retain capital, but make it more effective for well-being by placing it under social control, and so "scatter plenty o'er a smiling land."

This great economic change, while it is justified and urged by economic considerations, has behind it ethical aims. The securing of plenty is only incidental; the elevation of man is the real aim. Wealth is only human character visualized. "Every atom of substance," says Ruskin, "of whatever kind, used or consumed, is so much human life spent; which, if it issue in the saving present life, or gaining more, is well spent, but if not, is either so much life prevented or so much slain." For the first time in the history of man, a revolution is proposed that has as its end not the substitution of one ruling class for another, but the destruction of class and the establishment of a universal humanity. It is often said of Socialism that it is the enemy of civilization; it claims instead to be the only true friend of civilization. Instead of leaving the benefits of human progress to be monopolized and enjoyed by a few, it proposes to extend them to all. Socialism is not even the enemy of aristocracy; it proposes to make it possible for all men to become aristocrats. A comfortable living will not make a gentleman, but you cannot have a gentleman without three generations of those who have lived in comfort. Socialism intends to supply the material basis without which aristocrats and gentlemen cannot be made.

Nietzsche and others have had much to say about the Superman whom the future is to produce, the man of to-day raised to the nth power, an exalted being who will express the capacity of the race for development. "A Superman, if you will," says Karl Kautsky, for the socialists, "not as an exception, but as a rule, a Superman as compared with his predecessors, but not as opposed to his comrades, a noble man who seeks his satisfaction, not by being great among crippled dwarfs, but great among the great, happy among the happy — who does not draw the feeling of his strength from the fact that he raises himself upon the bodies of the downtrodden, but because a union with his fellows gives him courage to dare the attainment of the highest tasks." Which offers the higher ethical ideal, Nietzsche or Kautsky?

II

The greater part of the critical objections made to the ideals of Socialism reduce themselves, on a slight examination, to variations of one formula: Socialism is merely a resplendent vision, a beautiful mirage, a perfect theory, but quite impossible of realization. In proof of the impracticability of Socialism, critics appeal to the irreconcilable differences between socialists; men of so diverse aims and policies, it is inferred, could never agree in practical action. Of course, socialists differ widely among themselves, and some of the details proposed by various groups are irreconcilable. But this is true only as to subordinate principles, or the application of fundamental principles to details. In other words, the things in debate are expedients merely. Here differences of opinion should be expected, and, it may be fairly presumed, they will prove no more formidable to socialists than such differences are to any men who undertake a common cause. Men will doubtless be no more unanimous under a socialistic system than they are now; discussion and experiment, and finally the will of the majority, will then as now have to be the reliance for the settlement of such differences. Present discussions of the details of a future socialistic order have an academic interest mainly, yet they are not entirely without value, because by such discussion an approach to unanimity may be secured as social evolution progresses.

M. Yves Guyot, one of the acutest critics of Socialism, objects: "No socialist has succeeded in explaining the conditions for the production, remuneration, and distribution of capital in a collectivist system." On the contrary, a large number of socialists have given such explanations, with superfluous and meticulous detail. Mr. Bellamy's romance, "Looking Backward," is an example. The defect of such explanations is that they have not been convincing, which is probably what M. Guyot means. But why should they convince? Economics does not profess to be an exact science, with power of accurate prevision, and why should Socialism, more than any other economic theory, be required to predict the future? Such explanations, or predictions, as M. Guyot challenges socialists to make are necessarily worthless, except in so far as they are understood to be a work of the imagination. To set forth, as Mr. Bellamy did, a picture of how Socialism might be supposed to work, is a valid reply to the assertion that Socialism is impossible. The illustration of possibility successfully controverts dogmatic denial of possibility, but it does nothing more. Can M. Guyot, or any other defender of Capitalism, predict what will be the organization of American society a century hence? Of course he can, anybody can, but with no authority superior to Mr. Bellamy's — that is to say, with none at all.

These objections to Socialism are ceasing to be heard in serious literature. They are entirely out of date, because they apply only to the Utopian schemes of the past. The objection of impracticability may be conclusive in the case of a Utopia; against an imaginary social order it is perfectly valid to set imaginary objections. But impracticability is not a valid objection to a Socialism that expects to be realized through a social evolution. The difference between a Utopia and an evolution is, that one is thought out and the other is lived out. Practicability is of the essence of evolution; every step taken must work or be abandoned. As Karl Marx puts it, the socialist is merely a sort of midwife, helping the old order give birth to the new with as little pain as possible. When a writer like Mr. Mallock, therefore, says of Socialism that it is impregnable as a theory, the only trouble being that it will not work, he is simply writing

nonsense. It will work; it must work; whatever does
not work cannot be evolutionary Socialism.

III

When we take up the details of Socialism, we quickly
meet a serious and perplexing question; namely, the principle on which the wealth produced by a coöperative
society is to be distributed. All socialists are agreed
that the distribution must be equitable; they are about
equally divided in opinion, as to groups, though perhaps
not as to numbers, whether "equitable" and "equal"
are synonymous. Will equal distribution satisfy the
average ethical sense of the future socialist community,
or will there be recognition of unequal service and therefore unequal reward?

There is much to be said, abstractly, for either principle.
It may be plausibly argued that, as men's services vary
greatly in value, they should be unequally compensated,
each receiving the real value of his service. There is
no such thing as equality in this world, and no possibility
of equality. Any attempt of Socialism to accomplish
human equality must be classed with Jack Cade's
promise that seven halfpenny loaves should be sold for
a penny, and the three-hooped pot should have ten hoops.
The modern socialist recognizes this necessary limitation,
and hastens to profess that the equality demanded by
him is equality of opportunity, equality of privilege.
But given equality of opportunity and inequality of
ability, and by inexorable logic and fact as inexorable,
there will result unequal achievement. Will Socialism
recognize such inequality and provide proportioned
(that is, unequal) rewards?   If not, is Socialism anything

but the attempt of the lame and the lazy and the inefficient to pull all men down to their level? Can a social
order be founded on such a basis? Will the men of
brains and energy ever submit to be robbed of the fruits
of their labor, that these fruits may be enjoyed by those
who have not produced them? So long as the world
stands, is it not likely that the man who can do things,
and does them, will be on a higher level than the man
who cannot do things, or is too indolent to try? Making
water run uphill would seem to be as easy a task as to
reverse this inevitable current of human affairs.

Moreover, as another practical difficulty, this should
be considered: in the case of purely intellectual services
there would be no little embarrassment in estimating
their value. Competition now fixes a market value, even
for intellectual services; but when there is no competition, how shall an immaterial service be equated with a
material reward? Some of the Marxians, if not Marx
himself, would cut this knot, not untie it, by denying
that any sort of labor is worthy of compensation but
manual labor. But we may be sure that this will not
be the solution of the future. Brains, not brawn, will
continue to rule the world, and, if they are not paid, they
will take their pay.

On the other hand, if the problem be approached from
the side of human brotherhood, the decision will be different. A father who loves his children equally divides his
property equally among them. Is not brotherhood a
better title to a share in the common product than service? We see that selfishness, pleading justice and amount
of service, will claim unequal division; love, recognizing common brotherhood, will concede equal division.

Which will conquer ?   Nobody can at present say ; but whichever way the final decision inclines, there can at any rate be no question which most accords with the funda- mental ideas of Socialism, as well as with the ethics of Jesus.   All men may not be equal, but all are equally men.

That equal division is in accord with the highest ethics, is confirmed by the fact that men always resort to this principle in extremes.   After the San Francisco earth- quake, food and stores were seized by the public author- ities and distributed to the people according to their need. Rich and poor stood in line and received their share in turn.   Shipwrecked men, compelled to take to the boats, divide food and water equally, and it is the unwritten law of the sea that he who steals from the common store for- feits his right to live.   Under great stress, the primal eth- ical instincts of the race, as well as the brute in man, assert themselves with unmistakable emphasis.   And such con- siderations as these lend great force to the reasoning of Enrico Ferri, one of the leading socialists of Italy, when he says, "When all men have given their best labor to society, each is entitled to an equal share of the product, since each has contributed equally to that solidarity of labor which sustains the life of the social aggregate." Unequal distribution may be a relic of individualism, which, though it now appeals strongly to many as just, will become less and less ethically convincing as we ad- vance toward the new social order.

Closely akin to the question of distribution is the ques- tion of compensation.   Socialism cannot realize its ideal, or even approximate it, except by expropriation of land and machinery.   Expropriation of land is already legal and common, under the so-called right of eminent do-

main — the theory that the rights and interests of the
whole people take precedence of the ordinary rights of
property. Socialism is merely demanding a wider application of this principle than has been usual, but proposes
no new principle. But such expropriation has thus far
implied compensation : the right of the people to resume
ownership of land, if needed for public purposes, has not
been pressed to denial of the right of the private owner
to receive a fair equivalent for that of which he is deprived.
Will Socialism enforce expropriation without compensation ? Does Socialism imply confiscation ?

Different answers are given by socialistic writers as to
what ought to be the socialistic policy in this respect. It
is at bottom an ethical question, but many socialists pre-
fer to discuss it as a question of expediency. Mr. Spargo
shows that compensation is entirely consistent with
socialistic principles, and that many socialists of authority
have actually favored it.[1] On the other hand, it would
be easy to cite many socialists of perhaps equal authority,
who have scouted all idea of compensation. Karl Marx,
who is to-day the most widely accepted authority among
socialists, does not apparently feel very strongly the
ethical obligation of compensation, but distinctly favors
it as most expedient : "It will still be, if we can proceed
by compensation, the cheapest way to achieve the revolution." That is, he believes that compensation will not
only involve less danger of bloodshed and suffering, but
would be economically preferable, because a peaceful
revolution does not suspend the wheels of industry a
single day, while a revolution by violence inevitably sus-
pends the productive processes and makes a people just

[1] "Socialism," pp. 333–337.

that much poorer.   Expropriation and spoliation are not, therefore, identical terms.   It should seem that socialists will do well not to permit them to become synonymous. Nothing would do more to retard the progress of Social-ism, if not to make its victory impossible, than to let it be understood that everybody who has anything to lose must lose it, in order that those who have nothing to lose may gain all.   Considered simply as a matter of tactics, which is the way that Marx chooses to consider the ques-tion, socialists would be mad to suppose that they can ever persuade the Haves to give all to the Have-nots. Or that, failing to persuade, they can compel.

But it should also be understood that, in demanding expropriation without compensation, socialistic writers are not reckless of ethical principles.   We shall not get their point of view unless we comprehend that they urge this as the only ethical course.   What the capitalist calls confiscation, they call restitution.   They hold that the capitalist is a robber; that his wealth has been stolen from the producers.   They deny the right of the capitalist to demand compensation for his past robbery and his loss of the privilege to rob for the future.   To those bred in the ethics of Capitalism, these ethics seem monstrous, a mere specious apology for wholesale rapine and plunder; but the world is beginning to question whether the ethics of Capitalism are true ethics.   Some think that the cap-italist has set the worker a shining example of rapacity without conscience and of profligacy without shame; and that the capitalist should not wonder if the worker now says with Shylock, "The villainy you teach me I will exe-cute, and it shall go hard, but I will better the instruc-tion."   For generations, says the socialist, the capitalist has taken, by force and fraud, the lion's share of the product of labor, and has added insult to injury by maintaining that it was justly his. He has procured the enactment and enforcement of stringent laws to protect him in the enjoyment of wealth so ill gotten. Is it any wonder that the man whose labor is the source of all this wealth now hopes for the day when this spoil shall be snatched from the robber and restitution made to the wronged; or that he laughs at compensation, as one would laugh at the proposal to compensate a highway robber from whom a stolen purse had been wrested? We may not accept that point of view; we may find some defect in such ethics; let us at least make the effort to comprehend both, and then ask if there be no truth in either.

IV

It is objected that Socialism is economically infeasible, that the only result to be fairly anticipated from socialized production and equal distribution would be such a reduction of per capita wealth as would mean universal poverty, the total destruction of all that we mean by civilization. Huxley has put this objection with peculiar emphasis and point: "So long as unlimited multiplication goes on, no social organization which has ever been devised, or is likely to be devised, no fiddle-faddling with the distribution of wealth, will deliver society from the tendency to be destroyed by the reproduction within itself, in its intensest form, of that struggle for existence the limitation of which is the object of society."[1] This is our old friend Malthusianism with a

[1] "Evolution and Ethics," p. 212.

new face.   Enough has perhaps been already said about
the defects of this theory, yet it may be well to direct
attention anew to its weakest point: reproduction, as
matter of fact, is far from unlimited; it has many effective limitations.   According to universal present experience, in every civilized country, the birth-rate increases as we go down the economic scale, and decreases
as we go up.   The more any class advances in comfort,
the less becomes its fecundity.   Why, then, if the whole
of society should become comfortable, should we not expect from our present experience that its fecundity would
rather diminish than increase?

If it be replied that Socialism proposes to remove all the
restraints of prudence that now lead the well-to-do classes
to decline to bring into the world more children than they
can properly rear and educate, it may be rejoined that
prudence cannot be the real cause of the decrease of fecundity in the higher classes.   For the rich are restrained
by no such considerations of prudence; they have the
means to rear and educate large families, but it is among
those who have the largest means that the birth-rate is
smallest.   The very rich have smaller families than the
moderately rich.   Is not the real danger of society, as it
advances in economic comfort, that which President Roosevelt pointed out under the term "race suicide"?   May we
not rationally anticipate that the effect of Socialism would
be rather under-population than over-population?

Assuming this to be no serious difficulty, it may be
arithmetically proved that Socialism is economically possible.   The official statistics of the present production of
wealth in the United States show that if the product were
equally divided, every individual would have something

over $300 a year, or $1500 for each family of five.[1] This would insure a fair average of comfort. But with every able-bodied person a producer, which is the theory of Socialism, the amount of annual wealth would be incalculably increased. Far less than half of the able-bodied population are now engaged in production, and the doubling or tripling of labor would produce astonishing results. Better organization and direction of labor would enhance the result. There can be no reasonable doubt that from four to six hours' work a day — intelligent and hearty labor — would suffice for the support of a people in ample comfort, and even insure as much luxury as is compatible with the maintenance of good physical and moral conditions.

There is practically no limit to the productiveness of the soil under intensive cultivation, and the food supply can always be made to exceed the need of population.[2] There need be no fear of starvation under a socialistic régime, and there is plenty of starvation now. There is a similar possibility of indefinite productiveness of manu-

---

[1] The figures are as follows: value of farm products, $7,848,000,000 (I give only round numbers) ; manufacturing products, $14,802,000,000 ; value of gold mined, $96,000,000; of silver, $27,000,000; of other minerals, $1,506,000,000; making a total of $24,279,000,000. As some of these figures are from later statistics than 1900, the population may be estimated at 80,000,000 (for the United States proper, to which the above figures apply), and the result is $303 per capita, or $1515 for each family of five.

[2] " A trustworthy estimate of the relative efficiency of agriculture as at present pursued — trustworthy, because based, not on guesses, but on careful scientific tests — is that in the culture of potatoes the average efficiency of the United States is 19 per cent; in wheat culture the average is only 28 per cent; in cotton culture average efficiency is even less, but 17.5 per cent." — Harrington Emerson, "Efficiency as a Basis for Operation and Wages," pp. 76–79.

U

facturing labor.   Mr. Edison is not a socialist, and he will probably be accepted as having a right to predict the industrial future, if any man has such a right.   "There will be no poverty in the world a hundred years from now," says Mr. Edison.   "There is no limit to the cheapness with which things can be made.   The world will soon be flooded with the cheap products of machinery — not the poor products, the cheap products. . . .   Poverty was for a world that only used its hands.   Now that men have begun to use their brains, poverty is decreasing.   Think how long the world has stood, and then recall that practically everything we know to-day that is worth while we have learned within a hundred years. . . .   We are learning how to control the forces of nature.   As we learn, we shall transform the world." [1]

Capitalists are beginning to recognize that their plants do not produce nearly to the limit of capacity.   The result of the treatment of laborers as beasts of burden or as machines has been a disastrous limitation of production. [2] Every resource has been exhausted to increase the efficiency of machinery, but the efficiency of men has been neglected, and the principles of "business" have discouraged efficiency in the laborer.   The unions are sometimes charged with a responsibility that belongs elsewhere ; it is asserted that the tendency of these organizations is to reduce all

[1] "The Wonderful New World Ahead of Us," in the *Cosmopolitan* for February, 1911, p. 306.

[2] English workmen have made the capital mistake, from the economist's point of view, of deliberately limiting production.   Their unions establish not only a minimum wage, but a maximum day's work, and no member of a union can be induced to do more.   The result is that the English worker's efficiency is as 1 to $2\frac{1}{4}$ of the American's.   But he has something to say for himself in justification of his policy that we need not pause to examine.

wages to the capacity of the least efficient, so that all
motive to excel is destroyed. The unions concede the
fact, but deny the inference : the fault is not theirs, but
the employer's. The union merely demands that men
shall be paid a minimum wage; it has no objection to
the paying of higher wages to the better workmen; but
the employer has deliberately made the minimum wage
the maximum. Moreover, if in any factory or shop, some
men do much more work than the average, either this is at
once exacted by the employer as the standard for all, or
else wages are cut. When "piece-work" is the rule, the
result is similar : if some workers earn much more than
the average wage, the price is cut for all. The employer
has, by this policy, ingeniously destroyed every motive
for efficiency in his best workmen. A good man knows
that if he really exerts himself, he hurts all his fellows
without benefiting himself.

Capitalists are now beginning to realize the results of
this policy, and careful experiments are making in scientific efficiency, with the end not only of determining what
is a precise standard of a day's work, but of giving the
worker the benefit of his increased efficiency in increased
wages. Workers must be treated as individuals, and with
some rudiments of justice, if capitalists would increase
their output; by their short-sighted rule of fining efficiency, instead of rewarding it, they have doubly punished
themselves. Men who have made a study of scientific
efficiency have concluded that few manufacturing plants
suffer a loss of less than 30 per cent of possible efficiency,
as a result of the ignorance and unwillingness of workers.
One of the chief authorities on this subject has recently
declared : "The actual and potential wastes in each year

amount to as much as the total accumulation of wealth, and if all the possessors of accumulations were left in undisturbed possession, and the wastes of current production and use eliminated and the gain equitably apportioned according to meed and deed, no woman or child would need to do mill or factory, store or office, work, no superannuated man or woman need toil, no young man need delay marriage, nor any head of a family be torn by anxiety as to the feeding, the clothing, or the housing of his dependents." [1]

There is no disposition on the part of socialists to minimize the importance of this matter; practically every socialist writer of note agrees with Kirkup, when he says: "The claims of Socialism must rest on its superior efficiency, from an economic, political, and moral point of view." Great losses that are to-day inseparable from the clumsy action of the "law" of supply and demand might be prevented by the greater fluidity of a system that would insure a better adjustment between need and production. The Trust has shown what economies of production are possible, even under our present system, by such adjustment. The Sugar Trust closed three-fourths of its factories, and fully maintained its volume of production, with an immense saving of cost, and, of course, corresponding profit. The Whiskey Trust acquired eighty plants at its organization or soon after, closed all but twelve, and produced more whiskey than ever; greatly to the scath of the people, but as greatly to the profit of the Trust.

Some of the elements of cost under the present system that would be eliminated under Socialism are: insurance;

[1] Emerson, "Efficiency," p. 16.

all losses of the community, by fire or death, would still fall on the community, in some form, but only the actual loss would be borne, not, as now, a tax enormously greater. The middleman and the broker would disappear, and, becoming producers, would add to wealth instead of being a heavy tax on production. All advertising, and the other costs of selling goods, which now fully double their cost to the consumer, would be saved. The great evil of adulteration would vanish with competition, which alone supplies the irresistible motive. No laws against adulteration can be more than palliative, while this powerful motive remains in full force.

v

Another much urged objection to Socialism: Experience thus far shows that private enterprises are conducted with greater energy and economy than public. But is that true? Would it not be more accurate to say that some private enterprises are conducted with more efficiency and at less cost than some public enterprises, and *vice versa?* Was the digging of the Panama Canal conducted with more efficiency under the corporation organized by de Lesseps than now under the United States government? It is notorious that enterprises managed by the engineering corps of the United States Army are conducted more efficiently — as measured by quality of work, time consumed, and cost — than any other engineering work in our country. How about the Post Office — is its service exceeded in accuracy, promptness, and cheapness by the express and telephone services conducted by private corporations? Could the average citizen be convinced that the postal service would be better done by a private corporation? Let anybody try it who thinks he could. Where there seems lack of economy, in public as compared with private service, the reason generally is that there has been a desire to administer, not for the lowest cost of service, but to give the greatest amount of service regardless of cost.

Since this is above all a practical question, let us take a severely practical case. Up to 1892 the city of Nashville was lighted by a private company, with 382 arc lights and 437 gas lamps, at an annual cost of $65,000. The city then acquired the plant and did its own lighting. In 1896, with the same plant, the cost of operation, including interest on the value of the plant, was $53,698, or $11,301 less than was paid under contract to the private company. Moreover, the city had maintained during that year 848 arc lights, and 652 gas lamps, making its actual saving for the year $48,982. No doubt cases are producible in which municipal lighting has resulted in loss, rather than in so large a gain. But a single instance like that of Nashville is enough to dispose of the *a priori* objection that private enterprise is less costly than public. Public enterprises may be conducted in so dishonest and inefficient a manner as to become a tax on the community; if so, it is evidently the community's own fault, and the remedy is in its own hands. But how can a community protect itself from a rapacious corporation that charges an extortionate price for its services, and is protected in so doing by the possession of a virtual or actual monopoly? This is the problem that many municipalities are facing just now, and the only effectual answer appears to be, in the majority of cases, municipal ownership. And if, in such case, a municipality should fail to secure the expected economies, it will at least have the satisfaction of knowing that it is no longer plundered and oppressed for the profit of others, but is getting something like a dollar's worth for a dollar's expenditure.

A certain practical difficulty will emerge in the evolution of Socialism, and on its solution will largely depend this question of efficiency : How can the men best fitted for direction be secured under a socialist system ? The necessity of such directing does not need arguing, and very ominous is the disaster of so many attempts at co-operation, because of the lack of proper direction, the failure of the enterprise to evolve men of the intelligence to perceive how labor could be profitably expended, where a market for the product could be found, how the process of making could be conducted with least waste, by what inventions it might be facilitated, and how several hundred workmen could be so organized and supervised as to produce the best results.

The socialist is not obliged by his theory to find answers for all such practical problems, and probably the best answer to this one is, We do not know. If, three hundred years ago, the wisest man had been asked what sort of a system could be worked out for the most effective use in production of a host of labor-saving inventions, he could not have predicted the modern Trust. We have come to that result by a process of social evolution, every step of which is plain enough now that we look back on it, no step of which could have been anticipated generations ago. As society continues its evolution towards the socialistic organization, assuming that to be its goal, other methods will be evolved as needed. The mere fact that men cannot now predict what the methods will be is no reason to doubt that they are possible.

But the socialist can suggest certain rational lines along which the course of future evolution may conceivably progress. The national postal system points out a way by which the best men could be found in every department of industry, namely, by promotion from the ranks up to the highest positions of those who proved themselves worthy of advancement by their capacity and service. A way of securing the best men for direction might thus be devised that would be impartial and almost automatic in its action. And, as in the post-office now, so then in all forms of industry, the main question would not need to be, Will this pay? but, Is this best? What private corporation would ever introduce free rural delivery? The unprofitable enterprises would be maintained by the profitable, as is the case now to some extent. For example, when one pays two cents postage on a letter, he pays about half a cent for the actual cost of delivering that letter, and a cent and a half tax to make up in part the deficit caused by doing other post-office business at a loss. The post-office in many ways illustrates how all business would be done under a socialistic régime: for the common good, at common cost or profit, as the case might be.

VI

It is further objected to a socialistic system that it would take away what has hitherto been the greatest motive to human exertion, the possibility of acquiring wealth, and would put no adequate motive in its place. This is Mallock's heaviest indictment of Socialism. But how great is its weight? What does "the possibility of acquiring wealth" mean? What has it meant? It means and has meant the possibility that a few men, by superior shrewdness and good fortune, might obtain a vastly disproportionate share of the wealth produced. That such a possibility may exist, it is necessary that the great majority shall get a very small share of the product. Can society progress only by allowing the strong to exploit the weak? Is life worth living only on the condition that most men must lose in order that a few may gain? Is it not just possible that a higher economic efficiency in society would result if every man had the certainty that his material reward would be commensurate with his effort?

The answer to these questions cannot be a simple Yes or No, for the problem is greatly complicated, not simple. It is historically true, perhaps, that the spur of want on the one side and the hope of gain on the other have produced most of that individual initiative which has been the chief lever of human progress. But it does not follow that the desire of wealth, or what economists call self-interest, is the whole of the kinetics of civilization. It may be granted that there has been a tendency in mankind to be as worthless and lazy as circumstances would permit, and that no strong race has developed, except where a stern struggle for a livelihood was made necessary by an unsmiling nature, and still it may be doubted if this is a valid law of human nature for all time. Mr. Mallock sees in greed the one touch of nature that makes all men kin. Is not that a most unsatisfactory analysis of history and human nature? Love of country, love of wife and children, love of friends, love of mankind, love

of truth, love of beauty, love of fame, love of power —
these are motives that have been quite as powerful as
that love of gain which economists make the sole foundation of their systems.

Wealth is valued for the power that its possession con-
fers, for the luxury that it makes possible, for the social
distinction that it purchases. It is still more valued because it is the accepted test of success. To get rich is the
proving of one's manhood in a fierce struggle with his fellows; it is the demonstration of superior physical, mental, and moral stamina. For, though wealth is sometimes
acquired by immoral means, its acquisition demands certain moral qualities : self-control, persistence, integrity —
the latter not measured by abstract ethical standards, but
by the recognized rules of the game. Under Socialism
there will be the same opportunities of power, of distinction, as now exist. Leaders, directors, will be even more
necessary than under the present order, and the need will
certainly produce the men, as it has always produced
them. As for pride, the love of honor, it might be made
a thousandfold more effective than now, by providing
some system of public distinctions for those who give
exceptional service, or sacrifice themselves for the common weal. Among the Greeks, the crown of wild olive
was the highest of all distinctions, and to win it demanded
the best powers of mind and body from the best-trained
men the world has ever seen. The golden age of Athens
which produced literature and art never since surpassed
did not reach this apical achievement by virtue of any
money rewards. Phidias and Praxiteles received only
moderate sums for their incomparable statues. The architect who designed the Parthenon is said to have been

paid only twice as much as the stone-cutter who worked on it; the rest of his pay he received in the applause of his fellow-citizens. Æschylus, Sophocles, Aristophanes, were paid in fame, not in money, for their immortal dramas, and rich citizens were ready to spend large sums for the honor of staging such plays. Thucydides, Demosthenes, Sappho, Plato, never gained an obolus by their writings; public recognition and the joy of their work were their sole and sufficient reward.

The sheer felicity of exercising one's faculties would be motive enough for a vast number, especially in all lines of artistic endeavor. No artist paints, or poet writes, or orator speaks, chiefly for love of money. Under our present system he must have money to live, but the artist of every degree and kind would gladly be freed from all necessity of thinking of sordid gain, and do his best for his art out of pure love of the work. And this is as true of many engaged in the useful arts as of devotees of the fine arts. Many a mechanic, many a man of business, has the same feeling at the bottom of his soul, and toils for the pleasure of his work more than its gain. The medical profession affords a fine instance of a class whose chief motive is not greed, but the welfare of men. A large proportion of the work of every physician and surgeon, even of the greatest men in the profession, is given gratis to those who are too poor to pay. Hundreds of useful inventions in surgical apparatus have marked the progress of the art of healing, but the man who should patent such a device and by means of it exploit the afflicted for his gain, would be promptly ostracized by his profession. Literature is no exception to this principle. It is true that Dr. Johnson said, "Nobody but a fool ever wrote except for money," but, like many of his sayings, it was not true. On the contrary, one might say that nobody ever produced literature of the first rank who wrote chiefly for money. The rapture of creation is its own reward. One can distinguish in the work of Andrea del Sarto, for example, pictures that he painted because with all his soul he loved his art, and pictures that he painted merely for money, as tradition says, to buy jewels to adorn his worthless Lucrezia.

Next to the ecstacy of creation, the artist desires recognition, fame; money comes last of all. The man of science finds his chief reward in the discovery of new truth, and next to that in the recognition of his work by the learned world; as for money, it is hardly in his thoughts, except as a means of continuing his work. The delight of the statesman is in the exercise of authority, the direction of public opinion, the work of administration; the hope of gain comes last, if it come at all. Something of the soldier's stern joy of battle, something of his hope of promotion and honors, might well be expected to enter into a large proportion of the citizens of a socialized state. Indeed, an army helps us to realize many of the probable features of Socialism. An army's food, clothing, shelter, all material wants, are assured by the State; it lives and dies without hope or wish of wealth; but how cheerfully it gives its services, with what enthusiasm does it hail the day of battle! Under a social state that would assure leisure and opportunity of culture to all, not to a few, the individual bent would have such avenues of development and exercise, such prospects of usefulness and distinction, as would inevitably lead to the highest possible achievement in all departments of human activity.

Socialism may not be adapted to Orientals, who are credited by us with a specialty for indolence, but the Caucasian race is not inherently indolent. On the contrary, to a normal Caucasian nothing is more abhorrent than inaction. A child is the closest approach to perpetual motion yet discovered or devised. An adult must do things — if not work, then he must have "sport." But now, when men are compelled to work as they can, not as they would, what wonder they are listless, that they shirk, especially when they consider the social injustice of their lot, how their labor is rewarded. There might be reasonably anticipated in a socialistic system greater liberty of choice, hygienic surroundings, reasonable hours, a plentiful reward, everything that could make work attractive. When all men love their work as the artist loves his — and it is not unthinkable — the industrial problem will be a problem no longer.

The present and past incentives to effort for advancement have been and are : first, the pressure of necessity ; second, the hope of reward ; third, love of the work itself. It is a reasonable forecast that these motives will remain unchanged under Socialism, or will change only to become more effective. The pressure of necessity will be diminished as to the individual, not as to society ; all that man possesses he will still have to earn by sweat of brow and brain. The force of the second motive should be greatly increased, as hope becomes certainty, as men are assured that they labor entirely for their own benefit, and not for others. The third motive is at least capable of being made the strongest of the three.

One other important question remains to be asked before we leave this subject of incentive : What incentive for invention will there be under a socialized order? "I have but one light," said Patrick Henry, "by which my feet are guided, and that is the light of experience." Until recently the inventor has been little influenced by hope of gain. All the fundamental inventions on which civilization is built were devised by unknown persons under the prehistoric communism : such as the potter's wheel, the lever, the sail, rudder, loom, distaff, the smelting of metals, and the making of glass, parchment, and paper. And among prehistoric inventions not mechanical were such as the cultivation of cereals, the domestication of animals, as well as the elements of art — engraving, sculpture, painting, and, most important of all, writing. Love of gain played no important part in such inventions. There was little advance on these prehistoric discoveries until the Middle Ages, when the use of the lens was discovered, with its quickly following applications to the telescope and microscope. The mariner's compass and the art of printing followed. And the notable thing is, that in the case of all these mediæval discoveries, which determined the advance of knowledge and the progress of civilization for the next three centuries, we can no more certainly say who was the inventor of any than we can positively ascertain the inventor of gunpowder, which came into use at about the same time.

Even in the last great century of invention, when the monopoly of "patents" had become established, the notable prizes that fell to inventors were few, and did not always go to the most deserving. James Watt, the inventor of the steam-engine, and George Stephenson, the maker of the first locomotive, won but a modest competence as the result of a lifetime's work. Hargraves and

Arkwright, inventors of cotton spinning and weaving machinery, had their patents invalidated by legal proceedings and reaped little reward from them, though Arkwright made a fortune as a manufacturer. Eli Whitney, inventor of the cotton gin, obtained almost no reward for an invention that transformed the world's industries and produced a great civil war. The inventor of the slot machine, Percival Everitt, died a pauper, and his very name is unknown to the thousands that daily use his device. Morse, Howe, McCormick, Bell, Edison, Westinghouse, Pullman, were more fortunate and received princely rewards for their inventions, and these examples have dazzled many Americans and inspired the hope of other great fortunes, — hopes that would be moderated by a visit to the United States Patent Office at Washington. There is no more pathetic sight than that great collection of models of useless contrivances and blasted hopes. If an invention is successful, some capitalist nearly always contrives to cheat the inventor out of the financial reward of his work.

And what of the incentive of the author — for surely one may speak of the grievance of his own craft. Is the mere financial motive to write a strong one, when the writer knows that, unless he produce a book that will become one of the "six best sellers," he will be paid less for his labor than the unskilled immigrant who digs our ditches? Can it be truly said that our present system is peculiarly adapted to encourage these higher forms of human activity, or that society would be likely to suffer greatly if such incentives were removed? Nevertheless, though the incentives have always been small, the inventor has continued to invent and always will, irre-

spective of reward; the poet and the philosopher will
write and the artist will paint, though they live in beg-
gary and die in the poorhouse. Encourage invention,
literature, art? The world cannot discourage them by
anything short of hanging, and it is doubtful if even that
extreme penalty would be efficacious.

But there is reason to believe that Socialism would
greatly stimulate invention and all the forms of intellectual activity. We may rely upon it that all arduous work
would be speedily made less arduous, if every man were
required to do manual work. The powers of the brightest minds would be at once concentrated on the problem,
How to discover and apply labor-saving machinery and
methods. A few years would suffice to transform the
present methods by which the world gets its rough and
disagreeable work done into ways comparatively easy
and agreeable. Capitalism has introduced machinery
with a single motive: the making of a profit. Socialism
will consider, not profit, but benefit to man. Labor that
is interesting in itself men will always gladly do; labor
that is not interesting should be made as little onerous
as possible, and the same is true of labor that is unduly
exhausting. More and more we shall come to take the
human view instead of the financial, cease to look at the
dollar and look at the man.

In estimating the probable advance of invention we
must not fail to take into account the certain progress of
intelligence under Socialism. Mr. Lester F. Ward tells
us that "eleven times as many talented persons belong
to the wealthy or well-to-do classes as to the poor or
laboring classes, although the latter are about five times
as numerous as the former. Indigence is an effective

bar to achievement." [1] Mr. Ward holds that talent is distributed by nature about equally in the various social ranks, and that the only reason why the wealthy contribute more to invention than the poor is because their economic condition gives them the opportunity. Making all allowance due for the possibility of error, and supposing that there is only half as much talent in the lower classes as in the higher, it is evident that improvement in the intelligence and economic condition of the lower class would result in an enormous increment of inventive faculty in society as a whole.

VII

Much has been said, and said truly, of the lack of agreement among the advocates of Socialism, and many critics make merry over the contradictory arguments advanced by socialistic writers. Their mirth would be much diminished if they should examine more carefully the objections made to Socialism, for many of these flatly contradict each other. Mr. Mallock, as we have seen, fears that if Socialism should prevail, the world would go to the bow-wows, because men would no longer have adequate motive for exertion. Other critics fear that men would have too much motive for exertion in a socialized order — that the inevitable appeal to ambition would produce a system of Bosses. It is argued that the political corruption of the present would inevitably become worse with every enlargement of the scope of governmental activity. This objection will disappear when a

---

[1] "Applied Sociology," I: 529. What has been said above of invention would of course be true of literature, science, art, and all the higher callings in which talent is an indispensable requisite for success.

x

larger view of politics is taken and the cause of present evils is correctly diagnosed. The Boss exists only on the sufferance of the people and as an aid to Capitalism. Political corruption is directly traceable to the capitalistic system : its root is the effort of the capitalist class to promote their fortunes and retain power. Capitalism bribes voters to secure the election of its tools ; corrupts legislatures, in part to procure favorable legislation, in part to avert unfavorable. It is suspected of bribing courts, and more than suspected of packing the courts with its retainers. It subsidizes and controls a large part of the press, which conceals the worst of these facts from the public, and when the facts can no longer be concealed or denied, apologizes for them and resists reform or the punishment of the guilty. It has put the pulpit under bonds, by its support of the churches and its gifts to missionary enterprises, and has muzzled the teacher by endowments of educational institutions and pensioning of veterans. It must dominate government and control public sentiment or perish, and until now it has succeeded in dominating, but at what an ethical cost !

Within a few years, these abuses of the powers of government, and of social and educational institutions, have opened the eyes of many to the fact that we are ruled by a privileged class, by means of bribery, corruption, and intimidation. Popular rule is seen to be a joke in the United States ; we have a government of the "interests," by the "interests," and for the "interests." We call ourselves a republic and wonder that England still tolerates its House of Lords — not perceiving that we have a house of lords, self-made lords of industry ; that we pay in taxes what they choose to assess, that we have as laws what they are pleased to permit to be enacted; that we have no rights left but such as they have not as yet cared to take from us.

Now it is plain that the very first step towards Socialism would by just so much lessen all these evils; and every subsequent step would lessen them proportionally, by the removal of the motive for this corruption, and likewise the power by which it is sustained. With the disappearance of Capitalism the evils would disappear, for their motive would be lacking. The supposed objection to Socialism, when the facts are duly taken into consideration, becomes one of the strongest arguments in its favor. It promises the complete cure of a disease that is sapping the very life of the body politic. Men do not commit crimes against society, on any considerable scale at least, without an obvious and powerful motive. As for the Boss, he lives on corruption and would be impossible without corruption. We have been considering, not an objection to Socialism, but a bogey.

VIII

The promised order of the future is believed by some to be socially undesirable: it would produce a social condition of uniformity, monotony, stagnation. This objection takes a variety of forms. It is said that if the state is the only employer, talent could not get its fair price and its development would be discouraged; that no sufficient place is made in Socialism for the higher pursuits, the learned and artistic professions, and so on. It is evident that this objection to Socialism, like many of the arguments in its favor, is entirely *a priori*, and its validity can only be determined by experience. The only reply

possible at present is of the same *a priori* nature as the
objection itself. It seems reasonable that Socialism
might make possible greater variety and higher intellectual and artistic development than the present social
order, since it plans to give every human being opportunity to make the best of whatever capacity may be latent
in him. Some of the present professions might disappear
under Socialism, or at least be reduced to very small
limits — that of the law, for example. Lawyers and
courts would find their useful functions growing less, until
they finally approached the vanishing point. The profession of medicine might be reduced to the limit of actual
social usefulness. On the other hand, some professions
would probably be greatly increased in numbers and extent of usefulness, especially the profession of teaching.
Certain other callings, not now dignified by the name of
profession, would tend to disappear : the police, for example, would be far less needed ; firemen could be practically retired from business by the erection of fire-proof
buildings alone, with mechanical contrivances within
them for the extinguishing of any small fire that might
be caused by carelessness or accident.

The effectiveness of all professions might be greatly
enhanced in a socialized order, by having them composed only of volunteers, who should duly qualify themselves for practice and be licensed by authority. Men
and women of the professions would then do their work
as producers, like others, and spend a part of their leisure
hours in the study and practice of their chosen calling.
Men would not enter a profession then as a mere means of
making a living, which now causes every calling to be
overcrowded with incompetents, but because they had

a natural aptitude and liking for it ; and they would work, not for pay, but for the sake of their art or science. Why should not such a system produce far greater proficiency in all professions than is now known ? The medical profession even now witnesses to the innate capacity of men to serve their fellows from the highest motives. There is no reason to suppose that medicine attracts men of higher nature than law or literature ; it merely offers higher opportunities. In more senses than one men feel themselves to be the heirs of all the ages ; they know that we who are now here on the earth owe a vast debt to antiquity that we can pay only to posterity. The call to heroism still falls on men who have ears to hear — not in vain comes the summons to high endeavor.

> Then welcome each rebuff
> That turns earth's smoothness rough,
> Each sting that bids, nor sit, nor stand, but go !
> Be our joys three parts pain !
> Strive and hold cheap the strain.

Especially does this seem to be true of all forms and degrees of art. All artists should, and most artists do, love their art supremely. The constant plaint of the painter is that he must turn out pot-boilers when he would fain attempt a masterpiece — of the poet that he must do hack-work for a living instead of composing an epic. No doubt most artists deceive themselves about their capabilities ; pot-boilers and hack-work are a better measure of their genius than Madonnas and epics. Most of us who spoil good white paper by putting on it what we are pleased to consider our ideas could never, under any circumstances, write anything that the world would not willingly let die. The "mute, inglorious Miltons" probably never existed outside of a poet's lively imagination. But, at any rate, Socialism would remove this excuse — or this obstacle, as one pleases — and make it possible for any man who had anything to say to the world to express it at his best, on paper, on canvas, in marble.

For some professions, Socialism would be an emancipation. For example, journalism, in theory one of the noblest callings, in practice one of the vilest. It is now completely subservient to two masters, party spirit and Capitalism. Publishing a newspaper has become a purely commercial enterprise, and this is as true of the "religious" press as of the secular. A newspaper exists by virtue, first of its subscription list, recruited from a party or a denomination; and even for the so-called "independent" papers, whether religious or secular, there is a definite constituency who are more or less of a certain way of thinking. The paper must please them or lose its readers. The profits depend on advertisements, as the sale of the paper does not more than meet the cost of production, and seldom does even that. It is inevitable that the editing of the paper should be influenced by these considerations. The news and editorial columns tell, not the truth, but that version of events which will be most likely to please the readers and least likely to offend advertisers. In the case of many journals, they are openly edited from the counting-room, and make little pretense of a higher virtue than giving the people what they want. Others assume a higher virtue, without giving any evidence of possessing it. The business of the press as a disseminator of news is seriously impaired by this commercialism, and the proper function of the newspaper, as teacher and prophet, is nearly gone. None but the very ignorant, or the very credulous, permit themselves to be seriously influenced by what they read in the newspapers, because men have lost all confidence in the truthfulness and honesty of those who conduct our journals. The press is known to be as venal and corrupt[1] as the bosses whom it denounces with so fine a show of superior virtue. But in a socialistic order newspapers would belong to the community and would be published for the benefit of all. The temptation to falsify news and dissemble opinions would be removed; energy and talent could be concentrated in the collection and impartial interpretation of the world's news, and the press might become, what it ought to be, a people's university.

IX

Men complain of Socialism most frequently and most loudly, perhaps, that it will abolish liberty. Socialism is conceived as looking forward to a social condition in

---

[1] For example, the reciprocity bill enacted in 1911, to give effect to a treaty negotiated with Canada by President Taft, contained a clause for the free admission into the United States of Canadian wood-pulp used in the manufacture of the cheap white paper on which newspapers are printed. The bribe was sufficient. Carefully concealing from their readers the fact that they were beneficiaries, the newspapers of the United States, without regard to party, supported the bill and manipulated their news columns freely to create public sentiment in its favor. Canada rejected reciprocity, and the bill as a whole remains nugatory; but this single clause was made unconditional and went into immediate effect. The only newspaper that had courage to tell the whole truth about this disgraceful transaction was the *Outlook*, a religious weekly (strange coincidence!) that is printed on paper of too high a grade to profit by this change in the tariff.

which, in a sinister sense that the poet did not intend,

The individual withers and the world is more and more.

"Under Socialism," said a public speaker recently, "man would hardly own his own soul." To which a socialist might rejoin, that under Socialism a man would for the first time have a soul worth owning. The late philosopher, Herbert Spencer, was perhaps the most prominent in objecting to "the new slavery," as he was pleased to label Socialism.[1] In his earlier writings Mr. Spencer said many things that pointed in the direction of collectivism, but in his later years he conceived a violent dislike for the theory. Not long before his death he wrote to an inquiring friend a letter, summarizing his views, and authorizing their publication: (1) Socialism will triumph inevitably, in spite of all opposition; (2) its establishment will be the greatest disaster that the world has ever known; (3) sooner or later it will be brought to an end by a military despotism. Mr. Spencer might conceivably be right in the first prediction, and prove to be wrong in the other two. But without discussing the value of any of the predictions as such, do they not throw a strong light on a prevalent misapprehension regarding the nature of liberty, and the probable effect of Socialism, should that prevail?

It is the paradox of freedom that the less liberty a man

[1] Many of Mr. Spencer's admirers and echoes have failed to appreciate the fact that he criticised and opposed Socialism because he was essentially an anarchist. Anarchy is only the logical deduction, and it is the only logical deduction, from Spencer's premises of individualism and liberty. As Mr. Hillquit aptly says, "The theories of Herbert Spencer and those of John Most differ but in degree, not in quality." — "History of Socialism in the United States," p. 233.

has the more liberty he enjoys, the greater the number of his voluntary restraints the less he is restrained. Or, as Cicero put it long ago, *Legum omnes servi sumus, ut liberi esse possimus.*[1] Compare the liberty of the savage with that of the civilized man. For the savage there are almost no restraints save those of nature, but he speedily discovers that there is no despot like nature. Hence the savage has but a minimum of possibilities; he has no real liberty. The civilized man is surrounded by restraints — of habit, of custom, of law — but how indefinitely greater his real liberty, because of the indefinitely larger number of things he may do and enjoy. Freedom is not negative but positive; it is not mere absence of restraint, but presence of opportunity. If you give a poor man a thousand dollars, you have greatly increased his freedom, by multiplying the things that he can do. Other things being equal, the strong have more freedom than the weak, the educated than the ignorant, the rich than the poor. Civilization that frees us from restraints also multiplies restraints, but at the same time multiplies possibilities of action and enjoyment, and hence promotes freedom. The restraints of law are trifling in their pressure on the working-man, even in despotic Russia, compared with the restraints of poverty. To make a man, it is needful to make him rich — that is, give him enough to live a civilized life. It is not law, therefore, but poverty that hinders freedom in a civilized society, and Socialism is the attempt to release men forever from the restraints of poverty and correspondingly to enlarge real liberty.

Any price in the way of additional voluntary restraint that might have to be paid for such a result would be

[1] *Oratio pro Cluentio*, 53.

cheap, in any view of the case.   It is indeed possible that
the liberty of a few, of those who now enjoy most liberty,
might be somewhat curtailed in the course of socialistic
evolution, though it is not certain that any justifiable
and reasonable liberty would be lost by any; but the
vast majority of mankind would be certain to gain, and
the welfare of the vast majority must be the paramount
consideration.   For the working-man Socialism has no
possible terrors, not even extreme State Socialism.   Why
try to scare him by telling him that the State will dictate
to him what sort of work he shall do, and the number of
hours he shall do it?   Necessity has always dictated his
work, and his boss has dictated the hours.   He expects
to gain, not lose, by a change of dictation, and it is hardly
possible that he should be disappointed.   "Let no man
talk of the regimentation of the people under Socialism;
every shopman, clerk, or factory hand is drilled into
absolute uniformity of action now." [1]   A man chooses
his trade or occupation under the present system — in
theory; in reality, he takes whatever work he can get.
The number of those who can engage in a given occupation is now regulated by irresponsible individuals, namely,
those who choose to establish industries affording that
sort of occupation.   Does anybody seriously think that
the tyranny of a bureau,[2] conducted with some regard

---

[1] Villiers, "The Socialist Movement in England," London, 1908, p. 239.

[2] But why worry ourselves about a bureau — happy name! the thing
is so uniformly wooden — which is necessitated only by a single form of
socialistic theory, State Socialism.   State Socialism is paternal and autocratic; it would endeavor to regulate production by regulating persons.
Marxian Socialism, which has by far the larger number of adherents,
would regulate production and leave persons to regulate themselves.   The
former implies a bureaucracy, the latter is consistent with perfect democ-

to actual social conditions and subject to the people's control, would be worse than the tyranny of the present haphazard methods?

Why do men so generally dismiss their imaginations, and put their brains to sleep, when they begin the discussion of Socialism? Let us look candidly at this notion of the curtailment of the liberty of workers by Socialism. What is the daily life of the mechanic, the factory hand, the clerk, the unskilled worker? They rise, snatch an early breakfast while many of us are asleep, and are at their tasks by seven o'clock or earlier. They toil hard, many of them with only a half hour's intermission for rest and luncheon, until six in the evening or later. Many labor twelve and fourteen hours, fortunate are those who have only ten, and a few of the aristocracy of labor get off with eight. At the close of the day, most of them are utterly exhausted in body and stupid of mind — they eat their supper, smoke a pipe, or gossip a little, some of them stray away to the saloon for an hour or two; then they tumble into bed, and — *da capo*. Not only six days of the week, but many toil seven in this deadly round that ends only with the grave. The wives of men who thus labor are working equally hard in the home, often even harder, and always longer hours, for, as the old rhyme has it, "woman's work is never done." The children are taken out of school as early as the law permits, and too often earlier, and put to work, that they may add something to the slender income of the family. Is this any fancy picture? Those who know the life of

racy. The Roman Catholic Church, while suspicious of State Socialism, is not necessarily inimical to it, but it is irreconcilably opposed to Marxian Socialism. What it really opposes is not so much Socialism as democracy.

the working people know that it barely does justice to the reality.

Now to such a laborer, Socialism comes and says: "I offer you in exchange for this hard and joyless life of yours, ease and plenty and rational pleasure. You shall have a good house to live in, with abundance of light and air, and equipped with every comfort. You shall have as good food as anybody, as good clothes to wear. Eight hours shall be yours for sleep, and ten hours more a day for leisure, to be spent exactly as you please. Open-air recreations will be provided without cost; there will be lectures and theatres and whatever private social entertainments you desire. There will be libraries, where the best books can be had, galleries where the best art may be studied, concerts where the best music may be heard. If you have a thirst for knowledge, there will be universities in which you may be a learner, laboratories in which you may pursue investigations, not for four years merely, but as long as you please. If you have the creative impulse, you shall write books, or paint pictures, or mould statues, or invent new machinery, or compose music, to your heart's content. There is no limit to what you may do or what you may become, but your own desire and your own talent and industry.

"On your part, you must work for six hours, on six days of the week, or possibly for only four hours, at whatever labor may be assigned you. If you are put to farming, you shall have the best machinery and every facility for doing your work in the least laborious way. If you are sent to a mine, everything that scientific knowledge or engineering skill or mechanical ingenuity can do shall be done to make your work as safe and pleasant as it can be made. If you are assigned to a factory, it shall be well lighted and ventilated and warmed, and every appliance for safety that can be devised and all that sanitary science can suggest shall be supplied for the health and comfort of workers. Labor shall be freed from most of its dangerous and disagreeable features, and the process of making a living will be made comparatively safe, easy, and pleasant. Moreover, as all members of society will engage in useful and productive labor, work will be dignified and honorable. All that is asked of you in return for what is offered is, that you submit to competent direction and do your work faithfully; and so far as possible you will be assigned a task appropriate to your abilities and tastes."

Suppose the power to make this offer and to fulfil its terms. Would the world's workers part with any great amount of liberty in order to accept it? Would it be a hardship, would it be slavery, for any of us to live under such a régime? Undoubtedly a few of the rich would have to part with some of their present power and luxury, but how much better would be the lot of humanity as a whole! The greater portion of any community would be delivered from a present condition that is but one remove from slavery, and for the first time would become free men and women — as free as any can possibly be who live in a society, and therefore have obligations towards their fellows from which nothing can ever free them. This is what Socialism holds out to the worker. It is permissible to doubt whether such glowing promises can be fulfilled, whether so lofty a social ideal is realizable; but to call such an ideal slavery is surely the height of absurdity.

x

What effect may Socialism, if it becomes established, be expected to have on crime and vice? In the new order of society we may expect to see crime treated as we are coming to treat disease, the "great white plague," for example. The criminal is an abnormal person, and as such is dangerous to society; like a man with the small-pox, he is a source of infection to others. First of all he must be quarantined, and then, if possible, cured; if cure prove impossible, the quarantine should be made perpetual. In the family it sometimes happens that a member is not controlled by love but by selfishness; and if he cannot be won by loving persuasion to a better mind and a better conduct, there must be some exercise of authority for his restraint and punishment, as a means of winning him. So in the larger family, society, the selfish and the greedy and the violent must sometimes be restrained and punished. But force is to be used against the criminal, not vindictively, but in accordance with the law of love, to protect the weak and to win the erring to better ways.

A new criminology is one of society's greatest needs, and is even now on its way to recognition and establishment. By rational treatment crime may be greatly reduced, and in time may be expected nearly to disappear. All the present crimes against property would surely disappear with the temptation to commit them. Increasing refinement and training in self-control and the arts of social life would lessen the number and brutality of crimes against the person. All the social vices and most of the social crimes are greatly aggravated, if not

altogether caused, by the present keen struggle for existence. Yet there is grave reason to doubt whether vice
and crime will ever disappear, as a result of an improved
environment simply. In the unbridled lust of the flesh
among the rich and well-to-do, we find a large part of the
support of vice and the incitement to crime. Why should
we expect to see passion better controlled, merely because
all men have become well-to-do? Until men and women
are radically changed in character, we cannot expect so
radical a change in society.

And there is one class of evils that depend almost wholly
on the individual, very little on the environment — those
social wrongs that grow out of ambition, jealousy, hate,
lust. How can these be rationally expected to disappear
with advance of social comfort? So far as any of them
are aggravated by present economic conditions, we may
expect amelioration with economic advance, but the only
cure for evils is to cure their cause. That means, that
we must secure the regeneration of man. But that cannot be done by increasing his wealth, for it is by no
means the present experience that the richest are the
most ethical.

What effect may be fairly expected from the progress of
Socialism on the vice of intemperance, for example?
Socialists have been unwise thus far in not making active
war on the saloon, for, to say nothing of its incitement to
vice, all the evils of Capitalism are sublimed in the saloon.
Socialism, being above all a theory of the economic betterment of the whole people, cannot ignore the frightful
waste involved in the consumption of alcohol. A conservative estimate of the drink bill of the United States
is two billion dollars a year paid out by the consumers

of the liquors manufactured and imported. Sums so immense can mean nothing, until we find some unit of measurement that will bring them within our comprehension. Two billion dollars is a sum nearly equal to the entire gold and silver money of the United States; it is two hundred million dollars more than the combined capital of our national banks. Two billion dollars would pay our national debt twice over, and leave a surplus of two hundred millions; it would pay the total appropriations of Congress for about three years; it would build a fleet of two hundred Dreadnoughts, such a fleet as the world never saw or dreamed of; one sixth of it would pay for the Panama Canal; it is a sum exceeding the total assessed value of the property of Philadelphia or Boston, or of the States of Illinois, Indiana, Michigan, Minnesota, or Missouri. Owing to the flimsy construction of buildings, the loss by fire is probably greater in the United States than in any other country in the world; but we drink up in one year as much as fire costs our insurance companies in ten years. And this attempt to measure the drink bill, so as to make its extent comprehensible, excludes any estimate of the indirect costs of alcohol — what the taxpayer has to contribute for the prevention and punishment of alcohol-caused crime; for the relief of alcohol-made paupers; and the large voluntary tax for the support of asylums and hospitals, largely filled with the victims of alcohol. The cost of the criminal law and of charity is mainly chargeable to a vain effort of society to repair the damage that alcohol is doing every year.

All this is economic waste that can easily be expressed in dollars. But what shall we say of that other social waste that is expressible only in terms of life and happiness ? If alcohol only seized upon the vile and the vicious, we might look on with comparative equanimity, in spite of its enormous cost. But it clutches the brightest and best. Only the eye and mind of Omniscience can know and compute the greatness of this loss. But those who have lived long enough to see some of the most promising young men of their generation utterly ruined by intemperance can roughly estimate the loss to the world of these, and such as these for ages past. Minds that might have added to the happiness and extended the knowledge of mankind, or promoted the progress of civilization by invention and discovery, have brought to the world nothing but sorrow and shame. Men who might have become leaders of their fellows in State and Church, in literature and art, have died and left behind nothing but pain, and a memory that their dearest obliterate as quickly as possible.

Only recently have American socialists had the courage and wisdom to declare themselves in favor even of temperance, and they are openly opposed to prohibition. They have done good service, however, in emphasizing the fact that intemperance is greatly aggravated among the poorer classes by their poverty, and the squalor and misery that go with poverty in the great cities. Friends of the temperance cause must realize more clearly than they have in the past that closing the saloon will accomplish little good, so long as the demand for drink continues — the "speak easy" and the "blind tiger" in that case will simply take the place of the saloon, and the evil is hardly touched. They should not forget, as reformers have been too prone to do, that men must be won, not driven,

Y

to virtue — that reforms forced on an unwilling community accomplish nothing but revolt and ethical confusion
worse confounded. Better material conditions must be
provided for the poorer classes before marked improvement in temperance can be rationally anticipated. That
drunkenness is a cause of poverty is generally recognized,
but it is becoming clear that it is also an effect — men are
poor because they drink and they drink because they are
poor.

Alcohol in all its forms harms the working-man most,
because his organism is less strong and well nourished.
He may have as much muscular power as the man of the
higher classes, or even more, but he has not the same
toughness of constitution. The actuaries' tables of our
insurance companies show a marked difference in the
"expectation of life" between the upper and lower classes
of the American people. Alcoholic beverages injure the
laborer in another way than through their actual effects
on his body : they absorb money that he needs for nourishing food for himself and his family, and so he is still
further enfeebled by his indulgence. Yet it is easy to
comprehend the almost irresistible temptation of the
laborer to drink. He feels the need of exhilaration, something that shall dull his sense of suffering, relieve some of
his fatigue, slake the abnormal thirst created by some of
his employments. The wives of working-men are often
unfitted for domestic duties, wholly without training,
and do not know how to buy food to the best advantage
nor how to prepare it so that it shall be most palatable and
nourishing. Bad cookery has not a little to do with
driving men and women to drink.

The socialist, the prohibitionist, and the working-man

who is no sort of "ist," ought to join hands in united and determined effort to better these conditions. It is usual to object to prohibition, that a social vice like drunkenness cannot be cured by law; but it is a convincing reply that such a vice cannot be cured without law. True, men must be cured of the drink habit, the drink appetite, and that is a moral process, sometimes a therapeutic; but this cure can never be effected, in multitudes of cases, while a saloon on every corner continually appeals to the drinker's appetite. Existing laws are as sensible as it would be to set food before a starving man, at the same time saying to him, "If you eat that, you must pay a fine or go to jail." At the present time, the labor unions are in advance of the socialists in opposing the saloon. The constitution of the United Mine Workers forbids any member to sell any intoxicants, even at a picnic; and many of the most honored leaders of working-men have avowed themselves uncompromising enemies of the saloon and of drink.[1]

---

[1] Some official utterances by working-men's leaders: "Nothing has done more to bring misery upon innocent women and children than the money spent for drink. The laboring man has no money to spend on drink without robbing his family. I believe as the labor movement grows, so will the temperance movement grow." — John Mitchell, ex-president of the United Mine Workers. "Because the liquor traffic tends to enslave the people, to make them satisfied with improper conditions, and keep them ignorant, the leaders of the trade-union movement are called upon to fight the saloon." — Thomas L. Lewis, president of the United Mine Workers. "Who can deny that the liquor traffic is driving women to work in factories, in workshops, and at washtubs, who ought not to be there? The liquor traffic tends to reduce wages; never to increase them. The use of alcohol makes men less skilful, and drives them to lower scales of employment and reward. Every cent spent in the liquor business is wasted, bringing no social benefit or moral uplift." — John B. Lemon, treasurer, at the last convention of the Federation of Labor, in Toronto.

XI

An objection of the commonest against Socialism, and some esteem it the most serious of all, is that it would be destructive of the family. It is true that some socialists, regarding the family as the product of Capitalism and priestcraft, have declared for its abolition. Other socialists hold very different views. Mr. H. G. Wells says that Socialism, so far from destroying the family, "would make it, for the first time, so far as a very large moiety of our population is concerned, a possible and efficient thing." [1] With this Kautsky agrees, though he adds, "We expect that a new form of society will also develop a new family organization." It is vain to object that Socialism will destroy the home, when it is a fact that Capitalism has destroyed the home for millions, by reducing the laboring class to a degree of poverty that compels mothers to work in factories, and leave their families uncared for — that compels children of a tender age to work or starve. Destroy the home, forsooth! As if Socialism could possibly be a greater menace to the home than Capitalism now is. Nothing worthy of being called a home is possible to many millions of Americans under the industrial conditions of to-day. Not to mention that other enemy of the home, that the family can now never know security, being always haunted by the spectre of want. Greater than the actual misery of the worker's lot is this continual dark shadow of uncertainty that hangs over him and his — the possibility that he may lose his job to-morrow, that his union may declare a strike, or his employers decide on a lockout or on shutting down the works for an indefi-

[1] "New Worlds for Old," p. 131.

nite period, the prospect of sickness, injury, or disablement, and the certainty of old age and rejection everywhere. Lasting happiness is impossible with the wolf forever lurking just outside the door. It is difficult for virtue, impossible for contentment, to flourish in such an atmosphere.

In view of this often-urged antagonism of Socialism to the family, it is worthy of note that no current reforms engage the sympathy and practical coöperation of socialists more quickly and heartily than those that concern the problems of the home, especially the protection of women and children. One of the finest and most valued institutions in Germany is the forest home, near Berlin. Delicate children in the schools are sent, on the advice of physicians, to this out-of-doors school, and in a year or two most of them return, none the worse in their studies and greatly improved in health. The importance to the coming generation of such intelligent effort as this appeals strongly to socialists. The "fresh air" work in our cities meets with equally warm approval; only, socialists do not fail to urge that there is something better than such attempt to remedy the evils of the slums, and that is to do away with the slums, to secure fresh air, pure water, and clean surroundings for all. So socialists approve the attempt to prohibit child labor, but they also urge that it is comparatively useless merely to prevent the children from working and do nothing to uplift the families from which they come, for that is the wanton cruelty of condemning children to starvation and nakedness. Child labor is the direct product of social misery. Reforms cannot go single-handed, because social evils are interrelated in a complex system. Still, one must begin somewhere; we must strike at the nearest head of the hydra, and keep on striking, until the last one is killed.

It is hardly worth while to give serious consideration to the ideal community of the future, as some socialists have imagined it, so far as the treatment of children is concerned. That ideal might not be unfairly described as a great system of foundling hospitals, or Spartan barracks, in which all children shall be separated from their parents at a tender age and reared together under an ironclad system. If this seems to any people an improvement on the present order — even with plenty to eat and drink and wear guaranteed, and experienced nurses and teachers employed — one must infer that the present lot of the workers is fuller of misery than had been imagined, and that the present methods of rearing children are more ineffective than the sharpest critics have dared to charge; and also that parental love has declined to a degree that it shocks one to think about.

It is rational to expect a general uplift of the family through the effect that Socialism is likely to have on the status and character of women. The ideal of Socialism is the perfect equality of the sexes, but not the equality contemplated by existing laws. Legislation has thus far had as its principal aim the insuring of fair and free competition. Laws have been and still are like the rules of the prize ring or a Marathon race, merely an effort to secure a fair contest, and their spirit may be summed up in the phrase, "May the best man win." And it must be acknowledged that, under this free competition, the "best man" not infrequently turns out to be a woman. But while contests doubtless have their place in life, all life should not be a contest; and above all, it should not be a contest between men and women. A man may be compelled sometimes to fight, but there is something repulsive to healthy manhood in requiring, or even permitting, women to fight. It is because the present order of society makes life one long fight with one's fellows, in which the weakest go under, that the present order is radically and hopelessly wrong. In promising to make life a struggle for one's fellows, not with and against them, Socialism holds out a bright prospect of uplift for the whole race, and for woman especially.

By giving woman economic equality with man, Socialism would insure her equality in all things. But equality of right and opportunity does not mean identity of function. Nature has imposed on the race two imperative duties: to preserve life and to reproduce it. These may be called the primary duties of mankind. The chief burden of the preservation of life falls on man; the chief burden of the reproduction of life falls on woman. All those activities connected with the production and exchange of useful commodities, which we call "industry" and "business," are the special province of man, and the performance of his duties commands a return in money or money's worth. But there is no market price for maternity; a mother's fulfilment of duty can be paid only in love, in respect, in service. The relative incidence of these duties can never be altered; the future man, if there is to be a future man, must have a mother. And this means, inevitably, that women as a class can no more become the economic equals of man, in the sense of producing as much wealth as he, than a quart of milk can be made into a gallon.

No doubt, as Professor Densmore argues,[1] more hygienic training and outdoor life will make woman more nearly man's physical equal, without diminishing her charm; still, her sex function will prohibit her from equal competition or equal performance with man as a producer of wealth. But if nature has given to man superior strength, she has bestowed on woman the finer moral fibre and the higher spiritual endowment, —

> Her 'prentice hand she tried on man
> And then she made the lassie, O.

These gifts it is her privilege to use for her own generation, and her duty to transmit to posterity. This fulfilment of her function of maternity necessarily takes from the life of every woman who is a mother a large stock of her physical energy and a considerable portion of her labor-time. No other state of things is possible, or will ever be possible, if the race is to continue. Therefore woman can never equal man as a producer of wealth, but she is his equal in every respect in social function. Neither sex can be pronounced more indispensable to society than the other, both are equally necessary, and, therefore, both should receive equal social recognition. That is to say, both should receive an equal share of the results of their common labors.

The recognition of this perfect social equality, so far from threatening the permanence of the family, ought to increase it. Such condition will promote reasonably early marriages. Youth is the natural time for mating, but under present conditions only the imprudent poor

[1] "Sex Equality," New York, 1907, esp. Chap. III.

and the rich who do not need to be prudent venture to marry early. The average man must establish himself in some business or profession or trade, so that he can be reasonably certain of a good income, according to his social standards, and so be confident of his ability to support a family. When men and women are economic equals, and both are assured of a competence, earlier marriages may be expected, and offspring physically and spiritually superior to those of present-day unions, often concluded late and between persons who never should have been mated.

The socialist protests against a social order that virtually compels every woman to attach herself to a "bread-winner," with or without legal sanctions, or suffer heavy social penalty and perhaps actual want. Women cannot have the dignity that belongs to their sex function until they are given independence, economic and ethical, as well as legal. Are those marriages exceptionally unhappy now, or exceptionally likely to end in divorce, in which both parties are financially independent? If the wife has property and income of her own, does she love her husband less, or is she less devoted to her children, than the woman who must ask her husband for a nickel every time she wishes to take a trolley car? May we not fairly expect more marriages for genuine love, when, on the one hand, men are no longer tempted to be fortune-hunters, and no woman is compelled to marry for a home?

Those who first called prostitution "the social evil" spoke more wisely than they knew, for, seeking only a euphonious name, they hit upon an accurately descriptive epithet. It is almost wholly a social evil, due to the economic dependence of women upon men, and may be expected to disappear entirely under Socialism. Comparatively few women choose this life of vice because they are inherently vicious; it is for them a means of livelihood, often the only possible means. Rescue work makes no visible impression on this great social ulcer, because we are only fooling with the symptoms, providing soothing plasters, and lack courage to go to the root of this disorder. No doubt sexual immorality will continue, to some extent, under Socialism; but the great majority of men and women may reasonably be expected to love purely and to live unselfishly for the welfare of those whom they love, when they are on an absolute social and economic equality. The coming of children will bind a married pair still more closely together, in future as in the past, for neither Socialism nor anything else will materially change human nature. The love of parents for their children will be no less in a new society than it has been in the old. And while love endures, the family cannot fail; when love fails, the family cannot endure.

It is recognition of this principle that has led many socialists to favor the dissolution of the marriage bond, as soon as affection has ceased to bind husband and wife together. But this is not a view peculiar to socialists. In the divorce colony at Reno will be found many of the capitalist class, but few socialists. It is equally true that some socialists have advocated what is commonly known as "free love" for marriage, a more or less refined hetærism, or even promiscuity of the sexes. But these are mere vagaries of individuals or groups, that have no special affinity for the real principles of Socialism, since such individuals and groups are at least equally numer-

ous among those who are not socialists. Many opponents have been conspicuously unfair, to the verge of
deliberate dishonesty, in attempting to fasten upon
Socialism a theory of marriage that is no essential part
of the system.

XII

What effect would Socialism have on "society" in the
narrower sense, on the association of men and women for
mutual pleasure? It would probably have no direct
effect, and would seek to have none. Social intercourse
would continue to be arranged, as now, on voluntary
principles. Indirectly, however, Socialism might have
an effect, and, so far as one can forecast, entirely for good.
It would do away forever with those artificial distinctions
that rest on wealth, and social intercourse would arrange
itself on the basis of mutual affinities of character, tastes,
and pursuits.

The destructive effects of Socialism on our present
social customs are more easily predicted than the new
combinations that would be effected. The chief expenditure of those who now have means above their
wants is less on pleasure or luxury than on display.
These are sometimes hard to distinguish, it must be admitted, but are usually separable. Men buy automo-
biles and yachts, partly, of course, because they like
sports, but still more because engaging in these particular
sports marks them out as men of wealth and a certain
leisure, and so constitutes a claim to social eminence.
Women flaunt silks and velvets, diamonds and pearls,
partly because these are beautiful objects and are supposed to enhance the beauty of the wearers, but still more

because their possession is in itself a certificate of wealth and a title to social distinction. We all buy things more to impress Mrs. Grundy than to please ourselves. Has our neighbor a new parlor organ? We must at once have a piano, and thereby show our social superiority, even if no member of the family can play the new instrument. If Mrs. Smith has a new silk dress, Mrs. Jones across the street goes her one better with a sealskin coat. And so forth and so on, to the end of the social chapter.

Socialism would do away with the greater part of display, if not with all, by depriving people at once of the motive and the means. If men are conscious of economic equality, each will have the courage to be himself, to live his life in his own way, and the temptation to imitate or surpass his neighbor will be eliminated. Even if the disposition for display should remain, which is possible, the ability would be lacking. No one in a socialized community could greatly surpass his neighbor in the mere externals of living; if he wishes to surpass, he must surpass in real worth, in character, in attainments. And the higher forms of character, the best attainments, are rarely or never bred by the desire to surpass; they come through sincere love of the thing sought. It seems a reasonable forecast, therefore, that the ethical tone of society would be higher under the new order than it now is, and that there would be more real happiness, with less envy and jealousy — all, certainly, things most devoutly to be wished.

Social ostracism will probably be more effective than law in a new social order, for the repression of offences with which it may be inexpedient for the law to deal.

Even now this is sometimes the case. A woman known, or even suspected, to have lapsed from sexual virtue loses her social standing at once and can scarcely ever recover it again — even to be proved innocent does not always avail. A man caught cheating at cards will be expelled from his club and sent to Coventry by men who are not at all particular about most forms of moral transgression. This is a means of social discipline obviously capable of indefinite extension, if people choose to extend it. If society strongly disapproves a certain line of conduct, the remedy is in its own hands and can be applied without legislation at any time. Fines and imprisonments, and even death itself, are penalties no more feared than social disgrace.

IX

THE SOCIAL TEACHINGS OF JESUS — GENERAL
PRINCIPLES

BIBLIOGRAPHY

General works: —

BEYSCHLAG, New Testament Theology, 2 vols. Edinburgh, 1895.
WENDT, The Teaching of Jesus, 2 vols. New York, 1892.
BRIGGS, The Ethical Teaching of Jesus. New York, 1904.
GILBERT, The Revelation of Jesus, New York, 1889.

The Social Teaching of Jesus: —

Ecce Homo. Boston, 1896.
CANDLISH, The Kingdom of God. Edinburgh, 1864.
BOARDMAN, The Kingdom. New York, 1899.
MATHEWS, The Social Teaching of Jesus. New York, 1899.
PEABODY, Jesus Christ and the Social Question. New York, 1904.
JENKS, The Social Significance of the Teaching of Jesus. New York, 1908.
WESTCOTT, Social Aspects of Christianity. London, 1887.

IX

THE SOCIAL TEACHINGS OF JESUS — GENERAL PRINCIPLES

NOTHING is more encouraging in theological studies than the general recognition of the fundamental importance of candid, reverent, inductive study of the teachings of Jesus. That such study should have been postponed until our generation is the marvel of marvels. One would have reasoned that the paramount desire of Christians in all ages would have been to learn what was taught by him whom they professed to accept as Master and Lord. Much of value has already been accomplished in this study, but much remains to be done. It is so difficult a task to put away from the mind previous theological bias, and permit the words of Jesus to make their own impression, that the work cannot be accomplished in a single generation. Much critical study of the sources was necessary, and is still to be completed, before we can be assured that what purport to be the words of Jesus are really his words.

But any fruitful study of the teachings of Jesus must be truly critical, not pseudo-critical. No arbitrary rules can be suffered to decide whether a given saying is to be recognized as genuine, or should be excluded as a late tradition. Historical critics are prone to forget that what they call documentary evidence is only one of the criteria of truth. A method that rejects the parables of

the tares, the leaven, and the pearl of great price, because
they are found only in Matthew, or will not receive as
the words of Jesus the parables of the Good Samaritan
and the Prodigal Son, because they are found only in
Luke, certainly leaves something to be desired in ethical
insight and critical authoritativeness. Many of the
sayings attributed to Jesus in the gospels are so self-
evidencing to men of acute moral sensibility that external
evidence is dispensable. Even a critic like Schmiedel
comes near recognizing this : "We may accept as credible
everything that harmonizes with the idea of Jesus which
has been derived from what we have called the foundation pillars, and is not otherwise open to fatal objection."
Many offences have been committed in the name of criticism, but perhaps none have been more flagrant than the
rejection, for lack of fuller external attestation, of words
that nobody could have spoken but the Teacher of Gali-
lee. His ethical sayings are of so unique character that
they cannot be supposed to have been either imitated or
radically altered — they burned themselves into the memories of those who heard. We may allow something
for traditional or editorial modification of form, but most
of the words of Jesus given us in the synoptic gospels cannot be invalidated by any rational criticism. In a discussion like the present, results must be given, not processes ; but we must certainly have a wider basis for our
discussion than the nine "foundation pillars" of Schmiedel
or the "doubly attested sayings" of Burkitt.[1]

Careful inductive study of the ethical elements in the
teaching of Jesus is the more necessary, because it is

[1] Schmiedel, "Jesus in Modern Criticism," London, 1907. Burkitt,
"The Gospel History and its Transmission," Edinburgh, 1907.

notorious that even his professed disciples do not accept
his ethics as actual standards of character and conduct.
The Christian world has long been agreed that these
ethics are to be interpreted as counsels of perfection, as
ideals beautiful indeed, but forever unattainable. That
they are basic principles for the direction of life and conduct, few Christians believe and still fewer practice. The
Jesus of the gospels found his most formidable opponent
in the Judaism of his day; his chief present obstacle is
the Christianity of our day. We have to free ourselves,
therefore, from this unrecognized attitude of hostility
to the teachings of Jesus, before there is any reasonable
prospect of our comprehending them.

An immense work must be done, as indispensable preliminary to successful study of the ethics of Jesus, in
discharging our minds of prejudices and inherited ideas.
Centuries of dogmatic instruction have so warped the
mental operations and colored the imaginations of men
that it is almost impossible to see Jesus in the dry, white
light of truth. The very historic facts are so incrusted
with tradition that they are hard to come at, and so un-
familiar in form that they are even harder to comprehend.
Comprehension is an effect of sympathetic imagination,
and is impossible so long as we insist on subjecting the
Oriental mind to the psychological processes of the West.
Jesus was not a Western academic lecturer, but an Oriental popular teacher. We must expect to find him speaking in the sententious, enigmatic manner of other Oriental teachers. He does not pursue the scientific method
but the literary.[1] He utters pregnant sayings, not pre-

[1] As to literary form, much of the teaching of Jesus is in that rhythmic
style of the Proverbs and other Wisdom literature, generally termed

cise definitions. He speaks in bold metaphor, in start-
ling paradox. The West dotes on abstract ethics; Jesus
gave men concrete ethics. We should be prepared, therefore, to find many of his sayings relatively true, not
exactly true. And yet we must not rush to the opposite
extreme, and regard the teachings of Jesus as a series
of cryptic utterances, whose meaning is to be laboriously
puzzled out. They are brief, epigrammatic, often highly
figurative, illuminative, stimulating; "my words," he said,
"are spirit and life." To interpret his paradoxes and
metaphors as if they were rigid scientific definitions or
precise rules of conduct, is to fall into that very rigor of
legalism that he reprobated in the Pharisees, in the strongest invective that ever fell from the lips of religious
teacher.

More than grammatical exegesis is required to understand ethical precepts of this order, and to understand
them as grammarians will often be to miss their meaning
altogether. Nothing could be a more wrong-headed principle of interpretation than this suggested by an eminent
New Testament critic: "The only legitimate exegesis of
the passages is one that assigns to them their obvious literal meaning. Nothing else could have been intended.
In no other sense could they have been understood by
the original hearers or readers."[1] But the gospels make
it plain that the hearers of Jesus often misunderstood

"Parallelism"—the only poetry known to the Hebrews. It will astonish some to be told that Jesus was poet as well as prophet, but such
he was, if we have his words as he spoke them, though all translators and
editors have done their best — or worst — to conceal this fact from the
English reader.

[1] Orello Cone, "Rich and Poor in the New Testament," p. 214. New
York, 1902.

him, because they insisted on this principle of interpretation. Nowhere are sympathetic insight and sound judgment more necessary than in studying the words of Jesus. He himself often intimated as much: "He that hath ears to hear, let him hear."

Jesus taught ethics, not an ethic. He did not aim at clothing his precepts with scientific form, or giving them schematic completeness. He speaks a truth here, he tells a parable there, flashes of ethical light into the darkness of men's souls, rather than careful reasonings. We look to him for ideals and inspiration, not for systematic instruction. Yet though unsystematic, his teachings are not a haphazard collection of miscellaneous unrelated sayings; there is an organizing principle to be found in them, without long search or undue ingenuity. The followers of Jesus are under no obligation to do what their Master deliberately declined to do — construct a complete ethical system out of his detached sayings — but his teaching will be better understood by us if we see that there was an order in his ideas, and that his chief sayings stood in a sound logical relation to one another. For, though a concrete thinker, Jesus was not a loose thinker, and he was not content with the Emersonian rule of speaking what is true to the mood of the moment, trusting his sayings somehow to harmonize with each other, and despising consistency as the infirmity of small minds.

One other preliminary word should be said. Religion has to do with man's relation to God; ethics with man's relations to his fellows. Jesus was a teacher, not of ethics alone, but of religion — his ethics were grounded in his religion, were the necessary consequence of his religion. In the mind of Jesus the two appear to have been inseparable and the follower of Jesus can never consent to their separation. The one thing that was never absent from the thought of Jesus was his consciousness of God; and the one thing that cannot be eliminated from his teaching is the sentiments of dependence, of duty, of gratitude, of devotion toward that Soul of things known to us as the perfection of unity, power, wisdom, love, and law. But while the impossibility of an examination of the ethical teachings of Jesus, in which his religion shall have no part, ought to be apparent to any one who is at all familiar with his words, it is possible to give our main attention to the ethics.

I

In making an inductive study of the social teaching of Jesus, it is of the first importance to get his own point of view. How did he conceive of his mission? What did he believe that he had come into the world to accomplish?

If we approach the gospels with this question, we shall have little difficulty in finding an answer, for Jesus and the evangelists leave no room for doubt on this point. It becomes clear at once to one who studies his words that the social teaching of Jesus was no by-product, that his ethical precepts were no fortuitous *obiter dicta*, but that this was rather the essence, the burden of his message to men. He came to proclaim the Good News; of that we are so often assured as to leave no possibility of doubt that this was the way in which Jesus himself conceived of his mission. His message is still further described as "the Good News of the Kingdom of God," or "the kingdom of Heaven." The proclamation of Jesus was Good News to men, because it was the announcement that the great hope of the nation was on the verge of fulfilment: the kingdom of God was at hand.

The mission of Jesus is also described as "salvation" — he proclaimed a divine deliverance of both individuals and society, through the establishment of a new society, the kingdom of God. It was for this work that he was the Anointed of God. There was evidently in his mind no thought of a national restoration, a great political renaissance of Judaism, such as the Jew of his day ardently desired. For to the Jew, the kingdom of God had come to mean a revival of the monarchy by a son of the House of David. The kingdom indeed connoted the ideas of a commonwealth of righteousness, peace, and plenty, but only as a result of the triumph and worldwide rule of Israel. The Messiah was to supplant the emperor as sovereign of the world, and sway the sceptre of the nations from Jerusalem, and the foot of the Jew would be on the neck of the Roman. The current Jewish idea of the kingdom was, in a word, purely political and materialistic.

But to Jesus this was nothing. There were many zealots in Israel, after him, as well as before him, but Jesus declined to be a zealot. The kingdom in his eyes was one in which God should rule and righteousness prevail and good triumph, a kingdom in which the poor in spirit shall come to their own, the meek shall inherit the earth, the merciful obtain mercy, and the peacemakers be called children of God. The Jews expected a political deliverance, Jesus proclaimed a social. They scornfully rejected a kingdom and a Messiah so differing from their preconceptions. And yet if Jesus could have won the Jews to acceptance of his spiritual kingdom of God and a reorganized society, Jerusalem would have been saved and the Jewish race would have been promoted to the hegemony of the earth. They adhered to their dream of world conquest and world empire at Jerusalem, and their city was lost and their race scattered.

The certainty, confidence, and persistence with which Jesus proclaimed this idea of the kingdom is the most striking fact in his ministry. It is the dominant note of his teaching; it is set forth as the supreme quest of every disciple. And this, the most comprehensive term that we have for the mission of Jesus, marks his teaching as fundamentally a social teaching: for the conception of a kingdom is the conception of a society, ordered by law. But what kind of a society? What did Jesus mean by the kingdom of God? He has told us this plainly in the prayer that he taught to his disciples: it is a kingdom of God, for in it God is to be more fully revealed to his children as their Father; it is God's kingdom, inasmuch as his children are to honor him more fully, because more intelligently, as Father; it is God's kingdom, since in it his will is to prevail completely, as it now prevails in heaven.[1]

The kingdom is the master-word of Jesus, the root idea of all his teaching; we shall seek in vain to comprehend his ethics, unless we grasp this word and all that it implies. We must first of all see this world reconstituted, as Jesus in imagination saw it, so as to consist of a society of renewed men, men who have experienced the blessedness of a new life — a life imparted by God, and hence lived in harmony with God; a life ruled, guided, as God himself is guided, by the law of holy love. It is a king-

[1] Matt. 7:21; 18:14; Luke 12:47; 22:42; Mark 3:35.

dom impossible to the natural man, so to enter it he must be born again from above. And this is an experience impossible to the proud, the self-righteous, the self-satisfied, so that only those who are meek and teachable in spirit can ever learn the secret of Jesus and obtain entrance to his kingdom. Men cannot compel the coming of such a kingdom of the spirit, though they can do much to hasten it; God alone can set it up; the kingdom and the power and the glory are his.

This conception of the kingdom, fundamental in the teaching of Jesus, marks his Good News as a social gospel in its very essence, not in any occasional and accidental way. From a previous tendency to overlook the social nature of the teaching of Jesus, the pendulum is now swinging rapidly to the opposite extreme, and the tendency is strong to treat his teaching as wholly social, and social in a very literal and narrow sense, as concerned mainly with the material welfare of men living in social relations. Historical Christianity has without doubt erred in its overemphasis of the individual; the Protestantism of the last two centuries has gone to the very extreme of this assertion of the importance, the sacredness even, of the individual soul. It is the marked feature of the teaching of Jesus that he holds in just equipoise the two great, elemental, equally necessary ethical truths: first, that society cannot be regenerated except by the birth of individual souls into a new life; and, second, that the individual cannot exist apart from society and cannot be saved apart from his social relations.

The Good News of Jesus is spoken to individuals. The purpose of its proclamation was first of all to transform

single lives.   Jesus made all his appeals to the individual,
elevated the soul to new dignity, rediscovered the worth
of personality.   Such a message was of the more value
to his age, as the tendency of Roman imperialism was to
subordinate the individual to the State.   Nothing could
well be more emphatic or impressive than this side of
the teaching of Jesus.   The kingdom is the reign of God
in the individual soul, the supremacy of his righteous will
acknowledged and obeyed, followed out in all conduct, at
whatever cost of opposition or suffering.   A supernatural
revolution of the individual is the necessary condition to
a natural evolution of society.   The shepherd went out
into the wilderness to find the one sheep that had
strayed; the woman swept her house with lighted lamp
to find the single coin she had lost.   In all the teaching
of Jesus, the most resonant and thrilling note struck
is this worth of the individual soul.   The gospel is, as
Harnack says, "a question of God and the soul, the soul
and its God." [1]

But this is only half the content of the gospel.   Men
are saved singly, soul by soul, just as truly as men are
born singly into the world; but, on the other hand, every
regenerate soul is born into a society, as truly as every
human babe.   The gospel is as fundamentally social as it
is individual.   The two elements are no more separable
in religion than they are in any other part of human life.
Man is a social animal on the spiritual side, as completely

---

[1] "What is Christianity," p. 56.   Christianity has no necessary affinity
with economic individualism.   In his eternal relations to God and righteousness, Christianity teaches that each individual soul stands or falls
alone.   In his relations as a man, in the actual affairs of life, Christianity
insists that no man lives to himself, that we are all members one of another.

as on the physical. In transforming a human life, Jesus transforms all its relations. "On the one hand," says Dr. Peabody, "the kingdom is an unfolding process of social righteousness, to be worked out through individuals; on the other hand, the individual is prompted to his better life by the thought of bringing in the kingdom." [1] No better suggestion, perhaps, is possible of the practical reconciliation of the social and individual elements in the teaching of Jesus. Beginning in individual hearts, the kingdom is intended to work outward like leaven, until all society is affected. Insignificant as the mustard seed, it shall become a tree. It shall make the disciples of Jesus the salt of the earth, the light of the world. The world shall eventually be transformed into the kingdom.[2]

The ignoring of either of these two principles will lead to speculative error and practical disaster. The message of Jesus loses its reality, if we forget his estimate of the infinite value of the individual soul; the individual loses his significance and his very salvation becomes impossible, unless we hold fast to the idea of his social relationships, as Jesus taught them. The idea of salvation is a necessary synthesis of individualism and socialism; no soul can be saved but by personal, vital contact with a Saviour; life can be communicated only by contact; —

[1] "Jesus Christ and the Social Question," p. 120.

[2] It is often urged that the collectivism of Socialism is opposed to individualism, but a reconciliation or synthesis may be found. The conflict between individual interests and collective is no greater in society than in the family. Both individualism and collectivism find their place, and are easily reconciled in family life, provided only the family is ruled by the law of love. Socialism merely proposes to extend the family, until a nation, a race, become one great family, with common interests, a common life, and a common purse.

there is no long-distance gospel. But Jesus did expect society to be regenerated; he did look to see the kingdom of God prevail; he came into the world to insure its victory over the powers of evil. The kingdom was not a mere figment of the imagination to him, but the royal rule of God actually established in the earth. He looked forward to a social future of which Isaiah's glowing prophecy was so far from seeming exaggeration that it rather disclosed the poverty of language for an adequate description.

The teaching of Jesus regarding the kingdom struck at every form of privilege. There was no longer a privilege of birth: men did not become members of the kingdom by descent from Abraham, but by a transformation of character, a new birth of the spirit. There was no privilege of wealth and social position: all members of the kingdom became brothers, with equal rights and equal duties. There was no privilege of priesthood: every man could go direct in prayer to his Father, and worship God in spirit. There was no privilege of learning: the Pharisees who knew the law were no better than the *am-ha-arets* whom they despised, possibly not so good as he. And because this was the teaching of Jesus, because he was the great Leveller, all who were concerned in the maintenance of privilege conceived a great, a deadly hostility to him. He was the great Revolutionary of the ages, and he knew it. "I am come to cast fire on the earth," he said. Not peace, but a sword, was his greatest gift to man, for every great idea is a sword, and his was the most militant idea ever made known to men. No more revolutionary teaching could be conceived. Jesus clearly implied the reconstitution of society as organized under the Roman Empire; and he equally implied the reorganization of society as it exists to-day throughout the civilized world. Renan exaggerates little, if at all, when he says, " A great social revolution, in which distinctions of rank would be dissolved, in which all authority in the world would be humiliated, was his dream." Such teachings as his could no more be made compatible with any form of society yet known to man than a piece of unfulled cloth could be made to agree with an old garment. New wine put into old wineskins would no more certainly burst the skins than this teaching of Jesus would rend asunder old institutions.

They miss the mark altogether, therefore, who say that Jesus was concerned solely with the world of spirit, that he endeavored to found an exclusively spiritual community. To accept his teachings was and is impossible, without making an attempt to carry them into every relation and detail of life. The teachings of Jesus are spiritual, no doubt, but their effect, just so far as they really prevail, is necessarily to reconstitute the individual spirit not only, but to reconstitute the society in which Christian spirits dwell. Yet it is true that Jesus had no more intention to furnish a programme of social reform than he had to teach a system of theology. His work was to declare principles, to awaken consciences, to inspire effort, not to work out polities and constitutions. We need not stumble if we find him at times hard to reconcile with modern thought. He must speak to his own age, if he was to speak to any age; could he have spoken as a man of the twentieth century to men of the first, he could not have made himself understood, and his life would have been lived in vain.

We cannot pass on without brief consideration of another notion regarding Jesus and his teaching about the
kingdom that has lately won considerable acceptance,
not to say enthusiastic advocacy, in "critical" circles.
Bousset, for example, maintains that Jesus conceived the
kingdom as something in the future and wholly miraculous.
It was to come suddenly and with a great display of power.
The apocalyptic ideas that we find in the discourses recorded in the thirteenth chapter of Mark's gospel, and
in the twenty-fourth and twenty-fifth of Matthew's, dominate all of the thinking and teaching of Jesus. If this
view is correct, and Jesus believed in an immediate and
catastrophic consummation of the kingdom, after his
lifetime yet near at hand, the remote future is excluded
from the scope of his ethical teaching. In other words,
all his teaching is of a temporary character, intended to
govern his disciples during the brief time that was to
elapse before the end of the age — interim ethics, not
universal.

In this view of the case, Jesus not only did not teach
any absolute ethics, valid for all subsequent ages, but
he had no intention of doing such a thing. For all that
we know, therefore, his sayings may have no application
whatever to the conditions of the present age. Then, if
Jesus was only an apocalyptist, and his ethics were only
interim ethics, what concern have we with his teachings,
or what difference does it make to us what he taught?
If he was so entirely and hopelessly astray about the
whole subject of the kingdom and its coming, as events
proved him to be on this hypothesis, his opinions cannot
matter to us more than those of any crack-brained enthusiast. Not merely the divinity of Christ, but any real

significance or authority of Jesus as an ethical teacher, absolutely disappears if this theory is accepted. We had better turn to Aristotle, who at least tried to establish ethics on a basis perpetually true.

But when we come to examine the gospels, it is evident that this theory cannot possibly be held, without a ruling out of one-half of the evidence. That the kingdom proclaimed by Jesus was apocalyptic and catastrophic exclusively, is a theory flatly contradicted by fully half of the sayings attributed to him. If we take into consideration all the evidence as given to us by the gospels, we find him describing the kingdom as both present and future — that is to say, a present possession whose full consummation lies in the future, when God's love shall have completely conquered the evil in the world and restored men to his likeness.[1] "The kingdom of God is at hand," "The kingdom of God is within (or among) you," are sayings that cannot be fairly ruled out, and they cannot be reconciled with an exclusively apocalyptic conception of the kingdom. The parables of the sower, the seed, the tares, of the mustard seed and the pounds, are not easily reconcilable, to say the least, with the idea of immediate catastrophe.[2] Bousset does attempt to explain the parable of the mustard seed in this sense: since the mustard plant in the Orient attains its great size in a single summer, therefore Jesus expected

[1] Matt. 8:11; 13:43; 25:34; 26:29; Mk. 14:25; Luke 13:28; 22:18-29, 30.

[2] This idea is even less sustained by the latest documentary criticism than by the gospels as they stand. Neither Schmiedel nor Burkitt seconds Bousset. The apocalyptic element is not prominent in the "nucleus" of Flinders-Petrie; it is wholly absent from the Sermon on the Mount, which gives the core of Jesus's teaching regarding the kingdom.

the kingdom to reach worldwide extent and power in a few years — an exegesis as far beside the mark as the inane objection of earlier critics that Jesus committed a scientific blunder in this parable, since the mustard is demonstrably not "the least of all seeds."

II

The significance and worth of the kingdom, in the mind of Jesus, consisted in the fact that it was the kingdom of God. The deepest need of man's nature is to know God, and this knowledge men sought after, longed for, but never fully attained, until the coming into the world of Jesus of Nazareth. For he first clearly made known to men a God who is our Father in heaven, a Being whose inmost nature is holy love. Gods who hated the world, men had believed in ere this, and trembled before them. A Creator of the world, an omnipotent King, terrible in righteousness, merciful only to the one people whom he had chosen out of the nations to be peculiarly his — such a God the Jews had believed in and slavishly obeyed. But a Father,[1] a God who loves all the creatures he has

---

[1] Father is as distinctively the Christian name for God as Jehovah is the Jewish. "Father" as a name for God occurs about a dozen times in the Old Testament, and over two hundred times in the New. Five prayers of Jesus are recorded, and in each of these he addresses God as Father (Matt. 11 : 25–27; 26 : 39, 42; Luke 33 : 34, 46) and in the longest of these the name is thrice repeated. The disciples are bidden to follow his example (Matt. 6 : 9; 23 : 9). This was not the current Jewish habit, as the prayers of the Pharisee and Publican testify (Luke 18 : 11–13). The fourth Gospel greatly emphasizes the Fatherhood idea, using the term about ninety times. If any deny that this gospel gives an accurate historical reflection of the ideas of Jesus, it must at least be allowed to measure how deeply he had impressed this idea on his disciples.

made — all, not a chosen race, nor a chosen few — and with parental solicitude ever seeks the good of all: of such a God the world had not so much as heard. It can hardly be said to believe in such a God now. Good News like this seemed too good to be true. Yet Jesus habitually spoke of God as "my Father"; in his teaching he spoke of him to men as "your Father"; and he taught his disciples to pray to God as "Our Father, who art in Heaven." Aristotle, one of the wisest of pagans, said, "Love to God does not exist; it is absurd to talk of such a thing, for God is an unknowable being."[1] But Jesus came to reveal the Fatherhood of God, and so to make the love of God not only possible but normal, since he is in every way worthy of our love, the one Being who is absolutely and unchangeably good.[2]

Will it be believed that learned Doctors of Divinity are still arguing whether Jesus warrants anybody but a Christian — *i.e.* a professed follower of his — in calling God "Our Father who art in Heaven"? To Christians, they say, he is indeed a loving Father; to all others he is still the same terrible hater of iniquity and punisher of the evil-doer, that men thought him to be before the coming of Jesus. One wonders if such disputants ever read the parable of the Prodigal Son! So little as that do Christian teachers, in this twentieth century, yet comprehend the kind of God that Jesus revealed to us: the Father of all men to whom he has given life, who, as their Father, desires with all the power of an infinite and holy

---

[1] " Magn. Moral." ii. 11. Plato is a little more hopeful — "God, the father and creator of the universe, is hard to find, and, when found, impossible to impart to all." To use modern nomenclature, Plato is theist, Aristotle Deist.   [2] Mark 10 : 18.

love the well-being of every child of his; who has no favorites among his sons; whose heart yearns over the erring and sinful, and precisely because he is a Being of infinite moral perfection, holy and righteous altogether, hating with all the energy of his nature that which is impure and unrighteous, longs, not to punish his erring and disobedient children, but to restore them to the joys and privileges and purity of the family of God. This is God as Jesus reveals him to us, not only in his words, but in his character, at the same time assuring us that "he that has seen me has seen the Father."

That God was the Father of Israel is an idea that the prophets should have made familiar to every Jew, but the conception of God as the Father of all mankind, of each human being, was first set forth with unerring certainty by Jesus. And if God is the Heavenly Father of all, it follows that every man is still his child, however sinful, wandering, or degraded. We may deny our sonship, we cannot lose it. Each human life, in the light of this truth, becomes a thing of priceless value, of unspeakable worth, so that there is joy in the presence of God over a single wanderer who returns to home and love. To be "lost" is to be in the far country, away from the Father's house, separated by our own act from the Father's love; to be "saved" is to be brought back to our Father's house and love, and restored to all the privileges of sonship. Only the cross could add anything to the idea of God's Fatherhood that is given in the parable of the Lost Son.

We see, therefore, in the teaching of Jesus a message that was not Jewish, not national, not racial, but universal. This element is apparent in many single sayings, as well as in much of the parabolic teaching, like the great supper, the marriage of the king's son, the wicked husbandmen. It is even more manifest in his conduct. He never turned away a gentile : the Samaritan woman, and the leper of the same race, the servant of the centurion, the daughter of the Canaanitish woman, appealed not in vain to his sympathy.[1] In every possible way and on all occasions, he taught that the brotherhood of those who are children of the common Father cannot be bounded by race or color; it must be as wide as the Father's love. Brother is not only fellow-disciple, it is fellow-man; neighbor is not he who lives next door, nor co-religionist. Who is my neighbor? asked the lawyer. And in the parable of the Good Samaritan, Jesus made answer, "Anybody who needs you; anybody whom you can help."

Mr. Blatchford says that he cannot believe in the existence of a Heavenly Father, such as Jesus reveals, and sees no signs of him anywhere.[2] But to most of us the difficulty is rather not to believe in a Heavenly Father, for we see signs of him everywhere. If there is no mercy, no goodness, no Fatherhood, at the heart of things, how did we, merely what this universe has made us, come by such ideas as goodness and mercy and fatherhood, and how is it that we are in some measure good and merciful and fatherly? Can the stream of human nature rise higher than its source? Can we be good, and yet derive from no source of goodness? To believe in the earthly fatherhood and deny the Heavenly is the most monstrous of all irrationalities.

[1] John 4; Luke 17 : 18; Matt. 7 : 26; Mark 7 : 26.
[2] "God and my Neighbor," pp. 73–78.

> From the first Power was — I knew,
> Life has made it clear to me
> That, strive but for a closer view,
> Love were as plain to me.

But, men object, you are anthropomorphic when you call God your Father. The objection is true, thus far: we express the highest spiritual verity that we can conceive in terms of man, but how else could men express their ideas? The words in which we vainly try to clothe our religious ideas do not so much testify to the poverty of our language as to the majesty of our thought. When we call God Father, we affirm our conviction that there is at the heart of things a Life from which all things else proceed; a Mind, not less conscious and intelligent than ours, but infinitely greater in scope, whence proceed unity and order and beauty; a Goodness, of which ours is but a dim reflection, the source of all righteousness and justice; a Love that is dimly shadowed in the present human affection, and which seeks the highest welfare of all creatures. Religion is the seeking of oneness with this Life, this Mind, this Goodness, this Love.

The Fatherhood of God is the one thing of which Jesus claimed unique and conclusive knowledge. And it is this knowledge of God as Father that constitutes his the one heart pregnant with celestial fire, that makes him not only the purest but also the strongest among the sons of men, that gave to the world one life which both illustrates and justifies the daring words of the Hebrew poet: —

> When I behold thy heavens, the work of thy fingers,
> The moon and the stars, which thou hast ordained,
> What is man that thou art mindful of him,

Or the son of man that thou visitest him?
And yet, thou hast made him little less than God,
Thou hast crowned him with glory and honor.

From Jesus we first learned that the true humanity is the
divine in man. His sonship, according to the gospels,
consisted in a perfect consciousness of moral union with
God, so that in all things the Father's will was his, not
in a metaphysical union such as the creeds vainly attempt to set forth in words. This was a relationship
manifested in his boyhood consciousness, that grew with
his growth. We need not pause to debate the question
of the sinlessness of Jesus; but the record of his life dis-
closes this fact, unparalleled in the history of the world's
teachers: he never betrays the slightest sense of guilt,
while he shows the highest conception of goodness. In
this he differs from the most saintly men, whose shame
at wrong-doing is always proportioned to their saintliness.

III

Jesus, then, proclaimed to men a God who loved the
whole world. No other view of his mission is contained in
the early Christian literature. All who stood near Jesus,
and had opportunities of learning his teaching, are a
unit in this presentation of the matter. They all exalt
before men, as worthy of their worship and obedience, a
God whose nature is everlasting, boundless, holy love.
What do we mean when we say that Jesus reveals God
as "holy" love? Something higher, purer, something
more worthy of our reverence and imitation, than the
mere passion or affection that we too commonly have in
mind when we speak of love. "Holy" love implies

something of higher ethical value than emotion; it implies a principle of action that controls all thinking and willing and doing. It describes the self-imparting principle, that quality in the nature of God that impels him irresistibly to give himself to others. This is the significant thing in the revelation of God as Father made to us by Jesus: out of the heart of the infinite God, there wells up an inexhaustible, an everlasting fountain of love, in whose lifegiving stream the whole world is bathed.

The object for which this love is imparted to man is described as "salvation," deliverance. The method of this deliverance Jesus describes in varying terms, all of which have in common the element of spiritual change. On one occasion he said, "The truth shall make you free." The man who is living an evil life is in bondage, he is a slave, for there is no bondage like the liberty to be only vile, and

> He knows a baseness in his blood
> At such strange war with something good,
> He may not do the thing he would.

Jesus promises to free him through the truth — to make him free in the only real sense: free to love, free to do justly, free to hear and obey the highest dictates of his nature, not the lowest.

Again, Jesus speaks of salvation as conditioned on repentance — a change of attitude towards God and man, something within the power of man. He recognized the fact that man is more than a congeries of thoughts and emotions, that he is ruled by will, that he has a purpose. And he also recognized that man does not acquire goodness by endosmosis, but by volition, or rather, by a series of volitions, until a habit of right-doing is established. The Prodigal's "I will arise and go unto my Father" was a determination quite within his own power, resting on a sense of wrong-doing, "I have sinned against heaven and in thy sight." It was the constant endeavor of Jesus to induce men to turn from the life of the mere human animal, that he might lift them into the life of the sons of God.

Again, Jesus declares that the secret of deliverance hangs on faith, trust. But what sort of trust? Preachers and theologians have taught that to be saved we must "trust in the merits of Christ" or "trust in Christ's atonement for sin," and the like. But Jesus never said these things. He said deliverance comes to man by trusting in Him and doing his commandments. The first is a legalistic conception of salvation, the second is vital. The one grows out of a system of theology, the other out of a sense of personal need. Trusting Jesus is deliverance, because it is spiritual dynamic; it brings man into vital relation with Jesus and his Father, involves a new life of love and righteousness, and insures power to continue in that life and develop into likeness to God.

Salvation by believing something has no place in the Good News — that was the error of the Scribes, as salvation by doing something was the error of the Pharisees. By "faith" Jesus did not mean pronouncing a series of formulas about him, he meant spiritual receptiveness. The people to whom he spoke were like present-day Christians, so self-satisfied, so blinded by religious conceit, clad in such an impenetrable armor of pride, that his Good News had no significance for them. His teaching could find no entrance into their minds, no echo in their hearts; hence it evoked no response. But sometimes he found hunger for the truth, spiritual receptivity, where he had least reason to expect it — as in the case of the centurion, of whom he testified, "I have not found such faith, no, not in Israel." This is the secret of his oft-repeated saying, that the kingdom must be received as a little child, with that receptivity of impressions of spiritual truth that is characteristic of childhood, the time when

> The earth and every common sight
> To them do seem
> Apparelled in celestial light,
> The glory and the freshness of a dream.

But we reach the heart of the teaching of Jesus regarding deliverance when he represents it as the impartation of life, eternal life. It is this element of his teaching that, when it has been fully apprehended, has made his Good News a message that finds the deepest longing of the human heart and fully satisfies it. "In bringing life and immortality to light," as the apostle phrases it, he brought to the world a draught for which it had been long athirst. For,

> Whatever crazy sorrow saith,
> No life that breathes with human breath
> Has ever truly longed for death.
>
> 'Tis life, whereof our nerves are scant,
> Oh life, not death, for which we pant;
> More life and fuller that I want.

But how often and for how long has this teaching of Jesus been misapprehended, since men have persisted in

thinking of the "eternal" life as the life of heaven, a life
of the hereafter that cannot begin until this life is ended.
Yet Jesus said explicitly, "He that trusts me (commits
himself wholly to me, becomes mine in thought and conduct) has eternal life." He represented the eternal life
that he came to impart as the present possession of every
one who truly became his disciple. And that meant
simply this: the purpose of God's love, the end for which
he is revealed to us in Jesus, is that we may be brought
into a character like his own. Nothing is more characteristic of the teaching of Jesus than this, and it is the
foundation of all his ethics. A single paragraph from
the Sermon on the Mount is representative of all: —

You have heard that it was said,
    "Thou shalt love thy neighbor
    And hate thine enemy."
But I say to you,
    "Love your enemies,
    And pray for your persecutors,
    That you may become children of your Father in Heaven;
    For he makes his sun rise on evil and good,
    And sends rain on righteous and unrighteous.
    For, if you love those that love you, what reward have
      you?
    Even the tax-gatherers do that, do they not?
    And if you are courteous to your brothers only, what are
      you doing more than others?
    Even the heathen do the same, do they not?
    Be you therefore perfect,
    As your Father in Heaven is perfect.[1]

Deliverance consists, therefore, in being changed from
what we are into what God is. We are "saved" when

[1] Matt. 5:43-48.

we begin to manifest a character of holy love. And Jesus promises to impart this life, this character, to every disciple ; he has engaged to supply just what every man is conscious of lacking, not ethical ideals so much as ethical power. Jesus makes it possible for every man to have this life, and to have it abundantly — that is to say, to realize fully, not in some small measure merely, this ideal of character. The cynic who says, "You can't change human nature, it is bound to remain selfish," and the enthusiast who seeks to build his Utopia on an unchanged human nature, are alike wrong. Jesus can change human nature, and on that changed nature a new social order may be built. He can and does change men from lovers of evil, doers of unrighteousness, into lovers and doers of the good and the true. Nobody can read a book like Mr. Begbie's "Twice-born Men" and have any doubt of that.

This it is to be a Christian : to make Jesus our Teacher and Exemplar, and to live his life among men. As he reveals to us a God of holy love, who unstintedly imparts himself to men, as he himself lived a life of self-sacrifice and service, so a disciple of Jesus to whom life has been abundantly imparted will be animated by a like spirit of unselfish love and service. Jesus was the great Deliverer, but every follower of his must be a deliverer also. Jesus gave himself to men, not only on the cross, on which the Christian world has too exclusively fixed its eyes, but in lowly service through his whole life, of which we are far too oblivious. "The Son of Man came not to be ministered unto, but to minister." Many a follower of Jesus has given his life for his fellows, in the very spirit of his Master, and the impulse to do this is inseparable from

Christianity.   Seeing in God their Father in Heaven, his
disciples must see in every man their brother on earth.

IV

And so Jesus summed up all religion and all ethics in
the twin precept : "Thou shalt love the Lord thy God with
all thy heart," and, "Thou shalt love thy neighbor as
thyself."   On these two commandments hang not only
all the law and the prophets, but all the Good News.
Love to God and man are the two hemispheres of duty.
Religion, in the conception of Jesus, consists in the service of man and the vision of God ; and commonly the
vision comes to us as the reward of service — as also our
own Longfellow has taught us.

This is the uniqueness of Jesus as an ethical teacher.
Instead of a bewildering subdivision of duties and commandments, a medley of great and small, inextricable
confusion of important and unimportant, Jesus gave men
one simple law, "Thou shalt love."   Love, as he used
the word, does not depend on the lovableness of the
object, but on our will ; it is not, as we have seen, primarily, an emotion or sentiment, but a principle of conduct, a habit of unselfishness, of kindness, of ministry.
We cannot will our emotions, but we can will our conduct.
And perhaps it would be as well, as has been suggested,
if we could substitute for the word "love," which has
come to have all sorts of misleading connotations, the
term "good will."   We are resolutely to keep ourselves in
an attitude of good will towards all.   "The man is most
truly a man in the attitude of good will ; and he is at his
best for every kind of successful effort when his good will,
ruling every impulse and appetite, compels the whole

menagerie of animal forces within him to do the work of his manhood." [1]

When Jesus repealed the ancient law of hate, and said, "Love your enemies," he commanded the Jew to cherish good will towards the Roman. Nothing but a change of nature, a complete reversal of ethical standards, would enable a Jew to do that. When Jesus says to the men of to-day, "Love your enemies," he commands the working-man to cherish good will towards the capitalist. Can that be obeyed without a change of nature? But to carry this spirit of good will into all social relations is the idea of the kingdom of God that Jesus proclaimed. The highest test of character is not loving friends, or even helping the needy, but in manifesting good will to those who have wronged us — not merely foregoing revenge (though that is noble), but suppressing just resentment of injury and actively doing good to him who has done evil to us. "The everlasting rule," says Trench, "is that thou render good for the brother's ill; the shape in which thou shalt render it, love shall prescribe." Though Jesus gives many precepts, they are all facets of the one precious jewel, love.

The chief of all possessions is self-possession, but that a man may truly possess himself he must first have renounced self. The greatest good that God has bestowed on man is life; but in order to find his life a man must lose it. The desire of distinction is probably the most imperious of all social impulses; but to be great in the kingdom is to be servant of all. This Great Paradox of Jesus is a corollary from his law of love, and is the profoundest of his social ethics.

[1] Dole, "The Coming Religion," Boston, 1910, p. 64.

> Till this truth thou knowest:
> "Die to live again,"
> Strangerlike thou goest
> Through a world of pain,

says Goethe, though his life gave little token that he had himself learned a truth that he so clearly expresses. By performance of a menial service, according to the fourth gospel, Jesus illustrated this idea of the practical outcome of love in our relations to our fellows, as, girded with a towel, he washed the feet of his disciples. In this labor, usually relegated to a slave, he visualized the nature of that which he inculcated as love of the brother.[1]

"He that loses his life for my sake shall find it," is not a barren counsel of perfection, but a social law, verifiable as such by every man for himself. Life cannot be really lived unless it is lived for something that death cannot destroy. But a life lived for self will soon be destroyed by death — only a life lived for others leaves behind it permanent results. It is Tolstoi's great merit to have perceived this; it is his great defect that he could not perceive one thing more: that Jesus inculcated renunciation as a spirit, not as a law. "To renounce everything," he says, "therefore, could not, it seemed to me at first, be an absolute condition of salvation. But the moment this ceased to be an absolute condition, clearness and precision were at an end." The root of the great Russian's difficulty was that he insisted on finding in the discourses of Jesus what Jesus never put there, the clearness and precision of a legal code.

---

[1] John 13 : 4–11. Like the story of the woman taken in adultery, this incident authenticates itself as certainly true, because impossible of invention.

But Jesus did not give us a code; nothing was further from his intention than that; he taught us to live the life of the spirit. And living that life, no man can find fulness of life by living to himself; only as he lives in and for others does he truly find himself. Yet the renunciation in which Jesus tells us that we obtain our greatest blessedness, is not that renunciation of the world which ascetics of all ages and of all faiths have falsely taught, but renunciation of self. There is no virtue in what men commonly call self-denial, but all virtue is comprised in what Jesus called denial of self. And as man finds himself in finding the meaning of love, the meaning of life is disclosed to him in service. He discovers that the service of God is the service of his fellows. The realization of his neighbor's claims on him is a man's first true self-realization. Once it was thought that the great thing was for the sinner to save his lost soul from the world; now we know the great thing to be for the saint to give his soul to a lost world, and that he saves both the world and his soul by the giving.

Not only does the man who devotes himself to the salvation of others get his own salvation on the way, and as it were incidentally, but he will often be surprised by its attainment. There is a fine, and even a humorous, touch in the parable of the sheep and the goats, in which Jesus illustrates this idea that we can serve God most effectively by being kind to God's children: the note of surprise in the words of those who are rewarded, "Lord, *when* saw we thee hungry and fed thee, or thirsty and gave thee drink?" They were rewarded for their service, because they had not been serving for a reward. They had done their duty simply, unostentatiously, as it came to them, and the modesty of real goodness had kept them from realizing that they had been good. Sham goodness, on the contrary, wishes all the world to see how very, very good it is. If by any possibility, sham goodness could be conceived among that throng on the Judge's right hand, it would not be astonished at the reward, but would complacently accept it as a proper recognition of merit, and even wonder why it was not larger.

Men are more religious than they suspect, incurably religious, even men who tell us that they have no religion — they often practice what they do not preach. Whoever loves and serves is so far one in spirit with Jesus and his Father. Whoever listens to the voice of duty is listening to the voice of God, and in his obedience makes himself one with the eternal and universal Life of power and goodness in whom inhere all the real values of the world. For in such obedience fear has vanished, and the peace that passes understanding takes its place — the fundamental fact of all religious experience, which is none the less a fact if it be admitted to be inexplicable. To do the will of God the Scriptures represent as the end of all religion and the condition of all blessedness.

V

And here we see the reconciliation of idealistic and rationalistic ethics, long supposed to be at opposite poles and in deadly conflict. Both are right, and so far from contradicting each other that they offer each other mutual confirmation. The strongest argument of ideal ethics is, that we are compelled to posit an eternal distinction between good and evil, founded in the nature of

God, whose moral law is but the transcript of his character. The basal principle of that law is love — love of
God, love of man. The best statement of rationalistic
ethics is that right and wrong are ideas that derive their
validity from social well-being. Right is conduct favorable to the preservation and progress of the race; wrong
is unfavorable conduct. But love is the only conduct
that is favorable to the race; altruism is the necessary
condition of human progress. Recognition of human
brotherhood is, on either theory of ethics, the foundation
of all right conduct between man and man.

This has been vehemently denied by the German
philosopher, Nietzsche, among others. "Life," he says,
"is essentially the appropriation, the injury, the sub-
duing of the alien and weak. It is suppression, compul-
sion, the enforcing of its own forms. It is assimilation,
and at the least and gentlest, exploitation." He scouts
altruism: "The weak and crippled should go to the wall:
that is the first principle of our philanthropy." "Do I
counsel you to love your neighbor?" asks Zarathustra;
and this is his answer, "Nay, I counsel you rather to shun
your neighbor, and to love those farthest away." Nietzsche preached unadulterated selfishness: "One must
learn to love himself, with a wholesome and healthy love,
so that one is sufficient to himself, and does not run about
in ways that are described as love of one's neighbor."
And he professed to found his ethic on the results of
science, the law of evolution and the survival of the fittest:
"Sympathy opposes, in the main, the law of development,
which is the law of selection. It preserves what is ripe
for destruction, it operates to defend the disinherited
and condemned among men. This disheartening and

contagious instinct . . . is . . . a chief instrument in the advance of decadence." [1]

It is doubtless quite true that the only practicable ethics in a society organized on the principle of competition are the tooth-and-claw ethics of the jungle. The Golden Rule is impossible in such a society. Jesus and Socialism alike demand the abolition of competition and the substitution of some form of collectivism, which is simply brotherhood applied to economics. Nietzsche clearly perceived this essential affinity of Christianity and Socialism, and he therefore hated both with an impartial and undying hatred. But Marxian Socialism should have been welcome to him. The present evils of society are caused by selfishness and greed, and the remedy that Marx proposes is — more greed and selfishness, the class struggle. *Similia similibus curantur !*

But Nietzsche's philosophy has resulted from a misreading of the facts of the universe, a misunderstanding of the law of selection, an interpretation of Darwin that is both narrow and false. Tennyson is responsible for much of this popular misunderstanding of evolution, and his stanza of "In Memoriam" —

> Who trusted God was love indeed
> And love Creation's final law —
> Tho' nature, red in tooth and claw
> With ravine, shriek'd against the creed —

is challenged as sharply by science as by theology. This

---

[1] The climax of Nietzsche's insane conceit is reached in this saying on the ethics of Jesus: "Believe me, my brethren ! He died too early; he himself would have revoked his doctrine, had he reached mine age ! Noble enough to revoke he was !" *Also Sprach Zarathustra*, First part, "Of Free Death," *et al.*

2 B

idea of a universal ruthlessness of struggle is not the Darwinism of Darwin, but of some unwise interpreters. "Those communities," says Darwin himself, "which include the greatest number of the most sympathetic members, would flourish best and raise the greatest number of offspring." [1]   Love is the law of the universe, not of human life only.   Much warfare of extermination does go on in the lower forms of life, but there is at the same time much of mutual support, aid, defence.   Maeterlinck has opened our eyes to this in his book on the Bee. Those animals that live in groups or societies, and acquire habits of mutual aid, are the "fittest" for life's struggle.   Competition exists in nature, but progress is made by the elimination of competition and the growth of coöperation.   Not strife and death, but peace, helpfulness, and love is nature's way upward.

And this has been conspicuously true of man, in all stages of his development.   "The first men who substituted the state of mutual peace for that of mutual war," says Huxley, "whatever the motive which impelled them to take that step, created society.   But in establishing peace, they obviously put a limit upon the struggle for existence.   Between the members of society, at any rate, it was not to be war *à outrance*.   Of all the successive shapes which society has taken, that most approaches perfection in which the war of individuals is most strictly limited." [2]   The survival of the fittest is in no way incompatible with the gradual improvement of all, as Huxley shows in his description of that conduct which is ethically best : "In place of ruthless self-assertion it demands self-

[1] "Descent of Man," Chap. IV and V.
[2] "Evolution and Ethics," p. 104.

restraint; in place of thrusting aside or treading down all competitors, it requires that the individual shall not merely respect but shall help his fellows; its influence is directed not so much to the survival of the fittest, as to the fitting of as many as possible to survive. It repudiates the gladiatorial theory of existence. It demands that each man who enters into the enjoyment of the advantages of a polity shall be mindful of his debt to those who have laboriously constructed it; and shall take heed that no act of his weakens the fabric in which he has been permitted to live." [1] No better exposition of the element common to the teachings of Jesus and the aims of Socialism has ever been made than this, by one who was neither Christian nor socialist. The philosophy of Nietzsche was refuted before it was stated.

That God is our Father, that this is God's world, that we are all God's sons, bound by the tie of brotherhood into one great family — these are the corner-stones on which all the social teachings of Jesus rest. It was because he believed these things so firmly that Jesus had the courage to attempt the establishment of the kingdom of God, a society ruled by God's spirit of unselfish love. His social ideal may be summed up by saying that his aim was to make all men brothers, by making them consciously sons of God; and that his firm conviction was, that only by brotherly love, thus implanted and sustained in human hearts, can the problems of society be solved.

VI

Aristotle founded his ethics on the abstract idea of the *summum bonum*, which he decides is happiness. His

[1] *Ibid.* p. 20, 81.

whole scheme of moral principles and moral duties is logically deduced from that abstract idea. Jesus does not discuss abstract ethical principles: What is the *summum bonum?* What is conscience? Has man free will? He begins with a concrete conception of human society, in which love or mutual good will is the universal law, and all his other precepts ray out from this.

The result of the principle of love in human conduct, Jesus uniformly calls "righteousness"; and as love has its two hemispheres, so has righteousness. By this comprehensive term Jesus means, first a right relation to God, and second, right conduct to man. The right relation to God consists in recognition of his Fatherhood, and the correlative duty of sonship. For, though all men are sons of God, and can be nothing else, by becoming disciples of Jesus and receiving the life that he imparts, they become sons of God in a more intimate sense. The Prodigal was a son in the far country among the swine, but not until he arose and went to his father, confessed his fault, and received his father's forgiveness did he know the depth of a father's love and enter into his real sonship. The first part of the Sermon on the Mount is mainly given to teaching this righteousness toward God. We need pause only to note how flatly Jesus contradicts the Jewish ideal of righteousness: that outward ritual, formal piety, constituted conduct that would win the favorable verdict of God. The righteousness of his disciples must exceed the righteousness of the Scribes and Pharisees, because it must take account of the spirit of religious and ethical precepts, not of their mere letter.

In the second part of the Sermon on the Mount the manward side of righteousness is expounded, and from the same point of view: it must be genuine, not formal. It is so easy to exaggerate the value of the external and formal, to atone for a lack of spirituality by laying an additional stress on ritual. But righteousness is something deeper than its outward expression, else goodness might be capable of scientific determination in terms of kilowatts, and we might express love in amperes or volition in voltage. Formalists, legalists, Pharisees, continually attempt this identification of the outward with the inward, until the latter is altogether denied and righteousness comes to signify an act and not a state of soul. It was the first work of Jesus to correct this error and to recognize the true nature of righteousness, as proceeding from love, good will.

Jesus differed from other ethical teachers in that he aimed not merely to change conduct, but to transform character — to transform character as the only effective means of changing conduct. He goes behind the outward act to the hidden motive; make the tree good and the fruit will also be good. He concerned himself primarily, not with what a man does, but with what he is. While others sought to impose on their followers an elaborate code, he sought to create a new man. Righteousness is goodness; it springs out of love, and shows itself in deeds of mercy and compassion to men, not in ceremonial exactness. "Ye must be born again" is fundamental; "conversion is the only means by which a radically bad person can be changed into a radically good person." [1]

Jesus clearly perceived that the Pharisees, though they opposed the worldly-minded Sadducees, were not them-

[1] "Twice-born Men," p. 17.

selves spiritually minded. To them righteousness was legalism, formalism, individual. They had no conception of solidarity, brotherhood, of conduct as affecting others and determined as to its ethical character by its effect on others. In their conception, righteousness was entirely a matter between man and God, and had nothing to do with a man's relations to his fellows. The pure soul of Jesus loathed the Pharisee who could practice iniquity toward the poor six days of the week, and on the seventh make long prayers and prate of righteousness. The Pharisee practised a scrupulous religiosity. Jesus lived religion.

Some will have it that Jesus differed from the Pharisees only in giving a new set of rules for human conduct, whereas the real difference was that the Pharisees taught rules, while Jesus taught principles. He came not to give laws but to give life. They were concerned with the fruitage of evil only; he struck at the root of the great Upas tree of evil. And so he declared that inward purity takes precedence of outward, that filial love is more important than gifts to the Temple, that mercy is more worthful than sabbath-keeping, that truth and justice are more to be sought than accuracy of tithing. Such teaching was fitted to exert a blissful emancipating effect. The legal servitude was to be exchanged for filial relationship, love was to take the place of fear, a sense of freedom and gladness would replace the old consciousness of the curse of the law. Truly, as compared with the Rabbis', Jesus might call his yoke easy and his burden light.

The Jew, under the lead of the Pharisees, had come to neglect social righteousness altogether; he had substituted ritual for brotherly love. He had forgotten, if he ever knew, that a man cannot be right with God and wrong with his fellow-man; he tried vainly to atone for social unrighteousness by piety toward God. That is where many are making a similar mistake to-day — those Christian Pharisees who believe that they can cheat their fellows and make it right with God by building a church or hospital or endowing a college. It was not because they tithed mint, anise, and cummin that Jesus condemned the Pharisees, but because they neglected justice and mercy and faith. He did not find their ethics too strict, but too lax. Men who boast that "their religion is the Sermon on the Mount" do not understand the first word of Jesus. He not only did not destroy the law, — the Jewish ethics that he found, — but he filled it full. He gave a keener edge to every precept, he put a new intensity of meaning into every "Thou shalt not." But he went further: for the "Thou shalt not" of Moses he substituted his own "Thou shalt." He saw that ethical perfection is positive, not negative; it is more than mere sinlessness, it is victory over the powers of evil. We ascribe to Jesus the perfect character, not because he avoided the ethically bad, but because he constantly overcame evil and did the ethically good. For this reason, Christianity is not merely a new ethic, but a new life, the continued presence in the world of a vivific Personality.

No such lofty ethical ideal was ever proposed before, and Christians have spent a large part of their time and thought ever since in explaining away, and lowering to what they are pleased to account a practicable standard, the teachings of that incomparable discourse. Yet the very loftiness of the standard is its chief practical value. To take but a single instance: it is conceivable that a man may never commit an overt act of impurity, and yet his soul be a raging hell of lust and passion during his whole life. Is such a man righteous? The world says, Yes. No, says Jesus. What, says the world, is it not enough that the man outwardly keeps the law of social righteousness? No, says Jesus, for though such a thing is conceivable, it is most unlikely to happen. The inward righteousness is the only sure foundation of the social. The fires of passion are likely at any time to burst through the thin crust of conventional correctness of conduct, and then we see one of those volcanic outbursts of social unrighteousness that issue in a terrible tragedy and astonish and convulse a whole community. In ethics, though not in nature, grapes may sometimes be gathered from thorns and figs from thistles — or what are passable imitations of grape and fig — but the crop is scant and very uncertain. On the whole, the words of Herbert Spencer hold good: "There is no political alchemy by which you can get golden conduct out of leaden instincts." [1]

Jesus finally presents, as a convenient summary of the law of love, a practical maxim that should control all conduct of man towards his fellows, "All things therefore whatsoever ye would that men should do to you, even so do ye to them." We need not waste time in discussing whether the Golden Rule was original with Jesus, whether Confucius and other sages had anticipated him in whole or in part; the chief thing is to note that the rule has been accepted from then until now as the highest ethical

[1] "The Coming Slavery," *Popular Science Monthly*, April, 1884.

truth. And it is substantially this that socialists propose as the principle that must underlie the new order,
and guide men as brothers in all their relations. But
Socialism has done Christianity good service in pointing
out the difficulty, not to say the impossibility, of obeying
the Golden Rule in a social order that is founded on selfishness and mutual hostility. No life of ethical perfection is possible for any man until it has been made possible for all men, because, as members of society, our
interests are so mutual and so complex that no man can
live to himself if he would, and no man can be saved by
himself or for himself. To live the Golden Rule with
any approach to completeness demands the reconstruction of our social conditions.

This becomes plain if one considers his normal life for
a single day. The clothing that one dons on rising in the
morning — do we ever realize how it has been produced
and by what means it has become ours? Do we ever stop
to think that the sweat and the tears and the very life-
blood of men and women have gone into the making of it,
and did we ever try to compute how much cruel injustice
and oppression and cheating have accompanied the various transactions that brought the garments to us?
Has not our only thought been how cheaply we could buy
them and how becoming they are to us, careless how this
demand for beauty and a good bargain might affect our
fellows? The coffee that one drinks at breakfast, the
sugar one puts into it, the roll and the beefsteak, or the
eggs and bacon — if one knows anything of the methods
of modern business, he knows that every article of food
on the table represents a host of wrongs, which he is helping to keep alive and pass on by consuming the viands.

Some of these wrongs have been done to us, others are wrongs done to our fellows. The wrongs done to us may usually be measured in the increased price one pays for his food, but many of the wrongs done to our fellows are measurable in deepest human misery. Can we, does anybody, live the Golden Rule under such conditions? An angel from heaven could not do it.

The breakfast is eaten, and men and women go to their daily tasks. How many things in the comprehensive word "business" will bear the test of the Golden Rule? How many men excuse themselves every day for things that will not bear that test, things from which their own not-too-sensitive consciences revolt, by saying, "If I don't do it, somebody else will." And it is absolutely true, *somebody else will*. We need not complete the analysis; let any one follow himself through the day to the evening meal, the evening amusements, the bed in which he sleeps — everywhere the same conditions! The man most disposed to live the Golden Rule cannot do it by himself, for it is a social rule. Society must be delivered, society must be regenerated, or the individual cannot maintain a regenerate life — society will prove too powerful for the individual, and will drag him down with it in a common ethical ruin. Either the love of God must prevail in this world, or the sin and misery from which God would save the world must prevail. Which? That is the problem of this age, as it has been the problem of all the ages.

This problem is the common ground of Christianity and Socialism. And it soon transpires, on survey of the ground, that there is both agreement and disagreement between the ethics of Jesus and the ideals of Socialism.

The agreement has been perceived by many socialists, who have professed admiration for the social teachings of Jesus, and some even profess to accept the teachings for their own. But these socialists, even when their sincere acceptance of the ethics of Jesus is beyond question, see in him only the Teacher, not a Saviour. They do not recognize that the real lack of the world lies not so much in ethical ignorance as in ethical impotence, that it needs regeneration more than enlightenment. The world has always had high moral ideals — not the highest always, but still high — what it has lacked is moral dynamic. The chief significance of Jesus in the history of mankind is that he is a Saviour, that he offers men deliverance.

VII

The message of Jesus to the world, therefore, is that social reform is possible only through spiritual renewal. To have a new society, there must first of all be a new man. The wiser socialists perceive this to be true, but hope for the renewal of man by evolution. Others put their trust, as did Owen, in education. Many reformers are busily trying to make men sober and peaceful and just and intelligent by legislation. Education and legislation are far from despicable as aids in the reorganization of society; but why expect from them what nothing short of Omnipotence can do? Education is only the training of the life that is, not the impartation of new spiritual life. Legislation, at the best, can only restrain men from doing the wrong; love of the right and impulse to do the right must come to men from a source entirely different.

Jesus is unique in his method of righting social wrongs. He proclaimed revolution by spiritual renewal, not by blood and barricades. But for this it would be hard to understand his indifference to organization, his disregard of the institutional side of religion, his aloofness from the temporal and political affairs of his age. He walked upon the waves of social agitation and unrest; others were submerged by them. Others had attempted to regenerate society by providing it with new forms; he saw that the only regeneration was to breathe into it a new spirit. Others had led a movement and founded a sect; he brought to men a new life, which could be trusted to find for itself appropriate outward forms. He saw into the heart of things, where most reformers see only the surface.

Here is an utter contrast of spirit and method between Jesus and present-day Socialism. Socialism seeks to attain the new society without the new man. The few who have insight enough to see that this is hopeless seek the new man by inadequate methods. In some vague way, undefined and indefinable, they trust to the evolution of the new man along with the new society. But man may be expected to evolve himself into the new man when we have discovered the secret of lifting ourselves over a fence by the straps of our boots. Only Jesus has shown the world how the new man may be produced, he alone possesses the secret of regeneration. And history proves abundantly, as does present experience, that the method of Jesus is practicable, that it is efficient, that it really accomplishes what it professes to do; while experience and history alike establish the negative conclusion, that no other power under heaven has been able to regenerate a man or a people. Improvement of social conditions demands, as a precedent condition and as a concomitant, better character. The teaching of Jesus tells how better character may be had, the only effective way yet known to mankind. Given a better man, a better social order is inevitable.

"To be converted," says William James, "to be regenerated, to receive grace, to experience religion, to gain assurance, are so many phrases which denote the process, gradual or sudden, by which a self hitherto divided, and consciously wrong, inferior and unhappy, becomes unified and consciously right, superior and happy in consequence of its firmer hold upon religious realities."[1] Whence we see indeed that the new psychology differs very little from the old gospel. In a letter written and published not long before his death, Count Tolstoi said to a friend, "I assert and will never cease from saying, that the only radical means for opposing the oppression of the masses by the idle minority is the religious rebirth of the individual. Further, the founding and fostering of religious brotherhoods is the only social activity that is suited to our day for the man of conscience who will not be an oppressor. I agree with you that the establishment of these religious communities can relieve the distress of the poorer wage workers. But I do not believe that a brotherhood movement can develop religious sentiment out of itself. On the contrary, the new birth alone can strengthen and fortify the movement."[2] Belief in the necessity and effectiveness of spiritual rebirth is not peculiar to revivalists and "orthodox" Christians.

[1] "The Varieties of Religious Experience," New York, 1902, p. 189.
[2] Printed in *Record of Christian Work*, July, 1910, p. 437.

Only a superficial student of social conditions can doubt that the chief ailment of society to-day is not deffective organization but moral weakness. If this is an accurate diagnosis, the methods advocated by Socialism are nothing better than a plaster applied to a cancer — the plaster may alleviate pain, but cannot cure disease. Jesus says, "Except a man be born from above, he cannot see the kingdom of God." Socialism says, Except society be reorganized, man can never be happy. The two sayings do not contradict each other — they are in different planes — but which is the profounder teaching? Which best corresponds to man's experience, present and past? A large part of social ills proceed, not from maladjustment of social institutions and forces, or from the maladjustment of the individual to his environment, but from the maladjustment of the individual to himself — in other words, they proceed from his own evil passions, impulses, character. Moral evil is not a theological abstraction, or an ethical theory, but one of the elemental facts of human experience. Socialism has no place in its philosophy or order for incurable moral perversity. But this exists; it must be reckoned with; a remedy for it must be found. Some socialists would treat this perversity, like crime, as a department of pathology. Pathology is all very well, as a preliminary. Before a cure for typhoid could be suggested it was necessary to learn the cause of the disease. But in every case the goal of medicine is therapeutics, not pathology, and Socialism has no moral therapeutics. Most socialists simply ignore the whole question — wave it gracefully aside, like Mr. Podsnap, and decline to discuss or even to recognize the difficulty. But moral perversity has an uncomfortable way of forcing itself on the attention of the world, and crime must either be cured or endured.

Jesus approaches the social problem from within; Socialism is endeavoring to solve it from without. The socialist would transform man's environment, hoping that this would work a change in man himself; Jesus would transform man, and leave him to deal with his environment. The method of Jesus is sound; that of Socialism illusory. But while the method of Jesus is indispensable, the method of Socialism is not hostile to it. Socialists and Christians are natural allies, not necessary opponents. The changes in social institutions that the socialist proposes are a wholly desirable complement to the spiritual change contemplated by Jesus. The kingdom that Jesus proclaimed and the social order to which the socialist looks forward are, so far as material conditions are concerned, indistinguishable. The liberty, fraternity, equality, resulting from the recognition of universal human brotherhood, that is the ideal of Socialism, is also the ideal of Jesus.

Yet socialists in large numbers continue to contradict Jesus, and to maintain that man can live by bread alone. While there are many socialists who are altruistic and spiritual, deeply in earnest in their efforts to lift up humanity, it is evident that the peculiar strength of Socialism has not thus far existed in these exalted sentiments. Most socialists are frankly selfish and materialistic. The working-man is a socialist, as a rule, not for what he hopes to give, but for what he hopes to get. He looks for a great improvement of his material conditions. He believes firmly with Jacob that gain is godliness; he has much need to learn, with the apostle, that godliness is gain.

Socialism tends to substitute itself for religion, says En-rico Ferri, "since its aim is for humanity to have its own 'earthly paradise' here, without having to wait for it in the hereafter, which, to say the least, is very problemat-ical." Is it necessary to point out that such a saying shows an entire failure to comprehend the teaching of Jesus? He desired, he expected, the coming of the "earthly paradise" in this life, so far as that means that all men should share equally in the bounty of their Heavenly Father, but he differed entirely from the mod-ern socialist as to the path that would lead men to the desired consummation. "Cleanse first the inside of the cup and platter," says Jesus. Only polish the outside well and the inside can take care of itself, retorts the socialist. The problem of readjusting the social environ-ment, of recasting social institutions, is a new problem for every generation; the problem of reconstituting a man is the same problem from age to age.

Materialism is really incompatible with Socialism. It is his materialism, partly enforced on him by circum-stances, that is the laborer's worst foe now. The deadly dulness, the benumbing routine of the working-man's life in the present factory organization, is the most formidable obstacle between him and a higher life. Mr. Markham has given a true, if terrible, picture of incarnate material-ism in his poem, "The Man with the Hoe": —

> Bowed by the weight of centuries he leans
> Upon his hoe and gazes on the ground,
> The emptiness of ages in his face,
> And on his back the burden of the world.
> Who made him dead to rapture and despair,
> A thing that grieves not and that never hopes,

Stolid and stunned, a brother to the ox?
*   *   *   *   *   *   *

Is this the Thing the Lord God made and gave
To have dominion over sea and land;
To trace the stars and search the heavens for power;
To feel the passion of eternity?
Is this the Dream he dreamed who shaped the suns
And marked their ways upon the unknown deep?
Down all the stretch of Hell to its last gulf
There is no shape more terrible than this —
More tongued with censure of the world's blind greed —
More filled with signs and portents of the soul —
More fraught with menace to the universe.

It is the chief praise of Socialism, as some teach it, it is the hiding of its power, that it can transfigure even such a life with the glory of a new hope.   But Jesus offers a loftier hope than that of mere personal betterment; an interpretation of life in terms higher than the senses; a view of present duty and of future destiny far more inspiring than Socialism can offer.   Many socialists are trying to make a religion out of their philosophy, and the devotion to the welfare of their fellows that it may inspire. But considered as a religion, Socialism is as a tallow candle to the sun when compared with the religion of Jesus. Such power as it has is derived, not from the gross materialism and the cruel class selfishness of its programme, as interpreted by Marx and Kropotkin, but to the sentiments of justice to all men, recognition of human brotherhood, self-sacrifice of the one for the good of the many. In a word, the moral power of Socialism is due to elements borrowed from the ethics of Jesus; and the goal to which it looks forward, a sort of golden age of universal equity

2 C

and equality, is essentially the millennium of Jewish prophets and Christian sages.

From our discussion this conclusion emerges : that the social teaching of Jesus has regard, not to form and mechanism, but to spirit and aim. Socialists commonly make too much of mechanism, of organization, and not enough of spirit. There is a larger place for personality in the philosophy of Socialism, and in its practical aims, than many socialists recognize. Here is where religion and Socialism, different planes, intersect. Socialism as a philosophy can find realization in a social order only through personality. The moral elevation of the great mass of mankind must go along with the establishment and maintenance of any form of collectivism. But while Jesus has thus one method and Socialism another, they are neither contradictory nor mutually exclusive, but rather complementary. As the bird's two wings sustain him in the air and propel him in his flight towards his goal, so these two methods seem necessary to the sure and stable progress of society. We may, therefore, and we should, approach the study of social problems, not as Utopian dreamers, but with a courage born of a justified and constant optimism.

X

THE SOCIAL TEACHINGS OF JESUS —
APPLICATIONS

BIBLIOGRAPHY

On Marriage and Divorce: —

WRIGHT, Report on Marriage and Divorce in the United States, 1867–1886. Washington, 1889.

Report of U. S. Bureau of Labor on Marriage and Divorce in the United States. Washington, 1891.

HIRSH, Tabulated Digest of the Divorce Laws of the United States. New York, 1901.

HOWARD, History of Matrimonial Institutions, 3 vols. Chicago, 1904. (Contains very complete bibliographies.)

BISHOP, Commentaries on Marriage, Divorce, and Separation, 2 vols. Chicago, 1891.

LICHTENBERGER, Divorce: A Study in Social Causation. New York, 1909.

WILCOX, The Divorce Problem, "Studies in History, Economics, and Public Law," published by Columbia University, 1894.

On Wealth: —

CONE, Rich and Poor in the New Testament. New York, 1902.

CARNEGIE, The Gospel of Wealth. New York, 1900.

JENKS, Great Fortunes: the Winning, the Using, New York, 1906.

The Liquor Problem: —

HORSELEY AND STURGE, Alcohol and the Human Body. New York, 1908.

BARKER, The Saloon Problem and Social Reform. New York, 1905.

War and Peace: —

GENERAL HOMER LEA, The Valor of Ignorance. New York, 1909.

GENERAL CHITTENDEN, War or Peace? Chicago, 1911.

ANGELL, The Great Illusion. New York, 1911.

NOVICOW, War and its Alleged Benefits. New York, 1911.

ADDAMS, New Ideals of Peace. New York, 1907.

HULL, The Two Hague Conferences. Boston, 1908.

X

THE SOCIAL TEACHINGS OF JESUS—APPLICATIONS

FROM our study of the general principles of his social ethics, we have reached the conclusion that, while Jesus aimed at social reform, he was not a social reformer. The social reformer is always mainly concerned with institutions; Jesus was chiefly concerned with men. His mission was not to be a reformer but a revealer — to make God known to men, and so bring men into right relations with God, as a condition precedent to right relations with one another. He was not agitator but prophet. He sought the betterment of society, indeed, but only through the spiritual uplifting of the individual man. He therefore maintained an attitude of aloofness and detachment from some of the chief social problems of his day, refusing to be tempted from the proclamation of his spiritual Good News into the arena of personal and political squabbles. Yet it was evidently no lack of sympathy with the suffering poor that made Jesus decline the rôle of a social reformer. His method does not imply denial of social wrongs, or minimize their importance; it merely places first things first, and emphasizes the fact that the direct righting of social wrongs was not his mission. His method was one of indirection, but none the less, rather all the more, effective.

This method of Jesus differentiates him from all other religious and ethical teachers and makes him unique.

Other great teachers of mankind have inculcated precepts, bound their followers by moral rules, drawn up ethical codes, sought the direct reform of abuses. That was the method of Confucius, of Moses, of Buddha, the three greatest teachers of the world before Jesus. They have left ethical codes that are still the standards of millions of the race. But the method of Jesus was other and more puissant; he confined himself to the inculcating of ethical principles, that are of eternal validity and of universal adaptation, principles that if faithfully applied and obeyed would long since have righted every social wrong. The superiority of the method is indisputable and transcendent. It is the secret of the inexhaustibleness of the ethics of Jesus; for, as Romanes appreciated, his teaching is notable for what it did not contain. There is nothing in his ethics that the progress of mankind has compelled his followers to surrender or modify. Codes become obsolete with lapse of time and change of social conditions; a true principle is always true. It is this characteristic of Christianity, more than any other, that fits it to be a world religion, beyond any of its rivals. Even when Jesus seems to depart from this method, and to lay down hard-and-fast rules of conduct, the departure is only a seeming one, and the rules are not rules. What he really does is to give occasional illustration of the way in which the primordial law of love is applicable to the complex details of a social relationship.

And let us remind ourselves again that the social ethics of Jesus are the very substance of his teaching, not an excrescence. Though he lived at times on the heights and in the silences, alone with God, for the most part he was a man among men. No visionary dreamer he, but a man who had a passion for truth and reality, for the practical and possible.   Not in the least austere or harsh, his nature was attuned to the finite as to the infinite, and in the presence of human need was vibrant with sympathy.   The common people among whom he moved, simple-minded, easily receiving his Good News, were the "little ones" whom it was the greatest of sins to cause to stumble.   To the outcast and lost he brought a message of hope and rescue.   He seemed peculiarly drawn to those whom the good society of his day had placed under its ban; and so, it was exaggeration, but not slander, when his enemies represented him as the friend of publicans and sinners.   Exaggeration, because he sought no one class of men, invited no favored few to enter God's kingdom.   He might be said to have begun his mission by preaching to the better classes, the regular attendants on the synagogue worship — if not actually Pharisees, well disposed towards Phariseeism.   But he was not content with this, and deliberately went to the outcasts with an assurance that it was possible for them to amend their lives and become members of the kingdom.   He does not seem to have made any permanent impression on this class, though he gained certain individuals from among them; but by such social ethics he estranged the cultivated and the well-to-do.   As a result, all but a select few from both strata of society rejected both him and his teachings.

I

The social unit is the family, not the individual — you must have two persons before you can have a society. The ethical ideas of Jesus were cast in the mould of the family, and were obviously colored by his personal experience. He spent the greater part of his life as a member of a Jewish family, participant to the full in its domestic life. Though himself a celibate, he was no ascetic. His ethical generalizations are based on the particulars of such experience. Love of man must ever begin in love of men. Even the kingdom, as Jesus conceives it, is the family of God — God himself Father and Protector of all, and all the world brothers and sisters because of their relationship to God. Therefore the practical ethics of Jesus are the ethics of the family life enlarged — as brothers and sisters the whole world are to live together in peace and mutual helpfulness, conscious of a common interest, and fully aware that the welfare of one is the welfare of all. Selfishness is excluded, because it is destructive of family life, which demands unity, and therefore the constant voluntary sacrifice of the individual for the common good.

The family rests on the institution of marriage; for scientific research has assured us that no considerable progress beyond barbarism was made until the family was evolved. The ultimate basis of the family is even more physiological than social. The young of the lower animals gain their growth in a few weeks or months, with few exceptions, and are then able to care for themselves. A permanent family is of no use in the perpetuation of such races, and therefore has never developed. But the human young require many years for their growth to a self-supporting age, and while it is not possible to fix any exact time when the boy passes into the man or the girl becomes a woman, the arbitrary rule of the civil law that manhood begins on the twenty-first birthday and

womanhood on the eighteenth, is near enough to physiological facts for practical purposes. It is to insure the
protection of children until they thus become men and
women, and so to perpetuate the race, that the family
was first instituted or developed, and this is still its chief
social function.

The teaching of Jesus regarding marriage is, therefore,
his most weighty and important social teaching. His
doctrine is comprised in few words, but it lacks nothing
in either clearness or emphasis. In his view, marriage
is a divine institution — God, and not merely social
custom, or civil law, joins man and woman in wedlock.
It is not, therefore, a contract that may be made and
terminated at the mere will of the parties concerned.
The civil law recognizes that marriage differs from commercial contracts, in that it establishes a *status*, in which
the rights of children and the interests of society at large
are involved; and that such a unique contract cannot be
terminated at will like other contracts. In no way interfering with or contradicting this principle, Jesus places
marriage on a wholly different plane, and a far higher.
It is here that the Roman Catholic Church finds its best
justification for regarding marriage as a sacrament; and
the teaching of Jesus indeed falls little short of this, for
the difference between a divine institution and a sacred
ordinance is hardly greater than that between tweedledee
and tweedledum.

The second teaching of Jesus regarding marriage is that
the institution is rooted in human nature, "male and
female created he them." It is not a concession to the
weakness of the flesh, as the early Fathers taught, but
results from the very constitution of man. The differ-

ence of sex is primary, and it is not merely a physical difference, it is an intellectual and ethical difference as well; and it is this fact that makes marriage, in any true sense, possible. For if the union of men and women were no different from the unions of the lower animals, it would not be worthy to be called marriage. No man knows, feels, or wills precisely like a woman, and it is these spiritual unlikenesses that condition marriage and give to it both its charm and its value. It is doubtless true that the ethical in marriage is linked to the physical, but the physical ought to be transfused and transfigured by the ethical.

Marriage thus has its foundation in the most imperious of natural propensities, the desire of every normal man or woman for the complement of self, the "affinity" to which each is irresistibly drawn. We may comprehend, though we cannot approve, the tendency of the early Church to condemn as essentially sinful a propensity in man which was the cause of so much unethical conduct in heathen society, in such condemnation losing sight of the distinction between the normal and lawful and the abnormal and lawless satisfaction of all human desires. And because of this error, the Catholic Church came to exalt virginity above marriage as the state most pleasing to God and most conducive to all virtue. But the Church in general has seen with clearer vision the truth taught by Jesus, that the natural desire of men and women for each other is an integral factor of human nature, implanted in the human constitution by the Creator; and that marriage was from the beginning intended to be the field for the satisfaction and exercise of God-given faculties. It is the plain teaching of history that when marriage has been forbidden in the name of religion, this negation of the facts of man's constitution has inevitably been futile, and has inevitably resulted in frightful immoralities. Jesus did not forbid marriage, nor did he recognize any higher state. He himself lived the celibate life, and he recognized that exceptional men may be divinely appointed to the celibate life for the sake of the kingdom of God. But marriage is the normal state for men and women; celibacy is the exceptional, and so far abnormal.

The only bond of marriage recognized by Jesus is the mutual love of one man for one woman — a love so dominant as to override that relation otherwise most sacred, the one human relation sanctioned in the Decalogue and also accompanied by a promise. Beyond and above the obligation to honor father and mother is the obligation created by sexual love, finding its fruition in marriage: "For this cause shall a man leave his father and mother, and shall cleave unto his wife." It is almost a profanation of love even to discuss the question of monogamy versus polygamy. Luther, in a great crisis of his life, taught that since polygamy was permitted to the patriarchs, and is not explicitly forbidden in the New Testament, it could not be inherently wrong, and might, therefore, be permitted to princes, lest they commit a worse sin, but even then under the bond of secrecy. His insistence on secrecy is a clear proof that his argument did not satisfy his conscience, and that he was deliberately conniving at what he knew to be an ethical wrong. Jesus did not explicitly forbid polygamy, it is true, because he had no occasion to do so, as it was not practised in his day, either among the Jews or the pagans in the Roman Empire. But he did exclude the very possibility of polygamy by confining his language to one man and one woman, and by describing a union that is impossible between one man and two women, "so that the two shall become one flesh."

After his usual manner, Jesus does not go into the details of the ethics of matrimony, but leaves his followers to deduce for themselves the ethical details from the general principle that mutual love is the bond of union between every married pair. The principle of mutuality is fundamental. Each party to the relation surrenders a portion of the hitherto complete and independent personality, for on no other terms can the two become one. If only one yields, while the other preserves full individuality, the result is a state of servitude, not of marriage. Jesus evidently presupposes something other and higher than mere physical attraction: the spiritual unity, the love that is beyond and above the somatic magnetism of each sex for its opposite, gives marriage most of its value and all of its dignity. Marriage that is founded on nothing more than sensuous charm cannot rationally be expected to endure after passion cools and beauty fades; but a marriage that is founded on mental and moral affinities, a choice of mates dictated by reciprocal perception and valuation of character, each expecting and hoping to give the other more than is received, to find happiness in making the happiness of the beloved, "will begin with the glory of the dawn and have shed over its last years the softened radiance of the afterglow." There is no painful disillusion, no sickening disgust, no deadly boredom and final despair in such unions. They never end in the divorce court. The death of passion and the inevitable fading of beauty are often the beginning of the truest love — of self-forgetfulness, self-control, self-sacrifice, which overleap such barriers as differences of temperament, culture, and habit, and gradually draw husband and wife together into most intimate and indestructible union. And this occurs the more surely, if the earthly love is rooted in the heavenly. Faith in the eternally true God of love makes the human love a symbol of its power and glory.

II

Though he usually avoided decision of specific ethical problems, there was a question on which Jesus did not decline to speak, namely, the question of divorce; and we are carefully informed that his teaching astonished the people. This part of his social ethics is of special interest to all who are concerned about the well-being of society, for cheap and easy divorce is as rife among us as it could have been among the Jews in the first century. The state of legal confusion that now obtains in the United States is partly the result and partly the cause of ethical uncertainty and social degeneration; and if not soon checked, promises soon to issue in social anarchy.

The teaching of Jesus is found in the following passages: Matt. 5 : 32, 19 : 3–9; Mark 10 : 2–12; Luke 16 : 18, and is accepted by nearly all critics as part of his undoubted words. But from very ancient times there has been division as to the proper interpretation of these words. The majority of interpreters, including most of the Greek and Latin Fathers and those who to-day call themselves Catholics, whether Greek, Roman, or Anglican, agree that Jesus forbids all divorce from the bond of matrimony, for any cause whatsoever. On the other hand, the majority of Protestant exegetes during the last four centuries, and a minority of the earlier Fathers, insist that Jesus permits divorce from the bond of marriage for adultery, but for no other cause. Here is an apparently irreconcilable conflict of opinion. Nevertheless, agreement is not impossible, for the Catholic exegesis has never been pronounced *de fide*, and the fallibility of all human opinion is part of the Protestant creed.

This is one of those rare cases in which both disputants seem to be wrong, because a common error underlies the exegesis of both parties. Catholic and Protestant alike have neglected the fundamental principle of exegesis: mere words mean nothing. Before we can interpret words, we must ask, Who speaks? To whom? For what purpose? If these questions had been asked and candidly answered, there must have been agreement in the exegesis.

The most elaborate teaching of Jesus on the subject was delivered in response to the testing questions of the Pharisees. It was teaching given to Jews, living under the law of Moses, as modified by the later rabbinic teaching. The practice concerning which the men of that day were in doubt, and concerning which Jesus was questioned, was divorce for trivial causes: "Is it lawful for a man to put away his wife for every cause?" Divorce on various pretexts seems to have been prevalent at an early date among the Jews; and, it being impracticable to reform it altogether, it was ordained in the Mosaic code that a man who put away his wife should give her a writing, stating his reason for so doing. This was for the protection of the woman, and was intended to discourage divorce except for strong reasons. And even this, as Jesus said, was because of the hardness of heart of the Jewish people, who were not ready for a stricter law. But Jesus goes back of the law of Deuteronomy to the older tradition of Genesis. The time has now come (he says, in effect) for a return to the original law of marriage; the primal institution is to be reënacted. Any man who henceforth puts away his wife, as allowed by the Law and the rules of the Rabbis, really violates the law of God; and if he takes another wife, he commits adultery, as does he also who marries the wife so put away.[1] Marriage is of God; it is a sacred union; and what God has joined together let not man put asunder.

The other passages are to be understood in a similar manner; they contemplate the same state of affairs. They also are spoken to Jews, and are directed against the evil that actually prevailed among them — the same evil precisely from which we are suffering to-day — divorce for trivial causes. Such divorce Jesus forbade for all time, and to his loyal followers that prohibition will be final authority. He permits neither contemporaneous nor consecutive polygamy. He will not listen to the argument, so dear to many modern apologists for divorce, that the way to make marriage more sacred is to make it less binding. Not more sexual liberty, but less, was his teaching. He gives no encouragement to recent teachers, who declare that divorce is a symptom of social health, not of disease; and that the cure is to be found, not so much in stricter laws about divorce, as in safeguarding

---

[1] If the words "saving for the cause of fornication" are a part of the words spoken by Jesus, and not a later interpolation, the reference is evidently to prematrimonial unchastity. Compare Deut. 24: 1, with 22: 14-21.

marriage. Let us safeguard marriage, by all means, and if possible, make divorce unnecessary, but let us by no means make the fatal error of mistaking a disease for a cure.

Jesus did not say one word — not one word, at least, that has been recorded — on the subject of divorce for that sin whose very commission dissolves the bond of matrimony, and makes twain again of those who had become one flesh. There was no reason why he should teach anything on that subject; there was every reason why he should not. There was no such thing under the Mosaic law as divorce for adultery; the penalty for that sin was death, as every Jew was aware. Jesus had no need to say that the man wronged by his partner's unfaithfulness was freed from the bond of marriage and could marry again; that was a matter of course, for the man was promptly freed from the bond of marriage by the death of the guilty one. The teaching of Jesus does not permit divorce for adultery, and the Protestant exegesis is wrong in maintaining that it does. The teaching of Jesus does not forbid divorce for adultery, and the Catholic exegesis is wrong to maintain that it does. The teaching of Jesus has no relation to the subject; that was a matter settled by the Mosaic law, which Jesus did not undertake to modify, and which he had no occasion to discuss. What he forbids is, divorce for trivial causes.

It has been objected to this interpretation of the words of Jesus, that the death penalty was no longer enforced for adultery in the time of Christ. That is pure assumption, and no proof of such alleged fact is forthcoming. The famous *pericope* of John 7 : 53–8 : 11 is not easily reconcilable with the notion that adultery was no longer punished with death. It is true that this passage is an interpolation in the fourth gospel, but it is generally believed to be an authentic apostolic tradition — indeed, it authenticates itself.

But the question that Jesus had no occasion to discuss is the very question that we have urgent need to discuss; for a change in modern jurisprudence has put us in a different condition from that of the Jews, and the teaching of Jesus is not exactly applicable to our situation. His principle is clear, and still valid if he is an authoritative ethical teacher; but we must go beyond his teaching. Neither the Old Testament nor the New gives any help for the solution of our problem: Is divorce permissible for marital unfaithfulness, now that the adulterer is permitted to live, instead of being put to death? We are left to be guided in this matter by general ethical principles, and by the teaching of experience. Does experience confirm the idea that absolute refusal of legal separation is promotive of social morality? Our own ethical state is bad enough, but are we really in worse case than those countries in which the Catholic rule prevails and divorce is not granted for any cause? Since legislatures will never again be persuaded to make death the penalty for offences against the bond of marriage, to forbid the severance of the bond is to add to the command of Jesus a prohibition of which he never dreamed, — one that would have seemed as monstrous to his generation as it does to ours. For to offer a premium on infidelity, by not only sparing the guilty one's life, but compelling the innocent victim to bear the penalty, is a proposition shockingly unjust and opposed to the practice of the vast majority of mankind.

These ethics of Jesus are severe, but not too severe. They set up a standard for his kingdom no higher than is demanded by his fundamental law of love. This is how men and women ought to behave to each other, if they recognize the altruistic spirit as that which should govern their lives. If it is easier to be divorced than to exercise the graces of tenderness, consideration, and forbearance, why should the married greatly concern themselves about their conduct within the bond of matrimony? But if they understand that divorce is normally impossible, there results the greatest stimulus to the cultivation of all the arts and graces that can sweeten human intercourse and make the hard places of life more tolerable, if not actually easy. In other words, cheap and easy divorce is the offering of a strong inducement to marital careless-ness, brutality, and infidelity. It makes the problem of how to be happy though married almost insoluble.

The ethics of Jesus do not recognize any difference of sex, in the matter of violated law and penalty. From his teaching but one conclusion can be drawn, namely, that all impurity is sin, that man or woman who breaks the marriage vow is equally guilty. There is one holy law in his kingdom for all. Nevertheless, on other grounds than his explicit teaching it may be maintained that the world is right in affixing the heavier penalty to woman's offence. The moral guilt of the sexes is equal; the social guilt of woman is greater than man's. In view of the more serious social consequences, society is ethically jus-tified in regarding the impurity of a married woman as the greatest of social offences, to be punished by a social ostracism that is much more terrible than any legal pen-alty. It is not without reason that the unfaithful wife

receives the full measure of contempt, not merely from
men, but even more from her own sex.

III

The worth of the ethical teaching of Jesus is witnessed
by the singular persistence of his ideals of character and
conduct.   What is true of the relations of husband and
wife is true of all the family relations, for which he provides no specific instruction beyond his universal law of
love.   The family, as he conceived it, is only the kingdom
of God in miniature.   It is "the world's first and greatest
venture in altruism." [1]   The varied relations of parent
to child, of brothers and sisters, are founded on mutual
love, unselfish good will, giving itself freely, without calculation or stint.   The family cannot exist, unless its
members are constantly asking themselves, not what
they can get out of it, but what they can put into it.

The evils that menace the family, and especially the
modern divorce problem, have not yet been scientifically
studied.   We do not accurately know the economic and
ethical facts that are at the basis of certain observed phenomena, and until we do know the facts every attempt
to apply a remedy deserves the jibe that Voltaire aimed
at medicine : the art, as he said, of putting drugs of which
we know little into bodies of which we know less, to cure
diseases of which we know nothing at all.   But it is
definitely known that many of the dangers that menace

---

[1] Peabody, "The Approach to the Social Question," p. 149.   This
book and its companion, "Jesus Christ and the Social Question," abound
in suggestion and stimulus, and one willingly acknowledges an obligation
to Professor Peabody that cannot be adequately discharged by quotation
marks or footnotes.

the family grow out of the negation of love. The increase
of divorces is a symptom of a deep-seated ethical evil,
a perverted ideal of life, in that men and women have
come to seek personal happiness first of all, not the happiness of those with whom they are bound in the family
relation. The pursuit of happiness is the most illusory
of occupations. Happiness is a by-product, and to seek it
directly is to lose it altogether. "Happiness" has come
to mean to many people the unrestrained gratification of
every impulse. Every inability to gratify desire tends
to the unhappiness of such, more or less, according to the
strength of the desire. But in that sense happiness is
impossible to any living being, in any conceivable social
state, rich or poor, high or low, married or single.

Real happiness can be found only in the voluntary
limiting of desire. The reason why so many families are
unhappy is that the members will not see that the family
life is a constant discipline in self-conquest, in gentleness,
consideration of another, patience, and that true happiness is found in the encouragement and growth of these
virtues. The permanence of the family institution promotes the peaceable adjustment of those numerous differences, inevitable between any two or more persons, which
would easily give rise to separation if severance were
easily possible. Families are unhappy and disrupted,
because, instead of being "tied up in the bundle of love,"
they find themselves tied up in the bundle of selfishness,
which soon gives place to hate. In the family it is especially true that one must lose his life to find it, that one
can become greatest only by being servant of all. Children are reared to-day to expect happiness above all
things, to seek it as the best thing life can give, to expect

everything, to give nothing. What wonder that such children, when they come to establish families, make a ghastly failure of it ! The law of love, as applied to the family, demands clear recognition of the obligations that arise from the family relationships, and a ceaseless discipline of the will, until the habit is formed of respecting those obligations in the minutest incidents of family intercourse.

The teaching of Jesus and the teaching of the primitive Christians effected a vast and thus far permanent change in family life. It has been purified and sweetened to such a degree that one of the most effective agencies of evangelization in foreign missions is the object lesson furnished to the heathen by a Christian family. So long as the teaching of Jesus has among his professed disciples that real authority which issues in obedience, the family is in no serious danger. But the tendency to extreme individualism, on the one hand, and extreme socialization on the other, constitute dangers that should be recognized. Communism and the family life seem essentially incompatible, but not Socialism and the family. Inasmuch as Socialism lays special stress on altruism as opposed to selfishness, on the interests of society and not on the whims of the individual, it is fitted to increase the stability of the family relations. It is true that a certain school of German pseudo-scientific socialists hold that the family is inconsistent with Socialism, but this is chiefly because they hold a theory that the present property institutions grew out of the family and are bound up with it. But other socialists accept neither the premise nor the conclusion.

It has been urged by some that the teachings of Jesus

are really unfavorable to the perpetuation of the family.
"If any one comes to me, and hates not his own father,
and mother, and wife, and children, and brothers, and
sisters, and what is more, his own life, he cannot be my
disciple." [1]   This is of course a "hard saying" for the
literalist, but for nobody else.   Evidently, when Jesus
counsels a man to "hate" his own life, he is not advising
suicide.   And it is equally evident that when he says a
man must "hate" his whole family, he does not mean the
destruction of the family.   He uses the word "hate," as
it is usually found in the Scriptures, as the antithesis
of "love"; not a passion of resentment, not a bitter feeling.
Such passion he teaches his disciples to regard as virtual
murder. [2]   "Hate" is a principle of action, that profound
moral recoil which goodness experiences whenever it is
brought into contact with evil, the feeling of loathing
that comes over an ethically normal nature when con-
fronted with moral vileness.   Every man who has heard
or seen evil that has filled him with horror or disgust, so
that he has shrunk from even the thought of it, knows
what this sort of "hate" is.   It is perfectly compatible
with love, with pity for the evil-doer, and a desire to
rescue him from unrighteousness.   It is "that chastity
of honor," as Burke so finely says, "that feels a stain like
a wound."

And what Jesus commands, therefore, is simply this:
whenever the family relations, though the most sacred
thing on earth, come between a man and his loyalty to
Jesus and his teaching, they cease to be the chief good of
life and become a snare to the soul, a lure to evil, some-

[1] Luke 14 : 26.
[2] Matt. 5 : 22; cf. 1 John 3 : 15.

thing that must be renounced and forsaken, a thing to be avoided like contagion by a man who has learned from Jesus what the love of God and man means. God must have all of a man's allegiance or none. And it is a matter of history, of observation, that the disciples of Jesus are sometimes compelled to make this choice — to be faithful to him they must forsake father and mother, wife and child, property and prospects. And many have done it. But it is only when this last cruel necessity of choice between family and Jesus is pressed upon him that a man is to "hate" his family; normally, a man can choose Jesus and keep to his family.

IV

Jesus has been claimed as the first socialist, the first spiritualist, the first Christian scientist, and so on. But the fact that emerges clearly from a careful study of his teachings is that he was no "ist" and taught no "ism." There are points of contact, real or apparent, between his precepts and many "isms," but his teaching was too broad and comprehensive to be circumscribed by any sect or party. Others have gone to an opposite extreme, and since they could not find a point of contact between their fad and the doctrine of Jesus, have denounced him because he did not sufficiently denounce social evils and champion reform. Jesus was too sane to be a reformer. Every great reformer has been more or less a lunatic; for to succeed as leader of a reform movement a man must be obsessed by one idea so that he can see, think, speak nothing else. He becomes utterly incapable of seeing truth as a sphere; it presents itself to him as a sharp sword, whose keen edge is fitted only for the destruction of evil. His passionate desire for the righting of the one wrong prevents him from seeing social facts in their true relations. He is useful and prevails, precisely in proportion to his narrowness; but he is not a safe ethical teacher.

Jesus did not abstain from the career of a reformer because there were no great social evils in his day. On the contrary, there was one that has no equal in modern times, the institution of slavery, universal in the Roman Empire, and affecting every detail of social life. Negro slavery, as it was known in the nineteenth century, which saw the last great struggle for its abolition, was a trifle as compared with slavery in the early Christian centuries. Originally captives in war, the slaves of the Roman Empire were in large part of equal race, of equal culture, with their masters. Æsop and Terence were slaves. Most of the business enterprises of imperial Rome were conducted by slaves. An uneducated brute might, and often did, hold in bondage a man fitted to be a university professor, a poet, a sculptor, a skilled man of affairs. The demoralizing effects on the upper class were far greater than those of negro slavery, great as the latter were. The injustice, the ethical wrong, of holding one's brother man in bondage was as great then as now. But Jesus did not denounce slavery; he did not command his disciples to free their slaves, if they had any; his most authoritative followers exhorted Christian slaves to be obedient to their masters, and not even to desire freedom for themselves, but to be content with their condition. Paul sent a runaway slave back to his master. William Lloyd Garrison lost faith in Christianity because Jesus did not pronounce slavery to be ethically wrong, and because his apostles condoned so great an ethical evil.

But Jesus and his apostles taught a principle with which slavery was utterly incompatible, when he told men that they all belong to the family of God. "One is your Father, and all you are brothers" was his unwavering utterance. When his disciples really comprehended the meaning of this teaching, how could one of them hold another in bondage? Slavery was certain to fade away just as rapidly as this principle of brotherhood was recognized. And in the earliest legislation of the first nominally Christian emperor we find edicts recommending and making easy the manumission of slaves. It is probably true, as later historical investigators urge, that slavery would not have disappeared so quickly, or so completely have given place to serfdom, if economic conditions had not coöperated with ethical motives; but the ethical motives were there, and were powerful. To ascribe this great social change mainly to economic conditions would be as true as to say that the abolition of slavery in our own country was due to economic motives alone.

We see here the immense superiority of Jesus over Mohammed as an ethical teacher. Mohammed undertook to be a social reformer; he was a social reformer. By divine revelation, as he professed and his followers believed, he obtained certain specific statutes regulating the evils that prevailed in his time concerning marriage and the ownership of slaves. Without doubt, his legislation elevated the condition of woman and improved the lot of slaves; he accomplished something of real social value in both directions. But he did so at the cost of legalizing both polygamy and slavery forever. No Christian can believe either to be right; no Mohammedan is free to believe either to be wrong. The ethics of Jesus are incompatible with either; the ethics of Mohammed recognize and perpetuate both.

Drunkenness was a great social evil in the time of Jesus, and he is criticised by some modern reformers because he not only did not denounce this vice, but even encouraged the moderate use of wine by his personal example. He made wine at Cana, according to the fourth gospel, and the language of the ruler of the feast plainly indicates that it would intoxicate, and that wedding guests were in the habit of drinking until they could not tell the difference between good wine and bad. That may not warrant the inference that at such feasts the guests became actually intoxicated, but it describes an indulgence beyond the bounds of moderation. Jesus deliberately avoided the life of an ascetic, and by so doing as deliberately challenged the condemnation of the censorious, as he plainly says: "For John came eating no bread and drinking no wine, and you say, He has a demon. The Son of Man came eating and drinking, and you say, Behold a glutton and a drunkard." The late Bishop Fowler, of the Methodist Episcopal Church, once publicly announced that he would refuse to believe in the divinity of Jesus Christ, if convinced that He made and drank wine that would intoxicate. Bishop Fowler lived and died a believer in the divinity of Christ, but he did so only by rejecting the plain facts recorded in the gospels. This is an example of the lengths to which fanaticism will lead a reformer; it shows how the vision of the kingdom can be quite eclipsed by holding too close to the eye some wholly desirable social change.

The truth is, that around the ethics of Jesus an artificial code has been built up by tradition, as the Pharisees built up an artificial code about the code of Moses, and one of its rules is: *All use of alcohol is a sin*. No exception is made by the extreme fanatics for even the medicinal use. And to make such ethics possible, they have been forced to explain away the facts about the teaching and practice of Jesus, by a system of lying exegetics that proves the existence of two kinds of wine mentioned in the Bible: one unfermented and harmless, the other fermented and harmful. Jesus, according to these theorists, made and used the unfermented and harmless wine; alcoholic wine is everywhere condemned in the Scriptures, and especially in the New Testament. This interpretation of the Scriptures to support the two-wine theory is beneath contempt as to its scholarship, and deserving of the strongest reprobation for its unethical handling of an ethical question.

The apostles were not more explicit in their teaching than Jesus, who was content to leave the whole subject to be worked out under his general law of love. One who loves God and his brother will be temperate in all things, and will never use alcoholic beverage to excess, nor will he eat to excess, or do anything else to excess. He will be temperate in his thoughts and words, as well as in his drinking, and will not think to promote ebriety by an inebriated vocabulary. But the apostles do indicate some explicit corollaries from the general principle of their Master. No drunkard can enter the kingdom of God, is one of the deductions of John, and is plainly an authorized deduction; for a drunkard has forgotten the law of love and has indulged in a vice that is hurtful both to himself and to society. Paul draws another corollary: "I will neither eat meat nor drink wine, if thereby my brother is made to stumble;" and though he undoubtedly means abstinence from wine that had been offered to idols, rather than wine in general, the principle holds universally good. Abstinence in the spirit of asceticism is anti-Christian; abstinence for the sake of the brother is profoundly Christian.

But though abstinence is thus commended, and is becoming more and more recognized as the higher Christian ethics in our age, it is not possible for one who accepts the teaching and practice of Jesus as his authority to condemn the moderate use of wine as a sin. It may be inexpedient under our present social conditions; it is not *per se* wrong. To say that it is wrong, is to say that the Master himself taught less than the perfect ethics and gave us an example of less than perfect conduct. But science has thrown new light on what constitutes moderation. The latest physiological researches into the effects of alcohol lead to the conclusion that it is not a stimulant, as medical science has long taught and practised, but always a narcotic poison. A small quantity, not exceeding two ounces a day, is oxidized in a normal body, and so far supplies the place of the carbohydrates, sugar, starch, etc. But before it can be oxidized it produces certain physiological effects, that may be recognized as incipient narcotism. The feeling of exhilaration that at first follows the ingestion of alcohol is also produced on many people by opium, and on nearly all by nitrous oxide in small doses — called for this reason "laughing gas" — both of which, in larger dose, produce profound narcosis, in the case of nitrous oxide lasting but a few minutes (whence it is much used by dentists in the extraction of teeth), while the opium narcosis persists for hours. A quart of whiskey taken at once has frequently produced immediate death — it is a more quickly fatal poison than opium, though not more certain in its action.

If a man would never take fermented liquors except with his dinner, and then not more than a pint of ordinary claret or its equivalent, he would probably suffer no measurable harm, and this might be fairly called moderation. Yet experiments show that, with even this indulgence, for several hours after such dining a man's physical and mental powers are sensibly diminished; and in the case of some susceptible persons the effect would be felt even on the following day. But how many who permit themselves the use of alcoholic beverages do or can hold themselves to so strict a moderation as this? Practically all use of alcohol is excessive use, as the most recent scientific experiments prove beyond a reasonable doubt. Only an abstinence virtually total will keep a man surely within the limits of scientific moderation.

Of course, in view of the acknowledged evils of the drink habit to-day, to plead the authority of Jesus against the regulation or suppression of making and selling intoxicating beverages, and especially against the closing of the saloon, is futile and absurd. When in our cities the majority of polling-places are located in saloons, and a citizen must enter a drinking-place in order to cast his ballot, the evil demands abatement, without regard to abstract ethics. When our towns have, in some cases, a saloon to every eleven voters, a social condition exists that calls for prompt action, not ethical discussion. The organs of the liquor traffic are wasting their time when they attempt to persuade decent people that their business has the approval of Jesus, or of any ethical teacher in the world's history.

V

Nothing in the social teaching of Jesus is of greater present interest and importance than his sayings regarding the possession and use of wealth.   It is easy to misunderstand his· teaching by listening to one sort of sayings only among his recorded words.   Like everything else in his doctrine, Jesus derived his views of property from his conception of the God of love.   This is God's world; it is God who made it, who rules it, who clothes the grass with greenness and the lilies of ·the field with a beauty exceeding royal splendor.   It is God who sends the rain and makes the earth fruitful, and causes the sun to shine on just and unjust alike; for the gifts of God, though priceless, are without price.   His tireless care and all-seeing eye watch over all that he has made.   Not a sparrow can fall to the ground without your Father, said he; the very hairs of your heads are numbered.   Hence Jesus was the great optimist, for he rested on the conviction of the Father's love and the Father's power and the Father's wisdom.   "Fear not, little flock, for it is your Father's good pleasure to give you the kingdom" are the words in which Jesus puts the truth expressed by his greatest disciple, "for we know that all things work together for good to them that love God."   This is as far as possible from that shallow good-nature and happy-go-lucky improvidence that is often miscalled optimism.

Be not anxious for your life, what you shall eat,
Nor yet for your body, what you shall wear;
For life is more than food,

And the body than clothing.
Mark the ravens, that they sow not, nor reap,
Which have no storehouse nor barn,
And God feeds them.
Of how much more value are you than birds!

* * * * * * *

And seek not what you shall eat
And what you shall drink,
And be not tossed about with cares.
For after all these things the nations of the earth are eagerly
    seeking,
And your Father knows that you have need of these things.
Nay, seek his kingdom,
And all these things shall be added to you.

While Jesus was not a socialist, in the sense that he had
no economic theory concerning society, he comes very
close to the ideas of modern Socialism in this teaching
regarding Providence. Men are not to be anxious about
the things of the present life, but seek first the kingdom
of God, for in the new society to which this seeking will
give rise, the law of love will be the universal solvent of
difficulties and no social problems will be perplexing.
This has been described, like so many of the precepts of
Jesus, as a counsel of perfection merely, a thing to be
preached but not practised, not a rule adapted to actual
life, but only the sublime expression of the most profound
religious mood — mystical moonshine, in short, to which
a man of sense need pay no attention.

"Be not anxious" is, of course, a precept addressed
to disciples, not to the world; spoken to those presumed
to be ruled by the law of love, it is an integral part of a
great ethical idea. Jesus did not say that all the rest of

416 SOCIALISM AND THE ETHICS OF JESUS

the idea and its applications could be disregarded, and
that this would then work by itself. As society is now
constituted, with its complete rejection of the ethics of
Jesus, men cannot escape from carking care, and that of
itself proves that our society is not the society that Jesus
contemplated. Men should be able to exist without
anxiety, for their Father's bounty is sufficient for all; it is
our fellows that compel care, not God. "It is obvious,"
says one, "that in this workaday world such principles are
impracticable; no business can be conducted on these
lines."[1] Undoubtedly. But the question then arises,
Shall we reject Jesus or reform "business"? A society
so organized that the precepts of Jesus cannot be obeyed
in it has no claim whatever to be considered a Christian
society.

In a really Christian society there would be no occasion for any man to worry about food and clothing and
shelter. The world produces enough for the wants of
every living being, and wisely directed industry would
increase its productiveness tenfold. Humanity is rich;
men are poor. Why? Because some have, by reason
of their superior strength of body or mind, obtained
possession of an undue share of the common bounty of
nature; a few men have stolen and keep to themselves
what God gave to the many. He feeds the birds, that
neither sow nor reap; but the birds, not being rational
creatures, have not intelligence enough to defeat the
Heavenly Father's plans. There is none among them
capable of organizing a "corner" in worms or fruits of
the field, none to seize the woods as his possession and
charge "rent" for all who would roost in them, and so

[1] Harnack and Hermann, "The Social Gospel," p. 59.

they all come alike to the table that God has spread for them, and each one gets his share of whatever there may be, and there is abundance for all. But we, being so greatly the superiors of these "lower animals," in that we have reason, and are not guided by mere instinct but by sense and foresight — we men have contrived in our wisdom that some of us shall have more than we know how to use of the Father's common provision, while the rest of us have barely enough to keep ourselves alive, and sometimes perish in our need.

The peculiar note of the teaching of Jesus regarding wealth is its sanity. His ability to take an all-round view of so complicated a question is most impressive as well as most instructive. Ethical teachers in many instances have failed just there, and by fixing their attention on a single phase of wealth have become extremists and fanatics. Jesus does not say that wealth is bad, and therefore to be shunned; he does not say that wealth is good in itself, and therefore to be sought; he recognizes in the possession of wealth great possibilities of both good and harm. He exhorts men to "make friends by means of the mammon of unrighteousness." He warns them against "the deceitfulness of riches."

The conduct of Jesus interprets his teaching. He had among his disciples men of wealth, like Matthew and Zaccheus; he had wealthy friends, who possibly became his disciples also, like Simon and Nicodemus and Joseph of Arimathea. He showed neither social predilections for the rich nor social prejudices against them. He required none of these to renounce his wealth, though he commended Zaccheus for his restitution and generosity. He recognized the fact that men of wealth may be men

2 E

of lofty and spiritual nature, and he loved the rich young
ruler who came to him asking the way of eternal life.
But, as we may gather from the story, in this particular
case wealth was a deadly snare, and this young man could
become a disciple of Jesus and obtain eternal life only by
renouncing that which stood between him and the kingdom of God.   It was the only case [1] in which such renunciation was made a test of discipleship, and Francis of
Assisi went beyond what was written when he made this
a general rule, though in so doing he had the approval
of Catholic exegetes and theologians, who commended
highly a precept that they had no intention of obeying.

Yet there may well be many cases like that of the rich
young ruler, in which no palliative treatment will answer.
We may suspect that wealth often becomes a man's ruin,
that the very weight of his possessions may be crushing
his spiritual life and making impossible his entrance into
the kingdom.   In such cases, as for that young man, renunciation may be the only safety.   Does not experience
fully confirm the following saying of Jesus : "How hardly
shall they that have riches enter into the kingdom of
God"?   And we may be certain that in this version we
have his real words, rather than in the softened form given
by Mark, "How hard is it for *them that trust in riches* to

[1] It is amusing to note how promptly every exegete and student discovers, and how emphatically he announces, that the words of Jesus to the
rich young ruler were not instruction for disciples in general, but discipline
suited to this particular case.   Very true, but why so uniform a stopping
here, so general a neglect to inquire how numerous are the other cases that
need the same treatment?   Did Jesus never call but this one man to
forsake all and follow him?   Or is the painfully correct exegesis of this
text not so much an attempt to comprehend its real meaning, as anxiety
to find an excuse for not making a wider application of the principle of
Jesus to the facts of social life?

THE SOCIAL TEACHINGS OF JESUS 419

enter into the kingdom of God." It is like a camel trying
to pass through a needle's eye; for all practical purposes
the thing may be pronounced impossible.

There is in Luke's gospel a passage that has been confidently asserted to be evidence that Jesus was hostile
to wealth and laid down a general law of renunciation:
"So therefore whosoever he be of you that does not renounce all that he has, he cannot be my disciple." An
easy and short-sighted literalism may deduce a general
law of renunciation from these words, but this is precisely
one of the cases in which, as Jesus himself assures us, the
letter kills, but the spirit gives life. We must, of course,
understand this saying in the light of the other teaching
of Jesus and of his conduct. If we avail ourselves of this
light, it will become plain that this saying, like those accompanying words, "Whosoever does not bear his cross
and come after me cannot be my disciple," is intended
to describe a spirit, not to impose a rule of action. The
literalism that takes such words, as the French say, "at
the bottom of the letter," and the indifference that evac-
uates them of all meaning as "orientalisms," are equally
to be shunned. The saying about the taking up of the
cross obviously does not mean that every disciple of Jesus
must actually die a death of shame, nor does the saying
about renunciation mean that every disciple must formally renounce all his possessions; in both cases Jesus
is telling us what sort of spirit his disciples must possess,
of what sort of conduct they must be capable in emergency. They must so highly esteem his kingdom, and
so rate the privilege of being his disciples above everything earthly, that they shall be willing to renounce
property and life itself for the kingdom's sake. Many

will never be called on to make the actual sacrifice, "the readiness is all."

Luke's gospel contains the clearest and most precise teaching of Jesus regarding wealth. "Lay not up for yourselves treasures upon earth," is not to be taken as a prohibition of wealth, but as an exaltation of the spiritual above the material, as is shown by the words following: "Lay up for yourselves treasures in heaven." And this will lead any man to a true valuation of wealth, and to comprehension of the distinctive teachings of Jesus on this subject: that by a member of his kingdom wealth is possessed but not owned. Individualism says now, as it has always said, "Is it not lawful for me to do what I will with mine own?" but the ethics of Jesus says, No, for it is not your own, and if it were, you might not use it save to promote your brother's welfare equally with yours. Disciples of Jesus are stewards of wealth, not owners. And the question for stewardship is not, How much of my wealth must I give to God and my brother? but, How much of God's wealth am I justified in using for myself?

This doctrine of stewardship is the chief contribution of Jesus to the ethics of property. According to him a man owns nothing; he owes everything. Wealth is a trust. The doctrine is set forth with profusion of illustration, in the parables of the talents and the pounds, the unrighteous steward, and the like. Trusts differ in amount, not in character — stewardship is the universal fact. Anybody who possesses anything is, according to the ethics of Jesus, a rich man and a steward. Wealth, being a trust, imposes special responsibility. Our conventional ideas need much revision to make them correspond with the teachings of Jesus. The rich man is a steward, but so is he whom we call the poor man — perhaps the poor man is in the greater danger of the two of neglecting his stewardship. Not to be envious of the rich is hard. It would be exceedingly difficult to guess how much of the present social unrest and the popularity of the ideals of Socialism has no better foundation than the envy of those who have by those who have not. Many a man who is not worth a dollar is as abject a worshipper of Mammon, as true an adorer of wealth, as the most purse-proud millionnaire. It is not necessary to be rich, but only to desire riches as the chief earthly good, to become a subject of Mammon. And upon a world that desires God *and* Mammon, Jesus presses the choice of God *or* Mammon. This is why Jesus does not call on the rich to divide their wealth with the poor; he calls them into his kingdom of the spirit, confident that if they really learn his secret, they will feel and act on his saying that "it is more blessed to give than to receive." Thus far most men believe this to be true only of kicks and cuffs.

It is in accordance with the ethics of Jesus, if not in consequence of them, that a great change is visible in the social estimation of the rich. Formerly they were measured solely by the amount of their wealth — how much is he worth? was the form of words, in which it was implied that a man's value was exactly proportioned to his property. Now the rich man is coming to be more and more measured by his social usefulness, how much he is "worth" in service, not alone in money. In other words, the standard of value is coming to be a man's actual contribution to the social order. He must justify his existence or go. Men of wealth are beginning to recognize more clearly the equity of this standard, to acknowledge the extent of their social obligations, and not a few are honestly asking for the best way in which these obligations may be discharged. If they have made their money under a bad system, that is no more their fault than it is the fault of others; if they are seeking to use their money for the good of their fellows, that is certainly their virtue.

VI

One reason why there are not more striking socialistic elements in the teaching of Jesus regarding wealth may be that there was so large an element of Socialism in the Jewish system, which was an underlying assumption on the part of himself and his hearers. The Jewish land tenure, as has often been pointed out, was essentially socialistic, with its provision of reversion to the original owner in every jubilee year. Modern society shows a tendency to come back to the Mosaic doctrine that rent and interest are in their nature immoral. But again, we are assured that "business" could not be carried on without them. It is perfectly true, and perfectly conclusive proof that modern business ought not to be carried on.

Man's life does not consist in the things that he has, says Jesus, but neither does it consist in the things that he has not, as says the ascetic. Real wealth is in the man himself. Who was ever poorer than Jesus, as men count wealth? Who was ever so rich as Jesus, in character, in spiritual influence? Men must have a motive independent of the outward good, in order to attain the outward good; for it is precisely the seeking of outward good for its own sake and for self that confines its attainment to the few and denies it to the many. Jesus, therefore, bids his followers shun the low places of what the world calls success, to renounce that which the world rewards with honor and applause, and patiently essay with him the difficult heights of love and fidelity and humble service.

But how serve one's fellows? What is doing them good? The Christian centuries have replied by what they have called "charity." And for this the followers of Christ can apparently plead the words of their Master. "Give to him that asks" is one of the practical applications of the great law of love made in the teaching of Jesus. But by what right have interpreters of Jesus, from the early Fathers to Tolstoi, restricted the scope of these words mainly to the gift of money? Give to him that asks, yes, give him the only gift worth your giving or his accepting, give him love, give him yourself. The teaching of Jesus is that all our life is to be a giving of self to the needy, the motive of such giving love, and its purpose the saving of our brother. "Sell all that you have and give to the poor," was given as a way of perfection to the rich young ruler, not so much for the sake of the poor, as for the sake of the giver — it was good for this man's soul that he should dispossess himself of that which hung like a millstone about his neck. The value of personal ministry, as distinguished from the giving of money, is highly emphasized in the parable of the sheep and the goats. Those on the left have been selfish, hard-hearted, not merely stingy. Likewise, what is condemned in the parable of Dives and Lazarus is no specific sin, such as drunkenness and gluttony, but heartlessness. The offence of Dives was not that he fared sumptuously every day, but that he had no thought for the poor beggar at his gate. The very dogs were kinder to Lazarus than feasting Dives, and, therefore, the rich man found no place in Abraham's bosom, the symbol of God's kingdom of love. We see the modern parallel daily, in the people of Fifth Avenue and the people of the East side — Dives still has not found the joy of service and of sacrifice, and he will therefore miss its reward. Yet we need also to remember that there is no moral quality in poverty, by itself, more than in riches; it is only more favorable soil for the growth of the humbler virtues.

The Church of the Middle Ages shows us what must be the result of the literal interpretation of the injunctions of Jesus. That Church greatly magnified almsgiving, as not merely a Christian virtue, but the means of salvation. By literal obedience to the words of Jesus, as the Church taught them, the mediæval world did its best to reduce all men to a common level of poverty. Such giving exhausts the source of supply, without visibly bettering the condition of the poor; and men have come to see that giving, which makes a brother a parasite on society, saps his manhood, ruins his character, cannot be the giving that Jesus commanded in the name of love. For if this is to love one's brother, what would it be to hate him?

On the other hand, even more blameworthy is that hard-hearted turning away from misery and distress, on the plea that giving might harm the recipient. Our danger is not of giving too much, but of giving too little. We have not learned the secret of Jesus until, seeing him in our distressed brother, we give ourselves to the Christ in our brother. Almsgiving is no incidental and voluntary thing in the life of a Christian; it is one form of that universal service of their fellows which Jesus calls all his followers to render cheerfully for his sake. And, accordingly, a follower of Jesus will give, not to promote his own sanctity or to save his own soul, but to save his brother. The one question that he will ask under all circumstances — and its answer will be the solution of most problems, if not of all — is, What and how shall I give so as most effectively to help my brother?

Nor is the disciple of Jesus to look for gratitude in return, else the giving is not gift but barter. And a large part of our giving is unconscious barter. We have classified the poor as the "deserving" and the "undeserving." Such a division is neither Christian nor rational; what we ought to recognize is that the needs of men are different. One needs money or food most, another most needs love and sympathy, another needs to be taught self-help most of all. To give lazily, selfishly, indiscriminately, harms ourselves quite as much as it can harm the receiver, though it is often ruinous to him. We recognize the demoralizing effects of charity on our brother much more clearly than on ourselves; it is ever the easier task to cast the mote out of another's eye.

And let us comprehend, if we can, that what the poor ask of us, what they have a right to ask, is not "charity" but justice. Charity is simply an attempt to compound our social sins, to help the wounded and crippled in the battle of life; but what we are called to do is, to stop the battle. If bullets continue to fly, somebody must be hit and hurt.

VII

The teaching of Jesus regarding the state is of the brief-
est, comprised in a single saying, but it covers the whole
ground.   It was given in reply to the sly Pharisee who
asked him whether it were lawful to pay tribute to
Cæsar.   The trap was skilfully contrived; and answer
would, it seemed, impale him on one horn or the other of
a dilemma.   If he said Yes, the Pharisees could turn to
the crowd with, This man cannot be the Messiah, for he
is neither patriotic or pious.   If he said No, they could
denounce him to Pilate, as advocating sedition.   "Show
me the tribute money," he said; they brought him a
denarius.   "Whose is the image and superscription?"
he inquired, and they replied, "Cæsar's."   The dilemma
no longer existed; by their production of the denarius
and their recognition of the imperial tokens, the Pharisees
had convicted themselves of acknowledging the Roman
political authority.   The further word of Jesus, therefore,
was not so much an escape from the snare they had set
for him, as a declaration that their conduct was better
than their theory, that there was no contradiction then
and need never be any contradiction between a man's
religious and his political duties: "Render therefore
unto Cæsar the things that are Cæsar's, and unto God
the things that are God's."   Under the law of love there
is no distinction between the sacred and the secular;
the religious is the political and the political is the religious.   As Paul afterwards correctly interpreted and
enlarged the principle, "the powers that be are ordained
of God"; he has established civil government; the magistrate is his minister.

If Jesus and Paul could say this of the despotic rule of

imperial Rome, surely it may be said of every other form
of government.   But shall we interpret these words with
such literalness as to find in them a command to endure
without resistance every form of oppression by government?   Do they contain a denial of what it is the fashion now to call "the sacred right of insurrection"?   Des-
potisms, and their minions, have so interpreted the words
in all ages, and have used the authority of Jesus to maintain themselves; but it is impossible to think that Jesus
or Paul intended to teach anything that so flatly contradicts fundamental ethical instincts.   No, what is here
described is the normal conduct of the followers of Jesus
under normal government.   When government fulfils its
natural functions of preserving peace and administering
justice, even though it be a despotism, forcible resistance is not justified.   When a government fails to fulfil
its function, and neither preserves peace nor adminis-
ters justice, even though it be in name a republican
democracy, forcible overthrow of such a government is
justified.   Again the law of love, the principle that bids
one consider the welfare of all, and not merely his own,
comes in to modify the rule of obedience to magistrates.
It is not the duty of followers of Jesus to submit to unjust government, to permit political institutions theoretically good to be so administered as to harm the entire
community.   It is, on the contrary, the duty of Christians to reform such abuses, peacefully if they may, with
violence if they must.[1]   Let justice prevail though the
heavens fall has been a valid principle of ethics for many

[1] This is by no means equivalent to adopting as our ethical standard
the words of Kant: "Thanks to Nature for intolerance, for envious
and emulous self-seeking, for the insatiable desire to have and to rule !
Without this, all the desirable qualities of humanity would lie eternally

centuries, and though something hackneyed, has not lost
its force.

But, it may be asked, does not this contradict other
teaching of Jesus? Does he not counsel submission to
oppression, non-resistance to evil-doers in all cases?
Apparently he does. "If any man would go to law with
you and take away your tunic, let him have your cloak
also," seems to mean that a man is not to defend himself
against injustice. "And whosoever shall compel you to
go one mile, go with him two," seems to exhort to submission, however oppressive government may be.
While "Resist not him who is evil, but whosoever smites
you on the right cheek turn to him the other also" seems
to forbid any protection of self or others from personal violence. But such literal interpretation has been advocated by not a few Christian sects, as well as by individuals of influence, without finding favor among Christian
people at large.

There is a twofold difficulty in the way of adopting
this extreme literalism as a standard of interpretation.
First, the conduct thus seemingly required was not the
conduct of Jesus himself. When he was smitten on one
cheek in the court of the Sanhedrin, he did not turn the
other to the officer, but claimed to be heard and condemned before he was punished. It was contrary to the
Jewish law to strike an uncondemned prisoner, and Jesus
stood on his rights as a Jew. We are warranted, therefore, in concluding that Jesus is, as usual, stating a principle, not a rule; inculcating a spirit to be cherished, not
giving a precept to be exactly followed in all cases. Men

undeveloped. Man wants peace, but Nature knows better what is necessary for him — she wants strife."

are too quick to resent injury, to resort to violence, to rebel against oppression; what they need is restraint as to these things, not encouragement. And so Jesus suggests that men are to be slow to resent, to rebel, to use force; that they are to bear insult and oppression as long as possible, and to claim legal rights and repel violence with violence only as a last resort, after all other means have been fully tried and failed. He taught this truth, the lesson that men most require to learn, by precept and example : —

> The best of men
> Who e'er wore earth about Him was a sufferer;
> A soft, meek, patient, humble, tranquil spirit,
> The first true gentleman that ever lived.

Our second difficulty is that the supposed teaching of Jesus contradicts a primal human instinct, the instinct of self-protection, and a primal Christian virtue, the protection of the weak by the strong. Primal instincts are never wrong. It may be, it generally is, a question how they may be lawfully exercised, but the instincts themselves are sound. This is equally the belief of the Christian and the evolutionist. The Christian believes that God made man in his image; therefore, the basal facts of human nature are of divine origin, and unless it can be proved that an instinct is induced by sin the presumption is that it is healthy and to be followed. The evolutionist believes that all these instincts have been developed by the experience of the race, and for that reason following them is the line of safety, hence ethical. Natural science and Christian ethics alike, therefore, affirm that the impulse toward self-defence is not unethical but ethical.

Not only is self-protection a primary human instinct, but protection of our brother is a necessary inference from the law of love. A teacher so sane as Jesus cannot be rationally supposed to have intentionally contradicted either the instinct or the inference. An interpretation of his words that contradicts both *must* be a false interpretation. He cannot possibly have counselled a cowardly abandonment of duty towards the victims of wrong-doing, for that would be a breach of the law of love. And there is this difference between the instinct to protect one's self and the inference that it is a duty to protect the weaker brother: self-protection is a right that may possibly be waived, while protection of another is a duty that cannot be ethically evaded. A man may perhaps submit to violence done himself, if he will, but he may not permit violence to be done to his neighbor whom it is within his power to protect. It is fairly arguable also, that, while as a purely personal question, a man may elect to endure rather than to repel violence, in many cases such submission would be unethical. For it would encourage in rudeness and brutality one who for his own sake, and for the sake of other possible victims, ought to be effectually taught to behave himself peaceably. There is truth in the old quip, that if we wish peace we must be ready to fight for it. To believe that Jesus commands his followers to stand by inactive and see a child or a woman suffer physical violence from some brutal fellow, is incredible. The least we can say of the great Teacher is that he was a normal man, and no normal man could do or teach that. Tolstoi would perhaps approve of a man's remonstrating with the evil-doer in such a case, but the only effectual remonstrance with a brute who will abuse woman or child is remonstrance with fist or club.

It is also too often forgotten — Tolstoi always forgets it — that physical force is not the only possible form of violence. Words often hurt worse than blows. "I will speak daggers though I use none," says Hamlet. To turn the cheek and yet speak stinging words, is to obey the doctrine of non-resistance in the letter and violate it in the spirit. The scathing rebukes of Jesus must have seemed much more formidable to the Pharisees than the whip of small cords in his hands; neither can be reconciled with the interpretation that some would put on such a maxim as, "Resist not the evil man."

If violence is not absolutely prohibited between individuals, it cannot be unlawful between nations. That is to say, war is lawful in self-defence, or for the protection of a weak people against the aggression of a stronger, if it is lawful for an individual to protect himself or another by force. And as we have concluded that the latter is lawful, in extreme cases, and may even in some circumstances become a duty, the same conclusion follows regarding war. That the American colonies were justified in renouncing their allegiance to England and fighting for their independence, failing peaceful means of redress, is a proposition defensible in accordance with the principle of Jesus. That it was the duty of the United States to intervene and prevent the further oppression of Cuba by Spain is an even plainer ethical proposition. With regard to two other wars in which our country has been concerned, it is a fair question whether they were not unnecessary, whether conflict might not have been averted by more tact and patience; and that the Mexican war was ethically indefensible is now admitted by every candid American historian.

What we thus find to be true regarding our national history, is true of the world at large. Many wars have been due to unjustifiable aggression, others grew out of haste and passion and might easily have been averted; a small residue were justifiable. The thesis sometimes propounded by extreme advocates of peace is indefensible : "There never was a good war nor a bad peace." The memory of any reader of general history will supply instances that confute both clauses of the thesis. But that the greater part of the fighting that history records was unnecessary, unjustifiable, and valueless, is a thesis proved to be true by a host of examples.

Quite apart from what we may learn from history, however, the case against light or frequent recourse to arms in the settlement of international disputes is very strong. When nations acknowledged no ethical obligations, when there was no code of things that it is forbidden nations to do, enforcible by the common conscience of the civilized world, each nation was compelled to enforce its claims by the sword or submit to have its rights trampled upon without redress. But as civilization has progressed, the idea of national honor and national duty has strengthened; a code of international obligations and conduct has come to be recognized as binding on all countries that aspire to be ranked among the enlightened and honorable nations of the world ; and each decade sees this code enlarging in scope and becoming more accurately obeyed. Means of enforcement there are none, beyond the appeal that the code itself makes to the conscience of every people and government. And just as disputes between individuals, in every enlightened country, are now submitted to the arbitration of courts, instead of being set-

tled as of yore by personal combat, and just as the willingness of men to submit their differences to this peaceful
arbitration is now recognized as one of the chief tests of
a people's progress in civilization ; so, it is more and more
felt, should be the case with disputes between nations.
Few questions can now arise between civilized countries
that might not be peacefully and honorably decided by
a competent and impartial tribunal, provided only that
both parties to the dispute are willing to submit their
case and abide by the decision. It is an augury of the
future peace of the world that the President of the United
States and the Foreign Minister of Great Britain have
publicly announced as their policy the negotiation of a
treaty of arbitration, without limit to the questions
arising. War can never decide the justice of a nation's
cause ; war can only show which is the stronger of two
disputing nations. International arbitration and universal peace is a movement in strict accord with the ethics
of Jesus ; for his law of love bids either individuals or
nations avoid strife and bloodshed, whenever peace is
possible without sacrifice of a larger duty imposed by
the same law.

Universal peace is also the ideal and aim of Socialism.
It proclaims a worldwide brotherhood of man that is
incompatible with warfare. The waste of wealth inseparable from war is abhorrent to Socialism ; and the
constant preparation for war is possibly a greater burden
than war itself. Not only the actual taxation imposed
on the peoples of Europe by armaments, but the permanent withdrawal of one-third of the population from productive activities, constitutes a burden that, when prolonged for a generation, may well amount to more than

2 F

the cost of a short, sharp, and decisive conflict, such as modern wars have come to be. Civilization is being crushed under its burden of militarism, and none sees this more clearly than the socialist, none is more insistent that a remedy must be found. Many socialist writers find as bitter things to say of "patriotism" as of religion; and the boastful, swaggering, bullying Jingoism that is commonly confounded with patriotism certainly deserves all their reprobation. Here is a point where the forces of Socialism and of Christianity converge, and against their combined energy, if it be but wisely directed, the advocates of militarism will contend in vain.

XI

THE SOCIAL FAILURE OF THE CHURCH

BIBLIOGRAPHY

On the early institutions of Christianity: —

HARNACK, The Constitution and Law of the Church in the First
Two Centuries, Crown Theological Library. New York, 1910.
——, The Expansion of Christianity in the First Three Centuries,
2 vols. New York, 1904.
WERNLE, The Beginnings of Christianity, 2 vols. New York, 1903.
WEIZSÄCKER, The Apostolic Age, 2 vols. New York, 1899.
SCHMIDT, Social Results of Early Christianity. London, 1885.
ULHORN, Conflict of Christianity with Heathenism. New York,
1879.
——, Christian Charity in the Ancient Church. New York, 1883.

On the teachings of the Apostle Paul: —

WEISS, Biblical Theology of the New Testament, 2 vols. Edin-
burgh, 1882.
SABATIER, The Apostle Paul. London, 1896.
WREDE, Paul. Boston, 1908.
STEVENS, The Pauline Theology. New York, 1892.
PFLEIDERER, Paulinism, 2 vols. London, 1877.
——, The Influence of the Apostle Paul on the Development of
Christianity. New York, 1885.

On Church and State: —

GEFFCKEN, Church and State, their Relations Historically Con-
sidered, 2 vols. London, 1877.
HERGENRÖTHER, The Catholic Church and the Christian State.
London, 1876.

XI

THE SOCIAL FAILURE OF THE CHURCH

FAILURE may be absolute or relative. Christianity began with a distinct consciousness of a social mission. No one who reads the history of Christianity with a candid mind will question the absolute achievement of the Church in righting social wrongs and ameliorating social evils. If it has not accomplished all that too partial advocates have sometimes claimed for it, it has accomplished much. But when we ask whether it has realized the ideal of Jesus, it is no longer a question of what Christianity has done, but of how much it has left undone, and even unattempted. The same candid mind that will frankly recognize the worth of the actual achievement must also conclude that the Church has not come within measurable distance of the ideal of Jesus, nor even made a serious attempt to realize that ideal.

Whether the gospels give us the actual words of Jesus, or teachings greatly modified by oral tradition before they were brought into their present form, is immaterial for our purpose. For it cannot be denied that in the gospels we see, as in a mirror, the ideal of the character and teaching of their Master that the Christian churches had come to cherish toward the close of the first century. The social ethics that they recognized as true, and at first attempted to realize, are embodied in these writings.

And from this point of view the fourth gospel is just as historical and valid evidence as the synoptics. The only difference is that it illustrates the development that Christianity had undergone in the course of a generation or so after the synoptics were completed. And that difference is significant, for the fourth gospel shows that the idea of the kingdom was already fading from the consciousness of Christians. The synoptics agree in representing the mission of Jesus to be the establishment of the kingdom — an unmistakably social ideal; the fourth gospel represents Jesus as coming into the world to impart life to men, abundant life — an individualistic ideal. The two methods of representing the life and teaching of Jesus are not irreconcilable, but they are distinctly different.

Jesus declared that his kingdom was not of this world, that he came to establish a spiritual kingdom, not a political; but from all his teaching it is plain that his kingdom was to be in this world. In the beginning he seems to have hoped for an ethical reformation of the Jewish people. When disappointed in this, he centred his hopes in a small group of carefully picked disciples, whom he might prepare by his instructions to continue his work when the enemies he had provoked should succeed in cutting short his own career. But there is nothing to indicate any purpose of Jesus to found a Church. Nobody would ever conclude from the study of the gospels that he had any intention whatever of establishing a special organization for the propagation of his teachings. The only sayings that look in that direction are in the gospel of Matthew, and the doctrine of the Church that has been deduced from them must be either a misunderstanding of something that Jesus did say, or the putting into his mouth by a later generation of something that he never said and that never entered his mind.[1] He desired a new social organism, not a new organization, an entire regeneration of mankind, not the association into a close corporation of a regenerate few. All outward, formal organization is foreign to his ideas, as the gospels make him known to us. It was Paul who introduced into the Christian assemblies the synagogue organization, according to the Christian records as we have them.[2]

The consciousness of this social mission persisted in the minds of the followers of Jesus throughout the apostolic period; the churches of the first generation or two of disciples retained much of the spirit and aims of their Master. For, though the apostolic letters mention the kingdom rarely, but speak often of the church, the writers had not forgotten the teachings of the Lord, and the church meant to them a visual realization of the spiritual ideal of the kingdom. They saw in organization only an effort to give external reality to an internal fact; in their view, the churches existed to hasten the consummation of the kingdom. And at its beginning, organized Christianity was full of enthusiasm and spiritual energy. The organization was of the simplest, just enough to insure social cohesion, and the new life began at once to clothe itself in appropriate forms and find practical outlet in social service. It was the social element in the new

[1] Nevertheless it is probable that he expected that a community of some kind would be the result of his teachings, and the Greek word *ecclesia* is the equivalent for words used in his native tongue to describe the community of Israel, a people called out from the heathen and separated unto Jehovah. If Jesus ever used the word "church," it must have been in that sense.   [2] Acts 14 : 23.

faith that at once made the church at Jerusalem communistic. And yet, strictly speaking, "communism" is a misnomer as a description of the facts, sanctioned though it is by generations of usage. There was no economic theory behind the new conduct, and there was no equal division of property. Private property was neither condemned nor approved. The disciples at Jerusalem were comrades, face-to-face with an emergency; they divided their goods as men always divide in the presence of a common need or a common peril. The disciples were so ruled by the spirit of Jesus that whatever each one possessed was at the service of his brother. "Thou shalt love thy neighbor as thyself" was not among them a mere form of words — to which men give perfunctory assent, followed by instant disobedience — but was the actual guiding principle of life. "And they sold their possessions and goods and divided them all, according as any man had need." The mention afterward of the cases of Ananias and Sapphira and Barnabas makes it plain that we are not to understand the method to have been a simultaneous sale of all possessions and an equal division of the entire proceeds, but a sale from time to time of property possessed by some, and distribution to those in need from the sums thus contributed to the common treasury. Each member continued to hold his own property, but he held it subject to the needs of the whole body of disciples. In that sense they "had all things in common," because they "were of one heart and soul," so that "not one said that aught of the things that he possessed was his own." To such a point the teaching of Jesus about the stewardship of wealth and love of the brother had brought his first disciples.

This communistic principle was more enduring in early Christianity than many have realized. The Epistle of Barnabas says, "Thou shalt communicate in all things with thy neighbor; thou shalt not call things thine own; for if ye are partakers in common of things that are incorruptible, how much more of those things that are corruptible?" Justin says, "We who were before occupied by preference with possessions and goods, now bring what we have to the community, and share it with every one who has need." From the later Fathers scores of sentences like the following may be culled: "Private property is the root of all strife." "Possession in common, that is, equal ownership, is the natural and original order of things." "Beyond what a man requires for his absolute needs, all that he has belongs to the poor." "The luxury of the rich is the robbery of the poor." "What the poor ask is not thine, but their own." [1] It was because sentiments like these survived in the Church, in spite of the apostacy of the institution as a whole, that Monachism became so great an institution; for Monachism was Socialism plus piety, as piety was then conceived. Nor are we entirely dependent on Christian sources for our knowledge of this matter. Lucian, in his merry satire on "The Death of Peregrine," says: "It was impressed on them by their original lawgiver that they are all brothers . . . with the result that they despise all worldly goods alike, regarding them merely as common property. Now an adroit, unscrupulous fellow who has seen the world, has only to get among these simple souls and his fortune is made; he plays with them." [2]

[1] For the social teachings of the Fathers, see Harnack and Hermann, "The Social Gospel," Crown Theological Library, 1907, p. 33.

[2] Fowler, "Works of Lucian of Samosata," Oxford, 1905, IV: 82, 83.

The early organization of the churches shows plain marks of the social purpose of the new brotherhood. The democratic polity, recognizing the equal privileges of all members of each assembly of believers, and the entire freedom of each assembly from external control, approaches the perfect social liberty proclaimed as ideal by the anarchist. There is no domination of the churches, even by the apostles, and no conception of the churches as united in a single corporate body, such as was indicated by the epithet "catholic" introduced in the second century. No purer democracy has ever been seen, and democracy is the most entirely social of all forms of government.

The first officers of whom we have any record were appointed because of a social need, and their functions were at first purely social. Because of dissatisfaction with the distribution from the common fund, the apostles caused the election of deacons to attend to this matter, in order that they might be left undisturbed to their spiritual function of teaching. We have no hint of any enlargement of the functions of deacons, as such, during the apostolic period; for that one of the seven at Jerusalem, Philip, was afterwards conspicuously useful as a missionary was manifestly due, not to the fact that he was a deacon, but to the fact that he was Philip. In the second century, when the first simple organization began to take on greater complexity, the *episcopos*, who became elevated above his fellow-presbyters in rank and authority, was important for his social rather than his spiritual functions. Religious instruction was given by those who bore the various names of apostles, evangelists, prophets, teachers; and the bishop was the treasurer, the almoner, of the

Church. Even so late as the time of Irenæus, his functions were administrative, and the teaching office was discharged by the presbyters. It was not until the third century that the bishop became recognized as the chief teacher of the Church, his spiritual functions then for the first time becoming more important than the social.

We see the same social features everywhere in the apostolic churches. The *agapæ* were preëminently social meals, and it was out of their social character that such abuses grew as those so emphatically rebuked by the apostle Paul in his first letter to the church at Corinth. The meetings of the early churches for worship were social, if we may judge from the hints about them in the same letter — as far as possible removed from our formal and solemn Sunday services, and more like a modern prayer-meeting than anything else found in the Christian churches of to-day. There was no confining of prayer and prophecy and exhortation to appointed officers, but a free participation on the part of any who might suppose themselves to be qualified — a participation so free that Paul was obliged to warn the Corinthians against disorder in their meetings.

How has it come about that Christian communities, at first so simple in organization, so flexible in ritual, so entirely social in spirit and aim, should in so short a time have been completely transformed into the complex organization, the stately and inflexible ritual, and the anti-social spirit of the Holy Catholic Church of the third and succeeding centuries? For it cannot be denied that there was a transformation, so complete that the very recollection of what the apostolic churches were was blotted out of the memories of men, and has never been recovered. It is doubtless true that the Church never ventured formally to repudiate the teachings of him whom it acknowledged as its Founder, but it practically denied them, by putting first things second and second things first. It has so overlaid the teachings of Jesus with glosses and interpretations, as to give them a wholly different meaning — Jesus himself was not a Christian, according to the tests that his Church soon came to impose. No doubt the full meaning of his teaching could not be understood until time had given it a better perspective and experience had better interpreted it. But it is also true that all subsequent development of Christian ideas must be carried back to the teaching of Jesus and tested by that as a norm. Jesus is the one final authority on the meaning of Christianity, to which all other authority must be subordinated. And for this principle we have his own warrant: "Call no man Rabbi;" he alone is the Teacher who can speak with supreme authority to his disciples. And it is one of the most terrible ironies of history, undeniable by any one who has studied the origins and development of Christianity, that the One whom millions of Christians profess to adore as their divine Founder, would for more than a thousand years have imperilled his life had he come again as man and proclaimed his doctrine in one of the churches dedicated to his Name!

Nowhere in history can one find an instance of more complete perversion of an institution than in the history of the Christian Church. Nowhere can one find a better example of the overlaying of an original simple teaching with other doctrines and ideals, so that the first becomes lost to sight. Why did such a distorted view of God and man come to prevail, that now to many earnest souls to love the one seems impossible without hating the other? How were the social ethics of Jesus so travestied and nullified that, to many honest minds, the Christian religion of to-day seems the chief obstacle to the progress of the brotherhood of man, and the Christian Church looms up as the most formidable barrier against the prevalence of social righteousness?

I

First among the forces that deflected Christianity from its original line of progress was the preponderating influence of the apostle Paul.   An intellect of the first order, a soul of the noblest type, zeal and activity never surpassed, made this man the chief force in the initial attempts of the new religion to find itself.   In the first great internecine conflict of the Church it would have been an incalculable disaster if Paul had not won, for in that case, so far as we can see, Christianity would never have become differentiated from Judaism; it would have struggled on for a time as a Jewish sect, and then would have disappeared, as did the Essenes.   Paul saved Christianity from perishing in the cradle.   But it was almost an equal disaster that Paul did win; for, in becoming differentiated from Judaism, the new faith became the Christianity of Paul rather than the Christianity of Jesus.   From this Pyrrhic victory nothing could have saved him but to have received his training at the feet of Jesus, instead of at the feet of Gamaliel.   It was the chief, the irreparable misfortune of Paul not to know Jesus in the flesh, and the partial knowledge of Jesus in the spirit that he obtained was cast in the moulds of Rabbinism.   Or, to adopt the figure of Jesus himself, the new wine was put into the old bottles, with the result that was foretold.

There are two current methods of dealing with this divergence of Paul from Jesus, either of which is supposed by some to be more "orthodox" and "safe" than recognition of the facts. The first has at least the merit of simplicity; it is a flat denial that there is any such divergence. But this is becoming increasingly difficult, indeed impossible, in the face of the practically unanimous verdict of modern scholarship. And it is passing strange that any admirer of Paul should hesitate to admit a fact on which he himself insists, of which he almost boasts. He tells the Galatians that he did not receive his gospel from man, and was under no obligations to the other apostles. He had been fourteen years a proclaimer of the gospel before he had his first conference with an apostle. That he had somehow become possessed of the main facts regarding the life and teaching of Jesus is beyond question, but he seems to have taken pains to keep aloof from those who had been nearest to the living Jesus, lest his independent commission from the risen Jesus should be questioned or impugned.

Nor is the fact of divergence disproved by the allegation that the fundamental teachings of Jesus can be found in the writings of Paul. This may be conceded, as to most of the things that may be called fundamental, perhaps of all. But it is quite as true that much is to be found in Paul that is, to put it mildly, additional to the teaching of Jesus; and some of this additional matter is capable of an interpretation in a sense irreconcilable with some of the teaching of Jesus. In point of fact, Christian history shows that it was so interpreted, and that such interpretation made of Christianity something utterly different from the religion that Jesus taught and exemplified. Only by ignoring a considerable part of the teachings of both Paul and Jesus can they be brought into apparent accord. Such ignoring is an indispensable part of the apologetic that maintains Paul to be the legitimate expounder of the primitive gospel of Jesus, and not the preacher of "another" gospel.

The second method is less simple. It partially admits a divergence, at least an "apparent" difference, and offers as a means of reconciliation the doctrine of inspiration. As Paul asserted that he had the mind of the Spirit in his teachings, we must believe his word to be equally authoritative with that of Jesus, and we must receive this additional matter in his writings as an extension and official interpretation of the gospel, not contradicting the primitive message of Jesus, but complementing it. It is the office of exegetical science to interpret Paul and Jesus so that they do agree. But this explanation can hardly satisfy, unless one is capable of considerable intellectual and moral disingenuousness. For, according to the orthodox Christian theology, the Spirit of God dwelt in Jesus more richly than was possible in the case of any man, since Jesus was also Son of God; and superior authority must necessarily attach to the teachings of such a divine-human personality. And if it be insisted that inspiration is inspiration, that any degree of the indwelling of the Holy Spirit guarantees the truth of a message, we are once more reduced to the old shifts so repugnant to honest minds, for the reconciling of the irreconcilable. To reproduce the conviction that there is no difference between the teachings of Jesus and those of Paul has become forever impossible to scholars, and must now be left to those theologians who still go on complacently building their " systems," as if nothing had happened since the sixteenth century.

But even if such theoretic reconciliation as now seems impossible were entirely possible, it would not lessen to any degree the historical problem, pressed upon us by the fact that Paul was accepted by the Church, not merely as an authority equal to Jesus, but superior to Jesus. Paulinism did not supplement, it supplanted, the primitive Christianity; the later gospel completely eclipsed the earlier. So that the issue forced upon the Christian world became, and has ever since continued to be, Shall we place Paul before Jesus as an authority in religion? The cry "Back to Christ" raised in these latter years, so infuriating to many orthodox minds, has at least this significance: Once more it is clearly perceived that the words of Jesus ought to constitute the primary authority of any who call themselves Christians.

It hardly seems that such a proposition should be considered arguable; the mere statement of it ought to be as conclusive as an axiom of mathematics. Did Jesus come into the world to reveal God, and did he actually make the fullest revelation of the Father that man has ever had; or was his revelation but partial, and was he compelled to leave the fuller revelation to be made by Paul? Did Jesus proclaim a complete gospel of salvation, not exhausting the content of religious truth, but teaching everything that it is necessary for men to know and do in order to become sons of God; or did he leave the most precious and essential part of the gospel to be proclaimed and expounded by Paul? To those who insist so strongly on the authority of Paul that they would follow him rather than Jesus, one may quote the ironical words of the apostle to those who at Corinth would have unduly exalted him, "Was Paul crucified for you? Or were you baptized into the name of Paul?"

The teaching of Paul was the necessary result, on the one hand, of his birth and breeding, and on the other, of his personal experience. He was born and reared in a family of the well-to-do class, and never felt the bitterness of poverty; he was educated in the cities of Tarsus and Jerusalem, and the peasant life was unknown to him. He did not realize, as Jesus did, the perils of wealth and the sufferings of the poor. While there can be no doubt that the ethics of Paul were unfavorable to social evils, they were a softening of the principles of the gospel, and mark the first stage of departure from the character that Jesus had given to religion and ethics. The social questions of his day did not appeal to Paul, whose mind was preoccupied with intellectual problems. Yet the universalism of Jesus, the worldwide brotherhood that he came to establish, the oneness of Jew and Gentile in him, were to none of the immediate disciples of the Teacher so clear as to this man who had never been a disciple. It was not so much that Paul failed to comprehend the core of the gospel of Jesus, as that his rabbinic training encouraged too greatly a tendency native in him to speculate about the hidden mysteries. Such speculations he set forth in his writings, with the result that the Church came to identify those speculations with the gospel and finally to substitute them for the gospel.

In one important respect Paul was in complete sympathy with Jesus: in his opposition to Pharisaic legalism.

2 G

He had been bred in that school; he had sedulously practised its precepts and had vainly sought peace with God
by deeds of law.   Just as the original gospel of Jesus came
from his consciousness of Sonship, his relation to the
eternal God of love, an unbroken fellowship with the
Father, so the gospel of Paul was drawn from a bitter
experience of the impotence of the law to give peace of
mind and insure salvation.   Peace and assurance he
found through surrender to Jesus as Messiah and Lord,
and he was conscious that he had been made a new creation through the power of the divine Spirit.   He had been
delivered from the judgment of God, and Jesus was his
Deliverer; and Paul's whole theology was constructed
out of this personal experience.

For one constituted like him, it was not enough merely
to know that his surrender to Jesus had brought him
deliverance from sin and a peace of mind to which he
had hitherto been a stranger.   His intellect demanded a
theory to account for his experience, and a reconciliation
of the ideas derived from his Jewish training with his new
Christian ideas.   While the ground of his hope and joy
continued to be trust in a risen Christ, he found in the
death of the Christ the idea that was to be the organizing
principle in his thinking, and the means of reconciling
into a system ideas otherwise diverse.   Death must
have been essential to the mission of a Messiah, or Jesus
would not have died; but it could not have been necessary for the Christ himself; therefore, he must have
experienced death on behalf of others.   The sacrificial
ritual of his people had made Paul familiar with the idea
of vicarious death.   Gradually, therefore, the death of
Jesus assumed in his mind a wholly unique significance

and value, until the preaching of the cross becomes the central feature of his gospel.   While it is easy to trace this process of development, and even to see that it was necessitated, it is nevertheless undeniable that it leads to a type of teaching so different from anything that we find in the words of Jesus as to be in effect a totally new gospel.[1]

The divergence becomes the more unmistakable when we consider the teaching of Jesus regarding the forgiveness of sins, in comparison with that of Paul.   The teaching of Jesus is a corollary of his idea of the divine Fatherhood; forgiveness is the result of the willingness of God to pardon every son who seeks his forgiveness — the necessary outflowing of his bountiful, unmerited love. Jesus represents God as forgiving in precisely the way that an earthly father forgives, freely, without condition. The father of the Prodigal welcomes his repentant boy and grants him full absolution for his misdeeds without a word spoken; and so, is the evident implication, God forgives us.   But Paul is not content to take the bare fact of forgiveness; he must have a theory, a doctrine.   And he cannot free himself from the shackles of that legalism in which he has been bred; the concept of a holy law of God, which cannot be broken with impunity, is so ingrained into his mind that he cannot be rid of it; and he must have a forgiveness that somehow consists with the paying of due penalty for violated law.   And while Paul

---

[1] According to the gospels, Jesus conceived of his death as the necessary consummation of his work as Messiah, foretold by the Scriptures, foreshadowed by the fate of the prophets, and therefore a baptism of suffering from which he could not escape.   So the disciples at first regarded the subject (Luke 24: 26, 46).   The early discourses of the Acts are to the same effect (Acts 2: 23, 24; 3 : 14, 15; 4: 10, 27; 5: 29–31; 7: 52).

calls God Father, he does not conceive of him as Father, but as Sovereign, and as Sovereign he is the fountain of law. Sin is not merely alienation from a Father; it is an indignity done to a Sovereign's person and a Sovereign's authority; and the preservation of dignity and authority demands the infliction of appropriate penalty. Forgiveness must be compatible with the sanctity of law and the giving of penal satisfaction. Hence the Pauline doctrine of the atonement, the ground of which is the death of Christ, who thus bears the penalty of man's sin and makes satisfaction to the divine justice. At the cross mercy and peace have met together, righteousness and love have kissed each other. As a result of this atonement there is a forensic process of justification, a legal fiction by virtue of which what Christ has done in the sinner's behalf is transferred to the sinner, and he is judicially acquitted of guilt and his penalty is remitted. This is accomplished by "faith," belief in the teaching of Jesus, and surrender to him as Lord.

The divergence between Jesus and Paul is not invariable; often the two are in perfect accord. When Paul writes to the Galatians, "The fruit of the Spirit is love, joy, peace, long-suffering, kindness, goodness, faithfulness, meekness, self-control," he unquestionably has the mind of Christ and is teaching the very marrow of the primal gospel. But when he writes to the same Galatians, "Christ redeemed us from the curse of the law, having become a curse for us; for, it is written, Cursed is every one that hangs on a tree; that upon the gentiles might come the blessing of Abraham in Christ Jesus," he has gone beyond the gospel into the field of rabbinic subtleties and theologizing about the forgiveness of sins. So when he tells the Corinthians that love is the greatest thing in the world, greater than even faith and hope, and when he assures the Romans that love is the fulfilling of the whole law, he shows that he can comprehend the inmost secret of the teaching of Jesus. But when he writes to the Romans that God had set forth Jesus "as a propitiation through faith in his blood . . . that he may be just and the justifier of him who believes in Jesus," he is stating, not the gospel that Jesus proclaimed, but a speculative process by which he has made clear to his own mind the meaning of the gospel and its relation to his other ideas of God and the divine justice.

This theologizing of Paul regarding sin and atonement and justification so far fell in with the speculative tendencies of the time, so satisfied the ethical and spiritual sense of Christians for many generations, that it became and has remained until now the accepted orthodox content of the gospel. Such theologizing no longer satisfies an increasing number of Christians; and they are asserting their right to return to the simpler teaching of Jesus, and believe that God forgives sin, not because of an elaborate legal fiction, but because he is God. This they hold to be not only a more simple doctrine, but a more ethical and more profoundly spiritual. Paul's speculation satisfied only so long as men imagined that God was altogether such an one as themselves. When they once grasped the thought of Jesus that God is like none but himself, that he is the unique Being of the universe in his quality of holy love, they ceased to find illumination of mind and peace of soul in theories that conceived God to be no more than an almighty man, moved by human motives and subject to human limitations.

Jesus never attempted in his teaching to solve the riddle of sin; he was content to provide men with a remedy. He illustrates certain forms of sin in his parables, but he takes it for granted that men are conscious of their alienation from God, conscious of soul-sickness and disharmony of spirit, feeling the burden of guilt and unworthiness, sensible of their own impotence to escape from such a condition, and knowing their greatest need to be healing and deliverance and restoration to their Father's love. This Jesus came to bring to men, and he called it salvation, eternal life. He proclaimed himself to be the Way and the Life, and that the process of salvation was faith in him, that is to say, a trust or self-commitment, involving obedience to his law of love. By such faith only could a man learn the secret of the life that Jesus came to impart, become an imitator of him, learn from him the holy love of God, be so brought into harmony with the divine will as to receive the assurance of forgiveness of his sins, the inward peace that could result only from the restoration of spiritual harmony and deliverance from the power of evil. Only so could man ever come to comprehend the love of God as Father, or learn to love his God with all his heart and soul and mind and strength.

II

It is the historical fact regarding the teaching of Paul and its effect on Christian thought and Christian life that is here considered. The scope of the discussion excludes alike apologetic and polemic; it calls for no extended discussion of the truth of Paulinism *per se*, but merely for an evaluation of historic Paulinism, the interpretation given to his writings by the Church. Biblical theology, as among its most assured results, maintains that the Church got a different impression of the teaching and personality of Jesus from the fourth gospel from that which is conveyed by the synoptists; still another impression from the so-called "catholic" epistles; and one varying greatly from all the others from the epistles of Paul. And the historical fact is, that it was the Pauline view, as interpreted by the Fathers, that prevailed and made Christianity what it became and has remained — that his influence is as clearly preponderating and overwhelming as was the rod of Aaron when it swallowed the rods of the Egyptian sorcerers.

Not that this was the result of any conscious and deliberate effort on his part. Rather the contrary. Had Paul lived he would no doubt have been vastly surprised, and as much shocked, to know how completely he had supplanted and thrust into the background Jesus of Nazareth, the Christ of God, to whom he gave utmost reverence and loyal service unto the death. His training in the Jewish schools gave him a trend of thinking that made it impossible for him to appreciate and set forth the mission of Jesus as Jesus himself conceived it. His was a mind that exalted the theological above the ethical, the future above the present, the kingdom of God in its heavenly consummation above the kingdom of God as a regenerating force on earth. It would not be just to say that Paul was careless about the Christian life. Nobody who could write as he wrote to the Galatians of the fruits of the Spirit can be fairly charged with indifference to the practical side of Christian truth. But the relatively small place occupied by ethical teaching in his writings does warrant us in saying that he placed his main emphasis on the philosophy of religion, on doctrine rather than on life; not to the exclusion of life, but to its inevitable eclipse. Hence, while he was not without appreciation of the ethical teachings of Jesus, his mental constitution and training impelled him to give most thought to the speculative side of religion. The preëxistence of Christ in the "form" of God, the nature of the atonement, the forensic justification of the sinner, the real sanctification that follows, and the ultimate assurance of salvation in the divine election — questions like these occupy his thought and fill the larger place in his writings. Where Jesus is content to assume the fact of sin as a universal human experience, and point men to a remedy, Paul must find a historico-philosophical theory of the origin of sin. Where Jesus is content to teach the Providence of God, extending to the minutest affairs of life, as a justification of men's trust in their Heavenly Father, Paul is constrained to follow out the idea into a doctrine of the divine predestination.

And this seed fell into good soil. The predominant minds of the Church, after the apostolic age was well past, proved to be men trained in the Greek philosophy, accustomed to speculation, and delighting in it. Taking Paul as their guide, rather than Jesus, valuing dogma above ethics, they led the Church in no long time to believe that theology was more important than character, that a philosophy of religion was of more value than a life of religion, that Christianity was primarily a system to be believed if one would be saved. And so, from the second century onward, the Holy Catholic Church became an organization whose cardinal object was the statement and defence of sound teaching regarding Christianity.

There is no doubt that this tendency, which was already developed, received a great access of energy from the character of some of the teachings proposed in the name of Christ. Some of the early heresies were very naïve and crude, and it is difficult to comprehend how their authors ever conceived that they could find any place in a Christian system. Still, the tide of speculation once in motion, it was natural that cross-currents and counter-eddies should develop. Not all speculations would start from the same premises, or even reach the same conclusion from a common starting-point. That an attempt to assimilate the Pauline speculations with those of heathen philosophers was inevitable, follows from the fact that so many men like Justin Martyr were converted to Christianity in middle life, or after their education was completed and their mental habits established. While the life of such men was profoundly affected by the gospel, they were less affected in their thinking than we are sometimes inclined to suppose. And hence there began, at least as early as Justin's day, those speculations regarding the nature of Christ, and the union of the divine and human in his person, concerning which the Arian heresy and the council of Nice give us the first instance of an attempt on the part of the Church to determine authoritatively what should be taught and believed by all Christians.

Of course there were heresies and heresies. Some were comparatively innocuous, not affecting what were regarded as the fundamentals; others attacked points that were esteemed vital to Christianity. The Church was probably right in its estimate of Arianism as peculiarly dangerous, since it was a speculation inconsistent with the claim of Christianity to be the final revelation of God's nature and will, as well as the final word on man's duty. Christianity has no permanent mission, as Athanasius maintained, unless Jesus the Christ was God manifest in the flesh in some unique sense.   The speculations of Arius in a manner compelled contrary speculations, and forced on the Church the attempt to define the indefinable. And whatever objections may lie against the Nicene definition, it is preferable to Arianism in this: it at least makes an effort to preserve the essential thing in Christianity, that he who has seen and known Jesus has known and seen the Father.   This gone, there is no Christian religion left, only a system of altruistic ethics.

It is not necessary for our purpose to pursue further the details of the history of dogma.   Every reader will recall for himself how this was but the beginning of the Christological controversies, which were not finally settled until the close of the seventh century.   We see how this line of development in the Church came to divert men's minds from the ethical side of Christianity, and especially from the social ethics taught by him who was still nominally revered as Founder and Head of the faith. It may be pleaded by some apologist that such a diversion was historically unavoidable.   One need not be careful to answer, for the point is simply that it is actual.   To establish a fact we need not undertake to distribute blame.

III

Another influence was exceedingly potent in transforming the religion of Jesus into the Catholic Christianity of the second century, and that was paganism.   A host of religions and religious philosophies were contending for the mastery of the Roman Empire at the close of the first century — Manichæism, Gnosticism, the cults of Isis and Mithra, and many others. That Christianity was victor in the contest is the well-known historical fact. The traditional explanation has been that it conquered by the power of its superior truth, though some have been candid enough to admit that imperial favor turned the scale at a time when the issue was doubtful. But the more careful study of comparative religion, and the more thorough research into the origins of Christianity, have alike compelled the conviction that religious syncretism had much to do with the triumph of Christianity. The religion of Christ, in its struggle with other faiths, gradually adopted what seemed best in them, and not a little that was second and third best, and its success was in no small measure due to this method. That this was not so much a deliberately adopted policy, as the unconscious result of an assimilative process, natural and indeed irresistible under the conditions, did not make the result less certain.

One of the most striking instances of this syncretism is the worship of the Virgin, which, though favored by certain tendencies that developed within the Church, was little less than the grafting of the cult of Isis on the Christian faith. Readers of classic literature know how widespread and persistent this cult was in the first centuries of imperial Rome. Often the authorities became alarmed at its prevalence, and persecutions were from time to time instituted against the devotees of Isis, not less severe than the better-known persecutions of the Christians.[1] The Isis cult finally disappeared from the

---

[1] This was true of other cults also. Livy gives a circumstantial account of the excesses of the Bacchanalia in Rome in 186 B.C., as a result of which

empire, not because the laws were successful in extir-
pating it, but because the most essential feature of the
cult was incorporated into Christianity.   That essential
feature was the need felt by mankind for some recognition
in its religion of the female principle in the idea of divinity,
and the inculcation of the feminine virtues equally with
the masculine, as part of practical religion.   With this recognized in the worship of the Virgin, the Isis cult ceased
to have vitality enough to keep it alive.   Christianity
not only adopted the principle, but much of the nomenclature of Isis worship, and to Mary the Virgin were appropriated such phrases of the Isis worshippers as "Mother
of God," "Our Lady," "The Holy Lady," and the like.

The progress of Christological ideas was profoundly
affected by this syncretism.   Other religions than the
Christian had their Trinities; other religions had their
Saviours, together with doctrines of preëxistence of the
Deliverer, the virgin birth, and a resurrection after death.
For this reason, some have hastily leaped to the conclusion that Christians borrowed these doctrines from other
religions, and that the ideas we have been accustomed to
regard as uniquely Christian are in reality only a rehash
of Egyptian and Babylonian myths.   It is a superficial
scholarship that maintains such a theory.   A sounder
view, based on more thorough knowledge, is that there
was no conscious borrowing from other religions by Christianity; its chief features were independently developed
by its own teachers; but there was an unconscious assimilation of many parallel teachings and usages from the
other contending faiths.   Men trained in these pagan

the consuls enforced the law against illicit cults, and many offenders were
put to death.   Bk. XXXIX, Chap. VIII sq.

cults could not, at their conversion to Christianity, wholly divest themselves of ideas and customs ingrained into them from infancy; and Fathers like Clemens Alexandrinus, as well as heretics like Montanus, were more pagan than they suspected.

The same process is traceable in the institutions of Christianity. Other religions had their sacraments of baptism and a holy meal, and connected with them ideas of magical efficacy that were adopted by Christianity; and thus the simple symbols of the apostolic time were transformed into the wonder-working sacraments of the Catholic faith. The sacred festivals of the Church are either of demonstrably heathen origin, or were greatly modified by heathen influence. The Christian-Jewish passover feast had its counterpart in pagan celebrations of the vernal equinox, and many features of the pagan cults were made their own by Christians. The decking of the altars with flowers is a usage of the old pagan spring festivals, and the very name Easter is a testimony to this illicit marriage of heathen and Christian ideas. The Christmas festival is of so late origin that we can trace its progress in the Church, and be absolutely certain that it is merely a Christian adaptation of an ancient pagan festival, originally suggested by the winter solstice and the joy of men that the bonds of winter were broken and soon the genial summer would return. The popular features of the day — the feasting and merry-making, the exchange of gifts, the legend of Santa Claus — are all survivals of paganism, and have no claim whatever to a Christian origin, though in process of time a Christian significance has become attached to them.

How powerfully Gnosticism and Manichæism affected

Christianity, by securing the incorporation into its doctrine and practice of an ascetic ideal that found no countenance in the teaching of Jesus, and little recognition in the teaching of Paul, has long been a commonplace of historical studies. How the pagan revival, known as Neo-Platonism, affected the Christian ideas, has been so brilliantly set forth by Harnack and other learned investigators as to demand here no more than this word of allusion.

It becomes increasingly clear, as we study the development of Christianity, that in formulating the doctrines of their religion and working out its institutions and settling the details of its cult, the Christians of the second and third centuries did not draw their materials only or chiefly from the teachings of Jesus, or even from acknowledged Christian documents, but from the general stock of religious ideas, institutions, and customs then prevalent in the Roman empire. The right or wrong of this, whether it was part of a process of legitimate development, or the first stage of a degeneration, is not just now in question. The point of view now is, that such a process could not go on without a practical submergence of the teachings of Jesus in this accumulated mass of ideas more or less similar, more or less reconcilable with a continued profession of faith in him as the supreme Teacher as well as the Redeemer of men. That his ideas of human relations and of human society should be so modified by this syncretistic process as to become finally unrecognizable must be conceded to be the inescapable result. That this happened is certain, and that it happened should surprise no one who reads the early history of Christianity.

IV

A potent cause for the deflection of Christianity from the line of social regeneration on which it originally began was the fact that it was compelled to struggle during more than two centuries for its very life. We see the marks of persecution already in the later New Testament writings, especially in the Apocalypse, and the effect of persecution becomes increasingly evident in every decade of the second and third centuries. The new religion was put on the defensive, just so soon as its missionary operations had extended it throughout the Roman empire, and the imperial authorities had awakened to the fact of this wide extension. From their point of view, the new religion constituted a distinct danger to the imperial power; it substituted allegiance to Christ for supreme allegiance to the emperor and the law. Its strict monotheism made it intolerant of the imperial cult on which the state was now relying to furnish a bond of union between nationalities and religions so widely separated and discordant as those that constituted the empire.

It must be confessed that we get from the earliest Christian literature a very inadequate picture of the Christian churches and their environment, but some things are tolerably plain. Each Christian assembly of believers stood in the midst of a hostile community; the pagan philosophers were coldly critical; the priests of the pagan cults were at first contemptuous, then fearful, and always opposing; a superstitious people were ever ready to attribute disaster or calamity of any sort to the anger of the gods provoked by these "atheists"; the authorities were required by law to suppress this illegal sect, and suspected conspiracy in the private meetings. As we study this picture, we understand how and why the preservation of the unity of the organization came to seem the paramount necessity. Self-preservation made solidarity and compactness indispensable. Driven to rely on themselves, urged to mutual help and protection, Christians soon became acutely conscious of the organized power of the empire, and began to develop an equal perfection and extent of organization. The scattered churches came to self-consciousness as one Catholic body ; and soon it became evident that a universal Church was pitted against a universal secular power. In this struggle for existence was wrought out the strong ecclesiastical machine, with its hierarchy, its fixed canon of Scripture, and its rule of faith.

Unity of organization was, indeed, more insisted upon at first than unity of doctrine, as the more pressing need. The Ignatian letters are peculiarly emphatic in exhorting to unity under the authority and direction of the bishop, as the prime necessity appreciated by the author. Separation from the Church is the gravest fault of which a Christian can be guilty; disobedience to the bishop is only less grave. Such compactness of organization was made mandatory by the conditions under which the Church found itself. The growth of this institutional side of Christianity was probably certain in any case. It is hardly to be expected that the simple and incohesive organization of the primitive churches could have been permanent ; tendencies inherent in human nature, which have manifested themselves in other religions, would have brought about greater complexity. Nevertheless, the persecutions furnished conditions in which institutions grew as in a hot-bed, causing the development to outstrip all that might have been foreseen. It is easy to see how the turning of Christian activities into this channel left little energy for the following out of the social ideas of the first churches. That such a diversion was imperative, if the Church was to be preserved, and that it accomplished its purpose, making Christianity triumphant in the long struggle with the Cæsars, may do something to reconcile us to this distortion of our religion, but can do nothing to alter the fact that it was distorted.

But this compactness of organization, in a sect that professed supreme allegiance to another than the emperor, was so incompatible with the imperial ideal that it was the less to be tolerated the stronger it became. And so persecution was increasingly bitter, until it occurred to an emperor more astute than his predecessors that an alliance might be possible between the empire and the Church — an alliance that would never have been possible, had not the early teaching been already practically abandoned; for a social gospel, allied to religious fervor, would have been a menace to imperial despotism that no expedients could have lessened. We may perhaps give to Diocletian the credit of being the first of the Roman emperors to discover that Christianity could not be destroyed, but Constantine was the first to see that the new religion, so far from being destructive to the empire, might be made one of its chief pillars. Considered as a stroke of statesmanship, the union of Church and State, begun by him and completed by his successors, has no superior in the history of politics. It placed at the disposal of the emperors a system of administration admirably conceived, and soon as perfectly developed in all

2 H

parts of the empire as any ruler need have desired — a system that became the more efficient as a means of despotism because through their prelates the emperor was able to control the consciences of subjects as no heathen ruler had ever aspired to do.

This completed the transformation of Christianity. The kingdom that Jesus came to establish is hostile to this world, is endeavoring to supplant and transform it, and can accept no terms from it but unconditional surrender. But Constantine offered to make the Church rich and Christians respectable, and the offer was accepted with an eagerness that it is not difficult to comprehend, even while we deplore its results. The Church was too delighted to come out of the cave into which persecution had driven it, and bask in the sunshine of imperial favor, to ask or think about consequences. It gladly accepted what the State had to give, and before it realized the situation found itself compelled to do what its patron bade. It was not clear at the first, as it afterward became, that Constantine as friend was more dangerous to the Church than Diocletian as enemy.

And so we are brought face-to-face with one of the greatest anomalies in history: the religion of peace and righteousness and universal brotherhood becomes in a single generation the pillar of despotism and the foe of liberty, the apologist for every wickedness that may entrench itself in high places. The Church has, on the whole, kept its part of the shameful compact better than the State. It surrendered to the world and devoted itself to the task of justifying the world's life — a life that in every act and principle is an absolute negation of the teaching of Jesus. At the same time it impudently contends that the worldly life is in exact conformity to the teaching of Jesus, and has scrupled at no falsehood or forgery necessary to make out its contention. There is little injustice or exaggeration in Tolstoi's summary: "The Church so transformed Christ's teaching to suit the world that there no longer resulted from it any demands, and that men could go on living as they had hitherto lived. The Church yielded to the world, and, having yielded, followed it. The world did everything that it chose, and left the Church to hobble after as well as it could with its teachings about the meaning of life. The world led its life, contrary to Christ in each and every point, and the Church contrived subtleties to demonstrate that in living contrary to Christ's law men were living in harmony with it. And it ended in the world beginning not only to justify such a life, but even to assert that this was precisely what corresponded to Christ's teaching." [1]

There could be but one consequence of such union between Church and State: the complete disappearance of social ideas from the programme of the Church and even from its teaching. Socialism and imperialism are incompatible, but not more so than Socialism and sacerdotalism; and from the time of Constantine the sacerdotal spirit became rampant in the Church. Socialism means pure democracy; sacerdotalism means pure aristocracy. A Church that makes the sacerdotal idea part and parcel of Christianity is the necessary foe of all real social progress. Its true affinities are with the privileged classes, always against the people. It may be called a "democratic" Church, on the ground that a large num-

[1] "What I Believe," pp. 247, 248.

ber of poor people are found in it, but in organization and spirit it is fundamentally hostile to democracy. The poor are in the Catholic Church, but they are not of it; the doctrine and ritual and discipline of the Church are settled by its hierarchy, and the people have nothing left them but obedience. The instinct of the working people has not deceived them, when they have recognized the Church that has resulted from Constantine's policy as their enemy. The encyclical of Pope Leo XIII against Socialism, issued in May, 1891, was only the outspoken definition of an attitude that had long before been taken by the Church. And the vast majority of European working-men have had no experience of any other Church than the Roman, no knowledge of any other Christianity than that taught by the Roman Church. They have been quite justified in turning against the Christianity taught by a Church that publicly proclaims itself their uncompromising foe, that uses all its powers for the upholding of the present iniquitous social order.

From the time of Constantine, therefore, the ecclesiastical organization that constituted the corporate Church has remained on the side of wealth, on the side of privilege, on the side of organized injustice. The social mission of Christianity has been completely forgotten, or, if not forgotten, ignored. To undertake anything like a work of social regeneration, and still be the apologist and defender of imperialism, was manifestly impossible. Most of the clergy had the grace not to attempt such crass hypocrisy. Had the ideals of Jesus remained alive in what called itself his Church, it is manifest that every day must have witnessed their conscious violation, but it is only too plain that the ideals had perished. Henceforth, Christianity becomes an ameliorative force in the world, rather than a regenerative. It proceeded to accomplish many things for the benefit of men, but they were mere surface poultices. The deep ulcer of society remained unhealed. What the world needed was a transformation, radical, complete, such as the original Christianity was fitted to accomplish; what the Church now began to do, all that it was now fitted to accomplish, was to make social abuses a little less intolerable.

V

Persecution did more than modify Christian institutions; it had an immediate effect on the entire spirit of the Christian brotherhood. Men had so little to expect in this world that they came to do most of their thinking in terms of the world to come. The intensity of belief in the immediate coming of Christ visibly grows weaker in the early Christian writings, while the conception of the significance of the future life correspondingly enlarges. Hope of the consummation of the kingdom during their lifetime was finally abandoned by all Christians, and their hopes became fixed on the hereafter. The doctrine of the second coming, which filled so large a place in the literature of the apostolic and sub-apostolic age, has by the close of the second century become a department of eschatology. It is no longer a present reality, it is not even a definite hope; it belongs to heaven, not to this world. This gives an air of unreality to much of the Christian writings. We are accustomed to do so much of our thinking in terms of this life and the present world that it is difficult to read the literature of the early Christians sympathetically, or get the view of the writers.

They so emphasize the spiritual side of religion as often to forget that there is a material side to it, from which the spiritual can be separated only at the cost of reality. They no longer saw the spiritual in the material, no longer sought the material through the spiritual. The kingdom had no reality for them; its realization was not to be sought for or expected in this world. Men were therefore exhorted, not to seek a remedy for social ills, but to bear them patiently, in the hope of redress and reward hereafter. The greatest work of theology that the ancient Church produced, Augustine's "City of God," marks the complete passing of the ideal of Jesus.

But the transition to wealth and worldly power which is the striking feature in the history of Christianity from Constantine onward, gave new energy to a reaction from the material to the spiritual that had begun to manifest itself in the later part of the age of persecution. Men and women who revolted from a Church that was becoming so unlike its early ideal were unfortunately led into a wrong alternative by certain ideas that were derived from pagan sources rather than from the teachings of Jesus. A belief in the essential evil of matter, borrowed from Oriental religions, became gradually incorporated with Christian ideas, and while it did not perceptibly modify the formal theology of the Church, it profoundly affected the everyday thinking of all Christians. To the evil influence of matter was attributed the origin and continuance of sin; and the practical corollary was that the body is the source of all evil desire and unethical conduct in man. The practice of asceticism directly followed. Since the bodily appetites and desires are the root of sinful conduct, said men, let us by discipline of the body reduce moral evil to a minimum, and make the attainment of holiness by so much the less difficult. The institutions of monachism were only the visible embodiment of an ideal that substantially the whole Church came to cherish, of the most effective way, if not the only way, to live on a higher spiritual plane.

During many centuries it was taught without contradiction that the highest character could not be reached in the home, or in ordinary secular vocations, that a truly religious life could be lived only in the cloister. Men and women withdrew themselves from their homes and callings, abandoning with heartless cruelty those dependent on their love, that they might save their own miserable souls by prayer and mortification of the flesh in some monastery. That was to be religious. To live in the shelter of the home was a lower life tolerated by God in those who were too weak to choose the better part. How foreign such an ideal of the Christian life is to the teachings of Jesus there is no occasion to point out to any reader of the gospels. Yet it is the ideal still cherished by millions who call themselves Christians. The world has been right in concluding that this ideal is worthless, that a religion of this kind has no social value, but rather is full of possibilities of social injury. The Christianity that will not bear the test of the home, the shop, the market-place, the field, is not the religion of Jesus.

Monachism must be granted the praise of consistency and thoroughness. What the majority of men attempted to achieve by spasmodic fastings, and occasional austerities, the monks sought by a more logical and rigorous method. Monachism can be effectively criticised only by the denial of its premise. It is essentially anti-social and anti-Christian, because its aim is selfish, its chief object being the promotion of holiness and securing the ultimate salvation of those who engage in it; whereas Jesus exhorts to the unselfish life, the rescue of the other man, the love of neighbor. Monachism showed its unsocial character by withdrawing from the world the best and purest, or, at least, those who had the strongest impulse towards goodness and purity, and left the race to be propagated and the business of the world to be carried on by the worst. That the ethical deterioration of Europe during the mediæval period was no greater is the real thing to wonder at, not that it was so great.

VI

The social failure of the Church has been emphasized by Protestantism, which has thus far been as completely oblivious of the social teachings of Jesus as the Roman Church. This almost inevitably resulted from the conditions of its origin. Protestantism is part of the general revolt manifest in many forms throughout the whole of Europe from the fifteenth century onward, against the system of absolute despotism in Church and State, that had been built up and maintained during the mediæval period. That system at length broke down. Men refused to remain slaves and insisted on liberty — liberty to think, liberty to worship God, liberty to govern themselves, liberty to work and enjoy the fruits of their labor. The pendulum now swung in the opposite direction. For ages the thinkers among men had been finding arguments and excuses for absolutism; they now began to proclaim, defend, and expound the principle of individualism. The denial by the Church of liberty in religion led the

Reformers into the most extreme assertion of the rights of the individual soul, and opened the way for endless sectarian divisions and conflicts.

What is most surprising to the student of the Reformation is that so little was accomplished towards the rediscovery of Jesus and his teaching. But there is an explanation of a sort, if not entirely satisfactory, in the environment. Protestantism had the experience of Christianity in the first centuries, a fierce struggle during several generations for the mere right to exist. To conquer freedom of thought, freedom of worship, was its first task, and to do this required three hundred years. Religious liberty was practically unknown until the nineteenth century; and until it had been won men were not ready to raise or to heed the cry, "Back to Christ." It is difficult for us who rejoice in this heritage to realize how short is the time in which it has been possessed by men anywhere, and that it is not yet fully possessed except in America.

But aside from these outward conditions, the inward impulse of the Reformation was not directly favorable to the recovery of the social teachings of Jesus. Protestantism owes its characteristic form, and a trend that has lasted until now, to two factors : a personal, religious experience of Luther, and the revival of Augustine's theology by Calvin. Both were based on the teaching of Paul, not that of Jesus.

Luther's experience, though not unique, was most dramatic and impressive. It was the natural result of his idea of God — an idea not uncommon at the time, but nurtured to full growth in his mind by parental severity in his youth. God was to him, not a Father who loved all men with an everlasting holy love, but a Judge, who was full of wrath against men for their sins, holding them sternly to account for satisfaction to the uttermost. Conscious of sin, he vainly sought forgiveness and peace by the ways the Church recommended: confession, penance, good works. He rushed into the monastery in a panic of fear, and by severities that well-nigh cost him his life attempted to earn salvation, but found his agony of soul increased rather than diminished. From Augustine and Paul, but especially from Paul, he got the idea of forgiveness of sin through an act of faith, in virtue of which the merits of the sacrifice of Christ were transferred to him. This gave him peace of mind, and this gradually became to him the whole of salvation. Justification by faith, after this experience and as a natural result of it, seemed to Luther the core of the gospel; and to have this assurance of forgiveness was to be a Christian; this was to be saved.

No idea of the kingdom of God entered the mind of Luther. Regeneration as a means of entrance into this kingdom was not in all his thoughts. Here he was misled by the ancient Catholic teaching and never escaped from its error; regeneration was for him accomplished in baptism. The new life that is the essence of the teaching of Jesus was merely the result of this experience of forgiveness. Luther could speak lightly of sin, because, if one had faith, his sin was always forgiven. He never arrived at an adequate notion of the ethical obligation that rests on a follower of Jesus. In all his thinking, the Christian life and the Christian character fell into the category of second things. It is impossible for the believer to live without sin, and Luther at times implied that he need not try very hard, because he can always have recourse to faith and forgiveness. Hence arose a well-founded complaint that the Reformation was at first distinctly unfavorable to ethical conduct; and it was not until the gaps in Luther's teaching were filled in at the behest of experience, that the reproach was removed. Melanchthon agreed with Luther, as he showed in his "Loci Communes," in which he declared that the gospel is "the promise of grace or the forgiveness of sins through Christ." This describes Paul's teaching, not that of Jesus, whose Good News to men was the proclamation of the kingdom of God, with rebirth of the individual as the condition of entrance and the reorganization of society as its result.

The one party during the Reformation struggle that had some apprehension of the gospel of Jesus, that made some attempt to proclaim anew his teachings and to realize his ideals, the Anabaptists, were overwhelmed with obloquy and persecuted to extermination. It is quite true that they were not a homogeneous party, and that some among them gave just cause of offence by their fanaticism, their appeal to the sword, and their immorality. But these were not the real reasons why the Anabaptists were so reprobated by the reformers, so persecuted by all governments — these were merely the plausible excuses for the relentless bitterness with which they were suppressed. The Anabaptists were despised and rejected for the same reason that Jesus was rejected and despised — they announced a gospel that, if accepted, would have required and produced a reorganization of society on the principle of human brotherhood. Sixteenth-century Europe was no more ready for such a gos-

pel than twentieth-century Europe is.   Sixteenth-century
Europe was not ready even to permit the question to be
discussed, or to tolerate the existence of a party pledged
to the propagation of such ideas.   Four centuries have
resulted in so much of progress as this : Europe is now
listening to discussion of social reorganization, albeit reluctantly, and for the most part still returning no answer
but an angry negative.

The theology of the Reformers, and especially of Calvin, was possible only to men who had been bred under
aristocracy and monarchy.   From the ideas thus made
habitual to them, not even their tendency to magnify
the individual could free them.   The only theology they
could conceive was a theology in which individualism
could be reconciled with the divine Sovereignty.   They
thought of God as an absolute, despotic ruler of a world
that he had created "for his own glory" — a Being with
the united attributes of Pope and Emperor, raised to in-
finitude.   This God had decided of his good pleasure,
that is, in a wholly arbitrary manner, to bestow the blessings of salvation on a small number of persons, selected
without any reference to what they were or might do ;
and these should be called by irresistible grace, and should
in the life to come share with God in his "glory."   The
gospel that Jesus proclaimed was Good News for the
whole world ; the gospel according to Calvin was Good
News for the elect only — to all others it was a message
of wrath and condemnation.   The one was democracy
in religion, the other aristocracy.   It is no wonder that
Calvinism has done no more for the social uplift of humanity than Catholicism — it could not well do less.

We are at no great loss, therefore, to explain why the

Church has so long neglected the social mission with which the followers of Jesus are charged by the teachings of their Master. It would have been nothing short of a miracle if the Church had kept alive the ideals of Jesus during the ages of darkness and violence through which it has passed; and, if it had kept the ideals alive, it is hard to see what it could have effectively wrought towards their attainment, though it might have avoided some of its own deadly perversions. Now that the Church is slowly coming to a new consciousness of the meaning of Christianity as taught by its Founder, it is natural that there should be at first hesitancy and divided counsels. Christendom is still seeing men as trees walking, but it is beginning to see — that is the hopeful fact, and out of such sight much may come.

The most serious obstacle as yet to united and effective action is that the Church does not now see clearly, does not yet recognize the absolute need of social reconstruction, thinks that present institutions can be somehow patched up and made to serve longer. It has all along been treating the symptoms of social disorder, not understanding that society is suffering from a constitutional disease. It has been shown many times that there is such a thing as a collective Christian conscience, and that when it is once thoroughly roused, there is certain to be "something doing." But with regard to social evils, this collective Christian conscience has never been so roused as to go to the root of the matter. This is because of the confused ideas that have been entertained as to the real difficulty. The conscience is sound, the intelligence is at fault. A process of education is necessary in order to secure enlightened action and give

effective direction to the healthy ethical sentiment of
Christians. And to contribute to this education is the
pressing duty of every man who has come to see clearly
the truth as to social evils. It was once thought that
the office of religion was to fit men for heaven; men now
know that no man is fitted for the heavenly life until he
is fitted to live here among his fellows — the man prepared to live best is the man best prepared to die. It is
not by shirking one's duties on earth that one becomes
fitted to enjoy bliss above. To live this life aright, to
make the noblest and best of it, is man's whole present
concern. And men can live this life aright, can realize
their highest possibilities, only by accepting and following the teachings of Jesus.

We come then to this: the teachings of Jesus are utterly
incompatible with the present social order, and his Church
has entirely failed to accomplish the social revolution that
he anticipated as a result of the adoption of his precepts
as a rule of life. What then? Shall we abandon all attempt to live by the precepts of Jesus, or shall we try
as never before to reduce them to practice? Jesus or
the Church, the present social order or human Brotherhood — which? Shall we seriously make the attempt
to reconstitute the world according to the ideas of Jesus,
or shall we content ourselves with things as they are, and
go on saying that the ideas of Jesus are theoretically
admirable, but quite impracticable? Whence came this
conviction that Christianity must be denaturized before
it is fit for use? How can anything be pronounced impracticable until it has been tried? And no man can
point out a time or place or society that ever gave the
ethics of Jesus a fair trial.

If the ethics of Jesus are impracticable for the world as it is, such a fact is a condemnation, not of the ethics, but of the condition of the world. His ethics may be practicable ethics for such a world as should exist, a society ruled by the spirit of mutual brotherhood and good will. The world has always had its own Beatitudes: Blessed are the proud; Blessed are the self-complacent; Blessed are the self-assertive; Blessed are they that hunger and thirst after pleasure; Blessed are the cruel; Blessed are the lustful; Blessed are the violent and revengeful. Since Jesus deliberately challenged and reversed such ethics, it is not wonderful that the world pronounces his impracticable. The wonder is that the professed disciples of Jesus should accept the world's verdict and refuse to try their Master's principles. Of what use will it be to cherish orthodox beliefs as to the divinity of Christ, and his identity of essence with the Father, and at the same time contemptuously to reject his authority as teacher and guide? What avails it that Christians vociferate, "Lord, Lord," and yet do none of his commandments?

XII

THE ATTITUDE OF CHURCHES AND MINISTERS TO SOCIAL QUESTIONS

BIBLIOGRAPHY

PEABODY, The Approach to the Social Question. New York, 1909.
MATHEWS, The Church and the Changing Order. New York, 1907.
——, The Gospel and the Modern Man. New York, 1910.
ELY, Social Aspects of Christianity. New York, 1889.
RAUSCHENBUSCH, Christianity and the Social Crisis. New York, 1907.
CAMPBELL, Christianity and the Social Order. New York, 1907.
STELZLE, The Church and Labor. Boston, 1910.
——, Christianity's Storm Center: A Study of the Modern City. New York, 1906.
BROWN, The Social Message of the Modern Pulpit. New York, 1906.
HODGES AND REICHERT, The Administration of an Institutional Church. New York, 1906.
THOMPSON, The Churches and the Wage Earners. New York, 1909.
SPARGO, The Spiritual Significance of Modern Socialism. New York, 1908.

XII

THE ATTITUDE OF CHURCHES AND MINISTERS TO SOCIAL QUESTIONS

So numerous are the programmes offered for the regeneration of society, so confusing in their contradictions of principle, and so irreconcilable in their details, that it often seems to the bewildered mind as if the safest thing would be to do nothing. But this is really the most dangerous thing of all. The Church that adopts the Fabian policy is lost; it is a maxim of war that a defensive campaign invariably ends in defeat. But action does not necessarily involve a choice between these conflicting proposals. On the contrary, effective action may be taken with a strong conviction that no programme, made in Germany or elsewhere, for the complete and immediate solution of the social problem, is worthy of a moment's serious consideration by a serious person.

I

What attitude, then, is the Christian Church to assume towards proposals for social regeneration? What is a preacher to do towards solving the social problems of his time? No questions could be more practical; few could be more urgent; and some would think, none can be more difficult. But really, nothing could be more simple, if we first have fully settled in our minds what is the mission of a Christian Church and a Christian preacher in this world.

A Christian Church exists to hasten the coming of the kingdom of God among men, the development of that new social order that will inevitably result from the presence in the world of regenerated men, living in accordance with the rule of love that Jesus taught. The Church is not chiefly a hospital to which men are to take their spiritual diseases to be cured, though it must do a work of healing; nor is it simply a parlor to which people may resort to have their souls manicured, though spiritual culture is a part of its mission; it is first of all and last of all a propaganda of the kingdom idea and of the kingdom life. If it fails here, it fails altogether. The Church has no other legitimate purpose or aim than this. Whatever promises to promote the coming of the kingdom ought to have its sympathy, ought to be eagerly seized and made tributary to this single end. Whatever relates in no way to the progress of the kingdom, however desirable it may be in itself, is entirely outside the function of the Church. Here is a simple touchstone, by which every question of the duty of the Church may be tested; and the differences of opinion that will result from the honest application of this test will be both few and unimportant.

How far are Churches to-day using their spiritual resources and their manifold opportunities to promote the coming of the kingdom? Are they not cumbered with too many cares regarding the building up of the Church itself, the maintaining and perpetuating of the mere organization, which has no value save as a means to the great end? Is there not far too much sectarian activity and sectarian jealousy, and far too little zeal for the kingdom? What Church, what denomination, can honestly say that it is free from this sin, and who will believe it if it does say so ? May we not almost say that the Church, with its sacraments and its creeds and its liturgies, has done its utmost to shut out altogether the kingdom of God's love, to forget its divine mission to hasten the coming of the kingdom, and fallen to glorifying itself ? That it has not quite succeeded is perhaps the most convincing proof that God's love is invincible and that the Church has a divine mission. President Hyde, of Bowdoin, not long ago said, "A Church that has been reduced to a mere preaching station, and a repository of traditions, a performer of rites and ceremonies, is not far from its inevitable extinction." And he might have added, if the Church has sunk to the level of a mere social club, its case is no better.

Christianity has a message for the age, but for the most part the Church and the pulpit are not giving the age this message. The Church maintains a splendid ideal of the kingdom, but only as an ideal, something too spiritual to be expected in this life, a hope for the world to come, and as to this world it winks at all injustice and iniquity. To the demand for a practical Christianity, that will make a reality of the empty words "brotherhood" and " service," the Church still for the most part returns a dogged *Non possumus*. It will be vain for the Church to profess belief in the Jesus of the gospels, if by its conduct it continues to deny the gospel of Jesus. The piety that confesses Christ with the lips and crucifies him every day in the person of his "little ones" will be lightly esteemed by a cynical world. "Beware of the leaven of the Pharisees " was the warning of Jesus to his disciples ; and Phariseeism is to-day, as it was in the time of the great Teacher, his chief enemy and the unrelenting foe of his gospel. The Church is to-day in large part a collection of people who thank God that they are not as others — even as this socialist ! The indifferent priest and the hard-hearted Levite still throng the highways, but to many a man who has fallen among robbers and has been bruised and beaten and left half dead no good Samaritan comes with his oil and wine. The Church is too busy holding conventions and saving the heathen to attend to such small matters at its doors.

Shall we wonder that this profession of loyalty to Christ by a Church that persistently disregards the social teachings of Jesus, and reverently bows the knee to Mammon, is greeted only by the scornful incredulity of the world ? It was authoritatively stated a short time ago that Mr. Asquith's temperance bill was defeated in parliament through the opposition of clergymen who had invested their savings in brewery stock, the profits of which might have been lessened by the bill. At about the same time, the Archbishop of Canterbury publicly explained that he worked seventeen hours a day, and had no time left for the forming of an opinion on the labor problem. Whereto Mr. Keir Hardie made a reply, as unanswerable as it was stinging, that "a religion which demands seventeen hours a day for organization and leaves no time for a single thought about starving and despairing men and women and children has no message for this age." But that is England, and an established Church, and of course there is nothing like that in the free churches of America !

Men may surely be pardoned for thinking that what does not stand openly and strongly for justice and freedom and social righteousness cannot be of God and the

truth.   The Church is judged by the company it keeps.
And that company is the company of the rich and powerful, the class that has created and maintains all forms of
social unrighteousness, and now claims a vested interest
in their survival.   Some of our captains of industry have
no scruples against dealing in pitch, but are fastidious
about keeping their hands clean.   As Lady Macbeth said
of her lord, they "would not play false, and yet would
wrongly win."   Not virtuous at heart, they yet sedulously preserve the appearance of virtue.   They liberally
support the Church, and all religious and philanthropic
institutions, and thereby virtually control them.   The
millionnaire robber does not serve God for naught; he
goes to church that he may not go to jail.   He seriously
believes that "the more you put in, the more you will
take out."   It is a sound investment; for, as he views it,
religion is an excellent sort of insurance, good for both
worlds, and not costly.

What is the function of a Christian preacher?   It is
to be God's prophet.   He is not a mere orator on all kinds
of religious topics.   He is not a teacher of theology.   He
is not a lecturer on sociology.   He does not occupy a ly-
ceum platform, on which he is at liberty to discourse to
whoever will listen on everything knowable and several
other things.   He occupies a pulpit, in which he is Christ's
ambassador, and his mission is to beseech men in Christ's
stead, "Be ye reconciled to God."   To make known to
men the truth that God has revealed to him is his first
duty.   To teach men that God is a Being of holy love,
and to strive to bring men into moral fellowship with
God, is the practical side of his work.   He knows, or
should know, that to get men right with God is to get

them right with one another; and that, until they are right with God, they can never be really right with one another; but also, that until they are right with one another, they are not, and can never be, right with God. The two are one and inseparable, now and forever. If the preacher faithfully proclaims the gospel with which he has been intrusted, he will offer the world the most effective cure, the only effective cure, for all social ills. But it must be the gospel of Jesus, his whole gospel. Preachers are frequently exhorted to preach "the simple gospel," but that phrase is usually heard from the lips of simple people. The gospel is not simple but complex. Its principles are indeed simple; they can be comprehended by a child; but their application is as multifarious as the complicated concerns of modern life, and the preacher has to do with every one of these applications.

It is no part of the Christian preacher's mission, therefore, to preach Socialism or any other "ism." Nor is it his function to preach against Socialism. He moves in a different plane; he has another and a larger work to do. All "isms" are, for the preacher, errors. They are the worst heresies of which he can be guilty. That is because every "ism" is the narrow and fanatical assertion, the undue exaggeration, of something that, held in its right proportions, might be a truth, but in any case not truth which it is the preacher's business to proclaim. That is of sufficient importance to be said a second time: Let the preacher always remember that, even if they be true, "isms" are not for him. Larger truth has been intrusted to him, a greater work is before him to do; he cannot stick too closely to his proper function, and if that function seems to him sometimes to be narrow, let him realize that it becomes thereby the more intense and can supply his ministry the greater moral voltage.

Has the preacher been more faithful to his mission than the Church to hers? "And it shall be, like people, like priest." Look in the themes advertised in the daily press by the ministers of any of our cities, and the reports of sermons preached, and then say how far the minister of to-day remembers that he is God's prophet, Christ's ambassador. He has too often forgotten that the great need of the world is to know God, and to be brought into harmony with the infinite heart of love that beats at the centre of this universe. "God is an unnecessary hypothesis," said Laplace. "My heart and my flesh crieth out for the living God," said the Psalmist. "O God, thou hast made us for thyself, and our hearts are restless till they rest in thee," said Augustine. The Hebrew poet and the theologian of Hippo have better expressed the judgment, have more accurately voiced the cry of universal humanity, than the great mathematician. It is still the fool who says in his heart, "No God."

The preacher need have no fear that his occupation is soon to be taken from him by the prophets of Socialism. Some of them are confident enough of this result. Bebel boastfully declares: "Religion will not be abolished, or God dethroned [so good of him!]. . . . Without attack of force or suppression of opinion of any kind, religion will of itself vanish." [1] The prediction has a very familiar sound. Did not Voltaire predict something of that sort in the eighteenth century? Yes, indeed; he thought that to overthrow Christianity only five or six philosophers

[1] " Women and Socialism," p. 437.

who understood one another were necessary, and in one of his expansive moments he gave the Christian faith ten years more of existence. Bebel is wiser and sets no date. Christianity has survived many such predictions. And yet, we may consider it certain that if it finally proves worthless to the world, turns aside from its great mission to other ends, it will vanish. Only that which is permanently valuable remains permanently.

Those who expect to see a transformation of society without the influence of religion show a profound ignorance alike of history and of human nature. One has read the story of the past to little purpose if his reading has not taught him that religion unites the social group with a bond stronger than blood or language, as has often been shown when a difference in religion has rent asunder a nation, a tribe, or a family. That this, the strongest force in the world hitherto, is disappearing or likely to disappear, is the least credible of all prophecies. Some socialists are wise enough to see this, and, having lost faith in the Church, are trying to find a religion for themselves in their socialistic theories. "Socialism is at once a science and a religion," says Liebknecht; "in its appeals to the feeling and the conscience, it has the entire force of Christianity; in its appeal to the mind, it has all the strength of science." Such words could be written only by one who has never felt the appeal of Christianity, never heard the voice

> Saying, "O heart that I made, a heart beats here!
> Face, my hands fashioned, see it in myself!
> Thou hast no power nor mayst conceive of mine,
> But love I gave thee, with myself to love,
> And thou must love me who died for thee."

But religion is to be distinguished from its institutions. It is possible that the world will be saved, that it must be saved, apart from historic Christianity. The unethical religiosity that calls itself by that name has no salvatory value. Jesus taught that the test of institutions is their capacity for social service, "The Sabbath was made for man, not man for the Sabbath." The Church must sustain this test triumphantly, if it is to survive; if it cannot save, it must go. And it must save in a larger sense than the mere rescue of an individual here and there. It must save society. It is the business of the followers of Christ, not only to save sinners, but to prevent the regular and incessant manufacture of sinners. Believing with their Master that this is God's world, they must also believe with him that just because it is God's world, injustice and violence and greed and impurity are to give place to love and peace and brotherhood and righteousness.

More than once in the preceding discussions the necessity of regeneration has been mentioned, without any attempt to explain what was meant by that term. It means everywhere in this book just plain, old-fashioned regeneration, a radical change of heart, of motive, of nature, a change that can only be described as a new birth and can be ascribed only to the Spirit of God as cause. But, some reader may be asking, has not modern psychology thrown new light on this change, removed it from the realm of the mysterious and supernatural, and brought it wholly within the realm of natural law? Is what used to be called regeneration anything more than a psychological process that may be fully accounted for as a culmination of religious influences, which at a given time produce their legitimate effect in a way fully explicable,

like other less extraordinary psychological phenomena ?
Psychology has indeed thrown much valuable light on
regeneration, so that we comprehend the nature and con-
comitants of the change better than formerly, but it has
not explained the vital part of the process — the complete
and often sudden change of moral character. That part
of the process which is purely psychic — conviction of
sin, and the sudden transition to peace and joy, commonly
called an "experience" — is made much clearer by psychological investigation. But very little light has yet
been thrown on such ethical transformations as are related
in Mr. Harold Begbie's "Twice-born Men." The psychological "experience" is but too common without the
ethical change; yet in all ages, from Saul of Tarsus to
Jerry McAuley, there have been marvellous transformations of character for which psychology affords no explanation; and they have never been wrought save by
the power of Jesus and his teaching. Modern psychology
is as dumb before this marvel as the philosophy of the
past has been. And transformations as real, though not
so dramatic and striking as those related by Mr. Begbie,
are within the knowledge of every Christian; for, if he
has not experienced such a sudden moral renovation
himself, he has observed more than one such case in communities where he has lived.

II

The first and most practical duty of both churches and
preachers is to get a more intelligent and sympathetic
comprehension of the social problems of our day. Many
Christians are not yet aware that there are any social
problems, still more are not yet certain that the Church

and the ministry have any duty with regard to such problems. They are living in some past or future Golden Age of society and religion, dreaming perhaps of a restoration of apostolic Christianity. We can never have the apostolic Christianity again, because we can never again have the apostles and the conditions of their age— fortunately we never can ! "The mill will never grind again with water that is past." The world moves forward, not backward, and a man has begun to die when he has begun to live in the past. The institution that has "a great future behind it " is doomed. If the Church cannot prove its capacity to live in the present and for the future, it has ceased to be of any real value to the world, and must perish like any other effete institution. We must come as Christians to consciousness of our social environment, realize that the old individualism is as dead as feudalism ; and that a spirit and method that fitted social facts of two hundred years ago cannot be successfully related to present conditions.

New occasions teach new duties; Time makes ancient good uncouth ;
They must upward still, and onward, who would keep abreast of Truth.

Only by study both intelligent and sympathetic shall we succeed in getting the right point of view, in seeing things in their true perspective, which is the prime condition of mental sanity. To study unsympathetically or with little intelligence is to see things out of perspective, distorted, untrue, fatally deceptive. Ministers whose sympathy overbears their intelligence become, on the one hand rash and fanatical, reversing the conduct of

Balaam and cursing where they fain would bless; or they become cowardly, shrinking in dismay from an agitation that they do not understand and can, therefore, only fear. Those who study with intelligence but without sympathy become cold and barren theorists, whom nobody hears with patience or takes seriously. But to study with equi-balanced intelligence and sympathy means that one must not identify himself with any group or take an active part in social agitation. It is not merely wiser for the Church and the preacher to keep outside the whirlpool of class strifes; they can perform their proper function only by so doing. They are to be teachers and guides, not combatants. Their voice is ever to be raised in favor of justice and mercy and love, but it is theirs to imitate their Master in refusing to be judge of actual controversies.

This is not cowardly evasion of responsibility; this is not fear to incur danger; it is resolute insistence on doing one's own proper work, and declining to be tempted into side issues by plausible considerations. Judgment is not the function of Church and preacher, but education and training. Prophets of God and teachers of the world in righteousness, both by precept and example, is what Christians are called to be and do, and the world will respect them the more, not the less, if to all invitations to engage in other occupations they return the answer of Nehemiah to Sanballat, "I am doing a great work, so that I cannot come down; why should the work cease, whilst I leave it and come down to you?"

It is always a good rule to "do the next thing." Few of us have to go to seek duties; the providence of God thrusts them upon us quite as fast as we are prepared for them. To a certain extent, opportunism is the condition

of success.   Not an opportunism that disavows all guid-
ance by principles, and takes the line of least resistance
as conditions develop, no, not even if through all resulting
sinuosities of conduct the one goal be kept ever in sight
and some progress toward it be continually making.   But
an opportunism that recognizes the stone wall of certain
fact, instead of butting one's head against it ; an opportunism that comprehends that while principles are un-
changing methods may well be flexible.   Much effort by
the Church and preachers fails of any immediate and
visible result, whatever it may effect at some time in the
future, because of an uncompromising adherence to one
method, under the delusion that this is adherence to
principle.   Abstract ethical rules are seldom applicable
to concrete conditions in the same way that mathematical rules are applied, because ethics have to do with
those variable things, motive and conduct.   The chief
error made by churches and preachers with regard to
social questions is insistence on the ethically ideal, without consideration of the ethically practicable.   We should
always insist on the ethically ideal, in the sphere of the
ideal, but with clear vision recognize the ethically practicable in the sphere of the practical.

Before churches or preachers commit themselves to a
course of practical conduct, it is imperative that they ask
themselves this question : Is it rationally possible to
accomplish this thing, in this way, at this time ?   How
many failures and blunders would be avoided if this were
oftener done.   But, it may be asked, should the impossible never be attempted ?   Does not our Master bid us
attempt much that is rationally impossible ?   There can
be no question that the world would be incalculably

poorer to-day if there had not been men willing to lead
forlorn hopes, to face all but certain defeat; and that such
will always be the case cannot be doubted.   But let
us clear our eyes, and know what we are about.   Are we
seeking a practical success, or are we knowingly following
the truth at the cost of martyrdom?   The man who will
not flinch from duty, whatever the consequences, is wholly
admirable, but he does not deceive himself by looking for
success; he faces disaster or death, and expects nothing
else.   But the man who rushes blindly into a conflict,
without once looking at the forces arrayed against him,
or calculating the chances of victory or defeat, is not a
brave man, as he doubtless fancies himself to be, but
merely the common or garden variety of fool.   And oh,
in how many gardens does he grow and bloom!

Since the teaching of Jesus was so greatly concerned
with men's social relations, if the Christian preacher is
faithful to his Master his message must be preëminently
a social message, and the mission of the Church must be
at bottom a social mission.   Salvation begins with the
rescue of the individual man from sin and misery, the
impartation to him of a new life, so that he at once gets
a new point of view and no longer looks solely upon his
own rights and concerns, but upon those of his neighbor.
This results in giving him a new social status and imposing on him new social duties.   Until the preacher has
learned to conceive his religion and calling in this way,
he is quite unprepared for his work; when he has learned
so to conceive of work and religion, this new idea will inspire his message and determine his activities.   He will
see that his charge, as Christ's ambassador to beseech
men, "Be ye reconciled to God," is not a merely individual

matter, that he is aiming at something more than the salvation of individuals. His mission is to bring society and God together : and though he can do this only through bringing one man at a time to the knowledge and love and service of God, he is to keep the larger result ever in mind. It will make an immense difference to him and to the Church if they approach men in this spirit, and conduct their campaign of evangelism with this end in view.

III

If Church and preacher had always labored in this spirit, does anybody believe it possible that the working classes could have become so alienated from the Church as everybody knows them to be to-day ? Why has the proletariat come to believe that the Church is not its friend, but its foe ? It cannot be denied that the working people of all nominally Christian countries have become alienated from the Church, and the religion proclaimed and practised by the Church. This is as true of Protestant Germany and England [1] as of Catholic France and Italy. In the United States it is little better. The general growth of materialism and irreligion will account for some of this alienation, but the strongest influence is undoubtedly the growing conviction of the workers that the Church is either indifferent or hostile to their interests. Accordingly, their attitude is rapidly changing from one of indifference to open hostility.

[1] English Socialism is not entirely anti-Christian, however. The delegation of the English Labor Party that visited France and Belgium in the summer of 1910, three hundred strong, bore banners on which was inscribed : "We represent 500,000 English workpeople. One for all and all for one. We proclaim the Fatherhood of God and human brotherhood. Jesus Christ, the social Reformer, leads and inspires us."

2 K

The president of the American Federation of Labor not long ago said : "My associates have come to look upon the church and the ministry as the apologists and defenders of the wrong committed against the interests of the people. . . . They use their exalted positions to discourage and discountenance all practical efforts of the toilers to lift themselves out of the slough of despondence and despair." A labor leader recently said, "The American working-man hates the very shadow that the spire of the village church casts across his pathway." From still another comes this : "Some complaint has been made that working-men will not attend the church. Had the victim on the road to Jericho found in some of the chief seats of the synagogue the men who robbed him without mercy, and at the altar the priest and the Levite who looked upon him without pity, doubtless he would have gone his way sorrowful." Such sayings may be a trifle bitter ; they may not be entirely representative ; but who shall say that their feeling is without cause ?

It is easy to lay the burden of these things on an abstraction, and say that "the Church" is responsible ; but let us remember that the Church is only the aggregate of those "who profess and call themselves Christians." Working-men do not find that it is better, as a rule, to work for a Christian than for an unbeliever ; they do not find that they get better goods or juster weight or fairer prices from a Christian merchant than from a heathen Chinee. An orthodox church-member is as likely as any other man, when at the head of a corporation, to maintain company stores that rob his workmen, to resist just demands for higher wages, better hours, and more perfect sanitation. The presence or absence of righteous principles in a business seems to have little or no relation to the presence or absence in it of "Christians."

The working-man of to-day cannot see Jesus for the press, — the greed, the injustice, the oppression, the misery, of the present social order, — and there is no sycamore tree for him to climb. He can be cured of his indifference or hostility to the Church when the members of Christian churches show to him that the spirit of Jesus dwells in them, by living the Master's life and doing his works. The Church must let men see that it exists for the creation of a new social order, a new earth in which righteousness shall dwell. The condition in which the majority of our kind are compelled to spend their lives cannot fail to move the followers of that Jesus whom the spectacle of the social iniquities of his own time moved to the depths, so that he could not restrain his indignant rebuke of those whose selfishness made such suffering possible, even inevitable. Jesus deliberately turned from the ecclesiasticism and aristocracy of his day, and gave his life's best to the common people. If the world's workers reject Jesus now, they reject their best friend and hope.

Of course, the Church protests that it has been misunderstood, and what is even more important, that Christianity has been misunderstood. But who or what is to tell the world what Christianity is, if not the Church? And could the Church have been so fatally misunderstood, if it had been faithfully performing its social mission and delivering its social message? The answer cannot be refused: the Church has not been faithful, and it is more than time that it repented its unfaithfulness in sackcloth and ashes and began to bring forth fruits meet for repentance. It must make plain to those who do the world's work that the religion of Christ has not yet lost its early characteristic, that it has a message of hope and cheer for the oppressed and the exploited. It must resist the insidious temptation to espouse the cause of the moneyed class, merely because it can thus most easily assure itself of adequate financial support, or it is lost. The religion that Jesus taught will never perish; humanity will ever hunger and thirst for his message; men will always cry out for the living God, even though, like an infant crying in the night, they know not for what they cry. But the Church, institutional Christianity, has no such assurance of permanence; it appeals to nothing that is deathless in man; its existence depends wholly on its demonstrated utility. And if the Church allies itself with Capitalism, it will perish with Capitalism in the great social change that is surely coming. Men will turn with loathing and disgust from an institution that has so far departed from the spirit and aim of Jesus.

The present peril of the Church is curiously like that which befell it in the age of Constantine. Again an alliance is offered it with all that is splendid and powerful in our social order. And we are already well on the way towards an acceptance of the offer. The Church has practically consented to condone and hence to connive at social wrong, provided the wrong-doer will mitigate the wrong by a splendid and ostentatious "charity." Thousands of Christians will not permit themselves to consider the evidence that proves the maker of a great fortune to be ethically no more than a bandit, the Robin Hood of finance, because the millionnaire bandit does exactly what Robin Hood is said by tradition to have done

— he scatters a portion of his unjustly gained wealth
(nearly always an infinitesimally small portion) in public charities or education.   He thus doles out to the poor
— the poor whom he has made poor and keeps poor —
a trifle of what he has stolen from them by means more
or less legal, often so much "less" that he is saved from
punishment only by pleading the statute of limitations.
Is it putting the thing too strongly to say that a Church
guilty of condoning such commercial ethics as have
notoriously governed the accumulation of fortunes great
and small in the past half century, needs to repent and
bring forth the fruits of repentance ?   How can it otherwise make good its claim to be the representative on
earth of the Teacher of Nazareth ?

The world's workers, now in large part estranged from
the Church, will rally to the Church whenever the Church
shows that it fully accepts the gospel of Christ, and is
ready to apply its principles to the facts and conditions of
present-day life.   To-day the Church pardons, if it does
not encourage, ways of doing business totally irreconcilable with the gospel and at variance with fundamental
instincts of justice.   The Church has never had, in all its
history, a greater opportunity; the only thing doubtful
is its readiness to seize its opportunity and exploit it to
the utmost.

At the same time another social problem confronts the
Church: it is in danger of losing its hold on the more
scholarly and thoughtful class, that it could once count
upon as a main pillar.   Men and women who are trained
in our higher schools of learning, and taught to use the
scientific method in their investigation of all questions,
to search fearlessly for the truth and to accept nothing

on trust from the past, find it a matter of increasing difficulty to adjust their secular and their religious instruction.   It is not only students in theological seminaries,
but educated laymen in all callings, who are perplexed
with doubts and difficulties.   But the layman, while he
feels these difficulties as keenly as the theological student,
has little time to give to their solution; he looks to the
pulpit for help and enlightenment, and too often he looks
in vain.   He asks for bread and is given a stone.   The
old dogmas are pressed upon him, the old view of the
Bible is urged on him, and he is assured that his doubts
are only an evidence of depravity, certain proof that he
is morally aberrant, for if he were ethically right he would
have no doubts.[1]

Why should preachers wonder if men trained in the
modern methods of thinking and investigation turn in
weariness and disgust from such instruction? The
wonder is that anybody can be found to listen to it in this
day and generation; yet precisely such teaching is still
heard from the majority of pulpits of the United States.
It is no marvel at all that educated laymen are looking
elsewhere than to Christian ministers for their religious
instruction, and threaten to desert our churches in a body
unless there is a great change in the type and quality of
instruction.   They must have help in the solving of their
problems, and it is the duty of the preacher to give them
help.   The demand of the hour is for preachers who are
conscious of the existence of problems peculiar to this
age, who have themselves encountered these problems

[1] "If you pull up a doubt, you will find a sin at its root," said Dwight
L. Moody, and was quoted with universal applause by orthodox preachers
and the orthodox religious press.

and found a solution of them, so far as they are solvable, — preachers who have learned how to restate whatever of precious truth we have inherited from the past in the terms of present-day thought and experience.

This is far from saying that the preacher ought to look with contempt on the wisdom of ages gone, or discard lightly what has commended itself as true to men of other days who have walked with God and proved in their own experience the truth of his promises. But we are not to cast our thought in their moulds, we are not to expect altogether to duplicate their experiences. Nor is the preacher to announce himself as one who "knows all mysteries and all knowledge," an Edipus who can solve any riddle that the modern Sphinx may propound. He will do well to cultivate modesty, to recognize that religion presents insoluble problems; and for himself and his hearers, fall back on Bishop Butler's principle that probability is the guide of life — that in this world we are shut up to the necessity of choosing, not a course that is free from difficulties, but the course that presents fewest difficulties.

The estrangement of the professional classes is not entirely the fault of the Church. The educated man is by nature and training a Pharisee and aristocrat, even if he come from the plain people. This has been observed from the time of the Renaissance. Scholars, teachers, lawyers, physicians, and even the clergy easily become the champions of feudalistic Capitalism, in spite of the fact that most of them have risen from the homes of the poor. Learning was once supposed to be married to religion, but in these days it has contracted a morganatic union with wealth. It is the rich and the well-to-do that pay the salaries of the clergy and the fees of lawyers and doctors. "The ox knoweth his owner and the ass his master's crib."

The rich and well-to-do demand a gospel that shall support institutions as they are, that shall serve as an anesthetic to their consciences. They are, therefore, sturdy upholders of orthodoxy in doctrine, and demand that nothing else shall be proclaimed from the pulpits that they subsidize. The result is the flood of sermons every Sunday that are doing so much to make Sunday automobiling and golf and baseball popular. This is known in the circles of the elect as "preaching the old gospel," a holding forth on doctrines of sin and atonement and the inerrancy of Scripture, and above all, insistence upon "faith" and not works as the means of salvation, to the exclusion of all themes connected with men's present duty, and the careful avoidance of anything that might disturb confidence in existing social arrangements. Now it is doubtless true that a preacher's mind must have a theology, just as his body must have a skeleton, but it is no more his business to exhibit the one in the pulpit than the other.

The greatest lack in the preaching of to-day is reality. It is too much occupied with threshing over the chaff of long-past controversies, with pummelling men of straw, while real issues and dangerous foes go unnoticed. And reality is what modern education teaches men to see and demand everywhere. Educated men may sympathize with the preacher's purpose; they find it impossible to tolerate his method. Let the pulpit grapple bravely with present difficulties, and give information and help to the men and women who come to hear, not for men and women long since in their graves, and it will regain the respect of the educated class.   Men are ready to give a fair hearing, if not prompt reception, to any earnest message that comes home to their business and bosoms.

Meanwhile what is done to the few who try to live the life that Jesus lived, and to teach again to this age what he taught to his own?   They are accounted fools and dreamers, denounced as socialists and anarchists, esteemed to be the enemies of God and man, dangerous to society, men to be shunned and repressed.   And men are right in so treating them, if to preserve the existing order is the chief end of man.   For they follow the greatest revolutionary that ever lived, and they teach a doctrine the most subversive of the present order that was ever taught.

IV

It follows that it is the present duty of the Christian Church and preacher to leave no honorable expedient untried to regain its hold on both these classes, before it is too late.   Doubtless the Church might survive for a time without either the proletariat or the educated class, but what a Church!   The club of the rich, in which they would hear only a gospel of smooth things such as would not disturb their consciences; in which would also be tolerated on an inferior social footing their dependents and on-hangers, and such of the people in general as carefully train themselves to look upon business and religion as things quite distinct, and keep their secular and their religious ideas in separate thought-tight compartments of their brains, and so are able to hold comfortably any number of contradictory propositions without perceiving any conflict between them.   How long would it be before the kingdom of God would be brought to its consummation in this world by a Church like that?

There is but one way in which the Church can ever convince the toilers that it is their best friend, and that is by being their friend. It must show by its fruits that it exists in the world only to cause the prevalence of peace and justice, fraternity and equality, the liberty with which Christ makes men free through willing bondage to one's fellows. The Church that does this will not have to complain of the estrangement of the proletariat. The altruism of Jesus and the altruism of Socialism are proclaimed in terms identical; they profess aims that are indistinguishable. It is only in method that they differ. It is for the Church to prove, what it asserts to be the fact, that Jesus gives to his followers not only an ideal, not merely an example, but a vivific force that makes the ideal realizable. Abstract altruism has never yet moved any large number of men; the social altruism preached by their leaders has no attraction for the toilers. The element in Socialism that does appeal to them is not altruism, but class selfishness. It is the fundamental error of Socialism to assume that working-men are ethically superior to capitalists. In all labor disputes we hear tales of injustice and arrogance on the one side, and of dishonesty and shirking on the other, while each charges the other with bad faith. It is but too likely that the tales are all true. Why should they not be? Each side is frankly fighting for its own hand, trying to get as much for as little as possible, keenly watchful for a tactical error that will give an advantage. In such a contest, what becomes of the spirit of brotherhood, of self-sacrifice, of love? Either party would laugh in the face of one who spoke such words. It is the emptiness of mere words for socialists to prate of altruism among unregenerate men. Only the spirit of divine love can exorcise the demon of selfishness. It is still true that the name of Jesus is the only name given under heaven or among men, whereby they can be saved, for he alone can change men who hate into men who love their brothers.

In a word, then, the great need of the Church to-day is that it become more socialized in all its thinking and activities. Its influence ought to be much more widely felt in the direction of social betterment. It is right to insist, as the churches have always insisted, that to better outward conditions does not of itself better man; but it is time for the Church also to recognize that betterment of some outward conditions is an indispensable requisite to the betterment of man. Man needs something more than a spiritual gospel, because man is something more than a spirit — he has a body also, and, therefore, must live a life more or less material. A whole gospel will uplift the whole man, and the whole man cannot be uplifted in a slum. Those activities summed up in the phrases "the institutional Church" and "settlement work" are the first crude attempts of the churches to rise to their opportunities, and are praiseworthy as first attempts; but the time will come in the not distant future, please God, when we shall look back with a smile on the comparative futility of these beginnings. When the Church with her organized power, when all Christians with their latent enthusiasm, shall give themselves whole-heartedly to this work, there will be a transformation of society little short of marvellous.

The preacher can do much if he will get into closer

personal touch with the toilers. The men and women in
the factories will not come to church, it is said, and often
with truth. But some ministers have shown that it is
possible in that case for the preacher to go to the factory workers. Religious services can often be arranged
in the workshops or yards at the noon hour, and in cases
not a few remarkable results have followed the holding
of such services. Ministers and churches must learn to
dispense with some of their ribbons and starch, if need be,
and use the methods of the Salvation Army and other
successful workers among the masses. It has happened
that a preacher who has thus come into close touch with
the workers and gained their confidence because he has
spoken to them as man to man and has shown himself
to be in feeling and not merely in phrase their brother, has
been able to act as arbitrator between them and their employers and promote a peaceful adjustment of difficulties,
where without him strife and bitterness would have
resulted. These ought to be no sporadic cases. But
no preacher who is not a thoroughly manly man, and does
not in his heart of hearts think of the manual toiler as
his brother, should ever attempt such labors. Working-
men will be quick to detect, and equally prompt to resent,
the condescending coming among them of one who regards them as his inferiors and talks down to them from
a lofty height of superiority.

Christian churches and preachers may also do not a
little to make Christian sentiment felt in regard to social
legislation, for the amelioration of hurtful conditions of
life and labor. Not officially as churches and preachers
often, but as citizens, voters, and taxpayers, by speech,
writing, petition, private interview, they may influence

legislators and the press regarding the prohibition of child labor, better hours for women in factories, better sanitation of workshops, more effective protection against fire, and the like. It has been bitterly said that it is easier to interest good Christian women in a crusade against the alleged cruelties of vivisection than against the ill treatment of children in Southern cotton factories. Some eccentric bequests made by women in recent years give color to the accusation; for certainly, while our cities are overrun with children who are obviously ragged and dirty, and look half starved, a better use can be found for surplus money than founding asylums and hospitals for stray cats and dogs.

We must lay on the conscience of Christian philanthropists the duty of securing better housing for the poor. Berlin shows America what can be done in providing beautiful and sanitary homes for the working classes at reasonable cost, not as a strictly benevolent enterprise, but one returning a fair profit. Many foreign cities put to shame anything American. Indeed, as the result of a pretty wide inspection of European cities, one feels warranted in saying categorically that nowhere save in London may such wretched slums be found as exist in all the larger cities of the United States. Until recently it was true that the worst tenements in New York were those owned by Trinity Church; and only a persistent agitation in the newspapers and magazines finally aroused a sense of shame in that rich corporation such as to induce it to begin a reform. Indeed, its conscience had to be quickened by legal proceedings before it became really active. Many other tenements in New York, that are to-day a disgrace to that city, are owned by respected members of uptown churches; and, though a public nuisance and a menace to the health of the whole city, they are maintained in their squalor because they return a net income of fifteen per cent, while good uptown property will barely net its owner five. Our cities will vainly strive against the Great White Plague, while they suffer its chief breeding-places to exist untroubled. If love of our neighbor will not teach us better conduct, love of ourselves should.

The Church must also convince the thinking men and women that it is their friend. This is the easier task of the two, because they are thinking men and women. It is not very difficult to convince a thinker that he can be both happier and more useful in the Church than outside. The Church needs the educated sorely, but not more than they need the Church. The educated man who has become impatient with the Church and left it has hardly paused to reflect on the selfishness and ingratitude of his course. He has not remembered that he would not possess his present enlightened view of things but for the institution on which he has turned his back. He has forgotten how immeasurably poorer would be the community in which he lives if the Church were abolished. He does not consider what the Church is worth to him and his family, as a conservator of all that is best in our civilization, not to say the chief force by which advancement in civilization must be achieved. He has ignored the fundamental social need, as strong in religion as elsewhere, perhaps stronger in religion than anywhere, so that the Church is absolutely necessary as a means of keeping alive Christian ideals. It is impossible for the weak to retain their Christian faith and their Christian character without the fellowship of their kind, and even the strong are made stronger by fellowship.

Whatever of philanthropy there is in the world may be traced, directly or indirectly, to the Church, and usually the direct connection is patent and striking. Hospitals, asylums, schools, social settlements, temperance work, rescue work, lodging houses, dispensaries, the Christian Associations for young men and young women — would any of these exist but for Christian influences? Are they found anywhere in the world where the Church has not preceded them? Critics of the Church should not overlook these great agencies, in their aggregate a mighty force for the amelioration of social ills. The Church is doing less than her duty, no doubt, but only slander can assert that she is doing nothing in social service. Moreover, the Church is the one institution that is striking at the root of social ills, that is engaged solely in the work of regenerating men, of producing character, of inspiring high ethical conduct. Granted that the work is done ineffectively; the Church is doing it, in some sort, and if it ceases doing it, there is no institution to take its place.

The educated man cannot deny these things; the better he is educated the more he will be ready to admit that these things are so. Let the preacher press this view of the case on the mind and heart of the educated in his community. With all its defects and shortcomings, the Church is doing for the educated a work of inestimable value, and they are gladly availing themselves of the fruits. It is, therefore, the plain duty of every man or woman who values the character and ideals for which the Church stands to support the Church by membership,

attendance, and purse. Not to support it is the basest
ingratitude, as well as suicidal selfishness. Let the
preacher urge this view, and the educated cannot fail
to perceive the force of the argument, nor in the end will
they fail to acknowledge the obligation. Their selfishness is not deliberate, but unconscious.

At the same time the churches and preachers must
prepare to give as well as to receive. The educated ought
not to be expected to be solitary in unselfishness. Aside
from the good they receive from the general spirit of
brotherliness and helpfulness, they should not so frequently be sent away unfed as now. The preacher
should so live in the present and be so intensely a man of
his own day, so in sympathy with the thought of his own
generation, and so alive to its problems, that he shall be
both able and willing to state fundamental Christian
truth in accordance with the science and philosophy of
this time, and not in the terms of some age long past.
Only so can he have the intellectual respect of his trained
hearers, and bring to their sorely tried and troubled
hearts a message of help and cheer.

V

It is often asserted, by Socialists and Christians alike,
that Socialism and Christianity are incompatible.
"Christianity and Socialism are diametrically opposite
in method, aims, and spirit," says a Christian writer,
and therefore, "the Christian minister not only cannot
support it [Socialism] consistently, but cannot even be
in sympathy with it, and must oppose its extension." [1]
But this is a conclusion possible only to those who use

[1] Thompson, "The Churches and the Wage Earners," p. 125.

terms without defining them. Some forms of Christianity and some forms of Socialism are incompatible. But Nietzsche was more keen-sighted; he saw that the fundamental principles of Socialism and Christianity are not merely compatible, but identical, and included them in a common condemnation and opposed them with fierce and impartial hatred. The Great Paradox of Jesus is the corner-stone of Socialism: "If any one wishes to come after me, let him renounce self, and take up his cross and follow me. For whoever wishes to save his life shall lose it, but whoever shall lose his life for my sake and the gospel's, the same shall find it." The spirit of ministering and self-sacrificing love is fundamental in Christianity, and it is also what Socialism means by human brotherhood. It would be close to the truth to say that Socialism is more nearly a reproduction in modern terms of the gospel of Jesus than the system of rites and doctrines preached in his name in the so-called Christian churches of the world.

But it is to be borne in mind that, as the Christianity taught by Jesus cannot be identified with any existing Church or creed, so the essential thing in Socialism is independent of any particular economic or political programme. The Marxians to the contrary notwithstanding, it is not necessary to belong to a given party and speak an appointed shibboleth, in order to be a socialist; any more than one must belong to a particular Church to be entitled to bear the name of Christian. Both Christianity and Socialism, in their essence, signify the common brotherhood of man, with all the corollaries of equal privilege, equal sharing of all the common gifts of the common Father in Heaven. But organized Socialism will often have a different aim from organized Christianity, though the aims need not be incompatible. Socialism is, on its practical side, an economic scheme, and is concerned with environment; Christianity, on its practical side, is an attempt to regenerate man, and is concerned with character. Socialism is in the main materialistic, not excluding spiritual elements; Christianity is mainly spiritual, with a distinctly material goal. To recognize these differences clearly is to raise no objection to either, but rather to promote relations of mutual understanding, sympathy, and coöperation.

Socialism touches Christianity at many points, and may well influence deeply the thinking and preaching of a minister to-day. If he is alert and open-minded, he can hardly fail to be influenced. Socialism is proclaimed with an intensity of faith and an elevation of sentiment that are more characteristic of religion than of philosophy or economics — proclaimed as a new gospel, Good News for the poor and oppressed. It is a gospel of universal peace; it deprecates war between individuals and war between nations. It is a gospel of love, and exhorts men to cherish the spirit of universal brotherhood and to cultivate conduct in accord with that spirit. It is a gospel of hope, since it holds out to mankind the prospect of relief from the burdens of poverty and disease that now bear so heavily on the shoulders of the world's workers, and promises leisure and plenty to all. These are teachings with which the gospel of Jesus not only has no quarrel, but with which it fully agrees — they are "spirit of his Spirit and flame from the fire of his soul."

At these points, therefore, there is a possibility for Socialism and Christianity to become hearty allies, and no reason whatever why they should be enemies. The optimism of Christianity is fully as great as that of Socialism, and more intelligent, for it aspires not only to gratify men's physical needs, but

> to fill that deep desire
> The want that crazed our brain,
> Consumed our soul with thirst like fire
> Immedicable pain —

only, it denies that the pain is immedicable. Christianity, therefore, can neither offer nor accept a compromise with those socialists who flatly contradict the word of Jesus and ignore the spiritual need of man, teaching that the food is more than the life, and that man can live by bread alone. Many socialists are misdirecting their efforts and so wasting their energies; they will accomplish more for the uplifting of mankind when they shall succeed in teaching men to be less dissatisfied with their conditions and more dissatisfied with their character.

The preacher has something to offer the world that the socialist teacher cannot have, a remedy for social ills that will really cure. For while the socialistic ideals are practically those of early Christianity, Socialism has no potency to make its ideals workable. The machinery is all in place, the workmen stand ready at their benches, but there is no power-house — those who have planned the works have forgotten to put that in, and not a wheel will turn. Love of humanity, unless founded in love of God, is too weak a motive to endure the wear and tear of re-making a world. It is mere sentimentality that will disappear like the morning dew at the first touch of suffering, or the first chance of selfish aggrandizement.

Socialism and Christianity are not alternatives between which one must choose, still less antagonists of which if we love the one we must hate the other, but allies, since they avow the same essential ethics and seek in great part the same ends. They can mutually do each other good, for it is doubtless true that Christianity would be the better for being socialized, and it is certain that Socialism greatly needs to be spiritualized. The peril of Christianity is that men may be persuaded to attempt a divorce of piety from social righteousness; and the peril of Socialism is a bald, crass, brutal materialism. But though at bottom friendly, and capable of a close alliance and mutual helpfulness, Socialism and Christianity can never be identified. Christianity stands first of all for the redemption of the individual, for his emancipation from the slavery of sin to the status of a free man, for the restoration in him of the defaced image of God — this as an indispensable preliminary to a new social order, but certainly issuing in a new social order. It must continue to insist that the regeneration of the individual precede the regeneration of society; the new man must be born or the new society can never be. It is by this renovation of individuals, one by one, that society can be renovated, and there is no hope but this for the uplifting of the race. But it may be gratefully acknowledged that this work of individual renovation can be decidedly promoted by a general betterment of social conditions; the two lines of labor are mutually helpful, and mutually and continually interact; and at that precise point, therefore, Christianity and Socialism can join hands in common effort.

FOR A' THAT AND A' THAT,
   IT'S COMING YET FOR A' THAT,
THAT MAN TO MAN, THE WARLD O'ER,
   SHALL BROTHERS BE FOR A' THAT.

INDEX

THE MACMILLAN STANDARD LIBRARY

This series has taken its place as one of the most important popular-priced editions. The "Library" includes only those books which have been put to the test of public opinion and have not been found wanting, — books, in other words, which have come to be regarded as standards in the fields of knowledge, — literature, religion, biography, history, politics, art, economics, sports, sociology, and belles lettres. Together they make the most complete and authoritative works on the several subjects.

Each volume, cloth, 12mo, 50 cents net; postage, 10 cents extra

Addams — The Spirit of Youth and the City Streets. By JANE ADDAMS.

" Shows such sanity, such breadth and tolerance of mind, and such penetration into the inner meanings of outward phenomena as to make it a book which no one can afford to miss." — *New York Times.*

Addams — A New Conscience and An Ancient Evil. By JANE ADDAMS.

" A clear, sane, and frank discussion of a problem in civilized society of the greatest importance."

Bailey — The Country Life Movement in the United States. By L. H. BAILEY.

" . . . clearly thought out, admirably written, and always stimulating in its generalization and in the perspectives it opens." — *Philadelphia Press.*

Bailey and Hunn — The Practical Garden Book. By L. H. BAILEY AND C. E. HUNN.

" Presents only those facts that have been proved by experience, and which are most capable of application on the farm." — *Los Angeles Express.*

Campbell — The New Theology. By R. J. CAMPBELL.

" A fine contribution to the better thought of our times written in the spirit of the Master." — *St. Paul Dispatch.*

Clark — The Care of a House. By T. M. CLARK.

" If the average man knew one-ninth of what Mr. Clark tells him in this book, he would be able to save money every year on repairs, etc." — *Chicago Tribune.*

Conyngton — How to Help: A Manual of Practical Charity. By MARY CONYNGTON.

" An exceedingly comprehensive work with chapters on the homeless man and woman, care of needy families, and the discussions of the problems of child labor."

Coolidge — The United States as a World Power. By ARCHIBALD CARY COOLIDGE.

" A work of real distinction . . . which moves the reader to thought." — *The Nation.*

Croly — The Promise of American Life. By HERBERT CROLY.

" The most profound and illuminating study of our national conditions which has appeared in many years." — THEODORE ROOSEVELT.

Devine — Misery and Its Causes. By EDWARD T. DEVINE.

" One rarely comes across a book so rich in every page, yet so sound, so logical, and thorough." — *Chicago Tribune.*

Earle — Home Life in Colonial Days. By ALICE MORSE EARLE.

" A book which throws new light on our early history."

Ely — Evolution of Industrial Society. By RICHARD T. ELY.

" The benefit of competition and the improvement of the race, municipal ownership, and concentration of wealth are treated in a sane, helpful, and interesting manner." — *Philadelphia Telegraph.*

Ely — Monopolies and Trusts. By RICHARD T. ELY.

" The evils of monopoly are plainly stated, and remedies are proposed. This book should be a help to every man in active business life." — *Baltimore Sun.*

French — How to Grow Vegetables. By ALLEN FRENCH.

" Particularly valuable to a beginner in vegetable gardening, giving not only a convenient and reliable planting-table, but giving particular attention to the culture of the vegetables." — *Suburban Life.*

Goodyear — Renaissance and Modern Art. W. H. GOODYEAR.

" A thorough and scholarly interpretation of artistic development."

Hapgood — Abraham Lincoln: The Man of the People. By NORMAN HAPGOOD.

" A life of Lincoln that has never been surpassed in vividness, compactness, and homelike reality." — *Chicago Tribune.*

Haultain — The Mystery of Golf. By ARNOLD HAULTAIN.

" It is more than a golf book. There is interwoven with it a play of mild philosophy and of pointed wit." — *Boston Globe.*

4

Hearn — Japan: An Attempt at Interpretation. By Lafcadio Hearn.

" A thousand books have been written about Japan, but this one is one of the rarely precious volumes which opens the door to an intimate acquaintance with the wonderful people who command the attention of the world to-day." — *Boston Herald*.

Hillis — The Quest of Happiness. By Rev. Newell Dwight Hillis.

" Its whole tone and spirit is of a sane, healthy optimism." — *Philadelphia Telegraph*.

Hillquit — Socialism in Theory and Practice. By Morris Hillquit.

" An interesting historical sketch of the movement." — *Newark Evening News*.

Hodges — Everyman's Religion. By George Hodges.

" Religion to-day is preëminently ethical and social, and such is the religion so ably and attractively set forth in these pages." — *Boston Herald*.

Horne — David Livingstone. By Silvester C. Horne.

The centenary edition of this popular work. A clear, simple, narrative biography of the great missionary, explorer, and scientist.

Hunter — Poverty. By Robert Hunter.

" Mr. Hunter's book is at once sympathetic and scientific. He brings to the task a store of practical experience in settlement work gathered in many parts of the country." — *Boston Transcript*.

Hunter — Socialists at Work. By Robert Hunter.

" A vivid, running characterization of the foremost personalities in the Socialist movement throughout the world." — *Review of Reviews*.

Jefferson — The Building of the Church. By Charles E. Jefferson.
" A book that should be read by every minister."

King — The Ethics of Jesus. By Henry Churchill King.

" I know no other study of the ethical teaching of Jesus so scholarly, so careful, clear, and compact as this." — G. H. Palmer, Harvard University.

King — The Laws of Friendship — Human and Divine. By Henry Churchill King.

" This book is full of sermon themes and thought-inspiring sentences worthy of being made mottoes for conduct." — *Chicago Tribune*.

King — Rational Living. By HENRY CHURCHILL KING.

"An able conspectus of modern psychological investigation, viewed from the Christian standpoint." — *Philadelphia Public Ledger.*

London — The War of the Classes. By JACK LONDON.

"Mr. London's book is thoroughly interesting, and his point of view is very different from that of the closest theorist." — *Springfield Republican.*

London — Revolution and Other Essays. By JACK LONDON.

"Vigorous, socialistic essays, animating and insistent."

Lyon — How to Keep Bees for Profit. By EVERETT D. LYON.

"A book which gives an insight into the life history of the bee family, as well as telling the novice how to start an apiary and care for it." — *Country Life in America.*

McLennan — A Manual of Practical Farming. By JOHN McLENNAN.

"The author has placed before the reader in the simplest terms a means of assistance in the ordinary problems of farming." — *National Nurseryman.*

Mabie — William Shakespeare: Poet, Dramatist, and Man. By HAMILTON W. MABIE.

"It is rather an interpretation than a record." — *Chicago Standard.*

Mahaffy — Rambles and Studies in Greece. By J. P. MAHAFFY.

"To the intelligent traveler and lover of Greece this volume will prove a most sympathetic guide and companion."

Mathews — The Church and the Changing Order. By SHAILER MATHEWS.

"The book throughout is characterized by good sense and restraint . . . A notable book and one that every Christian may read with profit." — *The Living Church.*

Mathews — The Gospel and the Modern Man. By SHAILER MATHEWS.

"A succinct statement of the essentials of the New Testament." — *Service.*

Nearing — Wages in the United States. By SCOTT NEARING.

"The book is valuable for anybody interested in the main question of the day — the labor question."

Patten — The Social Basis of Religion. By SIMON N. PATTEN.

"A work of substantial value." — *Continent.*

Peabody — The Approach to the Social Question. BY FRANCIS GREENWOOD PEABODY.

" This book is at once the most delightful, persuasive, and sagacious contribution to the subject." — *Louisville Courier-Journal*.

Pierce — The Tariff and the Trusts. BY FRANKLIN PIERCE.

" An excellent campaign document for a non-protectionist." — *Independent*.

Rauschenbusch — Christianity and the Social Crisis. BY WALTER RAUSCHENBUSCH.

" It is a book to like, to learn from, and to be charmed with." — *New York Times*.

Riis — The Making of an American. BY JACOB RIIS.

" Its romance and vivid incident make it as varied and delightful as any romance." — *Publisher's Weekly*.

Riis — Theodore Roosevelt, the Citizen. BY JACOB RIIS.

" A refreshing and stimulating picture." — *New York Tribune*.

Ryan — A Living Wage; Its Ethical and Economic Aspects. BY REV. J. A. RYAN.

" The most judicious and balanced discussion at the disposal of the general reader." — *World To-day*.

Scott — Increasing Human Efficiency in Business. BY WALTER DILL SCOTT.

" An important contribution to the literature of business psychology." — *The American Banker*.

St. Maur — The Earth's Bounty. BY KATE V. ST. MAUR.
" Practical ideas about the farm and garden."

St. Maur — A Self-supporting Home. BY KATE V. ST. MAUR.

" Each chapter is the detailed account of all the work necessary for one month — in the vegetable garden, among the small fruits, with the fowls, guineas, rabbits, and in every branch of husbandry to be met with on the small farm." — *Louisville Courier-Journal*.

Sherman — What is Shakespeare? BY L. A. SHERMAN.

" Emphatically a work without which the library of the Shakespeare student will be incomplete." — *Daily Telegram*.

Sidgwick — Home Life in Germany. BY A. SIDGWICK.
" A vivid picture of social life and customs in Germany to-day."

Simons — Social Forces in American History. BY A. W. SIMONS.
" A forceful interpretation of events in the light of economics."

7

Smith — The Spirit of American Government. By J. ALLEN SMITH.

" Not since Bryce's ' American Commonwealth ' has a book been produced which deals so searchingly with American political institutions and their history." — *New York Evening Telegram.*

Spargo — Socialism. By JOHN SPARGO.

" One of the ablest expositions of Socialism that has ever been written." — *New York Evening Call.*

Tarbell — History of Greek Art. By T. B. TARBELL.

" A sympathetic and understanding conception of the golden age of art."

Trask — In the Vanguard. By KATRINA TRASK.

" Katrina Trask has written a book — in many respects a wonderful book — a story that should take its place among the classics." — *Brooklyn Daily Eagle.*

Valentine – How to Keep Hens for Profit. By C. S. VALENTINE.

" Beginners and seasoned poultrymen will find in it much of value." — *Chicago Tribune.*

Van Dyke — The Gospel for a World of Sin. By HENRY VAN DYKE.

" One of the basic books of true Christian thought of to-day and of all times." — *Boston Courier.*

Van Dyke — The Spirit of America. By HENRY VAN DYKE.

" Undoubtedly the most notable interpretation in years of the real America. It compares favorably with Bryce's ' American Commonwealth.' " — *Philadelphia Press.*

Veblen — The Theory of the Leisure Class. By THORSTEIN B. VEBLEN.

" The most valuable recent contribution to the elucidation of this subject." — *London Times.*

Vedder — Socialism and the Ethics of Jesus. By HENRY C. VEDDER.

" A timely discussion of a popular theme." — *New York Post.*

Walling — Socialism as it Is. By WILLIAM ENGLISH WALLING.

" . . . the best book on Socialism by any American, if not the best book on Socialism in the English language." — *Boston Herald.*

Wells — New Worlds for Old. By H. G. WELLS.

" As a presentation of Socialistic thought as it is working to-day, this is the most judicious and balanced discussion at the disposal of the general reader." — *World To-day.*

THE MACMILLAN FICTION LIBRARY

A new and important series of some of the best popular novels which have been published in recent years.

These successful books are now made available at a popular price in response to the insistent demand for cheaper editions.

Each volume, cloth, 12mo, 50 cents net; postage, 10 cents extra

Allen — A Kentucky Cardinal. BY JAMES LANE ALLEN.

" A narrative, told with naïve simplicity, of how a man who was devoted to his fruits and flowers and birds came to fall in love with a fair neighbor." — *New York Tribune.*

Allen — The Reign of Law. A Tale of the Kentucky Hempfields. BY JAMES LANE ALLEN.

" Mr. Allen has style as original and almost as perfectly finished as Hawthorne's. . . . And rich in the qualities that are lacking in so many novels of the period." — *San Francisco Chronicle.*

Atherton — Patience Sparhawk. BY GERTRUDE ATHERTON.

" One of the most interesting works of the foremost American novelist."

Child — Jim Hands. BY RICHARD WASHBURN CHILD.

" A big, simple, leisurely moving chronicle of life. Commands the profoundest respect and admiration. Jim is a real man, sound and fine." — *Daily News.*

Crawford — The Heart of Rome. BY MARION CRAWFORD.

" A story of underground mystery."

Crawford — Fair Margaret: A Portrait. BY MARION CRAWFORD.

" A story of modern life in Italy, visualizing the country and its people, and warm with the red blood of romance and melodrama." — *Boston Transcript.*

Davis — A Friend of Cæsar. BY WILLIAM STEARNS DAVIS.

" There are many incidents so vivid, so brilliant, that they fix themselves in the memory." — NANCY HUSTON BANKS in *The Bookman.*

Drummond — The Justice of the King. BY HAMILTON DRUMMOND.

" Read the story for the sake of the living, breathing people, the adventures, but most for the sake of the boy who served love and the King." — *Chicago Record-Herald.*

Elizabeth and Her German Garden.

" It is full of nature in many phases — of breeze and sunshine, of the glory of the land, and the sheer joy of living." — *New York Times*.

Gale — Loves of Pelleas and Etarre. By ZONA GALE.

" . . . full of fresh feeling and grace of style, a draught from the fountain of youth." — *Outlook*.

Herrick — The Common Lot. By ROBERT HERRICK.

" A story of present-day life, intensely real in its picture of a young architect whose ideals in the beginning were, at their highest, æsthetic rather than spiritual.   It is an unusual novel of great interest."

London — Adventure. By JACK LONDON.

" No reader of Jack London's stories need be told that this abounds with romantic and dramatic incident." — *Los Angeles Tribune*.

London — Burning Daylight. By JACK LONDON.

" Jack London has outdone himself in ' Burning Daylight.' " — *The Springfield Union*.

Loti — Disenchanted. By PIERRE LOTI.

" It gives a more graphic picture of the life of the rich Turkish women of to-day than anything that has ever been written." — *Brooklyn Daily Eagle*.

Lucas — Mr. Ingleside. By E. V. LUCAS.

" He displays himself as an intellectual and amusing observer of life's foibles with a hero characterized by inimitable kindness and humor." — *The Independent*.

Mason — The Four Feathers. By A. E. W. MASON.

" ' The Four Feathers ' is a first-rate story, with more legitimate thrills than any novel we have read in a long time." — *New York Press*.

Norris — Mother. By KATHLEEN NORRIS.

" Worth its weight in gold." — *Catholic Columbian*.

Oxenham — The Long Road. By JOHN OXENHAM.

" ' The Long Road ' is a tragic, heart-gripping story of Russian political and social conditions." — *The Craftsman*.

Pryor — The Colonel's Story. By MRS. ROGER A. PRYOR.

" The story is one in which the spirit of the Old South figures largely; adventure and romance have their play and carry the plot to a satisfying end."

Remington — Ermine of the Yellowstone. By JOHN REMINGTON.

"A very original and remarkable novel wonderful in its vigor and freshness."

Roberts — Kings in Exile. By CHARLES G. D. ROBERTS.

"The author catches the spirit of forest and sea life, and the reader comes to have a personal love and knowledge of our animal friends." — *Boston Globe.*

Robins — The Convert. By ELIZABETH ROBINS.

"'The Convert' devotes itself to the exploitation of the recent suffragist movement in England. It is a book not easily forgotten by any thoughtful reader." — *Chicago Evening Post.*

Robins — A Dark Lantern. By ELIZABETH ROBINS.

A powerful and striking novel, English in scene, which takes an essentially modern view of society and of certain dramatic situations.

Ward — The History of David Grieve. By MRS. HUMPHREY WARD.

"A perfect picture of life, remarkable for its humor and extraordinary success at character analysis."

THE MACMILLAN JUVENILE LIBRARY

This collection of juvenile books contains works of standard quality, on a variety of subjects — history, biography, fiction, science, and poetry — carefully chosen to meet the needs and interests of both boys and girls.

Each volume, cloth, 12mo, 50 cents net; postage, 10 cents extra

Altsheler — The Horsemen of the Plains. By JOSEPH A. ALTSHELER.

"A story of the West, of Indians, of scouts, trappers, fur traders, and, in short, of everything that is dear to the imagination of a healthy American boy." — *New York Sun.*

Bacon — While Caroline Was Growing. By JOSEPHINE DASKAM BACON.

"Only a genuine lover of children, and a keenly sympathetic observer of human nature, could have given us this book." — *Boston Herald.*

Carroll — Alice's Adventures, and Through the Looking Glass. By
LEWIS CARROLL.

  " One of the immortal books for children."

Dix — A Little Captive Lad. By MARIE BEULAH DIX.

  " The human interest is strong, and children are sure to like it." —
Washington Times.

Greene — Pickett's Gap. By HOMER GREENE.

  " The story presents a picture of truth and honor that cannot fail
to have a vivid impression upon the reader." — *Toledo Blade.*

Lucas — Slowcoach. By E. V. LUCAS.

  " The record of an English family's coaching tour in a great old-
fashioned wagon. A charming narrative, as quaint and original as
its name." — *Booknews Monthly.*

Mabie — Book of Christmas. By H. W. MABIE.

  " A beautiful collection of Christmas verse and prose in which all
the old favorites will be found in an artistic setting." — *The St.
Louis Mirror.*

Major — The Bears of Blue River. By CHARLES MAJOR.

  " An exciting story with all the thrills the title implies."

Major — Uncle Tom Andy Bill. By CHARLES MAJOR.

  " A stirring story full of bears, Indians, and hidden treasures." —
Cleveland Leader.

Nesbit — The Railway Children. By E. NESBIT.

  " A delightful story revealing the author's intimate knowledge of
juvenile ways." — *The Nation.*

Whyte — The Story Book Girls. By CHRISTINA G. WHYTE.

  " A book that all girls will read with delight — a sweet, wholesome
story of girl life."

Wright — Dream Fox Story Book. By MABEL OSGOOD WRIGHT.

  " The whole book is delicious with its wise and kindly humor, its
just perspective of the true value of things."

Wright — Aunt Jimmy's Will. By MABEL OSGOOD WRIGHT.

  " Barbara has written no more delightful book than this."